I0867848

The Art of Distances

The Art of Distances

Ethical Thinking in Twentieth-Century Literature

Corina Stan

NORTHWESTERN UNIVERSITY PRESS
EVANSTON, ILLINOIS

Northwestern University Press
www.nupress.northwestern.edu

Copyright © 2018 by Northwestern University Press.
Published 2018. All rights reserved.

Printed in the United States of America

10 9 8 7 6 5 4 3 2 1

Library of Congress Cataloging-in-Publication Data

Names: Stan, Corina, author.
Title: The art of distances : ethical thinking in twentieth-century literature / Corina Stan.
Description: Evanston, Illinois : Northwestern University Press, 2018. | Includes bibliographical references and index.
Identifiers: LCCN 2017049335 | ISBN 9780810136854 (pbk. : alk. paper) | ISBN 9780810136861 (cloth : alk. paper) | ISBN 9780810136878 (ebook)
Subjects: LCSH: European literature—20th century—History and criticism. | Ethics in literature. | Social distance—Philosophy.
Classification: LCC PN49 .S674 2018 | DDC 809.93353—dc23
LC record available at https://lccn.loc.gov/2017049335

To Alex, Eliza, and Mihai

Today . . . it is part of morality not to be at home in one's home.

—Theodor Adorno, *Minima Moralia*

CONTENTS

ACKNOWLEDGMENTS

This is a book about distance and proximity, community and tact; in a certain sense, people whose paths crossed with mine over the past few years have written it with me by offering renewed inspiration through gestures of kindness, friendship, and hospitality. It is hard to thank everyone, but here is a beginning:

I could not have wished for a more exquisite balance between involvement and detachment from my committee while I was writing the dissertation in the Duke Literature Program. I am very grateful to my adviser, Toril Moi, for her generosity throughout the years. She has spent much time reading each of the chapters, writing detailed comments, reading new versions, and writing more comments. Her advising truly is an "art of distances," balancing criticism, encouragement, and praise, engaging with the ideas, paying careful attention to her students' prose, and encouraging nuance. I must list my other committee members in some order, but what I have appreciated is how they have each offered something unique, therefore invaluable, to shape and support this project. After spending many delicious hours reading and discussing the poetry of Wallace Stevens and W. B. Yeats, or following closely the meanderings of Leopold Bloom in Frank Lentricchia's seminars, something about the imponderable temporality of fondling textual details in a quiet classroom is attached, in my mind, to his name, inextricable from an unfailing sensitivity to the practicalities of everyday life. Geoffrey Harpham's work on ethics inspired, in part, my own project. His claim, in *The Character of Criticism*, that ours is "a human practice of reflection and meditation that enlists every intellectual, affective, and experiential resource that a person has" made a deep impression on me as a student, as do, always, his unwavering commitment to the humanities, the thrilling nuances of his anecdotes, and the gracious, subtle ways of his tact. Ian Baucom and Fredric Jameson were the members of my committee most interested in asking the "big questions," hence the readers who encouraged me to think harder about the stakes of the project. Ian Baucom's elegance as a scholar, his professionalism, and the gentlest manner of guiding his students' thinking through difficult questions are still a model for me. Fred Jameson's intellectual range and dedication to the life of the mind are, as all of his students know, beyond impressive; I still think of him as my most demanding "implied reader." I also owe thanks to Michael Hardt, Alice Kaplan, Barbara Herrnstein-Smith, Valentin Mudimbe, James Applewhite, and Stephen Jaffe, who made intellectual life at Duke interesting in so many ways. And I return frequently to the work and ideas of Antoine Compagnon, my former adviser at the Sorbonne; and to what I learned from Paul Volsik and Catherine Bernard (Paris 7), as well as from Stefan Borbély and Sanda Berce (Babes-Bolyai). There is much gratitude suffused with sadness in the memory of Tudor Ionescu—my former French tutor, painter, novelist, and humorist—who modeled so compellingly the importance of not taking oneself too seriously.

I have discussed ideas and parts of this book with former students at Leiden University College the Hague (the moving excitement of Anna-Liisa Springham, Kristian Kristensen, Liam Klein, Jasper Ginn, and Barend de Rooj, among others, gave meaning to my time at LUC), the lovely graduate students at Duke who participated in the Community and Migration seminar (Taylor Ross, Jo Nopper, Austin Sarfan, Emma Goehler), and with the members of the research groups convened by Knut Stene-Johansen and Lars Saetre around Barthes's late lectures, and whose hospitality I have benefited from on more than one occasion, in Paris and in Bergen. Several colleagues in the English Department at Duke have read chapters or the entire manuscript, and I am deeply grateful for their support and collegiality: Sarah Beckwith, Thomas Pfau, Michael Moses, Tom Ferraro, Rob Mitchell, and Priscilla Wald. I feel privileged to call Duke my intellectual home, and I am appreciative of the funding that supported the completion of my graduate studies, offered by the Literature Program and the Evan Frankel Foundation. The dean's subsidy for the publication of a first book was instrumental in getting the manuscript into print. I also wish to thank the editors at Northwestern University Press, Henry Carrigan, Trevor Perri, and Nathan MacBrien; the two anonymous readers; the very efficient copyeditor, Christi Stanforth; the indexer, Steven Moore; and the team who made the publication of the book possible.

A question Fredric Jameson asked during my dissertation defense made me realize just how deeply personal this project was to me: "Why this preoccupation with distances? Is it distance from politics?" I grew up in Communist Romania, and while I was too young to truly understand this at the time, in such a context, a well-calibrated distance from politics, ostensibly not an option, is often a matter of the survival of one's soul. Later on, it was Milan Kundera's characters, especially Sabina in *The Unbearable Lightness of Being*, who shed light on the impatience I sensed around me as a child with the claustrophobic pressure of a society that requires full transparency—hence the need for distance, for the respect of privacy and of individuals' singularity. My parents' encouragement that I should learn foreign languages came from a subversive impulse, part of that histrionic practice that Czeslaw Milosz calls, in *The Captive Mind*, Ketman. This book is therefore also about sliding (often slipping) in and out of the languages I came to frequent over the years, in encounters and intimacies with words, books, people, and places. The schooling that Benjamin believed was required in order to "lose one's way in a city" (and also in another culture, I would add, including that of academia) happened in cahoots with friends and colleagues who had a great sense of humor and intriguing ideas and life-projects, and who often seemed too good to be true (yet they were). I learned much in conversations with my fellow graduate students in English and Literature; thank you, Tess, Rachel, Erin, Arnal, Magda, Anu, Shilyh, Michelle, Luka, Abe, Serhat, Veena, Brian, Alex, Sarah, and Russ. And then, there are the friends who are *always* there: Cecilia, Béatrice, Cristina and Brett, Luminita and Ioan, Chantal, Anne-Gaëlle, Gabriel, Daniela, Ksenia, Yi-Ping, Chunjie, Krista and Ish. The last thought of gratitude here (but otherwise always the very first) goes to my family: to Eliza, Alex, and Mihai, for our haven of unconditional love; to my parents, for all the dreams they invested in me and the infinite care they took that some of them, at least, might come true; to my brother Sorin, for being such an inspiration and a priceless friend, in spite of the geographic distance; to my extended family, always so supportive, gracious, and light-hearted.

Abbreviated versions of chapters 1 and 3 have appeared previously in print, as follows: "A Sociality of Distances: Roland Barthes and Iris Murdoch on How to Live with Others," in *Modern Language Notes* 129, no. 5 (2014): 1170–1198; "England (as if) through the Eyes of a Foreigner: George Orwell's *Masquerade* among the Poor of London," in *Études britanniques contemporaines*, no. 49 (2015); and "A Passionate Misunderstanding: Orwell's Paris, Miller's China," in *English Studies* 97, no. 3 (2016): 298–316. I thank the editors of these journals for their permission to reprint this material.

ABBREVIATIONS

The following abbreviations are used throughout the text and notes:

B	Iris Murdoch, *The Bell*
BC	Walter Benjamin, *Berlin Childhood*
CF	Virginia Woolf, "Character in Fiction"
CP	Elias Canetti, *Crowds and Power*
CVE	Roland Barthes, *Comment vivre ensemble*
DOPL	George Orwell, *Down and Out in Paris and London*
EM	Iris Murdoch, *Existentialists and Mystics*
ISR	Damon Galgut, *In a Strange Room*
IW	George Orwell, "Inside the Whale"
JD	Annie Ernaux, *Journal du dehors (Exteriors)*
L	Paul Morand, *Londres*
LT	Virginia Woolf, "The Leaning Tower"
LVE	Annie Ernaux, *La vie extérieure*
MC	Günter Grass, *My Century*
MEC	Elias Canetti, *The Memoirs of Elias Canetti: The Tongue Set Free, The Torch in My Ear, The Play of the Eyes*
MJ	Günter Grass, *Mein Jahrhundert*
MM	Theodor Adorno, *Minima Moralia*
N	Roland Barthes, *Le neutre: Cours au Collège de France*
PIW	Henry Miller, *Peace! It's Wonderful!*
RWP	George Orwell, *The Road to Wigan Pier*
S	Walter Benjamin, *Schriften*
TC	Henry Miller, *Tropic of Cancer*

The Art of Distances

Introduction

✦

Adorno and Barthes on the Question of the Right (Di)stance

In 1976–1977, Roland Barthes gave a course at the Collège de France under the title *Comment vivre ensemble: Simulations romanesques de quelques espaces quotidiens*, in which, refusing both didactic authority and a prescriptive moral standpoint, he intimated the idea of a community guided by the elusive principle of *délicatesse*, which he borrowed, intriguingly, from the Marquis de Sade.[1] A quest, an investigation, rather than the pursuit of a premeditated line of argument, the lectures were an attempt to answer the question "À quelle distance dois-je me tenir des autres pour construire avec eux une sociabilité sans aliénation et une solitude sans exil?" (At what distance should I keep myself from others in order to build with them a sociability without alienation and a solitude without exile?).[2]

Barthes claims that at the origin of his lectures lies the fantasy of a utopian community, a fantasy he explores as a collector of ideas, images, and passages mostly excerpted from favorite books like Defoe's *Robinson Crusoe* and Zola's *Pot-Bouille*, a Greek travelogue or a tome on Japanese culture—all cherished companions during summer holidays in the countryside. In the lectures, he orders his themes alphabetically as always expandable dossiers: "Akèdia, Anachôrèsis . . . Clôture, Colonie, Couplage, Distance, . . . Éponge . . . Marginalités . . . Proxémie . . . Règle, Saleté, Xénitéia, Utopie." It is as if Barthes created from the outset a space for the student—or the reader—to ponder his thoughts and pursue them in directions he could not have anticipated. The only caveat is that the subject of living together has to remain an open one: the "comment" (how) of the title registers a puzzling question, or even the impatient affirmation of impossibility, hence of utopia's necessity, and not a programmatic, or even descriptive, intention. Barthes offers much in the lectures, but then he retreats behind the openness he creates. He labels his inquiry "non-method" and readily qualifies it, because the negation appears too simple: "Il vaudrait mieux dire: pré-méthode. C'est comme si je préparais des matériaux en vue d'un traitement méthodique; comme si, à vrai dire, je ne m'inquiétais pas de quelle méthode ils vont être saisis. Tout est possible" (One had better say: premethod. It is as if I were preparing materials in view of a methodic treatment; as if I were not really concerned how they were going to be used. Anything is possible) (*CVE*, 183). What to make of Barthes's open-ended divagations so they do not remain, like Mallarmé's white water lily, only an "imaginary trophy"?[3] Research inspired by them begins under the auspices of an unconditional hospitality: *tout est possible*, he says in his concluding remarks.

The present book was inspired by Barthes's thought that we need "a science, or perhaps an art, of distances." The problem of distance is central to his "fantasme" because it involves eight to ten people, a number sufficiently small to allow for the cultivation of personal relationships that respect the singularity of each individual, but also large enough to require some principles that would facilitate their life together. In other words, his utopia straddles two intersecting philosophical territories: that of friendship, in which the number of people involved has always been a crucial question, and that of community, with its social and political dimensions. Barthes's use of the term *le vivre-ensemble*, often capitalized, which he ostensibly prefers to "community," suggests that his interest lies not in what these individuals have in common; rather, in what principles would make possible their harmonious coexistence. In this light, the theme of distance acquires in his lectures an aura that makes it impossible to miss its recurrence in the literature on friendship from Aristotle's *Nicomachean Ethics* to Nietzsche's *Zarathustra*, in the work of philosophers of community inspired by Martin Heidegger, in the sociology of class and distinction, and in the various grammars of anthropology, psychology, and political theory. Even the briefest overview of these clusters of texts shows that such an "art of distances" exists already in the interstices of a broader reflection on how to live with other people; and to highlight it is to emphasize the enduring importance that Barthes's question about the right distance has had, particularly in the last century.

When Zarathustra commends "love of the farthest" in "Neighbor-love," Nietzsche turns his back on a tradition of thought that for the most part took for granted the similarity of dispositions, tastes, and projects bringing together individuals in friendship.[4] Fissures in this expectation appear with Emerson's figure of the friend who comes from afar and thus disrupts the reassuring comfort of one's home, both because he is an event that "hinders [the host] from sleep" and because, once the novelty wears off, he is bound to disappoint in the trivial ways humans fail one another. A philosopher of process, Emerson reclaims his right to change and thus to be permanently at a remove from himself: after feverishly anticipating and preparing for a most special encounter, he praises the ideal connection with a friend who remains a spirit ensconced in distance, "forever a sort of beautiful enemy, untamable, devoutly revered, and not a trivial conveniency to be soon outgrown and cast aside." True friendship is conducive to self-transcendence and is paradoxically unafraid of solitude: "I cannot afford to speak much with my friend.

If he is great he makes me so great that I cannot descend to converse." With this, Emerson insists on self-reliance as the condition sine qua non of genuine friendship: "There must be very two, before there can be very one." Montaigne, whom Emerson had read and felt inspired by, also emphasized the irreducible singularity of each friend ("because it was him; because it was me"), but the distance that magnifies the figure of the other person is, in his case, imposed by death. "Of friendship," a eulogy honoring the memory of Étienne de la Boétie, also introduces in the philosophical conversation the idea of textual mediation—the discourse in language that interposes itself between oneself and another, interpellating one with the prophecy of a possible friendship to come. On certain readings, friendship is always the domain of the future, the *à-venir* that Derrida so often invokes in his lectures, reading and rereading Aristotle's paradoxical apostrophe: "O, my friends, there are no friends!"[5] In *The Nicomachean Ethics*, however, Aristotle casts friendship at the core of his vision of human happiness (*eudaimonia*), to be pursued both individually and collectively through an active cultivation of the virtues. Similarity of moral purpose—and thus proximity—is what holds the community together; distance, not so much.[6] Responding with characteristic eloquence—and a good measure of defiance—to this century-long conversation, Nietzsche was the first to denounce openly "communities of proximity,"[7] although his example was not the Greek polis, but the so-called stuffy horde mentality cultivated by the Judeo-Christian ethos which, Nietzsche claimed in *The Genealogy of Morals*, denied the diversity of life-forms and encouraged a narrow-minded, complacent form of love. In passages that echo Emerson's portrayal of the ideal friend as a "beautiful enemy," Zarathustra goes as far as to denounce the love of the neighbor as the "bad love" of oneself and advises "love of the farthest"—that as yet unfathomable difference that challenges, disrupts, and thrills the one committed to an ambitious project of self-fashioning. This conversation among philosophers, in which "distance" carries so many meanings and connotations—difference, respect, idealization, avoidance, futurity, death, self-overcoming, autonomy, mediation, and no doubt others—might have been at the back of Barthes's mind while preparing the lectures; if it was, he does little to show it. He only quotes briefly from *Twilight of the Idols*, moved by Nietzsche's attachment to the "pathos of distances" characteristic of any strong age, which he goes on to (mis)read in a creative manner that bears his stylistic interpretive signature.[8]

Barthes was not a philosopher, but his approach to living-together does have philosophical echoes in more systematic efforts to rethink community, most notably among his contemporaries Jean-Luc Nancy and Emmanuel Levinas, who engaged with the thought of Martin Heidegger. In *Sein und Zeit*, the German philosopher famously insisted on the ontological primacy of *Mitsein* (Being-with), critical of the philosophical tradition inherited from Descartes that contemplates the subject "with its skin off," and then only piles up attributes onto its "substance," inevitably failing to give access to the involvements and modes of solicitude that make up human existence. Ontology is no concern to Barthes, but his subtitle, *Simulations romanesques de quelques espaces quotidiens*, does highlight the crucial link between living together and space that Heidegger describes as the spatiality of *Dasein*. Suggestively, seeing and hearing are in his account distance-senses (*Fernsinne*), "not because they are far-reaching, but because it is in them that Dasein as deseverant mainly dwells."[9] The vocabulary of distance is implied in deseverance (*Entfernung*) and directionality (*Ausrichtung*), in *Zuhandenheit* (readiness-to-hand—instrumental), and *Vorhandenheit* (presence-at-hand—reflexive).[10] *Zuhandenheit*, for example, foregrounds the immersion in the world, which exists as a repertoire of possible involvements with which any *Dasein* is familiar by virtue of living in a social environment, in a certain culture.[11] The world is always "on its way" to one, a movement which also characterizes social interaction, which Heidegger suggestively describes in terms of leaping (yet another spatial representation): *für jemanden einspringen* (to leap in for someone, a mode of solicitude in which the Other can become dominated), and *jemandem vorausspringen* (to leap ahead of someone, not taking away the "care," but helping the Other become free to engage with it).[12] Perhaps even more important in the rapprochement with Barthes's concerns are the critiques of Heidegger by Emmanuel Levinas and Jean-Luc Nancy: arguably, their conversation is not about community, increasingly deemed an inadequate term that refers to idyllic or dangerously ideological forms of living together, but about ethical relationality. Levinas, for instance, was bothered by the primacy of the "we" in Heidegger's notion of *Dasein*, claiming that by emphasizing the commonality (*mit*), it obliterates the Other.[13] Levinas thus places metaphysics before ontology and draws attention to the danger of Heidegger's closed community of *Blut und Boden*, which divides humanity into "natives and strangers."[14] His solution is to strip the Other of all singularizing features so that the ethical relation can be imagined in the infinite distance that separates one from (what becomes) a figure of radical difference. Nancy, on the other hand, found that "Heidegger's *Dasein*, far from being too communal, is by no means social enough" (Bax) because he failed to think through the notion of *mit* (with), the most basic feature of Being, its relational character. This absence, coincidentally, is what bothers Nancy in Levinas's account as well: in an effort to ensure unconditionally the utmost respect for the deindividualized Other, Levinas has diluted the social in the infinite distance of the ethical relation. The capitalized "Other," Nancy points out, appears to be in a relation of difference from the world, rather than an "alteration *of* the world"; his alternative, *être singulier pluriel* (being singular plural), signals the "contradiction in terms" that is a singular being, and leaves behind the term "community," the idealization of a form of social life that was never real in the first place.[15] Like Nancy, Barthes thinks singularity is crucial, hence his insistence on an interpersonal distance that stays safe both from the alienation of sociability and from the exile of solitude.

On this point, Barthes might have been interested in the work of Heidegger's contemporary, Helmuth Plessner, which offers a valuable entry point into a historical account of the emergence of the problematic of distance in the twentieth century—an emergence hardly distinguishable from the critique of community that we now mostly associate with the work of philosophers such as Nancy and Levinas. *Grenzen der Gemeinschaft* (*Limits of Community*), published by Plessner in 1924, only three years before *Sein und Zeit*, presciently offered not only a critique of the *Blutgemeinschaft* that Heidegger would embrace, but also a vigorous defense of social life and interpersonal distance, in stark contrast to Heidegger's critical view of the inauthenticity of everyday life and its *distantiality*.[16] Plessner's immediate context was Weimar Germany, and the target of his critique, the social radicals—the Youth Movement and the Communists—who posited the ideal of community as the exclusive form of social organization. Distinguishing between two types of community, *Blutgemeinschaft* (blood-based, relying on emotional bonds, mostly irrational) and *Sachegemeinschaft* (a community of the ideal, whose circumference can be expanded indefinitely through rational persuasion), Plessner showed that they were both problematic in their premises and pernicious in their effects on human individuality: their demands for sincerity and transparence are claustrophobic, denying the soul the space it needs for its natural and unpredictable transformation.[17] As Andrew Wallace notes, Plessner's critique emphasizes two problematic assumptions: that people are fully transparent to themselves and to others and that all problems can be solved rationally. Even if such transparence were possible, Plessner insists, it would not be conducive to human dignity and flourishing; impersonality, game-playing, rituals, masks, diplomacy, and tact are crucial. Very much an intervention of its time, Plessner's defense of society is premised on the fundamental artificiality of human sociability, which makes inauthenticity not something to be deplored, but a set of skills to be cultivated. In short, *Limits of Community* distinguishes between the sincerity demanded in a "warm" society and the hygiene of cool conduct, criticizing "all forms of unmediated directness, pleading for moderate temperatures and indirect lighting, for art and literature of whatever type as long as they eschew intimate self-revelation in favor of the regulating practice of distance."[18]

Plessner's critique is one of many similar contemporary interventions that Helmut Lethen takes up in *Cool Conduct: The Culture of Distance in Weimar Germany*, attributing the rise of interest in codes of conduct to the shift from a culture of internalized guilt to one of exteriority, a culture of shame, that required the elaboration of strategies of face-saving and performance of empowering masks: "The mask transforms a person who has been exposed in a shaming way into a shameless performer; it turns one who is afraid of being perceived as weak into someone who is seen and feared as being strong."[19] More generally, one can speak with Lethen of a privileging of civilization over culture during this period, and thus of behavior and social etiquette over moral values, interiority, and authenticity.[20] This shift creates a sense of affinity between modernism and the seventeenth century, of which the Weimar intellectuals' rediscovery of *The Art of Worldly Wisdom* (1647) by the Spanish Jesuit Baltasar Gracián is symptomatic. Lethen writes:

> In the course of retrieving the negative anthropology of the seventeenth century, the thirty years' war of modernism (1914–45) also involves a remarkable resurgence of rules of prudent behavior, likewise a growth industry in that catastrophic century. Having lost the mooring of an external metaphysics, people begin scavenging the ruins of historical systems for an orienting codex of conduct, which is to say, the tools of self-stabilization.[21]

The central image for such a society is traffic, an environment in permanent negotiation where one does not grow roots. It relies on ceremony, diplomacy, and tact to "regulate proportions of distance and closeness, objectivity and familiarity"; indeed, this reminds Lethen of Schopenhauer's famous parable of the freezing porcupines.[22] In *Civilization and Its Discontents*, Sigmund Freud would use the same parable of the porcupines trying to find the ideal distance (that would keep them warm enough, yet not uncomfortable from too much proximity), to illustrate the dialectical struggle of civilization between libidinal ties and aggressiveness, of which the "narcissism of minor differences" is the innocuous manifestation. For Plessner, "narcissism is a necessary and reciprocal element of the ego's awareness of its reflection in the mirror of others";[23] Heidegger's own term for it is "distantiality," which refers to a nagging urge to compare oneself to others. This permanent competition is what makes everyday existence inauthentic, hence not a good premise for community.[24] Perhaps not, Plessner would say; but it is a human fact, an aspect of social life that can be skillfully negotiated.

Roberto Esposito's critique of community also finds its point of purchase here. In the competition for power and prestige, he writes, "the only way to avoid a catastrophic outcome is to institute among them sufficient distance so as to immunize each from everyone else."[25] Summarizing some of the positions that define the tradition of negative anthropology (Helmuth Plessner, Arnold Gehlen, Niklas Luhmann), Esposito uses the vocabularies of distance and of immunization interchangeably. He shows, for example, that Gehlen grounded his "immunitary option" in a theory of institutions: "the exoneration from environmental contingency that institutions ensure coincides, for the democratic subject, with a taking of distance from the world in which he or she is rooted, and, for this very reason, with a relieving of that common munus that obligates him with regard to others." Esposito's own *Zeitdiagnose* is couched in terms of separation and distance, or an always more complex immunitary dispositif: "Everywhere we look, new walls, new blockades, and new dividing lines are erected against something that threatens, or at least seems to, our biological, social, and environmental identity."[26] In Esposito's account, community must be reimagined through a vigorous critique of the common (*co-munus*): rather than emphasizing shared traits, confronting the *munus* that is debt and openness to the Other.

These philosophical positions suggest that Barthes is in solid company when he speaks of his "domestic utopia" as a form of rebellion against oppressive social arrangements, suggested by two extremes, exile and alienation. Claude Coste's summary of Barthes's quest aptly captures the discontent with the traditional forms of community the French thinker tries to avoid (without necessarily articulating them explicitly): the alienation of a community that suffocates its members through too much proximity, transparence, and sincerity; and the exile of those who do not belong to the community, in short, who have nothing in common and are therefore excluded. These aspects are crucial to the critique of "community" in the past century. Like other thinkers who have variously distanced themselves from the idea of *Gemeinschaft* (Plessner), or the suspect "nostalgia for a more archaic community that has disappeared" (Nancy), from Heidegger's community of *Blut und Boden* (Levinas), or from any notion of community premised on a misunderstanding of its etymology (Esposito), Roland Barthes—albeit in less methodical or self-consciously philosophical fashion—highlights attention to relationality and distance, to the ethos of openness to contingency and difference (suggested by his preferred formulation *le vivre-ensemble*), and, perhaps most importantly, to the singularity of everyone involved. This is to point out the acute relevance of *Comment vivre ensemble*, in which these ideas are not grounded philosophically, but simply expressions of discomfort, of common sense, and (as we shall see shortly) of a sensibility both discreet and delicate.

In Barthes's lectures, distance is also understood as a gesture of self-removal from the histrionics of everyday interaction, born not out of cold, strategic calculation but out of a protective impulse, that of allowing the others to live in the absence of mutual interpellation. This brings Barthes in proximity to Pierre Zaoui, who, in *La discrétion, ou l'art de disparaître* (*Discretion, or The Art of Disappearing*), speaks of discretion as an art, a practice, rather than a disposition. All cultures have imposed "a separation or an adequate distance not only in interpersonal relationships, but also in the relationship with God or nature, even in the relationship to oneself."[27] The exception, notes Zaoui, is Western morality in the version critiqued by Nietzsche: "La conscience occidentale avec ses rêves de sincérité totale, de petites communautés transparentes, et sa condamnation du théâtre, des masques, de toutes les formes de la représentation en général, c'est-à-dire de la distance de soi aux autres" (Western consciousness and its dreams of total sincerity, of small transparent communities, and its condemnation of theater, of masks, more generally of all forms of representation, that is, of distance between self and others).[28] There is, however, an immemorial morality of discretion, and Zaoui finds it exemplified in the work of Claude Lévi-Strauss, in practices that one refrains from, not in order to avoid danger for oneself, but to avoid hurting others. Thus in the Amazonian myths narrating the voyage of the Moon and the Sun in a boat, the world can only exist if it travels at the right distance from both of them: too much proximity to the Moon would make it silent, raw, and dark, while the Sun, too close, would burn the world, blinding it. Evoking this myth from *Le crû et le cuit*, Zaoui extrapolates discretion to encompass morality:

> Or dans un tel voyage tous les sens de la discrétion semblent se condenser: la Lune et le Soleil, l'un à la proue, l'autre à la poupe, sont dans des positions dissymétriques qui leur interdisent de se voir en face à face (discrétion visuelle); ils ne doivent pas faire trop de bruit pour ne pas effrayer les poissons (discrétion auditive); et ils ne doivent pas remuer sous peine de chavirer (discrétion gestuelle). La discrétion n'est donc plus simplement exigée pour certains moments ou certains rapports particuliers, elle n'est pas une obligation morale spécifique, elle est la morale elle-même.[29]

> Or in such a voyage all the senses of discretion appear condensed: the Moon and the Sun, one at the prow, the other at the stern, are in dissymmetrical positions that forbid them to face each other (visual discretion); they must not make too much noise lest they should scare the fish (auditory discretion); and they must not move lest they should keel over (gestural discretion). Discretion is therefore not just simply required by certain moments or contexts, it is not a specific moral obligation, it is morality itself.

Barthes's elaborations on *délicatesse*, we shall see shortly, are very much in accord with Zaoui's apology of discretion, often formulated in terms of a quest for the right distance; and his insistence that, in a world of visibility and surveillance, discretion has a political dimension, resonates with Barthes's own intuitions.

Whether a mask worn in order to conceal one's vulnerability, as in Plessner's analysis, or restraint practiced with an eye to the well-being of other people, as in Zaoui's, interpersonal distance often has as a corollary distance(s) within oneself. This impersonal "one" might not be *one* after all, but multiple in its singularity, as Nancy's formulation *singulier pluriel* suggests. "I would no longer be a human," he muses, "if I were not a body, a spacing of all other bodies and a spacing of 'me' in 'me.' "[30] We gain this view by coming in close—that is, microscopic—proximity to nonhuman entities as well. In *La naissance de la physique*, Michel Serres explains that "things are born from distance [*l'écart*]," from the declination and fall, or clinamen, of atoms in the void. Gilles Deleuze and Jean-Luc Nancy use the term "clinamen" to describe the inclination of bodies (both human and nonhuman) toward others through the slight detachment of atoms that are no longer under control:[31] a certain deterritorialization, to use Deleuze and Guattari's term, of the peripheries of a body, a loss of the proper and a coming into contact with other entities, bodies, or realities. Elaborating on Nancy's use of clinamen as contact, "which involves touch and the withdrawal of that touch: 'gestures, encounters [*rencontres*], approaches, distances [*écarts*],'" Irving Goh argues that clinamen may be the point of departure for a figure of thought that comes after the subject, the reject.[32] The latter manifests itself in three turns: a passive one, which designates the reject as that which is marginalized, repudiated, oppressed or discriminated; an active one, in which the reject retaliates against these external forces; and a generative one, in which the reject turns the force of rejection upon itself, becoming an auto-reject. This last turn, Goh insists, is about "creative regeneration": a distancing not only from others, but also from one's self, from one's old values, habits, mode of being. It is above all an ethical gesture that could lay the foundation for a new way of thinking about community, religion, and politics, leading us into a posthuman—nonanthropocentric and nonanthropomorphic—future. The only principle that would govern this new world is the "law of the law," the awareness of the others' existence, a non-Kantian categorical imperative that asks for respect (*considération*), which Nancy describes in terms similar to Barthes's, of closeness (*proximité*) and spacing (*espacement*).[33]

In a world lacking shared moral norms, distance emerges as a problem. Barthes often uses the word in the plural, speaking of "a conjoining of distances"—as if there were a newly formulated ethical imperative, that he only hints at but cannot spell out, lest he should sound dogmatic. Having placed him in the company of other thinkers of community, it will be useful to provide some context to his lectures, whose specific stakes will emerge to a larger degree as a brainchild of their time from an encounter with one of his contemporaries, Theodor Adorno. If the fact that neither cites the other's work is an indication, we can assume they were unfamiliar with each other; yet these two important thinkers of the past century shared a preoccupation with the possibilities of an ethical life that they formulate in terms of distance(s) and that can be traced back to a concern with the right stance of intellectuals in a society tired of politics, or at least of certain kinds of ideological agendas that gave them reasons to pause as early as the 1930s. Once this context established, it will ground the point of emergence of the "art of distances" inspired by *Comment vivre ensemble*. It will then be convenient to outline the trajectory of the book, expanding Barthes's community to include other writers who believed, at a remove from their own time, that literature (perhaps even more than philosophy) could help us think about distances and living together.[34]

Like Stanley Cavell writing his memoirs, the Barthes of the Collège lectures seemed "free of the desire to persuade," determined to "leave people intact."[35]

These are Cavell's words, not Barthes's; yet Robbe-Grillet's evocation of his former professor suggestively uses the same word, "intact," to speak about the effect, on him, of Barthes's late teaching. In a recollection of the inaugural lecture at the Collège, he muses over

> the disturbing demonstration of a discourse which was not a discourse: one that destroyed, step by step, any temptation to be dogmatic. What I admired in this voice that had just kept us in suspense for two whole hours was precisely that *it left my freedom intact*—better still: at each twist and turn of phrase, it gave it new strength.[36]

The title *Comment vivre ensemble* situates Barthes's lectures in a world deprived of a shared morality in which "how to live with others" can no longer take the form of a teaching, but becomes a shared quest, a collective attempt to elaborate "a science, or perhaps an art, of distances." Gingerly referring to his lectures as "ma façon d'être présent dans les luttes de mon temps" (my way of being present in the struggles of my time), Barthes insists that the problem of distance is a contemporary problem, hinting at a globalized world in which space "has become the real luxury." The self-governing community he projects is an enclave in retreat from the world, an attempt to rethink and carry out an alternative form of communal life: a domestic, not even a social, utopia, Barthes warns, governed by the principle of *délicatesse*. As Robbe-Grillet's evocation suggests, the manner of delivery was a way of practicing this principle, of leaving people in-*tact*. But how exactly does Barthes define delicacy, and how is this a way of participating in contemporary struggles?

The lectures held in the course of the following year cite *délicatesse* as one of the instances of "the neutral," a notion that Barthes had developed as an alternative to Sartre's *engagement*.[37] To follow this trajectory, from the late 1940s when Barthes began to write the essays that would be published in the 1953 book-length response to Sartre's *What Is Literature?* (1947) to the late lectures at the Collège, is to discover a shift in tone: from the rhetoric of a deeply suspicious Cold War climate, in which none of the available options seemed viable choices to Barthes, to a more light-hearted, often playful, if still discreet stance, exploring the idea of delicacy through a proliferation of examples.

It is commonly acknowledged that, from 1975 onward, Barthes's work no longer relied on tutelary systems; Tzvetan Todorov goes as far as to apply, perhaps only half in jest, Barthes's claim that one could only be a terrorist or an egoist, to these two major phases of his work, pre- and post-1975. Yet Julia Kristeva, another of his former students, insists that Barthes's position was from the outset, and remained, one of rebellious delicacy. In an attempt to historicize the project of his first book, she evokes forcefully the context of the early 1950s in France, dominated by a "banqueroute des idéologies et la misère de la philosophie" (the bankruptcy of political ideologies and the poverty of philosophy), in which Barthes's elegant and timid personality was to become the figure of a subtle rebel. She acknowledges that in a society dominated by mass culture, his *délicatesse* might be hard to understand, especially when it manifests itself in the insistence that authentic culture keeps us alive on condition that we do not stop putting it in question.[38] Yet she insists on a connection between delicacy and revolt specific to Barthes, whose choice of *writing* as an object of analysis appears to her as a most radical, because invisible, form of politics in the world already saturated with images of the 1950s ("un univers spéculaire, saturé de visibilité"): "Son respect et son admiration pour l'écriture était immense, mais réglé, à partir d'*une distance subtile* que seuls certains malades savent préserver vis-à-vis du commun comme d'eux-mêmes" (His respect and admiration for writing were immense, but adjusted from a subtle distance that only certain sick people know how to preserve from the ordinary as well as from themselves).[39] Delicacy, writing, distance: contextualizing *Writing Degree Zero* should help shed light on these affinities.

Delicacy as the desire and cultivated capacity to make fine distinctions appears rebellious indeed in the polarized, Manichaean climate characteristic of the Cold War period in France. Tony Judt speaks of a half-acknowledged rage pervading the writings of French intellectuals at this time: using a moral vocabulary, "ils divisaient tout—l'expérience, les choix, l'humanité entière—en catégories binaires: tout était bon ou mauvais, positif ou négatif, dans un monde peuplé de camarades ou d'ennemis" (they divided everything—experience, choices, humanity itself—in binary categories: everything was either good or bad, positive or negative, in a world populated by friends or enemies).[40] In this context, Sartre's famous essays, published in the journal *Temps Modernes* between 1945 and 1947 and then collected in *What Is Literature?* (1948), as well as Barthes's articles, published in *Combat* between 1947 and 1953 and then in *Writing Degree Zero* (1953), read like attempts to negotiate an adequate stance for the left-wing intellectual unwilling to relinquish his autonomy by following the Communist Party line. This was, it bears emphasis, the second episode in the "querelle du réalisme" (realism quarrel), which had first broken out in Paris in 1935 in the wake of the adoption by the first Soviet Writers' Congress in Moscow of Zhdanov's program for a "socialist realism."[41] Typical of the polarized thinking of the times, Jean Kanapa, the main editor of *La Nouvelle Critique*, labeled as "fascists and enemies of humanity" the existentialists who refused to conform to the Communist Party dictates; however, the anathema is not only cast against the pessimism of existentialists, but also denounces the decadence of the bourgeois aesthetes (practitioners of the so-called *l'art pour l'art*) and the formalism of painters who disdain content in their works. Sartre's essays are a reclamation of distance: he does not reject the idea of commitment, but the intellectual, he claims, cannot sacrifice his autonomy to a party that, "progressive and revolutionary in its doctrine and avowed ends, has become conservative in its means."[42]

Usually opposed, Sartre's *What Is Literature?* and Barthes's *Writing Degree Zero* share a historicization of the literary scene since 1848 predicated on one of the favorite *topoi* of French culture since the mid-nineteenth century: the "hate of the bourgeois."[43] Opposing realism and the *art-pour-l'art* theory developed in the nineteenth century, Sartre sees in them defensive maneuvers of bourgeois writers who hate their social class and try to escape it—some by adopting an alleged objectivity that would enable the revelation of the world "as it is," others by taking refuge in an empty aestheticism. Sartre and Barthes agree that socialist realism is only the last offspring of bourgeois realism, but the way out of the impossible predicament in which the left-wing writer finds himself is differently envisaged. As is well known, Sartre saw in commitment the only way a writer could escape his bourgeois origins in order to join the cause of the exploited. Barthes, however, claimed that such "commitment" was still a betrayal.

The source of this disconnect lies in their different views on language and its rapport to the world. Distrustful of the "crisis of language," in which Sartre sees only the culmination of the intellectual's alienation in a bourgeois society, he insists on the importance of taking a "rhetorical" approach premised on the belief of the adequacy of language to the world. Opposing it to the "poetic," which he denounces as "terrorist," and refusing the "cult of silence" that the latter leads to, he reminds writers that not to speak is still to speak (with the implication that silence amounts to complicity with the enemy): "Si l'on se met à déplorer l'inadéquation du langage à la réalité, on se fait complice de l'ennemi, c'est-à-dire de la propagande. Notre premier devoir d'écrivain est donc d'établir le langage dans sa liberté" (If we start deploring the inadequacy of language to reality, we side with our enemy, that is, with propaganda. Our first duty as writers is therefore to establish language in its freedom).[44] Barthes replaces this model with a tripartite one, beginning his *Writing Degree Zero* with the postulation of three realities: language, style, and writing. Distinguishing between language, "a human horizon which provides a distant setting of familiarity," and style, consisting of "imagery, delivery, vocabulary [which] spring from the body and the past of the writer and gradually become the very reflexes of his art," "a vertical and lonely dimension of thought," "the decorative voice of the hidden, secret flesh," Barthes defines writing as the locus of moral responsibility. The Sartrian influence on the following passage is unmistakable, but it is equally impossible to miss that, while Sartre locates commitment at the level of style, Barthes takes the latter for the product of the biological and historical person of the writer (and is therefore inescapable), hence the necessity of a third reality, *écriture*. *Writing* is the conscious choice of literary form, therefore the writer has to be mindful of the imbrication of literary conventions in social and political history:

> Within any literary form, there is a general choice of tone, of ethos, if you like, and this is precisely where the writer shows himself clearly as an individual because this is where he commits himself. . . . the formal identity of the writer is truly established . . . where the written continuum, first collected and enclosed within a perfectly innocent linguistic nature, at last becomes a total sign, the choice of a human attitude, the affirmation of a certain Good. It thus commits the writer to manifest and communicate a state of happiness or malaise, and links the form of his utterance, which is at once normal and singular, to the vast History of the Others. A language and a style are blind forces; a mode of writing is an act of historical solidarity. A language and a style are objects; a mode of writing is a function: it is the relationship between creation and society, the literary language transformed by its social finality, form considered as a human intention and thus linked to the great crises of History.[45]

But as Barthes goes on to show, relying on Sartre's own analysis, 1848 marked the breakup of the bourgeois consciousness and of its concordant, unique mode of writing—Literature with a capital *L*—which put the writer in the impossible situation of having to choose between the values of his bourgeois class and thus write in the obsolete forms of pre-1848 literature, or else work on new forms (that have yet no connection to new social realities) and thus fall into the trap of a self-reflexive literature (following in the footsteps of Flaubert, whose work is decisively marked by the failure of 1848 and the "hatred" of the bourgeoisie). Realist literature, Barthes claims, is nothing but pretense, never more artificial than when it claims to be transparent: similarly, he charges, Sartre's *engagement* does nothing more than affirm its commitment, because it does not put into question the signs encoded in the formal choices it adopts. "White writing," a so-called degree zero of language—Barthes had developed it in the 1940s in an analysis of Camus's *L'étranger*, then attributed it to Jean Cayrol and Maurice Blanchot[46]—appealed to him with its promise to abolish the "fatality" of the literary sign (that is, the fatality of signaling a political or social allegiance) and thus intimate in the form of the work the vision of a utopian, classless society:

> The writers of today feel this; for them, the search for a non-style or an oral style, for a zero level or a spoken level of writing is, all things considered, the *anticipation of a homogenous social state*; most of them understand that there can be no universal language outside a concrete, and no longer a mystical or merely nominal universality of society.[47]

Aiming at a degree zero of writing—"aiming" because this practice remains a utopia—is the only way, according to Barthes, for the bourgeois writer to atone for his "essential inauthenticity." The neutral, to conclude provisionally, is thus not a way of sidestepping commitment, but a form of acknowledging that literature as a medium of commitment has its own implicit allegiances to social formations and therefore a way of refusing to participate inadvertently in the oppression one is engaged in denouncing: according to Barthes, the morality of political choice is, in a writer, a responsibility of (literary) form. Before turning to the later lectures—which still preserve something of the "hermeneutic of suspicion" characteristic of the Cold War rhetoric, but also go beyond it—I want to shift attention to the writings of a German intellectual, Theodor Adorno, who wrestled with similar concerns. Staging an encounter between the two thinkers, French and German, who were apparently unaware of each other (or at least do not engage explicitly with each other's work) will help articulate better the historical stakes of the questions that animated Barthes in *Comment vivre ensemble*, and, implicitly, of the art of distances we are pursuing here.

The reserved tone with which Barthes approaches the subject of living with others brings to mind *Minima Moralia*, the book of short, often cryptic essays Theodor Adorno wrote in 1944–1947, during his American exile. An allusion to Aristotle's *Magna Moralia*, Adorno's title refers to the "melancholy science" that has as its object "a realm which has counted, since time immemorial, as the authentic one of philosophy, but which has, since its transformation into method, fallen prey to intellectual disrespect, sententious caprice and in the end forgetfulness: the teaching of the good life. What philosophy once called life, has turned into the sphere of the private."[48] Although separated by three decades, *Minima Moralia* and *Comment vivre ensemble* obviously share a number of concerns, the first one articulated in the "Dedication" from which I have just excerpted the above passage: the loss of prestige of moral discourse, and the precarious status of its object, the "teaching of the good life." The "method" that both Barthes and Adorno distrust is that of a rational discourse with which modernity has prided itself since the Enlightenment, a discourse, one might add, that looked up to ideals of objective detachment, of distance.[49] Adorno's famous equation "rationality is myth and myth is already enlightenment," as well as his analyses of American consumer culture, chime with Barthes's insights into the logic of late capitalism relentlessly unveiled in the essays collected in 1957 under the title *Mythologies*.[50] The diagnosis of late modernity that Adorno spells out—and in this *Minima Moralia* appears as a companion to *Dialectic of Enlightenment*—suggests that, because institutions have espoused the logic of rationalization and capitalist reproduction, they are no longer available sites of practice and transmission of ethical values, therefore private life has to bear the burden of remaining the sole medium where ethical practices—themselves contaminated by the pervasive logic of rationalization, reification, and exchange—remain thinkable.[51] Adorno identifies a conflict between the universal (society) and the particular (the individual), otherwise formulated in the paradox that the very institutions that should provide the conditions of possibility for individual existence and self-realization are now at odds with it.

The grimness of the subtitle, *Reflections from Damaged Life*, is pushed to an unredeemable extreme when he announces that "there is nothing innocuous left" and proceeds to show that the damage affects all the spheres of human experience, from the way one handles objects to interpersonal relationships. In "Refuge for the Homeless" he formulates the only available solution: "The best mode of conduct, in face of all this, still seems an uncommitted, suspended one: to lead a private life, as far as the social order and one's own needs will tolerate nothing else, but not to attach weight to it as to something still socially substantial and individually appropriate" (*MM*, frag. 18, p. 39). Adorno claims that in the "total system" he describes—no stranger to the world shared by Sartre and Barthes in which not to choose, as the former put it, is still to choose (that is, to choose evil)—all the available options are compromised and therefore any choice would be complicit with a system that ended up in barbarism. The inescapable reference is Auschwitz, the event that constitutes in Adorno's account the absolute caesura of Western civilization. In such historical circumstances, intelligence has become a moral category, and lucidity a moral imperative.

The term "uncommitted" is particularly significant because it sends us to Adorno's essay from 1965, "Commitment," written in response to the English translation of Sartre's "What is Literature?" Faithful to his theory of a "total system" that permeates and mediates any experience, be it collective or personal, Adorno shows that Sartre's *engagement* is a form of accommodation to this compromised world, hence complicit in the pernicious mechanisms it seeks to denounce. While he grants Sartre the insight of art's autonomy, formulated in the notion of the appeal that issues from any work of art, Adorno crucially adds: "There is no straightforward relationship between this appeal and the thematic commitment of a work"; and later on: "Works of art that react against empirical reality obey the forces of that reality, which reject intellectual creations and throw them back on themselves."[52] These two reactions to Sartre's notion of commitment, Barthes's and Adorno's, are strikingly similar, but to juxtapose them is also to make apparent the more mysterious air that conceals the pernicious forces of which Adorno cannot be suspicious enough. And this reflects in the only salutary alternatives they propose: in Adorno's account, nonrepresentational art is the only acceptable solution, because its abstraction holds up a mirror to "the abstraction of the law which objectively dominates society."[53] Beckett and Kafka produce the "shock of the unintelligible," they "arouse the fear which existentialism merely talks about." It is not sure from Adorno's account how such works are produced—Fredric Jameson ironically suggests that their creation is "a little less than magical"—but they are characterized as instances of pure volition, managing to escape the mediation by the system.[54] The following passage is worth quoting in full, because it registers the point at which Adorno comes closest to Barthes's own response to Sartre and his notion of the neutral or white writing: "The moment of true volition [that produces nonconceptual art] is mediated through nothing other than the form of the work itself, whose crystallization becomes an analogy of that other condition which should be. As eminently constructed and produced objects, works of art, including literary ones, point to a practice from which they abstain: the creation of a just life."[55]

Strikingly, both Adorno and Barthes insist on a necessary restraint on the part of the writer, as a way of intimating discreetly a better alternative to an unjust society: what Barthes called the "responsibility of the form" (and Adorno would probably not have disagreed with the formulation) is an attitude that rejects mimetic forms of representation that are compromised—through their imbrication in the "total system," as Adorno puts it, by their association with bourgeois values, in Barthes's account. The writer does not create a "just society," but his austerity and asceticism anticipate it. Adorno locates this anticipation at the level of the creative act that refuses the accommodation to the existing conditions, as do Beckett and Kafka ("As eminently *constructed and produced* objects, works of art, including literary ones, point to *a practice* from which they abstain: *the creation of a just life*"), while Barthes goes a little further in the suggestion that the "neutral" writer actually eliminates formally the markers ("signs") of inequality and injustice, intimating the freshness of an Adamic language and of a utopian, equalitarian society. The subsequent fate of the literary texts that inspired the "solutions" provided by Adorno and Barthes—Beckett and Kafka did not escape recuperation by the "total system" incriminated by Adorno, and Barthes was himself disappointed by Camus's *La peste*, and subsequently expressed doubts about the aesthetic value of the Nouveau Roman that he had originally praised as "white writing" (notably Robbe-Grillet's novels)—points to the impossibility of these alternatives, to the utopianism inherent in the notion that one can actively refuse to choose among the available options and adopt a lucid, self-reflective stance that would be somehow relevant politically.

Yet there are moments in *Minima Moralia* and in *Comment vivre ensemble* that allow room for nuance in this regard, to be sifted from the ways these two texts register the self-reflective presence of their authors as historical individuals. By this I mean that both Adorno and Barthes make a case for the relevance of individual experience, for the exemplarity of the particular, when the universal subject of bourgeois culture has abdicated. Paradoxically, however, as the last and therefore nostalgic "remnants of the bourgeoisie," Barthes and Adorno retain from this repudiated culture the attentiveness to particulars that used to be one of its central principles and turn it into an ideal to be preserved at the core of an ethical life that has retreated into the private. I will briefly show how Adorno justifies his emphasis on the individual, then I will turn to Barthes's late lectures and articulate more clearly the effects of their shared nostalgia.

Adorno's life was marked by the rise of Nazism: his first book was published on January 30, 1933, on the day of Hitler's accession to power, and his thought developed to a large degree as a parallel critique of Nazification and American consumer culture. *Minima Moralia* often identifies mechanisms at the core of capitalism that are similar in their instrumentalization of people to the polarizing logic of the Nazi propaganda. "Passing muster," for instance, is the mental habit of the businessman, the manager, and the Nazi doctor alike; they all expertly divide people into binary categories, in a simple operation that reduces everyone to friends or enemies, insiders or outsiders, accomplices or victims:

> Anyone who has once made it his concern to judge people's suitability sees those judged, by a kind of technological necessity, as insiders or outsiders, as belonging or alien to the race, as accomplices or victims. The fixed, inspecting, hypnotic and hypnotized stare that is common to all the leaders of horror, has its model in the appraising look of the manager. . . . The last stage is the medical examination to decide between capacity for work and liquidation. (*MM*, frag. 85, p. 131)

Given that everyone is judged only as means, rather than ends, this "total system" cancels out the very possibility of the ethical life: "Thus impoverishment of the relation to others sets in: the capacity for seeing them as such and not as functions of one's own will withers, as does that, above all, of fruitful contrast, the possibility of going beyond oneself by assimilating the contradictory" (*MM*, frag. 85, p. 131).

Schooled by the dialectical method of Hegel's *Phenomenology of Spirit*, *Minima Moralia* takes the radical step of reversing Hegel's treatment of totality and his critique of the *für-sich sein* of subjectivity, insisting that "the whole is the false" (*MM*, frag. 29, p. 50) and that the individual is "a distorted fragment of the world through which the processes generating decay might be glimpsed."[56] Read in light of this claim, *Minima Moralia* appears as the self-reflexive gesture of an intellectual who analyzes his predicament as a symptom of larger forces of history: Adorno understands his exile as a general condition among his contemporaries, which affects not only estranged intellectuals but also the displaced and the homeless; his travelogue is therefore autobiographical without being personal. Its self-reflective asceticism is mirrored in its form, which points us back to the complex relationship to Hegel. In a letter to Adorno, Thomas Mann expressed dismay at the relentless negativity that permeates *Minima Moralia*; the author replied unapologetically that "only a trickster gives more than he himself has." On the other hand, he admitted that ascesis was for him an effort, the necessity of which he had learned from Hegel:

> If anything has penetrated my flesh and blood from Hegel and those who put him on his feet, it is the ascetic stance regarding the

> unmediated expression of the positive. This is truly an ascesis for me, believe me, since the other, the more unrestrained expression of hope, would be much closer to my nature. But I always have the feeling that, if one fails to persist in the negative or moves too quickly into the positive, one plays into the hands of the untrue.[57]

The choice of the fragment is a manifestation of this ascesis: a formal strategy of resisting systemic totality, which however does not exclude closure. Often reading like aphoristic pronouncements, these fragments are "powerfully dominated by an aesthetic of closure," like Benjamin's *Denkbilder* (thought-images).[58] In other words, Adorno performs the very neutrality (i.e., "uncommitted stance") he cryptically alludes to in both *Minima Moralia* and the later "Commitment" essay. A similar performance of the "neutral" occurs in Barthes's later work.[59]

In the 1977–1978 course *Le neutre*, the French theorist returns very explicitly to this early notion with the acknowledgment that the neutral "a pour référent, en moi, un affect obstiné" (has as a referent, in me, a stubborn affect). Defining it more clearly than before as a "choice on the side" (le terme qui déjoue le paradigme; un choix à côté), the third, nondialectical term, outside of a paradigm it aims to unravel, Barthes conducts his course as an investigation rather than in any disciplined, methodical fashion, as a typical university lecture.[60] Favoring culture over method (the distinction comes from Nietzsche, via Deleuze)[61] and arrogating his right to digress, he states his refusal to subject his audience to an authoritative discourse and, rather than a dictionary of definitions, he offers a constellation of *scintillations* in the form of fragments with thematic headings ordered alphabetically.[62] Two aspects require emphasis here, and both set him apart from Adorno: one is that Barthes's style, even as he marks his distance from the "system" (in this case the institutional setting, which is in accord with larger structures of power, reflected in Foucault's notion of "resonance chambers"), Barthes takes a hedonistic rather than ascetic stance; to the regimenting tendencies of the system, he opposes the idiosyncrasy of pleasure—that is, the pleasure of culture. The second aspect is the choice of proliferating fragments, which, unlike Adorno's, are meant to remain open, always incomplete. This method of presentation, Antoine Compagnon claims in *Les antimodernes*, reflects Barthes's reservations vis-à-vis the avant-garde, the very form of modernism he had earlier cited as exemplary of the "neutral." Whereas Adorno never took his distance from his modernist paragons (Kafka and Beckett), Barthes's attention to the changing nuances of the times caused his sympathies to shift. The lectures turn to culture as to a repository of interesting objects to be rediscovered and (in the sense of *inventio* in classical rhetoric, i.e., finding one's examples in the collective *memoria*), (re)invented as objects of study: a lover's discourse (1974–1976), living-with-others (1976–1977), the neutral (1977–1978), and the preparation of the novel (1978–1980). At the same time, central to this way of teaching is the practice of *paideia* applied to the self, that is, culture as *paideia*. We have seen the autobiographical dimension of Adorno's essays: this is Barthes's.

Political in its premises, his project is ultimately ethical: "Dans la mesure où notre Neutre se cherche par rapport au paradigme, au conflit, au choix, le champ général de nos réflexions serait: l'éthique qui est discours du 'bon choix' . . . ou du 'non-choix,' ou du 'choix-à-côté': de l'ailleurs du choix, l'ailleurs du conflit du paradigme" (Insofar as our Neutral tries to define itself in relation to the paradigm, the conflict, the choice, our general field of reflection is the ethical/ ethics, which is the discourse of "the right choice," of the "nonchoice," of the "choice on the side") (*N*, 33). Predicting with some humor that the ethical might become fashionable again, if only as a return of the repressed (i.e., "repressed" by a Marx or a Freud—"à surveiller!," he enjoins), he warns that ethics is inescapable: "L'éthique, ça existe toujours, partout; seulement, c'est différemment fondé, assumé ou refoulé: ça traverse tout discours" (The ethical, it is still there / is always there, everywhere; it is only variously grounded, assumed or repressed: it traverses all discourse) (*N*, 33). The shift of emphasis is most clearly indicated in a later passage, in which the notion of indeterminate differentiation (opposing the logic of identity characteristic of the late capitalist world) becomes central to an ethical (read: personal) life-project:

> En effet, je voudrais, si c'était en mon pouvoir, regarder les mots-figures (à commencer par le Neutre) d'un regard frisant qui fasse apparaître des nuances (denrée de plus en plus rare, vrai luxe déplacé du langage; en grec = *diaphora*, mot nietzschéen). Bien comprendre: ceci n'est pas la requête d'une sophistication intellectuelle. Ce que je cherche, dans la préparation du cours, c'est une introduction au vivre, un guide de vie (projet éthique): je veux vivre selon la nuance. (*N*, 36–37)

> If it is in my power, I would indeed like to examine the words-figures (the Neutral, to begin with) with a penetrating gaze that would make nuances visible (a more and more rare commodity, displaced luxury of language; in Greek = diaphora, a Nietzschean word). Important to understand: this is not a request of intellectual sophistication. What I am looking for, in the preparation of this course, is an introduction to living, a life-guide (an ethical project): I want to live in accord with the nuance.

A connection with Michel Foucault's late concerns is not easily overlooked here: Barthes's project bespeaks a certain *care of the self*, a project of paradoxically becoming "neutral"—also in a certain sense impersonal, in keeping with a modernist sensibility—out of a desire to flee dogmatism, and this by being increasingly aware of nuances, capable of finer distinctions: opposing the lack of difference (the indifference of the system to the individual in his or her particularity) with its indefinite proliferation.[63] One should readily add, however, that the lectures (or rather, seminars) court the ethical both in its dimension of rhetorical ethos (which mobilizes a certain pathos as well), but also as the genuine regard for the others (the audience). No trace of Foucault's solitude following the end of the lecture:[64] Barthes insisted on the collective character of the quest, repeatedly inviting the contributions of those present in the auditorium.[65]

Although interpersonal relationships do appear to be ancillary to the individual's well-being, *délicatesse* as the dominant practice within Barthes's ideal community ensures that, in tandem with care of the self, there is also regard for others. To recapitulate, before we turn to Adorno again: the ethical appears to be pitched against the political, as its radical, if discreet, subversion; Barthes dreams of a domestic, *not even social*, utopia, a community in which the ideal distance between self and others would be a given, like a fine balance maintained at all times. *Délicatesse* is already present in the thematic catalog of the lover's discourse, central as a principle (and form of behavior, of attention) to the ideal community, and an essential example in understanding the idea of the neutral.[66] Indeed, it might be central to the demystifying practices of *sémiologie* itself.

As we have seen, Kristeva also touched on the notion of distance as inherent to the practice of *délicatesse*, and its centrality to *Comment vivre ensemble* makes a return to it necessary. Initially, Barthes intimates that his understanding of delicacy draws its inspiration from the Marquis de Sade, who appreciated all tastes, however eccentric, because they all "go back to a principle of delicacy," that is, to a capacity to make fine distinctions.[67] This does not exhaust the possible ways of defining *délicatesse*, and soon enough Barthes shows that it is also related to the problem of finding the ideal distance between oneself and others:

> La distance comme valeur. Cela ne doit pas être pris dans la perspective mesquine du simple quant-à-soi. Nietzsche fait de la distance une valeur forte—une valeur rare: "l'abîme entre homme et homme, entre une classe et une autre, la multiplicité des types, la volonté d'être soi, de se distinguer, ce que j'appelle le pathos des distances est le propre de toutes les époques fortes." (*CVE*, 179)[68]
>
> Distance as a value. That should not be taken in the petty perspective of self-containment. Nietzsche makes of distance a strong value, a rare value: "the gulf between man and man, rank and rank; the multiplicity of types, the will to be one's self, to stand out—everything I call pathos of distance—is proper to every strong period."[69]

This quote from Nietzsche's *Twilight of the Idols* takes us on a path toward which Barthes gestures rather vaguely in *Comment vivre ensemble*, but which can be explored in light of a passage in his autobiography of 1975. I am referring to the desire for "distance" as a desire for personal space that, he claims, is a contemporary problem. If this is indeed so, there also lurks a more personal nostalgia: in *Roland Barthes par Roland Barthes*, another text organized around traits (there he calls them *biographèmes*), he wonders ingenuously whether one might not be able to enjoy the charms of the *art de vivre bourgeois* in a socialist society, as one would enjoy an exoticism; this is what he would call a "contretemps," an anachronism.[70] In other words, as "one of the last remnants of the bourgeoisie," Barthes wants to rescue the value of distance (that is, the aristocratic respect for distinction, for the particular) from this almost defunct culture. This justifies the paradoxical position emphasized by Compagnon in Barthes's desire to situate himself "à l'arrière de l'avant-garde." As Compagnon, a student of Barthes, says: "Not simply in the rear-guard, but standing back, at a distance, shuffling his feet, squinting backwards, exercising a right to look or to inventory, the way Sartre said of Baudelaire that he was moving forward while keeping an eye on the rear-view mirror."[71] The gaze backward, the expression of ambivalence, is motivated by the desire to retain something that has become very rare: the fine nuances of *délicatesse*.

Adorno seems to share Barthes's nostalgia, if in less self-conscious manner: *Minima Moralia* lingers in the moment just before the bourgeoisie's presumed demise, in an unacknowledged attempt to lift from its *art de vivre* a certain sensitivity to the singularity of the individual.[72] It is a curious feature of *Minima Moralia*, so relentless in denouncing the paradoxes of rationality-driven modernity, that Adorno looks back, like Benjamin in *Berlin Childhood around 1900*, to an epoch that made possible genuine luxury (that is, a luxury more attuned to the specific needs of the individual), without an explicit awareness of the reliance of social privilege on the many underprivileged:

> Rampant technology eliminates luxury, but not by declaring privilege a human right; rather, it does so by both raising the general standard of living and cutting off the possibility of fulfillment. . . . What made up the voluptuousness of travel, beginning with the goodbye-waving through the open window, the solicitude of amiable accepters of tips, the ceremonial of mealtimes, the constant feeling of receiving *favours that take nothing from anyone else*, has passed away. (*MM*, frag. 77, p. 119, my italics)

Adorno's use of "distance" is in many respects similar to Barthes's: against the "bad mediation" of society, which makes one believe that the easiest way to approach the other is by way of the straight line, the "recognition of distance" is vital if an ethical life, be it in the realm of the private, is to remain conceivable. In a passage echoing Marx's multifaceted analysis of alienation, Adorno shows how this mediation intervenes in the deceiving appearance of proximity characteristic of consumerism: "What has become alien to men is the human component of culture, its closest part, which upholds them against the world. They make common cause with the world against themselves, and the most alienated condition of all, the omnipresence of commodities, their own conversion into appendages of machinery, is for them a mirage of closeness" (*MM*, frag. 96, pp. 146–147).[73] This closeness is well illustrated by Charlie Chaplin in *Modern Times* in the dance with the machine that swallows him, and is compounded by the fungibility of objects and the utility principle, both immanent to consumer culture; all reflect back onto the way individuals treat one another. That society is "stamped by the economic principle" is obvious in the disappearance of genuine distinction and in the rampant anti-intellectualism that goes hand in hand with what Adorno calls "the progressive disappearance of differences in the mode of consciousness between [upper and lower strata]" (*MM*, frag. 120, p. 187). Another instance of the "pathos of distance"? Indeed, but Adorno reclaims it as the necessary acknowledgment of space surrounding the individual, for his (or her) "aura" to exist. He uses this Benjaminian notion not only in relation to physical realities (the mountains) or ancient objects (cult objects), but also referring to individuals:

> Intimacies estrange, violate the imponderably delicate aura of the other which is his condition as a subject. Only by the recognition of distance in our neighbour is strangeness alleviated: accepted into consciousness. The presumption of undiminished nearness present from the first, however, the flat denial of strangeness, does the other supreme wrong, virtually negates him as a particular human being and therefore the humanity in him, "counts him in," incorporates him in the inventory of property. Wherever immediateness posits and entrenches itself, the bad mediateness of society is insidiously asserted. (*MM*, frag. 116, p. 182)

Tact, like *délicatesse* for Barthes, is a practice that needs to remain meaningful; problematically, it is connected to (outmoded) ritual, therefore it is often lost on the logic of identity dominating late capitalist society, when it does not help to perpetuate injustice.[74] In other words, since tact is the capacity to grasp a situation with sensitivity, and see what rules need to be applied, or if necessary, overlooked, it risks becoming incomprehensible in the absence of codified morality or social convention: it is no longer recognized as a deviation from something generally accepted as the norm, but misunderstood as indifference or social ineptitude.[75] Similarly, Barthes speaks of *délicatesse* in relation to politeness:

> Politesse: n'est intéressante (pour nous, par rapport au principe de délicatesse) que dans ses traits excessifs (car sinon prise dans une

> gangue conformiste d'habitudes: ce qui doit se faire); la politesse n'est délicate que si, par l'excès, elle retrouve une inventivité au besoin confinant au farfelu. (*N*, 62)
>
> Politeness: it is only interesting (to us, in relation to the principle of delicacy) in its excessive traits (otherwise it is taken in a conformist gangue of habits: what one must, is supposed to do); politeness is only delicate if, by excess, it discovers an ingeniousness bordering, if necessary, the eccentric.

In providing other examples of delicacy, many of which he lifts from various literary sources, Barthes is hardly concerned with prescribing conditions of applicability for this principle: a playful, open, infinitely nuanced stance remains the requirement and privilege of *délicatesse*. The reason is spelled out by Adorno, in a self-reflexive commentary incidentally formulated in the language of distance: "keeping one's distance" is not just a historical imperative related to a political situation; it is also a measure of the authenticity of real thought which goes back to one of Nietzsche's fundamental insights, a premise of all hermeneutic of suspicion:

> Only at a remove from life can the mental life exist, and truly engage the empirical. While thought relates to facts and moves by criticizing them, its movement depends no less on the maintenance of distance. It expresses exactly what is, precisely because what is is never quite as thought expresses it. Essential to it is an element of exaggeration, of over-shooting the object, of self-detachment from the weight of the factual, so that instead of merely reproducing being it can, at once rigorous and free, determine it. (*MM*, frag. 82, p. 126)

It is worth interrupting this paragraph to note that Nietzsche haunts both Barthes and Adorno in ways they do not seem to care to spell out, in this particular case with the allusion to the famous essay "On Truth and Lies in an Extra-Moral Sense." Adorno's thought continues later with a scintillating claim that might seem to address itself directly to Barthes, specifically to the French thinker's elaborations on the sedimentation of history in linguistic form that we have discussed earlier with respect to *Writing Degree Zero*:

> Distance is not a safety-zone but a field of tension. It is manifested not in relaxing the claim of ideas to truth, but *in delicacy and fragility of thinking*. . . . The distance of thought from reality is itself nothing other than the precipitate of history in concepts. To use them without distance is, despite all the resignation it implies or because of it, a child's affair. For thought must aim beyond its target just because it never quite reaches it, and positivism is uncritical in its confidence

> of doing so, imagining its tergiversations to be due to mere conscientiousness. A transcending thought takes its own inadequacy more thoroughly into account than does one guided by the control mechanisms of science. (*MM*, frag. 82, pp. 127–128, my italics)[76]

Adorno's moments of utopianism, reflected in his negative critique, point us to a practice that Barthes, three decades later, put into the service of a personal phantasm, the ideal community whose image hovers in the filigrees of *Comment vivre ensemble*. *Délicatesse*, to translate his enterprise in Adorno's language, aims beyond its target, proliferating examples as a way of signaling the insufficiency of any one illustration. To the self-confident "distance" of positivism it opposes a "conjoining of distances": an unassuming, obliging openness.

Between Adorno and Barthes thus opens up the field of tension of an "art of distances" inaugurated by gestures of disavowal of a bourgeois culture, which then unfolds in repeated acknowledgments that not everything that is associated with it can be relinquished; it is the manifestation of a split consciousness. As we have seen, the "neutral" emerged from the impossible times of a radically polarized world, defining itself as a lucid uncommitted stance: a *neither/nor*. Strikingly, both Adorno and Barthes seem to think of the ethical (the personal) as resisting a pervasive "total" system, acknowledging however the precariousness of any reclamation of exemplarity. The lectures at the Collège de France register a shift of tone: the reticence to propose something concrete is still there, in a permanent retreat of the act of enunciation, in a deferral of meaning from an example to the next, but it is also distilled in the dictionary of *scintillations* that map out the thematic field of living with others. It is up to the reader to resume Barthes's research, and to uncover in the work of other writers of the past century, the hitherto unacknowledged science, or perhaps art of distances he suggested we need. The following pages engage in the pursuit of just such an art.

The first part of the book traces the emergence of the "art of distances" in the interwar period and focuses on the aftermath of major events from the first half of the century: the economic downturn, discontent with the "dirty work of empire," fascism, and the Second World War. The title, "The Pathos of Distances in 'a World of Banished People,'" conjoins Nietzsche's famous formulation with Elias Canetti's description of a generalized sense of exile, which coincides, as we have seen, with Adorno's experience. What Nietzsche paraphrased as "the abyss between man and man, class and class, the plurality of types, the will to be oneself, to stand out" was no cause for celebration for George Orwell and Elias Canetti, the protagonists of the first and second chapters, respectively. While serving in the colonial administration of the British Empire, Orwell came to see this "distance" as an oppressive injustice at the root of imperialism; he was further alerted to the many forms of injustice and inequality while working as a dishwasher in Paris, tramping in and around London, fighting in Catalonia, and sharing the miners' quarters in the North of England. Revisiting his largely forgotten first book, *Down and Out in Paris and London*, I show how such experiences led him to defamiliarize the notion of class and its attending principle of sincerity, thus detaching himself from the "political generation" of the 1930s, and imposing on later generations of intellectuals an "inescapable obligation of tactlessness."

Much like a compulsion of tactlessness, Canetti's moralizing attitude (a desire to "rub people's noses in their wickedness") was directly related to his experience of being a stateless person all his life. In his case, "distance" was not exclusively the reclamation of class distinction, or of a sense of superiority inherent to imperialism. Born in Bulgaria into a family of Sephardic Jews, and moving from the Vienna of his youth to Weimar Berlin and taking refuge in England during "the Blitz" and after, Canetti described "*all* life . . . [as] laid out in distances," experienced like thorns in one's flesh. In his account, this unsettling sociality of distances, which can only be annulled in the experience of the crowd, ultimately explains the "barbarism" of the past century. In "The Inferno of Saviors: Notes in the Margin of Elias Canetti's Lifework," I read *Crowds and Power* through the lens of his memoirs, and show how, in an unacknowledged dialogue with Freud's psychoanalysis, this highly controversial book proposes nothing less than a reformation of the social sphere. In so doing, I also discuss Canetti's relevance to the historiographic debates about the rise of Nazism and to the ongoing conversation about the legacy of violence.

Obsessed with the crowd, Canetti does not claim that it is a sustainable mode of living with other people; the ideal would be a finely measured distance, such as in the practice of delicacy, or tact. Differently put, the way to tolerate the "pathos of distance" is by rewriting it (with Barthes) as pathos *and* distance: Eros and Sophia, love and wisdom. I take up this idea in chapter 3, where I discuss the secular community that Iris Murdoch imagined in *The Bell* (1958) as a way to address critically "our facile notions of sincerity and authenticity." Murdoch, I show, gives philosophical weight to Barthes's question about the ideal distance between "a sociability without alienation and a solitude without exile," grounding it in a critique, on one hand, of the British empiricist tradition culminating in linguistic analytic philosophy and, on the other, of continental existentialism, notably in its Sartrian incarnation. Bringing together Platonism and Christianity, her notion of love as a moral ideal—whose difficulties are well illustrated in *The Bell*—appears to be a field of tension between closeness and wisdom, echoing Barthes's rewriting of the Nietzschean "pathos of distances." In short, the first part of the book follows the path of a dialectic: it considers first the power of distance that separates, often dehumanizing others; the distance-annulling virtues of the crowd; and dialectically, an *ideal* distance—living neither too close, nor too far from others—imaginable in a small community.

Part II, "'The World in Me': The 'Distantiality' of Everyday Life," turns to the experience of everyday life as recorded in (partly) autobiographical narratives for a rewriting of Heidegger's notion in an ethical key. Refuting Heidegger's claim that everyday life is a space of inauthenticity on account of a generalized competitiveness in which the others are instrumentalized only for the sake of self-appraisal, I document the tendency of autobiography in the course of the past century to shift from a focus on the self (the paradigmatic example is Walter Benjamin's *Berlin Childhood around 1900*) to a preoccupation with the lives of others: from Ernaux's *Journal du dehors* and *La vie extérieure* (1999), Grass's *My Century* (1999), and Damon Galgut's *In a Strange Room* (2010), the self emerges as a composite personality, as if traversed by others. I show how Ernaux expands the autobiographical genre spatially, to incorporate the *outside*, while Grass projects the everyday onto the long duration of the century, piecing together an intriguing biography of his *Jahrhundert*; finally, how the South African writer Galgut alternates in his novel between the first and the third person, straddling the memoir and the novelistic genre in order to probe the frontier between the self and an impersonal, shared humanity. I argue that the perspective adopted by these narratives fosters the creation of a space for the imagination to do its work of remembering that all the people, infinitely different, to which everyday life and travel expose one are singular human beings, protagonists of stories they tell themselves about their own lives. Attuned to the singularity and humanity of such stories, these chronicles of encounters with other lives by Ernaux, Grass, and Galgut model a different way of thinking about self, others, and the distance between: the others invariably bring one back to oneself, enabling the revelation of unexpected or forgotten inner distances, and enlarging one's sense of self through a paradoxical humbling. This is the "art of distances" these texts offer their readers as a morality—redefined—for the everyday.

As this outline suggests, the central narrative of the book follows a chronological arc that starts in the late 1920s and ends in 2010, identifying the emergence of an insistent preoccupation with interpersonal distance in the interwar period, and some of its discrete episodes in Orwell's critique of class in the early 1930s, Canetti's obsession with the crowd experience (intensified during Nazism), Murdoch's critique of the liberal notion of personality following the second world war, the revalorization of the everyday and of history from below (as reflected in autobiographical texts that read like chronicles of other lives), finally, of the happenstance of travel as a consequence of enhanced mobility in the global age. But this historical narrative also has philosophical implications: with their focus on interpersonal distance, these literary texts contribute to a rethinking of living with other people that parallels the systematic approach to the problem of community by philosophers of the past century such as Nancy, Levinas, Esposito, and Sloterdijk. They do so, on one hand, by way of a refusal of the traditional community (variously identified as *Gemeinschaft*, bourgeois morality, the sincerity paradigm . . .), that Adorno captures in "Refuge for the Homeless" in *Minima Moralia*: "Today it has become part of morality not to be at home in one's home," which is this book's epigraph.[77] Indeed, the writers or characters that will occupy me in the pages that follow are outsiders, exiles, or foreigners in their own homes: Orwell tramping in and around London, and inspecting the kitchens of luxurious hotels in Paris; Miller reveling in his rootless freedom; the stateless Canetti, bemoaning the fact that his was "a world of banished people"; Murdoch's characters taking refuge in their community because the world outside "offers them no home"; Ernaux, a "class-transfuge," attentive to fleeting encounters with anonymous others; Grass, writing history "from below," imagining the stories of "little people"; and Damon (Galgut), whose chronic restlessness finds momentary respite only in anonymous rooms. On the other hand, these authors implicitly or explicitly reflect on how to live with others through the pursuit of powerful commitments that involve other people: to the ordinary (Orwell), the crowd (Canetti), the particular (Murdoch), the everyday (Ernaux), history from below (Grass) and the happenstance of travel as a metaphor for an open (inoperative, *unworked*) community (Galgut).

When Adorno speaks of "not being at home in one's home," the word refers both to the physical dwelling, but also to the symbolic dimension of one's familiar ideological bearings. The paradox noted and illustrated by Barthes and Adorno—of being the last remnants of the bourgeoisie and its harshest enemies—is thus reiterated here in new form, affecting this time more directly the notion of "morality": if one redefines it, capturing a truth about contemporary experience ("*today*. . . ," Adorno says), does the new content not impinge upon the "old" name, "morality"? The question will receive attention in the third chapter: Iris Murdoch's philosophical project largely consisted in shifting the familiar frameworks of moral discourse by broadening them; in her view, moral philosophy must encompass the full range of experience, which is usually the realm of the writer of fiction. Strikingly, this registers a return to what philosophy used to regard as its object, the question of the examined life, of how to live well—now *with others*.

Part I

✦

The Pathos of Distances in "a World of Banished People"

Chapter 1

George Orwell's Critique of Sincerity and the Obligation of Tactlessness

The concern about the appropriate stance for an intellectual in the 1930s was shared not only by Theodor Adorno and Roland Barthes; it was much on the mind of other thinkers and writers of that decade. In England, the period registered the juncture of the first generation of modernists and the so-called political generation—"stung into class consciousness" (Virginia Woolf), and confronting "the invasion of literature by politics" (George Orwell).

Orwell illustrates better than anyone else the writer's conflicted position in this period. His life was to a large degree marked by the paradox articulated by Adorno, of being "one of the last remnants of the bourgeoisie" but also one of its harshest critics, a predicament that demanded uncompromising lucidity. It is as if the British writer had pursued as his life's motto the stern injunction against the enjoyment of one's home in *Minima Moralia*, "Today it is part of morality not to be at home in one's home": when Orwell returned from Burma, where he had served for five years in the colonial administration of the British Empire, he decided to "submerge [him]self, to get right down among the oppressed, to be one of them and on their side against their tyrants."[1] In fact, to say that Orwell *returned* from Burma calls for a qualifying reminder: He had left for India as Eric Blair in 1922, after his "lower-upper-middle class" family had come down and was struggling to keep up the appearance of respectability—a special case, indeed, of the pathos of distance. Increasingly disgusted with his involvement in the "dirty work of the Empire," during a leave home he decided that his life as a sahib was a thing of the past. Rather hyperbolically hailed as "Saint George," not for his asceticism but, paradoxically, for his "ethic of free participation in the full-blooded drama of life,"[2] Orwell spent the two decades following his return to England until his premature death in 1950 expiating an immeasurable sense of guilt: his tramping expeditions in and around London; his work as a dishwasher in Paris; the travel to the North of England, where he shared the miners' quarters; and his "fight against fascism" alongside the anti-Stalinist militias in the Spanish Civil War all speak to the commitment to the oppressed he made in the late 1920s.[3]

Recording his experiences of voluntary destitution on both sides of the Channel, his first published book, *Down and Out in Paris and London* (1933), reads like a fictionalized autobiographical reportage. Partly because it straddles uncomfortably several genres, it has a minor status in the literary canon of the period and in Orwell's career, overshadowed by his most prominent late novels *Animal Farm* and *1984*. Its significance, however, lies in marking the birth of the *character* George Orwell:[4] someone who would henceforth ground his politics in firsthand experience and who would tirelessly evoke his encounters with the oppressed in a prose with powerful ethical undertones. "Innumerable remembered faces," he writes, for example, in *The Road to Wigan Pier*,

> faces of prisoners in the dock, of men waiting in the condemned cells, of subordinates I had bullied and aged peasants I had snubbed, of servants and coolies I had hit with my fist in moments of rage (nearly everyone does these things in the East, at any rate occasionally: Orientals can be very provoking), haunted me intolerably. I was conscious of an immense weight of guilt that I had got to expiate. (*RWP*, 147–148)

Between the "innumerable *remembered* faces" and the generic one, "a boot stamping on *a* human face forever" that captures the experience of totalitarianism in *1984*, Orwell's literary career unfolded as a move away from the autobiographical in search of a literary form that would respond to the demands of an increasingly politicized world. As has been observed, the face was for Orwell the source of an enduring ethical appeal; it was also a synecdoche for the body, which, in *Down and Out in Paris and London* already, is a "measure of truth":[5] both the narrator's own body, immersed in the sordid realities of poverty, and the bodies of tramps, scarred and diseased, silent records of their misery. Symbolically, the body is a reminder of shared humanity, of what Orwell calls quite loosely the *ordinary*. His lifelong commitment (between the tramps in *Down and Out* all the way to the proles in *1984*) was to the ordinary man: not imagined, such as the "ordinary mind on an ordinary day" of Mrs. Brown or Leopold Bloom, but known concretely from the encounters with tramps, miners, workers that Orwell pursued.

These experiences not only defamiliarize class; they also blur the boundaries between the ethical and the political, and even unsettle the categories that ground common understandings of politics. Readers of various political stripes have variously called Orwell a socialist, a liberal, a postliberal, "a thorn in the side of the Left," a right-winger, "the dire anti-totalitarian prophet"; and, as Kingsley Amis points out, "if they [the readers, had] none, incidentally, this [was] as much Orwell's doing as anyone else's."[6] Many critics found it more cogent to associate his commitment to "the ordinary" with a moral stance: "Orwell's conversion," as Woodcock liked to say, "came from a far deeper experience—emotionally as well as intellectually and physically—than that which made the Spenders and Audens in their college rooms and parental country rectories declare a mental adherence to communism."[7] This insistence on the "deeper" quality of his experience, on its necessary immediacy as a precondition for writing that would be relevant to the specific problems of the times has been central to critical appraisals of Orwell's attachment to the ordinary in ethical terms. John Rodden endorsed the views of other critics, for instance, when he professed that the case of Orwell offers "not only a sociological but also *an ethical guide* to the contemporary relation of the intellectual and politics";[8] but this view does not yet intimate the large spectrum covered by critical appraisals of Orwell's "ordinary," from the indiscriminately reverent to the derisively negative. In the words of Stephen Spender, Orwell was an Innocent, "a kind of English Candide of the 20th century. The Innocent is ordinary because he accepts the values of ordinary human decency."[9] In *George Orwell: The Ethical Imagination*, Sant Singh Bal agrees with Lionel Trilling, who finds that the basic quality of Orwell's writing is "a sort of moral centrality, a directness of relation to moral—and political—fact," identifying the basis of Orwell's ethics in his acceptance of ordinary life, hence his "apotheosis of ordinary, commonplace virtues of England and daily pieties of civilized life."[10] Others, such as Samuel Hynes in *The Auden Generation*, claimed that Orwell mythologized ordinariness: "in a Myth of the Proletariat (where ordinariness was given a class identity) and in a Myth of the English people (where it was made a national characteristic)."[11] And in *The Writer and the Absolute*, Wyndham Lewis identified Orwell's "weakness" as his lifelong quest for the essence of the ordinary: although there was a certain "emancipation," from *Down and Out in Paris and London* to *1984*, even in his last book, Lewis regretted, Orwell imported his enthusiasm for the "Proles"—a "silliness," a "stupid affectation" born out of class snobbery.[12]

The fraught reception of Orwell's political and ethical position highlights the importance of focusing on his early career in the context of the English 1930s, which in turn sheds light on a generation of writers that defined itself primarily through its political consciousness, the outcome of a sense of guilt associated with their class affiliation. The critique of the traditional German community that Helmuth Plessner formulated in his 1924 book *Grenzen der Gemeinschaft* took here the form of a deep discomfort with a British tradition of intellectual moderation felt by the generation of the 1930s in the wake of unemployment, the rise of Nazism, and, soon enough, discontent with the Left. A lucid assessment of this situation, Orwell's essay "Inside the Whale" is also an unselfconscious testimony to the enduring habits of sincerity, the paradigm (following Lionel Trilling) that characterizes societies with recognized and accepted social hierarchies such as the English one: Orwell's passionate misreading of Henry Miller's *Tropic of Cancer* (1934), the American writer's own book of Paris, makes necessary a critical rereading of *Down and Out in Paris and London*. It throws into high relief Orwell's dismantling of class distinction, premised, he learned, on maintaining a safe distance from, even on dehumanization of, other people. He engaged in this defamiliarization both as a committed writer with an attachment to the ordinary man, and as an individual alienated from his own class who, alerted while living abroad to the injustice of empire, and more generally to inequality and humiliation, examines poverty among the English with the eyes of a foreigner. Through brief juxtapositions of Orwell's writing with texts by Henry Miller and Paul Morand, this chapter will map out various modes of detachment that intersected and partially overlapped during the transitional decade of the 1930s: a cosmopolitan ideal instantiated by romantic travel and illustrated by Morand; the "intestinal embrace" of the avant-garde, whose cosmological pacifism Miller shared with Yeats and other modernist writers; and the "equidistance" of the uniquely positioned Orwell, whose stern ethico-political assessments imposed, as George Steiner aptly put it, an "inescapable obligation of tactlessness."

The Tower, the Whale, and the Discomfort of Class Consciousness

Many chronicled the 1930s decade in England: those, like E. M. Forster, born in the nineteenth century; writers like Virginia Woolf, who spoke from the relatively privileged place of the Bloomsbury circle; political writers like Stephen Spender, who identified explicitly with the 1930s generation; and George Orwell, who was "in but never of" that group. A comparative reading of two essays that span this spectrum, Woolf's "The Leaning Tower" and Orwell's "Inside the Whale" (both 1940), offers a useful window into the challenges posed by this decade. Both authors gave their views on the two previous generations of writers, isolating and contrasting the 1920s and the 1930s, and speculated about the future of literature. Paradoxically, Woolf's prediction was optimistic—she anticipated a renaissance of literature in a classless society after the war, yet the following year she committed suicide; while Orwell's assessment pointed to the end of literature "as we know it," that is, as a literature of the era of liberalism, yet he continued to write, giving powerful expression in *Animal Farm* and *1984* to the 1940 foreboding of "an age of totalitarian dictatorships—an age in which freedom of thought will be at first a deadly sin and later on a meaningless abstraction."[13] These paradoxes are paralleled by the tension inherent to the essays themselves, between what is said and what is left out, expressive of an anxiety that must have been difficult to evaluate with clarity in that troubled year. The two metaphors around which Woolf and Orwell organize their essays, the tower and the whale, epitomize the authors' respective situations: both places of retreat for the writer, the former leans to the left and belongs to the past, whereas the latter advances through adversity.

Woolf's "The Leaning Tower" is a sequel to her earlier efforts to chronicle the contemporary literary scene. The 1923–1924 essays "Character in Fiction" and "Mr Bennett and Mrs Brown" had made a distinction between the Edwardians ("materialists") and the Georgians ("spiritualists"), postulating the break of 1910 when "human nature changed." In the 1940 essay she provides a retrospective account of the 1920s and 1930s generations, identifying a major break at the end of the 1920s when the writer's tower began to "lean to the left."[14] Unconcerned with more distant, yet famous tower dwellers such as Montaigne, Stephen Dedalus, or Yeats's poetic personas, Woolf minutely describes a specifically British tower, whose shadow extends across the hedges separating various social classes. If the 1910 break Woolf identified in her earlier essays had seemed radical from a social and artistic point of view, this time the change is more significant because it cuts across a longer duration: it concerns "all writers from Chaucer to the present day" who had enjoyed the privilege of being raised "above the mass of people upon a tower of stucco—that is their middle-class birth; and of gold—that is their expensive education."[15] The intellectuals who began to write about 1925, and who, she submits portentously, "came to an end as a group in 1939," were also highly educated and formed, like "a string of names—Day Lewis, Auden, Spender, Isherwood, Louis MacNeice and so on," a very cohesive group, yet they had a radically different experience: wherever they looked, they saw change and revolution. "In Germany, in Russia, in Italy, in Spain, all the old hedges were being rooted up; all the old towers were being thrown to the ground. . . . Even in England towers that were built of gold and stucco were no longer steady towers. They were leaning towers" (LT, 140).

Woolf's formulations are suggestive of a social geography mapped out horizontally by "old hedges," and vertically by (leaning) towers: in a time of political and social turmoil, all interpersonal distances shift, in a dramatic change of the social landscape. In Woolf's account, the awkwardness of the "leaning tower" experience, which made it impossible for these writers to "look any class straight in the face," led to "discomfort, pity for themselves, anger against society." The reader can only wonder how this appraisal bears on the position of Woolf's own literary coterie, which is left out of the picture: might the hyperbolic style in which she couches her condescension be an indication of her own discomfort? One has reasons to doubt it. Yet she repeats emphatically her moral verdict ("wrong . . . wrong . . . wrong"), and the insistent recurrence of passive forms culminates in a parallel construction, anticipating the downright dismissal of their work for lack of artistic value:

> It was wrong for a small class to possess an education that other people paid for; wrong to stand upon the gold that a bourgeois father had made from his bourgeois profession. It was wrong; yet how could they make it right. . . . Trapped by their education, pinned down by their capital, they remained on top of their leaning tower,

> and their state of mind as we see it reflected in their poems and plays and novels is full of discord and bitterness, full of confusion and of compromise. (LT, 142)

Eventually, labeling these conditions "Leaning Tower Influences," Woolf mitigates her judgment that "they have been incapable of giving us great poems, great plays, great novels" (LT, 147) by blaming their failure on their formative experiences.[16] "During all the most impressionable years of their lives they were stung into consciousness—into self-consciousness, into class-consciousness, into the consciousness of things changing, of things falling, of death perhaps about to come. There was no tranquility in which they could recollect," she adds on an objective note, with a wink at Wordsworth. Finally, in a feeble redeeming gesture toward the end of her essay, she acknowledges the honesty of self-appraisals in these authors' autobiographical writings, the genre that proliferated between 1930 and 1940—by far, following Woolf, the most successful. The Leaning Tower writer, she adds, had the courage "to throw the little box of toys [of the nineteenth-century writer] out of the window. He has had the courage to tell the truth, the unpleasant truth, about himself. That is the first step towards telling the truth about other people" (LT, 149).[17]

In a farewell essay to Virginia Woolf from 1941, E. M. Forster pointed out that a transitory situation required caution when evaluating the literary merits of recent and contemporary writing. "We are all of us upon the Leaning Tower, as she called it, even those of us who date from the nineteenth century, when the earth was still horizontal and the buildings perpendicular. We cannot judge the landscape properly as we look down, for everything is tilted."[18] Three years later, Forster cautioned again against dismissing the writing of the 1930s generation as a failure. "We are plunged in a terrific war, and our literary judgments are not at their best. All our criticism is or ought to be tentative," confessing his own impression that "the long week-end did valuable work."[19] In the 1951 memoir *World within World*, Stephen Spender blamed the economic situation of Woolf's circle for their lack of appreciation for the 1930s generation. They were "like a watered-down aristocracy," Spender writes; "certainly not malicious exploiters of their fellow men, [but] . . . decidedly unwilling to sacrifice their independence to the cause of the working-class struggle."[20] Hence their attitude toward the younger generation:

> To them there was something barbarous about our generation. It seemed that with us the thin wall which surrounded their little situation of independence and which enabled them to retain their air of being the last of the Romans had broken down. A new generation had arisen which proclaimed that bourgeois civilization was at an end, and which assumed the certainty of revolution, which took sides

> and which was exposed even within its art to the flooding-in of outside public events, which cared but little for style and knew nothing of Paris.[21]

"A new generation . . . [who] knew nothing of Paris": nothing similar to Eliot's encounter with Laforgue's poetry, which revealed to him his own poetic persona; nothing of the artistic revolution imported with the postimpressionist exhibition at the Grafton galleries in London, that had inspired Woolf's remark about the change of human character "in or around 1910." It was, rather, social and political revolution that Spender's contemporaries contemplated, shaping Orwell's confidence that "the invasion of literature by politics was bound to happen."[22] Critics like Virginia Woolf, Spender wrote, "failed to see that public events had swamped our personal lives and usurped our personal experience";[23] if "all social relations changed" (as Woolf memorably put it, referring to 1910), now it was because of "a sort of compunction which our grandparents did not have," wrote Orwell, "an awareness of the enormous injustice and misery in the world, and a guilt-stricken feeling that one ought to be doing something about it, which makes a purely aesthetic attitude towards life impossible."[24] Spender raises the same issue, asking rhetorically, "Why should he not refuse [the political nature of the age]?" The effect would not be isolation or naïveté; in 1936, to ignore "the sense of political doom, pending in unemployment, Fascism, and the overwhelming threat of war" would likely result in the diminished scale of one's writing.[25] Differently put, a purely aesthetic stance would mean being out of touch with reality, the very source of one's writing.

The magnitude of the change recorded by Orwell and Spender is probably best captured by Woolf's sweeping inclusion of "all writers from Chaucer to the present day" in her characterization of tower dwellers. It might sound like an exaggeration, but it refers to the perception of a historical phenomenon: namely that in England, the intelligentsia had for the most part been part of an aristocracy supportive of the status quo; unlike France or Italy, in the 1930s it boasted no tradition of intellectual dissidence. Alan Swingewood attributes intellectual moderation to a British tradition of "political stability, historical continuity, a gentrified bourgeois culture, the strength of philosophical currents relying on common sense, experience, and practicality (utilitarianism, empiricism), combined with the absence of a broadly based revolutionary socialist movement."[26] Concurrently, Noel Annan speaks of an "intellectual aristocracy" of families closely bound to the establishment and to one other, which, despite a certain proclivity to criticize, it has cultivated "the English habit of working through established institutions." This is, he adds, "an aristocracy, secure, established and, like the rest of English society, accustomed to responsible and judicious utterance and skeptical of iconoclastic speculation."[27] These are the very traits of English society that Lionel Trilling captured under the sincerity paradigm: an established and accepted sense of hierarchy and everyone's place within it, which allows space for criticism as long as it is on the community's terms[28]—the very type of "community" that would come under scrutiny in much of the philosophical and sociological literature of the past century.

A close look at the 1930s generation, particularly through the lens of memoirs, reveals a pattern in their evolution as a politically committed group that inaugurated what many take for the first significant movement of dissent: as sons of well-to-do families, most of the writers of this generation traveled abroad in the late 1920s—early 1930s, especially to Germany and France, where they became aware of the effects of the economic downturn, such as large-scale unemployment, and of the rise of National Socialism in Germany. This awareness led to a nascent middle-class guilt consciousness, which only intensified on their return to England, where the new economic circumstances forced them to take jobs as teachers, journalists, reviewers, and so on. "Politically indistinguishable," as Orwell would say, they all pledged allegiance to communism, "the God that failed" in subsequent years.[29] This led George Woodcock to single out, in 1946 already, George Orwell, Herbert Read, and Graham Greene as the only English writers of the 1930s who did not wear badly in the following decade."[30]

Curiously enough, Woolf does not even mention Orwell in her essay. It would have been only too easy to cite him as the counterexample to the Leaning Tower writers, as the one who had perhaps never been in the tower in the first place, who had trespassed well beyond the hedges that separated social classes. Rather than suggest, however, that Orwell's brand of commitment would have been incomprehensible to Woolf, it is more useful to remember Stuart Samuels's remark that Orwell was "in but never of his generation."[31] Not only did major differences in his life trajectory set him apart from his coevals (he was older than most, born into a poorer family, served the British administration in Burma instead of going to university, as most did), but Orwell's own awareness of his singularity turned his intellectual life into a critical negotiation of distance from the prevalent kinds of writing and political attitudes of the 1920s and 1930s.[32] "Inside the Whale" is an eloquent example of Orwell's attitude.

Like Woolf, he evaluates the writing of his predecessors, making a distinction between the 1920s and the 1930s generations; his criterion, however, is not aesthetic, but political, assessing the merits of writers through the lens of their attitude to historical events. On the whole, he says, the writers of the 1920s were "railing against the *strange disease of modern life*" (this was, he adds without a mention of the First World War, "perhaps the prevailing attitude during the last hundred years"); the writers of the 1930s, on the other hand, were "the 'progressives,' the yeasayers, the Shaw-Wells type, always leaping forward to embrace the ego-projections which they mistake for the future."[33] Orwell, in other words, was not willing to grant his coevals the merit of having broken with the "prevailing attitude" of the aristocratic intelligentsia, and derided them for their political enthusiasm. What he had to oppose to their perceived superficial allegiance to communism was ostensibly Henry Miller's quietism. Apparently, Orwell felt he was entitled to assess the political situation in Britain, and in Europe more broadly, by his first-hand experiences in Burma, London, Paris, the North of England, and Spain; these afforded him a double perspective, "at the same time inside and outside," and the power of distance—to use Anderson's words—from both. His early commitment to the oppressed—all the oppressed, included in the capacious category of the *ordinary*—and the experiences he undertook as a result placed him, he apparently felt, in a position of objective detachment.

Orwell's "political" contemporaries could only fall short of his ideal. Orwell derided them as a group for their communist allegiances, taking the latter to be solely the expression of a desire to believe in something, a form of anti-fascism at best. Theirs was a superficial commitment, Orwell charged, devoid of the genuine knowledge that comes from direct contact with the lower aspects of reality; ultimately, such a lack was to be blamed on the "curse [of] the British class-system," which "prevented members of different classes to meet."[34] In Orwell's view, the situation had not changed with the 1930s generation of writers, as Woolf had emphatically pointed out. In a short review-essay published in the same year in *The Tribune*, he maintains:

> The sort of person who has the leisure to write a novel nearly always belongs to the middle-classes. He can't make contact with the manual workers, even if he wants to, and the bulk of his own class, who are much more intolerant intellectually than the proletariat, look down on him as a "highbrow." Whether he likes it or not he is forced back into the sterile little world of the literary intelligentsia, with the result that novelists of real gift like Aldous Huxley and Virginia Woolf, are ruined simply by lack of subject matter.[35]

This is the closest Orwell probably came to showing what he thought about Woolf as a writer: gifted, but lacking the opportunity to get in touch with ordinary people, the only source of relevant writing.[36] More generally, throughout his writings Orwell formulated this critique against all intellectuals—liberals, socialists, and so on—repeatedly blaming them for the lack of meaningful contact with the lower classes.[37]

The only one to whom Orwell attributes this merit is not a fellow English writer, but an American one: Henry Miller. Oblivious to the fact that Miller did not live with "the curse of the British class system," Orwell praises Miller for his "courage to identify with the ordinary man" and for his acceptance of the impending end of the liberal age and of Western civilization. Henry Miller's lucid, even defiant stance of noncooperation is famously suggested by the metaphor borrowed from Miller himself, "inside the whale":[38]

> Where Miller's work is symptomatically important is in its avoidance of any of these attitudes. He is neither pushing the world-process forward nor trying to drag it back, but on the other hand he is by no means ignoring it. I should say that he believes in the impending ruin of the Western Civilization much more firmly than the majority of "revolutionary" writers; only he does not feel called upon to do anything about it. He is fiddling while Rome is burning, and, unlike the enormous majority of people who do this, fiddling with his face towards the flames. (IW, 243)

We are in a position now to place side by side these two metaphors of the writer's retreat, the tower and the whale. Woolf's tower is quite clearly a specifically British one: it is a tower with a view, way above the hedges that separate social classes. It is also a link with the past, a symbol of the continuity of an aristocratic intelligentsia to which she also belonged (with the caveat, of course, that she was a woman). Hence the scope of Woolf's assessment, which does not transcend the English locale, and the contextual guilt consciousness, tied up with notions of class. Orwell does not even hint at such guilt consciousness in his account: "stung in self-consciousness" as he was himself, perhaps even if he had been aware of the phenomenon, he might not have felt inclined to credit a whole generation with a feeling which was so intimately defining of his personal outlook. More striking, however, is his attempt to make Miller intelligible by placing him against an English background, and to the benefit of an English public, at a time when Miller's books were under censorship: a case of transfer of prestige.[39] Orwell displaces and radically changes the meaning of Miller's whale metaphor, setting it against the larger history of "human civilization" with a vague wink at the *translatio imperii*, from "Rome burning" to "a friendly American voice." Unlike Woolf's tower, in which writers had presumably worked in unselfconscious isolation from society, the whale appears as a place of deliberate withdrawal.

The question that bothered generations of writers after Orwell's passing was how someone as involved as the author of *1984* could have possibly commended "fiddling while Rome was burning." Had he forgotten his commitment to the oppressed? His appraisal of Miller, as we shall presently see, was based on a misunderstanding that goes back to his experience of voluntary destitution in Paris and London, soon after his return from Burma.

Down and Out in Orwell's Paris and Miller's China, or The Enduring Habits of Sincerity

"Inside the Whale" was typically understood by later generations as an endorsement of quietism. A different perspective emerges when we examine the genealogy of the essay, which evolved from a lukewarm review of *Tropic of Cancer* while the book was still banned, through a revision of his reticent appraisal in a new review occasioned by the publication of *Black Spring*, and finally to "Inside the Whale," in which Miller is praised for his "courage to identify with the ordinary man" in *Tropic*. In a well-meaning effort to make palatable to the English sense of propriety an American writer who was censored at the time, Orwell places the latter in a moral framework that was foreign to Miller, oblivious to their different cultural backgrounds, contrasted by Lionel Trilling under the paradigms of sincerity and authenticity.[40]

Following Trilling's account, a major concern with sincerity appeared concomitantly with the rise of society: one is true to oneself as a precondition of being true to others, or, differently put, society demands of its participants to present themselves as sincere as a condition of its harmonious functioning. Although this "sincerity" has the potential of becoming alienating in the theatricality of social rituals, it is valuable for Trilling because it makes possible the public sphere, where opinion and critique *on society's own terms* may lead to understanding and change. Intellectuals, those "who make it their business to scrutinize the polity," do so with the assumption that understanding "may lead to action: the idea of society includes the assumption that a given society can be changed if the judgment passed upon it is adverse. In the framing of such judgments the ideal of sincerity is of substantial importance."[41] It is in the sphere of intellectual commitment, understood in Trilling's terms, that Orwell's intervention can readily be placed. All the more so, since Trilling sees sincerity as the English national virtue par excellence, ascribed to the "archaic intractability of the English social organization," to the "impermeability of English society, the solidness of the composition, the thick, indubitable *thereness* which enforced upon its members a sort of primary sincerity—the free acknowledgment that in one respect, at least, *they were not free*, that their existences were bound by their society, determined by its particularities."[42] It bears emphasizing that what Trilling calls a lack of freedom, characteristic more generally of the paradigm of sincerity, is qualified by Robert Pippin as a classical or premodern view of freedom, as opposed to later, individualist notions of freedom (corresponding, roughly, with Trilling's authenticity paradigm): thus the classical/premodern notion of freedom, as the true realization of one's identity or nature "required finding one's place or role in something 'outside' oneself, first in the polis or social community, and ultimately in nature or the whole"; Pippin further notes that "the widespread collapse of the metaphysical support for such a view of an ordered, hierarchical cosmos or divine order . . . provoked the modern assertion of freedom as a radically individual self-determination," as the work of Charles Taylor, especially *The Sources of the Self*, eloquently shows.[43] Following Trilling, however, it is a characteristic of the English mind that a freely assumed sense of responsibility weighs all the more heavily as a substitute for lost religious belief. In the national life, it assumes the idea of task, whose cheerful undertaking is the very principle of civilization. "In the personal life it was the principle which guaranteed the trait on which the English most prided themselves, their sincerity, by which they meant their single-minded relation to things, to each other, and to themselves."[44] Sincerity is what binds the community together, from one's relationship to oneself to one's rapport with others. Ironically, when Orwell claims in 1940 that "the passive, non-cooperative attitude implied in Henry Miller's work is justified," his habit of sincerity betrays him: "Whether or not it is an expression of what people *ought* to feel, it probably comes somewhere near to expressing what they do feel" (IW, 249, italics in the original). In other words, while praising Miller for his attitude, which coincides with that of his countrymen, he gently chides the latter for having forgotten their duty toward society.

Attached to neat binaries and symmetries, Trilling contrasts these "English" characteristics with certain traits that define the American sensibility; "Inside the Whale" is the illustration of an encounter where such differences remained unacknowledged. On subtracting Miller from the moral framework in which Orwell tries to confine him, the metaphor "inside the whale" loses its relevance; in fact, Miller roamed too freely *outside*, reveled in his outsideness and flouted all forms of containment, belonging or attachment. There was no such commitment to a country or a people in his life in the 1930s (the later *The Air-Conditioned Nightmare* suggests a change); Miller even made his refusal of such involvement explicit, in an affirmation of autonomy and freedom: "Is it good here in France? It's wonderful. Marvelous. For me it's marvelous. . . . For a French writer it may be bad here, but then I am not a French writer. I should hate to be a French or a Russian or an American writer. It must be hell. I am a cosmological writer."[45] As a way of asserting his estrangement even more emphatically, he refers to Paris as China: not as yet another country or foreign culture or language, but as the epitome of estrangement and lack of attachments, of a nomadic existence.

> I am here in the midst of a great change. I have forgotten my own language and yet I do not speak the new language. I am in China and I am talking Chinese. I am in the dead center of a changing reality for which no language has yet been invented. According to the map I am in Paris; according to the calendar I am living in the third decade of the twentieth century. But I am in China and there are no clocks or calendars here.[46]

The dismissal of calendars and maps, a gesture symbolic of Miller's self-exclusion from the contingencies of historical events, bears here quite intimately on the necessary excogitation of a fresh artistic language, perhaps even of a poetic self-creation, autonomous and unattached. Trilling's second paradigm, authenticity, conveniently relates to the themes and stakes courted by Miller's writing. As a form of experience not encompassed by the social, authenticity points to "a wider reference to the universe and man's place in it, and a less acceptant and genial view of the social circumstances of life."[47] Authenticity is a reactive rather than affirmative principle: it erects itself against the constraints and demands imposed by society. From the perspective of Miller's ethos of authenticity, the framework of responsibility within which Orwell tries to place Miller's writing appears rather contemptible (this is, incidentally, how Miller took it); what Trilling has to say about "the leaders of the great modern movement of art" applies to Miller's own "implied outlook":

> They did indeed grant that the natural universe was there and they gave it a degree of notice, but they refused to be submissive and dutiful to it. They poured mocking laughter upon it: they dealt with it in irony and detachment, under no assumption that it was in earnest, that it had promises to keep or any disposition to allow the truth about itself to be discovered, if indeed there was any truth inherent in it.[48]

Indeed, these words describe well Miller's richly extravagant writing, the "cosmological" vision that underpins it, and in general the reasons behind Miller's "political quietism."

The unacknowledged discomfort pervading "Inside the Whale" appears more clearly in the juxtaposition of *Tropic of Cancer* with the book that remains unmentioned in Orwell's essay, his own *Down and Out in Paris and London*. It is in this book, as I have suggested at the beginning of this chapter, that Orwell had to show his "courage" to identify with the ordinary man. It is along the footprints of those years of deprivation that he sees Miller strolling, all the while deploring Miller's ignorance of the underworld of the working class which he had explored. Indeed, for Orwell, who had himself been a penniless writer in Paris, a book evoking the squalor of poor quarters with the gusto of *Tropic of Cancer* must have been a thrilling find. In providing his English reader with a context for Miller's novel, Orwell clearly drew on the memories of his own self-imposed exile in France; and the fact that he undertook it partly in the hope of becoming a writer only adds to the irony pervading passages like the following, where he derides the omnipresent aspiring artists roaming the streets of Paris:

> During the boom years, when dollars were plentiful and the exchange-value of the franc was low, Paris was invaded by such a swarm of artists, writers, students, dilettanti, sight-seers, debauchees, and plain idlers as the world has probably never seen. In some quarters of the town the so-called artists must actually have outnumbered the working population. . . . It was the age of dark horses and dark genii; the phrase on everybody's lips was "*Quand je serai lancé*." (IW, 210–211)

This is not Miller's Paris; it is the bohemian city of the "lost generation" of American literature, Hemingway's "moveable feast," also evoked in the prefiesta chapters of *The Sun Also Rises*, in Gertrude Stein's *Paris France* and *The Autobiography of Alice B. Toklas*, in Harry Crosby's diaries, Matthew Josephson's "life among the surrealists"; it is the background to Fitzgerald's "finest and saddest of all American-in-Paris stories," "Babylon Revisited," and to Faulkner's *Four Letters from Paris*; a city given more precise cultural, social, and political contours by Janet Flanner's journalism (her long-lived "Letter from Paris" in the *New Yorker*) and Anita Loos's *Gentlemen Prefer Blondes*; the city re-created aurally in Gershwin's 1928 orchestral composition *An American in Paris*.[49]

By 1929, when Miller's eleven-year-long French exile began, conditions had changed dramatically. As it turned out, Orwell continues,

> nobody was "*lancé*," the slump descended like another Ice Age, the cosmopolitan mob of artists vanished, and the huge Montparnasse cafés which only ten years ago were filled till the small hours by hordes of shrieking poseurs have turned into darkened tombs in which there are not even any ghosts. It is this world—described in, among other novels, Wyndham Lewis's *Tarr*—that Miller is writing about, but he is dealing only with the under side of it, the lumpen-proletarian fringe which has been able to survive the slump because it is composed partly of genuine artists and partly of genuine scoundrels. (IW, 210–211)

It suffices even a superficial look at Orwell's *Down and Out in Paris and London* to realize the extent to which Miller's evocation of poverty in Paris seems to come close to his own; when Orwell describes *Tropic* as "for the most part . . . a story of bug-ridden rooms in workingmen's hotels, of fights, drinking bouts, cheap brothels, Russian refugees, cadging, swindling, and temporary jobs. And the whole atmosphere of the poor quarters of Paris as a foreigner sees them. . . . It is all there, or at any rate the feeling of it is there" (211), he could as well have quoted from the first pages of *Down and Out*:

> It was a very narrow street—a ravine of tall, leprous houses, lurching towards one another in queer attitudes, as though they had all been frozen in the act of collapse. All the houses were hotels and packed to the tiles with lodgers, mostly Poles, Arabs and Italians. At the foot of the hotels were tiny bistros, where you could be drunk for the equivalent of a shilling. On Saturday nights about a third of the male population of the quarter was drunk. . . . It was quite a representative Paris slum.[50]
>
> The lodgers were a floating population, largely foreigners, who used to turn up without luggage, stay a week and then disappear again. They were of every trade—cobblers, bricklayers, stonemasons,

> navies, students, prostitutes, rag-pickers. Some of them were fantastically poor. (*DOPL*, 7)

There is more than just the realism with which Miller describes his surroundings in Paris that Orwell finds appealing; the pages of *Tropic* also abound with descriptions of prolonged hunger, which Orwell had himself experienced repeatedly while in Paris. A few pages into *Down and Out*, the reader is offered a lesson in the anatomy—or perhaps the physiology—of hunger:

> You discover what it is like to be hungry. With bread and margarine in your belly, you go out and look into the shop windows. Everywhere there is food insulting you in huge, wasteful piles. . . . You discover the boredom which is inseparable from poverty; the times when you have nothing to do and, being underfed, can interest yourself in nothing. For half a day at a time you lie on your bed, feeling like the *jeune squelette* in Baudelaire's poem. Only food could rouse you. You discover that a man who has gone even a week on bread and margarine is not a man any longer, only a belly with a few accessory organs. (*DOPL*, 17)

Miller's description of hunger, on the other hand, is colored by the self-ironic note of optimism which he maintains throughout: "How a man can wander about all day on an empty belly, and even get an erection once in a while, is one of those mysteries which are too easily explained by the 'anatomists of the soul' " (*TC*, 40). A few pages later he celebrates his "really superb health," by which he means a typically American brand of optimism:

> I'm a bit retarded, like most Americans. Carl finds it disgusting, this optimism. "I have only to talk about a meal," he'd say, "and you're radiant!" It's a fact. The mere thought of a meal—*another* meal—rejuvenates me. A meal! That means something to go on—a few solid hours of work, an erection possibly. I don't deny it. I have health, good solid, animal health. The only thing that stands between me and a future is a meal, *another* meal. (*TC*, 49)

These passages speak to the very different mind-sets accompanying Orwell's project and Miller's seemingly aimless peripatetics, respectively. For while Orwell imposed on himself the experience of poverty so he could write about it for the members of his own class, oblivious to such realities (hence the almost portentous tone of the interpellative "you," seemingly generic, with the implication "you, too—*hypôcrite lecteur*—might come down in life one day"), in Miller's case there is a pervasive sense of delight accompanying his hunger, his perambulations in Paris, the spectacle of which is absorbed with an interest and gusto completely devoid of Orwell's gravity. It is as if Miller's hunger and thirst can be appeased not only with food and drink, but with the materiality of the city itself:

> At the Cité Nortier, somewhere near the Place du Combat, I pause a few minutes to drink in the full squalor of the scene. It is a rectangular court like many other which one glimpses through the low passageways that flank the old arteries of Paris. In the middle of the court is a clump of decrepit buildings which have so rotted away that they have collapsed on one another and formed a sort of intestinal embrace. The ground is uneven, the flagging slippery with slime. A sort of human dump heap which has been filled in with cinders and dry garbage. The sun is setting fast. The colors die. They shift from purple to dry blood, from nacre to bister, from cool dead grays to pigeon shit. Here and there a lopsided monster stands in the window blinking like an owl. There is the shrill squawk of children with pale faces and bony limbs, rickety little urchins marked with the forceps. A fetid odor seeps from the walls, the odor of a mildewed mattress. Europe—medieval, grotesque, monstrous: a symphony in B-mol. Directly across the street the Ciné Combat offers its distinguished clientele *Metropolis*. (*TC*, 40–41)

Orwell had described—in the passage quoted in full above (*DOPL*, 7)—"a ravine of tall, leprous houses, lurching towards one another in queer attitudes, as though they had all been frozen in the act of collapse," but then he readily moved on to detail the social landscape, more interested in the lives "curious beyond belief" unfolding within those precarious walls. Collapsing buildings are at the center of Miller's description, too, yet in his text a teratologist's omnivorous gaze feeds quite indiscriminately on the confusion of the human, the animal and the inorganic, on the impressionist slipperiness of colors, contours, and sensations. It is a signature of Miller's writing to capture the world at moments when it reveals itself in its hypostasis of living, but ailing organism; when its everyday surfaces of streets, houses, people become momentarily translucent and morph into inner organs, as if protruding through holes in the text: arteries—that is, boulevards crisscrossing the city—exhibit themselves as heavy blood vessels, their rich ramifications taking the reader along from the sordid particularities of a street, through the city and then giving him a glimpse of the continent: "Europe: medieval, grotesque, monstrous," a symphony that leaves none of the senses untouched, unmoved.

In line with the symbolism of the title, in *Tropic of Cancer* bodily metaphors open up explosive meditations on health, history, and literature onto a very particular view of the relationship between art and life:

> The house in which I live is being torn down. All the rooms are exposed. My house is like a human body with the skin peeled off. The

> wallpaper hangs in tatters, the bedsteads have no mattresses, the sinks are gone. Every night before entering the house I stand and look at it. The horror of it fascinates me. After all, why not a little horror? Every living man is a museum that houses the horrors of the race. Each man adds a new wing to the museum. And so, each night, standing before the house in which I live, the house which is being torn down, I try to grasp the meaning of it. The more the insides are exposed the more I get to love my house. I love even the old pisspot which stands under the bed, and which nobody uses any more. (*TC*, 389)

We are far here from Benjamin's arcades—those reassuring, inviting even, inside-outsides made for strolling at turtle speed, a chapter in the German philosopher's esoteric science of thresholds,[51] and his inverted version of Heidegger's bridge as thing-as-gathering.[52] Miller's is a house, or rather, a world, in the process of being blown to smithereens, and if gathering there is, it is one of horrors, a conjuration of the dark episodes of human history: "Every living man is a museum that houses the horrors of the race." And this frenzy, not just of corpses but also of individuals thrusting themselves under one's skin, like geological intrusions, contaminates even the possibility of inoffensive interpersonal relations, of a livable life with others:

> People are like lice—they get under your skin and bury themselves there. You scratch and scratch until the blood comes, but you can't get permanently deloused. Everywhere I go people are making a mess of their lives. Everyone has his private tragedy. It's in the blood now—misfortune, ennui, grief, suicide. The atmosphere is saturated with disaster, frustration, futility. Scratch and scratch—until there's no skin left. (*TC*, 12)

Impossible to cure, the afflictions of Western civilization can only proliferate exponentially; yet the narrative voice, far from deploring such misfortune, celebrates it with the same excitement—a critic said, with bravado—with which it evokes the more or less successful consummation of numberless sexual encounters. For in Miller's world, destruction and re-creation are inextricable: like Stephen Dedalus, like Nietzsche, the Patagonian—as Miller often calls himself—needs a sundering from the world, then a regression into the womb. Tania becomes a symbol of boundless fertility, recalling "the sprawling women of Picasso":

> The world is a cancer eating itself away. . . . I am thinking that when the great silence descends upon all and everywhere music will at last triumph. When into the womb of time everything is again withdrawn chaos will be restored and chaos is the score upon which reality is written. You, Tania, are my chaos. It is why I sing. It is not even I, it

> is the world dying, shedding the skin of time. I am still alive, kicking in your womb, a reality to write upon. (*TC*, 2)

The womb is a visceral prison, yet this space "inside the whale" represents, rather than a place of safe remove from history, the source of "a larger reality" that Miller's aim is to create with symbol and metaphor.

In the spirit of Whitman, with whom he aligns himself, Miller defines health as a forceful attitude toward life, a vitalism. From a memorable page in *Tropic* emerges the exemplary figure of Whitman—invoked while contemplating the map of New York his friend Fillmore keeps tacked on the wall of his Paris room—as the exemplary "healthy" individual, the synthesis of American life, past, present, and future: "He was the Poet of the Body and the Soul, Whitman. The first and the last poet. He is almost undecipherable today, a monument covered with rude hieroglyphs for which there is no key" (*TC*, 240). And then, in a move similar to Deleuze's later claim about the "superiority" of Anglo-American literature, Miller muses:

> It seems strange almost to mention his name over here. There is no equivalent in the languages of Europe for the spirit which he immortalized. Europe is saturated with art and her soil is full of dead bones and her museums are bursting with plundered treasures, but what Europe has never had is a free, healthy spirit, what you might call a MAN. (*TC*, 240)[53]

Denying Goethe the privilege to be the kind of paragon Whitman represents ("Goethe was a stuffed shirt, by comparison . . . , a pedant, a bore"), Miller concludes: "Goethe is an end of something, Whitman is a beginning" (*TC*, 240).[54]

In *Sincerity and Authenticity*, Trilling contrasts various American and British authors as a way to consolidate the opposition between his two cultural paradigms: whereas the English are easily identified with the paradigm of sincerity (and thus with Hegel's "noble soul"), Americans map out a different phase in the emancipation of the Spirit—Trilling resorts here, like D. H. Lawrence before him, to Hegel's narrative—corresponding to the "disintegrated consciousness," hence more concerned with the values of authenticity. The latter involves leaving behind existing connections and attachments, and thus a radical "change of heart." This is also Miller's position in *Peace! It's Wonderful!*: "The whole damned universe has to be taken apart, brick by brick, and reconstructed. Every atom has to be rearranged" (*PIW*, 7). This rearrangement can only temporarily be an artistic endeavor, because even art is an indulgence, "only a makeshift, a substitute for the real thing. There is only one art which, if we practiced it, would destroy what is called 'art.' With every line I write I kill off the 'artist' in me. With every line I write it is either murder in the first degree or suicide" (*PIW*, 4–5). To which words Trilling might respond with a reminder of the violent meanings explicit in the Greek ancestry of the word authentic: "*Authenteo*: to have full power over; also, to commit a murder. *Authentes*: not only a master and a doer, but also a perpetrator, a murderer, even a self-murderer, a suicide."[55]

Fiddling, then, is with Miller an existential and an artistic choice. The gamble is not on the "power of the words" as used with the directness of sincerity, but, as Deleuze would later say, on the creation of affect, in the *becomings* of authentic existence. Or, to put it in the vocabulary inspired by Barthes's lectures, these are different kinds of distance: not the ideal of objectivity grounded in the commitment to, and direct confrontation with, society's moral codes, but the flight from them, and the pursuit of aesthetic detachment—so extreme that it is not just detachment from contingency by means of the aesthetic, but ultimately from the aesthetic itself, entertaining the threat of self-cancellation in an attitude typical, at least since Mallarmé's *Livre*, of the avant-garde.

Yet the work of Orwell is a tremendous enlargement of our literature, as Raymond Williams said. And so is Miller's, for rather different reasons, and here questions of value or hierarchy are out of place: one cannot compare Miller's "intestinal embrace" and Orwell's own "measure of truth" (i.e., the suffering body, not imagined, but real). These are incommensurable distances. Moreover, Trilling's neat contrast between sincerity and authenticity cannot accommodate the luxuriant complexities of Orwell's strained relationship with truth, which at the outset undoes, then confounds, Trilling's binary opposition. Orwell's project was originally one of refusal of sincerity (turning his back on what he came to see as the doubtful respectability granted by his social position: a sahib, a middle class, etc.), of antagonistic confrontation of society. But *Down and Out in Paris and London*, or what we might call his "project of authenticity," was one he denounced, years later, as "masquerade." One wonders if even that dismissal was not tainted by his assumption, this time, of the stigma of insincerity, which Orwell ultimately confounds with inauthenticity. *Down and Out*, as we are about to see, reads like the unfolding of this stigma.

The "Courage to Identify with the Ordinary Man": England through the Eyes of a Foreigner

The mind-set with which Eric Blair returned from Burma prompted, in 1927, his tramping expeditions in the East End of London, followed a few months later by a longer stay in Paris, where he worked as a dishwasher.[56] Orwell acknowledged that the French capital also lured him with the mirage of a city of bohemians: there is no doubt that this was the place where he hoped to find a new social and professional identity. In *Down and Out in Paris and London*, a book ostensibly concerned with poverty, Orwell selects and rearranges his autobiographical material, setting out to map various Parisian locales (his sordid hotel room, the inferno-like underworld of *plongeurs* in the insalubrious kitchens of luxurious hotels and restaurants), then his narrator returns "home" to England, which he rediscovers from the unusual perspective of a tramp.[57] Compared to the first part of the book, Stephen Ingle says in a reassessment of Orwell's work, the second half is "rather dull."[58] While this is attributable to the different stakes the "English half" must have had for Orwell, it is not difficult to see why the first, Parisian, part makes for a more exciting read. Orwell was not just writing about poverty, as he explicitly stated his aim in the first pages of the book; he was writing about the French poor, and there is a touch of exoticism about the marginal types he evokes. The sketches of characters he draws have potential for a veritable *comédie humaine*, and his text occasionally toys with the literary conventions of the French nineteenth-century realist novel. Among the most obvious influences often mentioned by critics, however, are a few texts bearing directly on the subject of poverty, all familiar to Orwell: W. H. Davies, *Autobiography of a Super-Tramp*;[59] Maxim Gorky, *The Lower Depths*; and Jack London, *The People of the Abyss*. When Blair was still at Eton, Bal points out, Seebohm Rowntree's *Poverty: A Study of Town Life* and Charles Booth's multivolume *The Life and Labor of the People of London* appeared, "which obviously drew attention of the political leaders and thinking men of the day to the problem of poverty and unemployment. The influence of these books [on *Down and Out*] is also quite obvious."[60] Originally written as social reportage, in the form of essays and articles that were published by journals and newspapers and now reprinted in the *Collected Essays*, Orwell decided to turn these experiences into a book, whose genre is ultimately undecidable: hovering between the conventions of the realist novel, autobiography, social documentary, political journalism, it has variously puzzled and frustrated numerous critics eager to place and judge it by recognizable literary norms.[61]

Reconsidering it in 1993 in *Partisan Review*, Steven Marcus is struck by the originality of the book, while also claiming that it is deeply rooted in a tradition of British writing.[62] In similar vein, George Steiner had written in a 1969 essay in the *New Yorker*: "In the midst of the grime and mendacity he made it his business to explore, Orwell maintained a natural poise. This curious mixture of grit and fastidiousness accounts for a distinct strain in English letters. It relates a Tory such as Swift to a Jacobin such as Hazlitt."[63] Yet other readers have pondered similarities and differences between Orwell's first book and other firsthand accounts of tramping or poverty like Knut Hamsun's or Jack London's, or compared *Down and Out*'s treatment of the tramp with Charlie Chaplin's portrayal of it in *Modern Times* (1936).[64] While there is much to gain from various exercises of comparison, it is also important to show the specific difficulties Orwell was bound to run into with the second half of his book, which defamiliarizes a certain view of England while subtly addressing itself to the middle classes whose mentality Orwell profoundly dislikes.[65] In fact, it is fair to say that it defamiliarizes class, exposing it as a way of creating and maintaining distance, often by dehumanizing the poor.

A few considerations about the first half of the book are in order. From the outset, Orwell plunges the reader straight into the world of poverty, describing the blurred boundaries between the public and the private as if he were sketching a medieval locale. The street is like a shared space where the private bursts out in unfriendly exchanges; the omnipresent bugs, the peeling wallpaper, the coarse language, all suggest a certain degree of dehumanization. In language still mired in middle-class moral standards, Orwell equates poverty with a passport to indecency:

> There were eccentric characters in the hotel. The Paris slums are a gathering-place for eccentric people—people who have fallen into solitary half-mad grooves of life and given up trying to be *normal or decent*. Poverty frees them from *ordinary standards of behaviour*, just as money frees people from work. Some of the lodgers in our hotel lived lives that were curious beyond words. (*DOPL*, 7, my italics)

Orwell's vocabulary circumscribes a social geography that stretches beyond the limits of bourgeois intelligibility. Unlike the upper classes who derive their identity from the auratic properties of an ancestral place, this is "a floating population, largely foreigners, who used to turn up without luggage, stay a week and then disappear again"; representing every trade from cobblers to prostitutes and ragpickers, some, Orwell remembers, were "fantastically poor" (*DOPL*, 7). It does take some courage—in the sense in which Orwell was praising Joyce and Miller for their "courage to identify with the ordinary man"—to get down among these individuals who, at least at the beginning, inspire awe in the narrator: for Orwell, the "descent" will take the form of an initiation into destitution, an experiment in giving up social distinction. The narrator's courtship of poverty carries him in a downward spiral, in the interconnected hierarchies of financial security, respectability, feelings of self-worth, eligibility as a male companion, and social validation as a moral person. His experiment makes for an interesting situation that Trilling himself does not consider in his study. He does discuss the consequences of upward mobility as an exception to the desirable coincidence between sincerity and authenticity in the situation of "being authentic because sincere."[66] As an example, he cites the case of an Englishman who is content with his class situation and therefore does not aspire to an upward social mobility that would force him to become *somebody else* through the artificial adoption of more sophisticated habits; such a person, Trilling explains, would lose both his sincerity and his authenticity. In *The Road to Wigan Pier*, Orwell conversely dwells on aspects related to efforts of downward connection, ultimately indicting the "only connect [with the lower classes]" impulse that most of the intelligentsia follow rather unthinkingly (Orwell's diagnosis is uncompromising, as usual: he calls it *snobbery*), because they don't know, Orwell charges, what connecting really means: giving up part of oneself (having to become inauthentic). It is to this necessary experience that *Down and Out* speaks.

Yet this disavowal of sincerity is further complicated by Orwell's own social background, by the specific predicament of the "lower-upper-middle" class to which his family belonged. If in *Down and Out*, the generic "you" that Orwell interpellates remains mysterious ("You have *thought so much about poverty*—it is the thing you have *feared* all your life, the thing you knew would happen to you sooner or later" [*DOPL*, 16–17, my italics]), this apprehension is qualified later, in *The Road to Wigan Pier*, where Orwell attributes it both to the unemployed and to the members of a decayed class, such as his family. First he acknowledges that he "knew nothing about working class conditions" or about the humiliations of "respectable poverty" (*RWP*, 149). "The frightful doom of a decent working man suddenly thrown into the streets after a lifetime of steady work, his agonized struggles against economic laws which he does not understand, the disintegration of families, the corroding sense of shame—all this was outside the range of my experience" (*RWP*, 149). Yet as Orwell sets out to explain his social background, in a perceptive analysis of the decay of the middle class, he shows that this phenomenon was, in a way, familiar:

> I was born into what you might describe as the lower-upper-middle class. The upper-middle class, which had its heyday in the 'eighties and 'nineties, with Kipling as its poet laureate, was a sort of mound of wreckage left behind when the tide of Victorian prosperity receded. . . . Or perhaps it would be better to change the metaphor and describe it not as a mound but as a layer—the layer of society lying between £2,000 and £300 a year: my own family was not far from the bottom. . . . The English class-system . . . is not entirely explicable in terms of money. Roughly speaking it is a money-stratification, but it is also interpenetrated by a sort of shadowy caste-system; rather like a jerry-built modern bungalow haunted by medieval ghosts. (*RWP*, 121–122)

For the impoverished layer of the middle class, "gentility was almost purely theoretical. You lived, so to speak, at two levels simultaneously":

> In the kind of shabby-genteel family that I am talking about there is far more consciousness of poverty than in any working-class family above the level of the dole. Rent and clothes and school-bills are an unending nightmare, and every luxury, even a glass of beer, is an unwarrantable extravagance. Practically the whole family income goes in keeping up appearances. (*RWP*, 124)[67]

Orwell understood at an early age that the foundation of the class system was pretense, exposed by the lack of financial resources. This biographical background gives reasons to pause on encountering critical opinions ironizing Orwell's "sly glee at having attained such a low social level" (Lewis),[68] or equating his voluntary experience of poverty with "an act of youthful rebellion against the class of his birth."[69] *Down and Out* zooms in on an experience whose coping mechanisms actually resemble the "nightmare" of keeping up appearances his own family had gone through: the "peculiar lowness," "the shifts that it puts you to," "the complicated meanness, the crust-wiping."[70] Orwell, who does not mince words here, gives a new meaning to Nietzsche's famous "pathos of distance": it is no longer simply the distance between class and class; it also captures the pathetic efforts involved in maintaining the appearance of social distinction.

An excerpt from *Down and Out* echoes quite eloquently the paradoxical situation of the lower-upper-middle class:

> You discover, for instance, the secrecy attaching to poverty. At a sudden stroke you have been reduced to an income of six francs a day. But of course you dare not admit it—you have got to pretend that you are living quite as usual. From the start it tangles you in a network of lies you can hardly manage it. . . . All day you are telling lies, and expensive lies. (*DOPL*, 16)

While the sensations triggered by chronic hunger are documented with precision—"You discover that a man who has gone even a week on bread and margarine is not a man any longer, only a belly with a few accessory organs" (*DOPL*, 17)—there is no romanticization of the poor: on the contrary, Orwell goes as far as to say that it is all "prosaic," even "boring." But this is obviously an empty boredom, a boredom of deprivation—as opposed to the *ennui* of fullness, of excess, of the bourgeois—one that has to be countered with strategies of getting by that one must learn.[71] And this might be the most important point Orwell drives home: that there is a limit to what one can learn even with the best intention to see what it feels like to be poor. The occurrences that lead to this discovery have a humorous and perhaps self-ironic tinge when they occur in Paris:

> You discover the extreme precariousness of your six francs a day. Mean disasters happen and rob you of food. You have spent your last eighty centimes on half a litre of milk, and are boiling it over the spirit lamp. While it boils a bug runs down your forearm; you give the bug a flick with your nail, it falls, plop! straight into the milk. There is nothing for it but to throw the milk away and go foodless. (*DOPL*, 16)

"Nothing for it"—perhaps not the reaction of a genuine down and out? Other times, the detached narrator, perhaps mindful of the middle-class reader, distances himself from the participant, as in the self-conscious comment about hunger making him oblivious of coquetry: "It is disagreeable," he says, "to eat out of a newspaper on a public seat, especially in the Tuilleries, which are generally full of pretty girls, but I was too hungry to care" (*DOPL*, 49). Finally, in chapter 22, before his "return" to England, he sums up rather unpretentiously his conclusions about the life of a *plongeur*, his critical remarks about the hierarchies built in the subcastes of the lower classes, and his suggestions for improving their lot, all from the perspective of someone having known firsthand what Marx had called before him "the hidden abode of production":

> To sum up: A plongeur is a slave, and a wasted slave, doing stupid and largely unnecessary work. He is kept at work, ultimately, because of a vague feeling that he would be dangerous if he had leisure. And educated people, who should be on his side, acquiesce in the process, because they know nothing about him and consequently are afraid of him. I say this of the plongeur because it is his case I have been considering; it would apply equally to numberless other types of worker. These are only my own ideas about the basic facts of a plongeur's life, made without a reference to immediate economic questions, and no doubt largely platitudes. I present them as a sample of the thoughts that are put into one's head by working in a hotel. (*DOPL*, 121)

Not yet a socialist, but definitely a socialist in the making, already thinking in terms of class and transcending the category of national affiliation: although in Paris Orwell can still find himself amused by certain aspects of French snobbery, he criticizes, albeit with some distance, a system that he observes as a dishwasher in a hotel but that is surely an epitome of capitalist relations everywhere.

In London, the stakes will be different. Orwell anchors the contrast by noting that while in France a poor man on the street might pass for a bohemian (Orwell himself calls the lodgers "eccentric"), in England he is called "scum"; that is, socially, morally, even humanly unintelligible. How then to write a book that would reveal to the middle classes their prejudice? That the English half of the book is "rather dull," which I take to mean: lacking the humor and exotic coloring of the first half, has to be interrogated beyond the implicit complaint about its failure to reward the reader. Whereas the Parisian half bespeaks a clear commitment to the working classes in general, it becomes, as we read on, a prelude to the English one, whose rhetorical force might be reliant precisely on the interest of the first half. Why, after all, did Orwell find it necessary to rearrange his material and, contrary to reality, present his Parisian explorations *before* exposing his readers to English poverty?

The fragment that connects the two halves of the book, in which the narrator crosses the Channel anticipating the joy of being at home again, gestures toward the symbolic act of shifting perspective, of looking at things from an unfamiliar point of view on which Orwell gambles the value of his book. The question how an unprejudiced foreigner might see England leads to the heart of his effort to demystify a certain idea of England, that of the rich, and unveil a country to which respectable people prefer to remain oblivious. The fragment reads:

> On the journey I fell in with a couple of Roumanians, mere children, who were going to England on their honeymoon trip. They asked innumerable questions about England, and I told them some startling lies. I was so pleased to be getting home, after being hard up for months in a foreign city, that England seemed to me a sort of Paradise. There are, indeed, many things in England that make you glad to get home; bathrooms, armchairs, mint sauce, new potatoes properly cooked, brown bread, marmalade, beer made with veritable hops—they are all splendid, if you can pay for them. England is a very good country when you are not poor; and, of course, with a tame imbecile to look after, I was not going to be poor.[72] The thought of not being poor made me very patriotic. The more questions the Roumanians asked, the more I praised England; the climate, the scenery, the art, the literature, the laws—everything in England was perfect. (*DOPL*, 126)

This journey fragment reads like the beginning of a meditation on a question that Orwell returned to more than once in his life: "What is it like to see England for the first time?"[73] Not just as a foreigner, as the fragment implies, but also as a British middle-class citizen, whose experience abroad—in colonial Burma, in the social underworld of Paris—puts his own country in perspective. It seems plausible that Orwell structured *Down and Out in Paris and London* in such a way as to create this de-familiarization effect for the reader; that is, to have his narrator—and implicitly, the reader—*repeat* his own return home from Burma, and stage the shock experienced at the discovery, while tramping, of an England that looked so different from the familiar one: after experiencing the double foreignness, social and cultural, of poverty in Paris, the narrator has the uncanny revelation that *home*, this "England" he mentions no less than seven times in the passage, can feel even more alienating when looked at from a particular vantage point; and like Orwell's narrator, the reader is invited to equate middle- and upper-class patriotism with oblivion and complacency.[74] To really see things, one has to cast on them an estranged look, see them through the eyes of a foreigner; this is, at least, what the narrator's reminiscences suggest, after praising the London statues to the two honeymooners:

> Then the boat drew alongside Tilbury pier. The first building we saw on the waterside was one of those huge hotels, all stucco and pinnacles, which stare from the English coast like idiots over an asylum wall. I saw the Roumanians, too polite to say anything, cocking their eyes at the hotel. "Built by French architects," I assured them; and even later, when the train was crawling into London through the eastern slums, I still kept it up about the beauties of English architecture. (*DOPL*, 126–127)

Significantly, the foreigners *say* nothing; but their presence is sufficient for the narrator to begin to see England through their eyes, less "patriotically": the admirable statues might silently voice the suspicion that perhaps patriotism, pride in the "greatness" of England is in fact the celebration of an "old England" that tends to recede into an ever more distant, auraticized past, while the striking comparison with "idiots over an asylum wall" might suggest a present showing signs of degeneration.[75]

In French, *plonger*—the verb related to *plongeur*, which Orwell prefers to *dishwasher* in *Down and Out*—has the quality of suddenness, of shock, preserved by the English verb "to plunge" (as in to immerse in a liquid); it can also be used about a tree, to say that it *plunges* its roots into the soil, which adds a dimension of temporal unfolding, sedimentation, and self-transformation. Orwell's direct immersion in the world of tramps had both the impact of a shock, and the incomplete duration of a becoming. A scene close to the beginning of the second half speaks to both of these aspects. On leaving a pawnshop, where the narrator has traded his decent clothes for a tramp's rags and a little change, a recognition scene strikingly inaugurates the difficult process of relinquishing his social identity:

> It gives one a very strange feeling to be wearing such clothes. I had worn bad enough things before, but nothing at all like these; they were not merely dirty and shapeless, they had—how is one to express it?—a *gracelessness*, a patina of antique filth, quite different from mere shabbiness. They were the sort of clothes you see on a bootlace seller, or a tramp. An hour later, in Lambeth, I saw a hang-dog man, obviously a tramp, coming towards me, and when I looked again it was myself, reflected in a shop window. (*DOPL*, 128–129, my italics)

In this mirror-stage scene in the life of Orwell-the-tramp, the garb that makes him look like a hangdog man has a stronger impact on his immediate perception than his familiar facial features and bodily characteristics; the shop window reflects back, at a first glance, his social prejudices: if he cannot look behind the garb of the tramp he sees in the window, most likely no respectable person will. He has become nobody with immediately identifiable features, *only*, and *obviously*, a tramp. When another tramp addresses him as "mate" right away, he acknowledges that no one had called him that before—an unsettling realization of having joined the society of those without attachments: in other words, a community of those without community.[76]

He continues: "Dressed as I was, I was half afraid that the police might arrest me as a vagabond, and I dared not speak to anyone, imagining that they must notice a disparity between my accent and my clothes. (Later I discovered that this never happened)" (*DOPL*, 129), and this was because in England, it became obvious, anyone could go down in life, including old public-school boys like himself. The world of tramps was one in which everyone was leveled out into a democratic equality, although some, as the staged encounter with the former Etonian in a Salvation Army suggests, have trouble acknowledging it. The tramp who recognizes the narrator's accent as cultivated suggests the two of them "should hang out together a bit" (*DOPL*, 159), and holds in very low esteem the rest of the men in the dormitory, dismissing them as "very low types . . . who couldn't come down if they tried." This encounter serves to confirm another aspect that becomes salient in Orwell's experience, and on which he dwells at length: "Why are beggars despised?" (*DOPL*, 174), he asks repeatedly; why is "tramp" such a dreadful name (*DOPL*, 192)?[77] Not only are they denied respectability (he analyzes the equation poverty = immorality, as the necessary negation of the prevalent money = virtue); but they are also denied humanity, usually compared to, and treated like, animals, or referred to by names evoking disposable residue ("scum," etc.): it is, he discovers, as if the middle and upper classes were grounding their claims to distinction in the denial of the tramps' humanity.[78]

Down and Out records the process of giving up distinction in putting up with homelessness, hunger, dirt, dubious company, and the disdain of respectable people. Proximity with the poor also affords the narrator glimpses into some of their lives, narrated, as if in hieroglyphics, on their scarred bodies: "A tramp's clothes are bad," Orwell notes, "but they conceal far worse things; to see him as he really is, unmitigated, you must see him naked" (*DOPL*, 147). The passage below seems underwritten by the narrator's realization that beyond a certain point, even the imagination—hence narrative—has to show restraint from what could only be tactless, inadequate speculation:

> Flat feet, pot bellies, hollow chests, sagging muscles—every kind of physical rottenness was there. Nearly everyone was under-nourished, and some clearly diseased; two men were wearing trusses, and as for the old mummy-like creature of seventy-five, one wondered how he could possibly make his daily march. Looking at our faces, unshaven and creased from the sleepless night, *you* would have thought that all of us were recovering from a week on the drink. (*DOPL*, 147–148, my italics)

It is difficult to see the "you" in the last sentence as generic; it subtly conveys Orwell's enjoinment to his reader to acknowledge that there are extremes of poverty that one cannot begin to fathom. In such moments, the narrator recedes into the background to allow these narratives of scars and diseases assert themselves as signifying. In this sense, Adorno's words have a sober adequacy: "The somatic stratum of life, bereft of meaning, is the theater of suffering."[79] It is precisely a theater stage that comes to mind when reading the following episode, one that Orwell refrains from commenting on: "In front of the fire a fully dressed man and a stark-naked man were bargaining. They were newspaper-sellers. The dressed man was selling his clothes to the naked man. [They bargain and agree on the price, "five and a tanner."] The clothed man stripped, and in three minutes their positions were reversed; the naked man dressed, and the other kilted with a sheet of the *Daily Mail*" (*DOPL*, 158–159). "Bereft of meaning": this naked man wrapped in a newspaper might well be imagined on a stage in a Beckett play; even there, it would be not a symbol but, as Peter Brook says, a "theater machine." Like the parents in the trash cans in *Endgame*, it issues a ban on interpretation, since it is meant to remain a social hieroglyphic, a self-reflexive *fait divers*, gesturing to its mere being. Bare life—in fact, nobody. To say nothing more is not a question of morality. One might say it has become a question of tact:[80] less a form of regard for the sensibility of the reader, since Orwell's purpose is to create a certain discomfort, than a gesture of respect for the humanity of these people.

Did Orwell succeed in looking at England through the eyes of a foreigner? A brief comparison with a foreigner's account of London is instructive. I have in mind Paul Morand's *Londres*, published in the same year as *Down and Out in Paris and London* (1933), and later translated as *A Frenchman's London*. A diplomat and writer, Morand confidently declared once that a foreigner was likely to give a better sense of a city than a local because he had more critical distance (*plus de recul*).[81] A keen observer, Morand shows himself critical of the cynicism with which British authorities handle the problem of poverty, to which he dedicates the whole of the second chapter. There is much that meets the senses in these pages, the unintended irony being that Morand tries to achieve a picture of utter deprivation through an abundance, even excess, of stylistic means (repetition, enumeration, similes, etc.):

> *Sans* aucun bruit, *sans* boire, *sans* jurer, *sans* un geste de révolte, la main au chapeau pour un salut: "Good night, Sir," les miséreux attendent l'heure du sommeil, *comme dévitalisés, écrasés par cette ville qui les rejette*. . . . L'odeur des désinfectants fait tousser. Là, à la nuit tombée, les pauvres de Londres viennent dormir, cachés dans l'ombre, *comme* les paysans des plus reculés Balkans, ou *comme* les hommes préhistoriques. Une seule lampe, au milieu du dortoir, pour tous *ces*

> *lits pareils à des cercueils*, où certains se couchent tout habillés et tout chaussés *comme s'ils* avaient peur d'un torpillage. (*L*, 86, my italics)
>
> No noise, no drink, no curse, no gesture of revolt, touching their hats in greeting: "Good night, Sir," the miserable wait for the hour of sleep, as if exhausted, crashed by this city that rejects them. . . . The smell of disinfectants makes one cough. There, at night, the poor of London come to sleep, hidden in the dark, like the most secluded peasants in the Balkans, or like prehistoric men. One lamp only, in the middle of the dormitory, for all these beds resembling coffins, where some sleep fully dressed with their shoes on, as if fearing a torpedoing.

> En visitant les asiles de nuit, je me demandais par quel prodige ces infortunés, *sans famille, sans foyer, sans argent ni travail, sans pain et sans amis*, pouvaient durer pendant des mois et des années, et ne pas céder au suicide ou au crime. (*L*, 94, my italics)
>
> Visiting the night shelters, I was wondering by what miracle these poor unfortunates with no ties, homeless, penniless and jobless, breadless and friendless, could last for months and years, and not give in to suicide or crime.

These examples should be sufficient illustration of the paradox unselfconsciously courted by Morand's text: an abundance of stylistic devices is meant to convey a sense of utmost destitution. The reader is drawn into the text and made to experience vicariously, as refracted by Morand's gaze, the condition of being poor. "The condition," it is important to emphasize, not the specific experience of any given individual: to Morand, who sets out to visit some poor London lodgings, "it is always the same setting, and almost always the same story. Too many children . . . hasty marriage [. . .] That's why the street," he concludes without mentioning unemployment in this context, "is full of violin players, of strolling performers, of apple or match sellers."[82]

By contrast, Orwell refrains from feeling for the poor. Closer to the tramps than the French traveler, sharing night-shelters, food and cigarettes, he is paradoxically also—one should probably say *therefore*—more detached, more realistic: when experienced, Orwell suggests, poverty does not inspire pathos; it is trivial, sordid, boring, degrading, and infinitely complicated, especially for someone who was born into a different condition. There is, in other words, nothing metaphysical about it (as Morand would have it), quite the contrary: a hungry man, Orwell quips, is nothing more than "a belly with a few accessory organs" (*DOPL*, 17). He also refrains from generalizing (for him, it is *not* "always the same setting and almost always the same story"); the second part of *Down and Out in Paris and London* is populated by a gallery of characters whose lives do not come together in the intimation of a few types. And although he writes for the middle classes, Orwell certainly does not attempt to bring the tramps back into the sphere of bourgeois morality. About the first tramp he got to know more closely, for instance, he concludes: Paddy Jaques "had the regular character of a tramp—abject, envious, a jackal's character" (*DOPL*, 153), while Bozo, the pavement artist, was unlike most tramps and their "ordinary abject worm-like gratitude" with which they accept charity: he had "the decency of being ungrateful" (*DOPL*, 167). This is, superfluous to say, no longer the morality of "sincerity," but, rather, one directed against it.[83]

The shifting use of pronouns suggests the same transformation: if in the early stages of his social unselfing, in the recounting of his misfortunes as a newly down-and-out the "I" often slips into a generic "you," thus surreptitiously suggesting the possibility of anyone losing the privilege of class (and the narrator's identification as a middle-class man), later in the book instances where the narrator clearly identifies with the tramps ("we," "us"), against the respectable people who humiliate them, are more and more frequent. Importantly, however, Orwell arrives at the conclusion of his travelogue about the tramps' suburbs with the awareness that he has only known "the fringe of poverty," and that his self-transformation is by no means complete: "I shall never again think that all tramps are drunken scoundrels, nor expect a beggar to be grateful when I give him a penny, nor be surprised if men out of work lack energy, nor subscribe to the Salvation Army, nor pawn my clothes, nor refuse a handbill, nor enjoy a meal at a smart restaurant" (*DOPL*, 213). Finally speaking in his own name—the "I" of the narrator-character as writer emerges here—and enumerating the hard-won truths in a series of personal pledges that run against impercipient bourgeois moralism, Orwell concludes *Down and Out in Paris and London* with a gesture of anticipation: "That is a beginning" (*DOPL*, 213).

The career in the pursuit of truth that followed is well-known, so it might come as a surprise that only four years later, in *The Road to Wigan Pier*, Orwell ironically dismissed the tramping expeditions evoked in his first published book as "masquerade." The tramp's garb he had put on in *Down and Out* seemed in retrospect a naive way of tackling the problem of poverty: by 1937, the earlier struggle for authenticity acquired in Orwell's eyes a quixotic quality.[84] Raymond Williams suggests, however, that such a disavowal of an early work was typical of Orwell's persistent conviction, throughout his life, that he had failed when in fact he had succeeded so much. It also matters, I should add, that his dismissal appears in a book commissioned by the Left Book Club, at a time when Orwell was fashioning his own, idiosyncratic brand of democratic socialism: "Unfortunately," he begins chapter 10 of this later book, "*you* do not *solve* the class problem by making friends with tramps. *At most* you get rid of some of your own class-prejudice by doing so" (*RWP*, 154, my italics). "You" again—now potentially as a reader interpellated into taking action, into solving a social problem; "at most"—as if getting rid of even *some* class prejudice were a small thing. Chapter 10 sets out to show the magnitude of this task, only confirming the value of what *Down and Out* had aimed to achieve:

> But unfortunately you get no further by merely wishing class-distinctions away. More exactly, it *is* necessary to wish them away, but your wish has no efficacy unless you grasp what it involves. The fact that has got to be faced is that to abolish class-distinctions means abolishing a part of yourself. Here am I, a typical member of the middle class. It is easy for me to say that I want to get rid of class-distinctions, but nearly everything I think and do is a result of class-distinctions. All my notions—notions of good and evil, of pleasant and unpleasant, of funny and serious, of ugly and beautiful—are essentially middle-class notions; my taste in books and food and clothes, my sense of honour, my table manners, my turns of speech, my accent, even the characteristic movements of my body, are the products of a special kind of upbringing and a special niche about half-way up the social hierarchy. When I grasp this I grasp that it is no use clapping a proletarian on the back and telling him that he is as good a man as I am; if I want real contact with him, I have got to make an effort for which very likely I am unprepared. For to get outside the class-racket I have got to suppress not merely my private snobbishness, but most of my other tastes and prejudices as well. *I have got to alter myself so completely that at the end I should hardly be recognizable as the same person.* What is involved is not merely the amelioration of working-class conditions, nor an avoidance of the more stupid forms of snobbery, but a complete abandonment of the upper-class and middle-class attitude to life. And whether I say Yes or No probably depends upon the extent to which I grasp what is demanded of me. (161–162, my italics)

Trilling could not have wished for a more perceptive analysis of the discontents of the sincerity paradigm, nor Bourdieu—for a more eloquent reflection on the effects of social distinction. To recapitulate the trajectory of Orwell's sincerity: it begins, on his return from Burma, with the denunciation of the insincerity at the very core of the civilizing project of the British empire; in contrast to Kurtz, the antihero of Conrad's *Heart of Darkness* (who in Trilling's account represents the paragon of authenticity for pushing the darkest impulses of civilized modernity to its extremes of horror), Blair returned to England and decided to deprive himself even of the meager social capital his "lower-upper-middle" class position could provide: a radical rejection of the doubtful privilege of respectability.[85] *Down and Out in Paris and London* might be characterized as the quest for a more authentic self, a pursuit against society and its attendant principle of "sincerity" through voluntary downward mobility, which shows, through the unmaking of social identity (in his case similar to the decay of the middle class his own family had experienced directly) that it is based on claims to distinction, mystification, and snobbery, and with respect to the tramps, on the denial of their humanity. Through close acquaintance with the poor, Orwell insists on the authenticity of suffering, taking the body—his own, theirs—as a measure of truth. Yet writing is a social act, and commitment, as Trilling does not fail to show, is inherent to the paradigm of sincerity; hence the conflict between Orwell's project of unmasking society and writing for it, with the purpose of triggering change. Differently put, cultivating the outsider stance typically associated with authenticity, not taking society on its own terms, yet challenging it to change: this is where Trilling's paradigms begin to lose foothold. Further along in Orwell's trajectory, in *The Road to Wigan Pier* he points to inauthenticity ("at the end I should hardly be recognizable as the same person") as the outcome of the effort to give up distinction, and warns against it, commending, rather, sincerity without the pretense, hence being authentic *because* sincere.

To place Orwell's situation in a broader context, it is worth returning briefly to Morand. If, like other intellectuals of his generation, he was "one of the last remnants of the bourgeoisie," the travelogue *Londres* does not suggest much self-consciousness about it. While he finds his place in the wake of a long tradition of romantic travelers in the pursuit of self-cultivation, a tradition of which Henry James took himself to be the last in line, he has certainly earned himself a place in the longer history of cosmopolitanism, a practice and ideal of reflective distance whose history goes back to the Cynics and Stoics, and of which romantic travel was a significant moment.[86] The field of inquiry that problematized the issues at stake in a travelogue like Morand's, and whose avowed ideal was cosmopolitanism, was, of course, anthropology. In *Culture and Anomie: Ethnographic Imagination in the Nineteenth Century*, Christopher Herbert identified the conflicted postures of ethnographic subjectivity, attempting to mediate between sympathetic immersion and detached analysis and judgment.[87] Orwell and Morand, however, show that experiences of "immersion" can be very different, depending on how close one is willing to get to the foreign Other (and Morand's British poor, as well as Orwell's French poor, are exactly that, both foreign and—socially—Other).

E. T. Hall's work on proxemics in *The Hidden Dimension* is useful here: following his attempts to interpret the various dynamics of sociality, he divides its spectrum into public, social, personal, and intimate distances.[88] For Morand, one might say, the spectacle of poverty remains *socially* removed; his allegedly superior capacity for detachment (*plus de recul*) relates both to his lack of complicity with the British class system (thus having no stakes in remaining oblivious of its oppressive character), but also to his lack of a sense of responsibility (his not being in a relationship of *sincerity* with British society, the way Orwell is). Does he qualify as the neutral visitor with an "unprejudiced eye" whose view Orwell sought? The obvious thing whispered loudly throughout the five chapters of *A Frenchman's London* is that there is no such thing as an unprejudiced—that is, fully objective—foreigner, especially when he has the upbringing, education, culture, and life that Morand had: *Londres* is framed by Morand's complex horizon of expectations, reflecting a perception shaped by his idioculture.[89] One might even say, amending the words of George Eliot, that the "appeals founded on generalizations and statistics" Morand addresses to his readers, however skillfully embalmed in pathos (in the rhetorical sense), "require a sympathy ready-made, a moral sentiment already in activity."[90] By contrast, Orwell's ethnographic project—"like a travel-diary," he writes at the end of the book—becomes a *personal* matter. Rather than putting himself in the tramps' shoes imaginatively ("how long the roads *must seem* [to the vagabonds]," Morand writes), remaining essentially at a safe remove on grounds of his cultivated detachment, Orwell puts on the garb of a tramp and engages in what might be called an ethnography of proximity.[91] (Interestingly, in the conclusion, he says he wants to deepen his familiarity with poverty and get to know more *intimately*—incidentally using Hall's last category—what tramps like the ones he has met might actually think and feel.)

To conclude, how are literature, politics and ethics, everyday life and the ordinary reconfigured in light of Orwell's early work? Raymond Williams's remark that Orwell's writing represents an enlargement of our literature strikes a compelling note: I read it as an invitation to unsettle established criteria of value and relinquish generic categories (for instance, in evaluating a book like *Down and Out*) in order to grant Orwell a prominent place in the republic of letters for what he is, or perhaps for what he did. With characteristic acumen, George Steiner went even further in pointing to literature as ultimately inadequate when considering someone like Orwell: "In the last analysis, literature did not matter all that much. . . . What mattered was the use of language to make human beings more humane, to impel them to right action. Indeed, too much of literature was sophisticated tinsel designed to make social injustice less visible."[92]

As we have seen, shunning abstraction is not just the attitude lying at the core of Orwell's conception of writing, but also one that guides his idea of politics. To quote Trilling's apt words, "At a time when most intellectuals still thought of politics as a nightmare abstraction, pointing to the fearfulness of the nightmare as evidence of their sense of reality, Orwell was using the imagination of a man whose hands and eyes and whole body were part of his thinking apparatus."[93] Trilling no doubt refers here to the importance attached by Orwell to direct experience, as a source of insight not only into the life conditions of the lower classes, but also in the compromised realities of political allegiances. Praising *Homage to Catalonia* as "a flawless book," Steiner saw well that "it was in Barcelona during the murderous Communist betrayal of the Socialist, Trotskyite, and Anarchist allies that Orwell, with a Fascist bullet lodged in his throat, realized where the only possibility of decency lay. It was there that he chose *the impossible middle, equidistant* from the lies and raptures of totalitarianism, be it of the right or of the left."[94] The negotiation of distance as a practice of lucidity that Steiner alludes to speaks not just to Orwell's political stance, but also to his life choices and self-presentation. The "possibility of decency" lies as much in unswerving lucidity as in a retrieval of middle-class values—the "ordinary decency of common men," less prone to contamination by ideology, intellectual and political abstraction, or even—as in *1984*—totalitarian regimentation. If these are the values of an "old England," they are nonetheless secular; Orwell's ideal was "a system of morality independent of heaven or hell."

A comparative analysis of the writings of Orwell, Miller, and Morand in the 1930s widens the historical background against which Adorno's aphorism about the morality of "not being at home in one's home" unfolds, pointing to this period as one of intersection between at least three modes of detachment. Orwell, our main figure here, was in principle in agreement with the main tenet of cosmopolitanism; in *Road to Wigan Pier*, he wrote: "It is only when you meet someone of a different culture from yourself that you begin to realize what your own beliefs really are" (165). Paul Morand, however, illustrates by comparison a mode of detachment, self-cultivation and sympathy reminiscent of romantic travel, in which not being at home is a matter of personal ethos, rather than of morality. *A Frenchman's London* ultimately aestheticizes the world, turning it into spectacle; and to point out that Morand ended up as a Vichy supporter suggests an affinity between romantic ideals and disastrous political choices in the past century.[95] While Morand thought of himself as a cosmopolitan writer, Miller delighted in the idea of being a "cosmological" one:[96] although they both reveled in their freedom, there seems to be a world of difference between the attitude of rootless, barehanded Henry Miller, the American who made of Paris his China, and the state of mind of a French aristocrat, a world-trotting diplomat like Paul Morand, whose symbolic will, in *Le voyage*, was that on his death a suitcase be made out of his skin.[97] The shared present of their books stretches both ways, between the barehanded strolling freely, looking to the future, and the traveler for whom the suitcase is not just the symbol of travel, but also the unacknowledged metaphor of a past he carries along. "Cosmopolitan" and "cosmological" share the cosmos as their ideal; but "cosmology" also implies a new *poiesis* of the world (out of an "intestinal embrace") after a violent rupture with the past, thus a problematic relationship to tradition and to the idea of history. Its ideal of artistic detachment is enabled by a "higher" perspective (the Chinamen's gay eyes cast on the stage of the world from the top of the mountain in Yeats's "Lapis Lazuli," Miller's "cosmological eye"), through extraction from the feverish temporality of historical events and the gamble on longer durations.

"The charlatan," writes Steiner in apparent agreement with Orwell, "levels at eternity and falls short; an honest writer is never afraid to date. Indeed, as Orwell assured a correspondent in the summer of 1934, 'anything worth reading always 'dates.' "[98] From the perspective of 1940, when he praised Miller's "implied outlook," however, he might have seen a different side to that, even if he remained loyal to his own, personal creed.[99] Unlike Morand's idea of truth as metaphor (something he's looking for symbolically standing for "the secret of London"), Orwell's truth—about imperialism, the poor, the miners, fascism, wartime—resides in the unfolding of experience, it is truth, to borrow Tiedemann's words about Adorno, "in the emphatic sense of the word, that is, a truth that does not just subsume its object under something more abstract but unravels its very core."[100] I take Orwell's persistent effort to attune himself to contingencies and see beyond them as an ideal of objectivity ("equidistance") that comes close to a notion of tact verging on tactlessness,[101] amending thus Stanley Cavell's tentative definition of tact as "the application of a tremendous amount of force [his uncompromising indictments] with a tremendous amount of precision [in the diagnosis, isolation, and treatment of the matter in hand]."[102]

The following chapter, on Elias Canetti, will unravel another episode in the history of tact and tactlessness, taking us from Weimar Berlin to postwar England.

Chapter 2

✦

The Inferno of Saviors

Notes in the Margin of Elias Canetti's Lifework

> It is not until one is oneself an exile that one realizes to what significant extent the world has always been a world of banished people.
>
> —Elias Canetti, *Neue Rundschau*, 1965

> Morality is narrow if one knocks against it. The real morality has become one's skeletal structure.
>
> —Canetti, 1980

In an intimate letter dated July 3, 1959—one of the four hundred found soaked in a Paris basement in 2003—Elias Canetti shared with his brother Georges the news that he had finally completed *Crowds and Power*, a vortex of a book that had absorbed not only thirty years of reading, research, and writing, but also, in symbolic form, the events with which its gestation was contemporary.[1] Understandably, the letter transpires a huge sigh of relief, exuding Canetti's sense of fulfillment; he declares himself "thoroughly satisfied," convinced that the book will have given meaning to his life and granted the recognition of posterity. Not only does he feel entitled to the Nobel Prize "either for literature or for peace," he also anticipates that his contemporaries will fail to understand, or in any case they will take a very long time to grasp his insights: "Of course I won't get it. But that doesn't matter: I *know* for myself that no one else has penetrated so deeply into the confusion of our century."[2]

The deeply ambivalent reception of the book confirmed his apprehensions, so his self-confident resignation turned into a felt need to write a companion to *Crowds and Power*: "I ought," he reflects in his diary, "to embed my ideas in their place of origin, to make them appear more natural. It is possible that by doing that, I would *give them a different accent*. I don't want to correct anything, but I want to retrieve *the life* that is part of the ideas, bring it in close and let it flow back into them."[3] The autobiographical tomes he set out to write—*The Tongue Set Free*, *The Torch in My Ear*, and *The Play of the Eyes*—remain thus in the shadow of his major book, a pedestal engraved with the words "How I Wrote *Crowds and Power*."[4] They are meant to enlighten (still) puzzled, or unconvinced readers, by giving the ideas "a different accent," that is, by retrieving the life—his life, which is the life of his ideas. Tirelessly he traces the germ of his lifelong obsession back to his first experience of the crowd in Frankfurt in 1922, when at age seventeen he witnessed the workers' demonstrations after the murder of Walter Rathenau; three years later we see him make formal plans for a book on crowds and begin to collect material. But the witness experience would not be the closest he would ever get to a crowd: on July 15, 1927, he joined the eruption of "leaderless" protests on the streets of Vienna, enthralled by the spectacle of the Palace of Justice burning. This experience, now an immersion, is going to be so memorable that it fills Canetti with the exorbitant confidence that he will never need to read anything on the French Revolution because he knew what the crowd—the experience of the crowd in history—meant: it was now all "in his bones." Hence his perplexity that no one had *recognized* the phenomenon, no one had explained it *from within*, from the perspective of a participant whose consciousness is altered, who becomes joyfully oblivious of the usual fears, claims to distinction and individuality. Since there were more and more crowds in Central and Western Europe in the following years, especially brown-shirted marchers and Nazi mass rallies, by 1931 Canetti realized that it was not only crowds he had to understand, but also power. These are, it seems safe to assume, the significant landmarks of the "life" he had hoped to let flow back into his ideas, and that would illuminate the book called *Crowds and Power*.

Do they provide "a different accent"? Do they alter substantially our understanding of the *Lebenswerk*, as he still called his book on crowds in the posthumously published *Party in the Blitz*?[5] Do they turn Canetti into a more sensible figure or a more compelling author, in the eyes of those who, reviewing *Crowds and Power*, dismissed him as a sorcerer (Jacques Cabau), a "grotesquely shambling figure," "the most decayed limb one can possibly imagine of the great German intellectual tree" (Tom Nairn)? Do they deepen, provide unexpected dimensions to the fascination of those who were grateful to the "solitary man of genius" (Iris Murdoch), *Kulturphilosoph*, *Dichter*, and polymath "deported of our history" (George Steiner), for producing a "magnificent anthropological-political treatise," "the only masterpiece of crowd theory" (John McClelland)? The deeply polarized reception of *Crowds and Power*, to this day a book hard to evaluate or even situate in Western culture, gives ample reasons for doubt. Granted, if we look for crowds and power in the autobiography, we begin to understand that the 1960 book is not just a random collection of idiosyncratic theories, not austere, sterile excogitations emerging from the solitude of a scholar's room: his ideas have a historical background. But if that is all we see, it is hardly an existential or scholarly justification for spending thirty years fine-tuning taxonomies of crowds and their symbolism over hundreds of pages, and especially there is no reason for the ruthless, unforgiving, raw *Weltanschauung* that Canetti presents us in the second half of the book, on "the entrails of power." Are human organs made exclusively for violence?—is life just "an intestinal tract," as a critic understood Canetti's views? What makes him draw such a picture of life, and what does he hope to achieve by conveying it as such to others? Why did he say that with *Crowds and Power*, he felt he had "grabbed the century by the throat"?[6] These questions demand a fresh reading of the autobiography, in search of other aspects that would shed light on the vision that Canetti canvassed in his magnum opus.

There is more than memories about crowds and scattered ideas about political power in the autobiography. In fact, power is not even so much present as political power, but rather as the forceful dynamic that permeates all social relations, the sphere of everyday sociality, especially as it is perceived by a rootless, footloose exile negotiating affecting experiences of displacement, miscommunication, and lack of recognition. Power is present in the distances that people create and maintain among themselves, which resonates with the inaugural axiom of *Crowds and Power*: all life, Canetti proclaims, is laid out in distances; and it is only to abolish distances that people congregate in crowds (*CP*, 18). Critics who have paused on this early moment in the book have suggested that Canetti refers here to the *principium individuationis*, the boundary-setting process of individuation accompanied by an (archaic) "fear of being touched" (Canetti's words), that sets apart individuals in everyday life and that the crowd inexplicably makes them forget.[7] Close reading of the autobiography, however, yields a more concrete, deeply personal, and historical meaning for this early moment in *Crowds and Power*: a veritable anatomy of social and interpersonal distances is insistently pursued, it becomes, one might say, the leitmotif of a life segmented by repeated displacements, exile, symbolic homelessness. "All life is laid out in distances" reads like an axiom, but the memoirs reveal it as a deeply personal conclusion. And this is no insignificant detail: in light of these disclosures, it becomes possible to identify a new, quite subtle scaffolding to *Crowds and Power*, and an overall underlying purpose that has so far been missed.

In this chapter I will argue that the memoirs inflect *Crowds and Power* with a moralistic "accent" vis-à-vis the perceived separateness of people and their hurtful involvements, which in Canetti's view always involve power. A moralistic position is usually associated with Canetti's persona, but not with the author of *Crowds and Power*. Yet by foregrounding this attitude, Canetti's ultimate purpose will stand out as nothing less than a reformation of the social sphere. Whereas most of Canetti's critics have situated him in the company of crowd theorists, political theorists, or theorists of totalitarianism, I will show how the memoirs highlight Canetti's investment in a critique of modernity modeled on Freud. Few people failed to wonder at

Canetti's glaring omission of Freud's group psychology; and there are sufficient passages in the autobiography to illustrate that Canetti thought of Freud as his adversary. This perception, however, was more of a love-hate relationship, and in the end Canetti saw his adversarial stance as a youthful rebellion; moreover, he came to acknowledge Freud as a model. He also understood that after World War II, the stakes of any work on crowds were significantly higher than whatever might have motivated *Group Psychology and the Analysis of the Ego* (1920); Canetti's underlying concern echoes rather the interrogative ending—added by Freud in 1931—of *Civilization and Its Discontents*, regarding the fate of human civilization. To this ambivalent question, already sounding a pessimistic tone, Canetti's response is an unsettling *Weltanschauung*, and an even more disturbing, perhaps hopeless, call for change.

For this view to appear in all its clarity, a summary of the book and a quick overview of the reactions it elicited are necessary, followed by a brief excursus through the autobiography, with a focus on its two major themes: distances and crowds. This analysis will reveal more explicitly the moralistic attitude that Canetti did not drop after his first (and only) novel, *Auto-da-fé*; if anything, this attitude only seemed to acquire more gravity: as we shall see, Canetti the *Dichter* also took himself for a redeemer of sorts.

In the Wake of *Auto-da-fé*

Crowds and Power *(Summary)*

Like the novel *Auto-da-fé* before it, *Crowds and Power* is an overwhelming book.[8] Not only is the scope of the investigation intimidating—Canetti combs all of the human cultures, East and West, and all realms of life, archaic and modern, in search of crowd phenomena and aspects of power—but the paratactic presentation excludes from the outset even the semblance of a rigorously conducted argument grounded in previous scholarship on the two subjects. "This work of a lifetime cannot be more easily summarized than *In Search of Lost Time*," said Pierre Nora.[9] Canetti's originality, moreover, manifests itself as defiance of the enshrined boundaries between various disciplines: one might see the book as an anthropology of crowds juxtaposed with a phenomenology and sociology of power, including ethnographic accounts that are richly symbolic and an implicit critique of historiography; style is in flux between the documentary, the scientific, the symbolic, and the apodictic, there being hardly a distinction noted between the factual, the interpretative, or the imaginary. The bibliography contains little that one would expect in a book about crowds and power—names like Michelet, Taine, Tarde, Le Bon, or Freud are conspicuously absent, as are his Canetti's contemporaries Durkheim or Foucault—but it includes an eclectic mix of titles that has reminded many readers of the library of the mad sinologist Peter Kien in *Auto-da-fé*.[10]

In the apt description of Hansjakob Werlen, *Crowds and Power* reads like an "ethnographic study and poetic speculation, chemical experiment and symbolic representation."[11] That the overall structure of the book—crowds in the first part, power in the second—is deceptively simple is amply demonstrated by the radically divergent readings and interpretations that have been proposed by readers of various persuasions since its publication.

The early chapters, devoted to a rich typology of crowds and crowd symbolism, bespeak an attitude toward crowds that is eminently different from that of most of his predecessors in the long tradition of crowd theory. Canetti develops a new vocabulary to describe crowd phenomena, and suggests that the latter have a more significant explanatory value than previously imagined, not only for twentieth-century events but also for our understanding of modernity, history, and collective psychology. Before Canetti, culminating in Le Bon's 1895 influential *Psychologie des foules*, the crowd had been perceived as atavistic, irrational, and disruptive, formed of the troublesome residues of a civilization that saw itself in evolutionary terms as superior to everything that preceded it, and threatened with regression by eruptions of violence that had to be kept in check.[12] Freud's *Group Psychology and the Analysis of the Ego* (1920), while not sharing the same dismissive attitude, theorizes crowd formation in terms of the defective ego of the participants who idealize the same person as the superego with which they identify: that Adorno enlisted Freudian psychology in his account of Nazism appositely carves out a space in which Canetti's utter singularity as a crowd theorist shines forth. In his elaborate account, the crowd precedes the leader (if it ever has one); it has emotions and a mind—or at least an imaginary—of its own, and it constitutes a category that enjoys precellence over time and space: history is not a narrative of class struggles, but an aggregation of *open* or *closed*, *stagnating* or *rhythmic*, *slow* or *quick*, *baiting*, *flight*, *prohibition*, *reversal*, *feast*, or *double crowds*; moreover, all life, visible or invisible, is a matter of congregations, from the millions of spermatozoa competing for fulfillment in the egg, to the heaps of corpses of everyone who has ever lived, the spirits of various religions, the invisible worlds of bacilli revealed under the microscope lens. As in a Brueghel painting that Canetti admired in his youth, *The Triumph of Death*, no crowd is ever tired of life, that is, of its *increase*—that is, self-reproductive—principle; and there are always *crowd crystals*, groups likely to rekindle the fire of a crowd. Invested in crowd symbolism, Canetti believes in an imaginary that is essentially collective, a deep source of irrational impulses that also binds individuals as members of a community (tribe, nation, but also humanity at large); in this sense natural elements that are masses of smaller units—sand, forest, sea, rain, corn, stone heaps, wind, a treasure—are anthropomorphized and partake of this generalized crowd-dominated sensibility. He shows that there are, of course, specifically modern crowd phenomena, such as the increase of capitalist production (with its attending malfunctions: depression, inflation, etc.) or the drastic diminution of populations through modern mass destruction; these provide, he claims, more accurate insight into virtually all the major events of the twentieth century, from the consequences of the Versailles treaty, inflation, the two world wars, the Holocaust, civil wars and revolutions, the threat of nuclear annihilation, the Cold War. Yet late modernity is not *explicitly* Canetti's object of interest, in the lengthy evocations of archaic rituals, religious and mythical beliefs;[13] and part 2, concerned with a minute dissection of power in its cruelest forms, relies even less on examples that might concern directly Canetti's contemporaries.

An astonishing physiology of power in its real and symbolic incarnations, the short chapter "The Entrails of Power" captures both the raw act of seizing, incorporation and digestion of animals, and, through an expansion of this imaginary body to the whole of human experience, the circulation of power in society in the elaborate forms of commands (to which I will return) and in the invariable ways various rulers have dominated, throughout history, large crowds of individuals, ostentatiously displaying their power by spending prodigiously or sending countless subjects to their death. "The instant of survival," Canetti authoritatively states, "is the instant of power," and he guides his readers in the footsteps of African kings and the sultan of Delhi, finally through the delusional world of Schreber's paranoia;[14] these ruler figures, Canetti shows, are all "survivors," real or imagined, of great heaps of corpses. If this panorama apparently culminates in the characterization of Hitler as a combination of Muhammad Tuglak, the megalomaniac sultan, and Schreber, Canetti is quick to deflect what might have been the climactic moment of the book in the much-delayed first mention of the name Hitler. To him, the Nazi *Führer* was only an accident of history, one of many a "survivor" in a field of animal corpses: this is because most people eat meat, and everyone, Canetti finds, entertains ridiculous dreams of revenge, of self-expansion, of domination, everyone experiences satisfaction while walking in a graveyard, the relieved contentment of having survived so many who are under one's feet.[15] The stories of archaic violence turn out to be all moral parables: Canetti warns that no one should feel superior to barbarism after the horrors of the twentieth century. Given the availability of the nuclear bomb, "one man today has the possibility of surviving at a single stroke more human beings than could generations of his predecessors together" (*CP*, 468); the "survivor," warns Canetti again, has grown to such monstrous stature that a correct *Zeitdiagnose* necessarily has to focus on him: "Whether there is any way of dealing with the survivor . . . is the most important question today: one is tempted to say that it is the only one. The fragmentation and fluidity of modern life blind us to the simplicity and urgency of this one fundamental issue" (*CP*, 469). The rather perplexing ending of the book might have something of an apotropaic gesture: "If we would master power," says Canetti having just pointed to the dangers looming large in the Cold War and the bomb, "we must face command openly and boldly, and search for means to deprive it of its sting" (*CP*, 470).

What exactly does that mean, and how is it to be done? The relevant insights are in two related sections, one on Canetti's theory of command, the other on *Verwandlung* (metamorphosis, transformation), the latter mostly consisting of examples he hoped to expand on in a second volume, never completed. In Canetti's rather dramatic account of social intercourse, any command—from those of parents to those of dictators—conceals a death threat; when carried out, each command leaves behind a sting. The stings of command accumulate and sediment in one's body, are carried along, sometimes all of one's life, only to be passed on to others.[16] Being in a position to give commands creates an "anxiety of command," an awareness of permanent danger from those who have had to carry them out; conversely, always carrying out commands turns one into a burdened individual. The only free person is the one who knew how to dodge commands;[17] and one possible strategy is metamorphosis. It is here that Canetti's book is at its most elusive because most symbolic, for the examples he gives are mythological (derived from anthropological accounts of the Bushmen), pathological (*delirium tremens*), or aesthetic (the actor, the writer). In Pierre Nora's suggestive summary, "Les conduites de fuite, ces morts masquées que sont l'hystérie, la manie, la mélancolie" (These behaviors of flight, these masked deaths we call hysteria, mania, melancholia). Of help are other moments in Canetti's writings where he tackles transformation: the book on Kafka, his essay on the writer, a "keeper of metamorphoses," and, of course, the memoirs.[18] Whether he talks about Gregor Samsa's transformation into something smaller, or about a cripple's ambition to master the Western philosophical discourse, thus turning himself from an object of pity into "a place where people go on pilgrimages," or even about the various characters an actor is able to perform, Canetti is convinced that metamorphosis offers the way out of imposed identities, stagnation and rigidity, self-complacency, and ultimately perhaps even death, and that we have to take advantage of the large repository of metamorphoses contained in our culture (starting with Ovid's *Metamorphoses*) in order to change our lives.[19] This plea for freedom, however, is not fully developed in *Crowds and Power*; it can only be inferred from his other writings.

Brief Reception History

The most fascinating and intriguing aspect of the reception of *Crowds and Power* is not that various readers could not agree on the meaning of the book—indeed, one could hardly expect a project of such magnitude and richness to yield a unified meaning—but that they failed to reach a consensus on whether it had any value or not. Its publication provoked reactions ranging between dismissive contempt, dismay, and hyperbolic praise. "How does one judge a large-scale theory of this sort?": most reviewers asked this question, often rhetorically, puzzled not only by the book's lack of engagement with previous crowd theories, but also by its withholding of a criterion of evaluation of its own. Iris Murdoch dismissed the idea that considerations of truth-value even had any pertinence: "Clearly, there is no point in just saying impatiently, well is it true or not?"[20] Yet many did ask the question of the truth of *Crowds and Power* in all earnestness, obviously relying on the assumption that this book, with its lengthy accounts of myths, legends, anthropological reports, musings on the workings of power in archaic times and in faraway regions that supposedly, and disquietingly, were relevant to their own mores and times, had to be a scientific work, not literature. George Steiner was the only one to caution his readers against such assumptions: "Dr. Canetti's book is literature. Emphatically."[21]

The early reviewers made various assumptions about Canetti's aims and the scholarly work on which he had passed implicit judgment. Murdoch began her article with a disclaimer, confessing she was not the polymath who should evaluate the work of "a mixture of historian, sociologist, psychologist, philosopher and poet."[22] Similarly, Pierre Nora suggested that comprehending Canetti's theories required the competence of an academy of historians, sociologists, psychoanalysts, and philosophers.[23] "Whether or not we agree, we have here that rare sense of being 'let out' into an entirely new region of thought,"[24] Iris Murdoch said; but this *new region* irritated some critics, who felt in it like in the land of a mad prophet ("un sorcier," French critic Jacques Cabau called Canetti),[25] while it enthralled others with its ruthless imaginativeness and arrogant defiance of scholarly protocol and boundaries. Steiner placed it in the Germanic tradition of *Kulturphilosophie*, with its "unembarrassed striving after total vision," deriving from Hegel, Nietzsche, Burckhardt, Freud, and present in the writings of Kraus, Benjamin, Adorno, and Arendt; French historian Pierre Nora called Canetti a Tocqueville of the twentieth century, one who saw the need for new methods, adequate to the "new times, and new crowds"; French writer Roger Grenier was most starkly reminded of Nietzsche, while Veronica Wedgwood, the British historian who had facilitated the publication of *Auto-da-fé* in English, saw behind his "unvarnished and telling directness" the etchings of Goya.[26] To others, Canetti's claims were eccentric nonsense, with no bearing on contemporary life (Tom Nairn, Cabau), or just clichéd thinking inevitably generated by such catchphrases as "crowds" and "power" (Frenzel and Pross),[27] hardly addressing important problems since it made no use of Marxist categories like "labor" or "alienation," for instance in its theory of transformation (Ernst Fischer).[28]

That Canetti's book was a spectacular failure for left-minded critics like Nairn or Fischer, while it appealed to historians like Nora and Wedgwood, as well as academics and writers like Murdoch or Grenier, is indicative of cultural and ideological anxieties that dominated the 1960s regarding the relevance of the human sciences to the rabble and disenchantment left behind by the wars, as well as to the new configurations of power and world order:

How to deal with the enormities of the recent past, which old categories had failed to prevent? How to avoid such catastrophes in the future, through ideological, scientific, and ethical vigilance, lucidity, and rigor? Nairn not only dismissed Canetti's work as nonsense but also diagnosed the praise bestowed on it as a symptom of decrepit liberalism and distrust of the common sense of English ideology. At the other end of the critical spectrum, Canetti's work appeared as promisingly bearing the seeds of new beginnings: Karl Rauch suggested that one could only do justice to Canetti's insights if they were going to constitute the groundwork for a team of researchers,[29] Wedgwood concluded that "the whole provides an astonishing and disturbing new perspective of the human scene," and interestingly, in light of recent scholarly developments, Steiner's last words were that *Crowds and Power* was "one of the necessary prefaces to a study of the inhuman."[30]

How did the book and Canetti's reputation fare after these early reviews in the 1960s? If, as Blöcker claims, in the German-speaking countries *Masse und Macht* seemed already forgotten by 1963,[31] the reissue of *Auto-da-fé* both in Germany and in other European countries as well as in America renewed opportunities to discuss Canetti's work as a whole, thus linking the book on crowds to the 1935 novel, whose popularity steadily increased. Hansjakob Werlen shows that even so, Canetti still remained a rather obscure figure in German literature, and that he found wider readership only with the publication of his autobiography. As is well known, in 1981 the Nobel Prize committee bestowed their accolade on him, thus fulfilling his own second-guessed expectation, yet Werlen points out that at the time of his death in 1994 "he was mostly known as an incisive chronicler of European—and specifically Austrian—culture of the period before the Second World War."[32] Noting the recent plethora of books and articles on Canetti, he adds: "It is unclear whether today's renewed preoccupation with this author, who acquired a reputation for being very demanding, is merely a prolonged eulogy or the result of a widening of the influence of his writings."[33] In a 1996 issue of *Thesis Eleven* devoted to a reevaluation of Canetti's work, the introduction casts doubt on both of these possibilities, noting that the Nobel Prize award was not followed by Canetti's adequate recognition as a "seminal cultural-diagnostic thinker of our century," and singling out the pioneering study of J. S. McClelland, *The Crowd and the Mob: From Plato to Canetti* (1989), for tackling the challenge of understanding the distinctive theoretical contribution of *Crowds and Power*.[34] McClelland explains that the "somewhat ponderously Leavisite title" of his contribution to the *Thesis Eleven* issue, "The Place of Elias Canetti's *Crowds and Power* in the History of Western Social and Political Thought," is meant to highlight the problem of Canetti's *Crowds and Power*: that is, finding "its place in our cultural landscape."[35]

An exhaustive review of the critical literature on *Crowds and Power* of the past twenty-five years could well be a book-length project and would require much comparative work in several languages.[36] For my purposes here, it will suffice to point out that this work has focused on the relationship between Canetti's work with political theory, particularly the tradition of crowd theory and theories of totalitarianism. In McClelland's view, for instance, Canetti's insights into the diversity of crowds, of which the nasty ones were the single and generalized object of crowd theory in the tradition culminating with Le Bon, is invaluable for its implicit critique of this tradition, more specifically for its participation in the justification of the power and rule of a so-called elite.[37] McClelland thus attributes to Canetti the view that to generalize from the crowd horrors of history, as his predecessors did, is "a mindless exercise in elitist vituperation, the language of which has not changed much since the grumbling oligarchs in ancient Thebes."[38] In a reversal of perspective, Canetti sees the crowd as victims: number, he claims, is "the obvious point of contact between power and the crowd," "the conditions of modernity greatly increas[ing] the scope of power for leaders."[39] What falls out of McClelland's reading is Canetti's insistence that power permeates all spheres of social life, that it is not just the privilege of rulers. Interestingly, not even his emphasis on Canetti's sympathetic attitude toward the crowd as victims, if qualified by the realization that Canetti does not see the crowd as blameless (because it has a mind of its own), is in harmony with how others read Canetti's book: Hansjakob Werlen, for instance, sees *Crowds and Power* as displaying "a deep ideological caesura" between the positive validation of the crowd formation in part 1, and the later insight, in part 2, into the complicity between rulers and crowds, which "cannot overcome Canetti's early enthusiastic view of the crowd-state as a redemptive alternative to the fate of petrified individuality."[40] In other words, the unresolved ideological tension throughout the book between the redemptive state of the crowd and its complicity in power results for Werlen in an aporia by the end of the study, "when the author's call to resist power is countered by the book's proclamation of the inexorability of the crowd-state."[41] Axel Honneth concurs, albeit with different arguments, with the view that Canetti's book is plagued by reductionism, incongruities, discontinuities, and illogical reasoning: "Among the many attempts undertaken since the middle of our century to explain retrospectively the emergence of totalitarianism, Canetti's *Crowds and Power* still assumes today an extreme and irritating position."[42] It is then with thinkers such as Adorno, Horkheimer, and Arendt that he sees Canetti (implicitly) conversing. A scientist "in no way identical with the writer," argues Honneth, Canetti "attempted to demonstrate *literally* what was intended in the *Dialectic of Enlightenment* only in a metaphorical sense; namely, that the state of civilization in the 20th century can be analyzed appropriately only if it is construed as the perpetuation of the human being's archaic state of nature."[43] Running counter to Honneth's claims, George Steiner's words come to mind: "It is naïve to quarrel with metaphor," with Canetti's thinking "by leap of image."

If among the early readers of *Crowds and Power* there were a few who, like Steiner, heeded Canetti's self-presentation as a *Dichter*, one who had the right to metamorphosis and metaphor (as well as the right to show distrust, even contempt, for theories that claimed to explain everything away), more recent critics are much less willing to grant him the right to idiosyncratic thinking and writing. The least that many readers expected Canetti to illuminate explicitly was the presence of crowds in the major events during the decades immediately preceding the publication of the book. In this account, the book, in the reading of J. P. Stern, fails completely: "The Hitlerian experience as Canetti describes it does not provide a political paradigm" because it misses the opportunity to clarify the values belonging to the "traditionally legitimated German and European ethos" that led to the formation of Nazi crowds.[44] The list of questions *Crowds and Power* generates but does not address, according to some critics, shows that in 2000, when Stern's article was published, there was no more consensus on the value and meaning of the book than immediately after its publication. "Why is 'the crowd' as Canetti presents it *always evil*, potentially destructive, threatening death or suffering it?" Stern begins to recapitulate these questions. Yet this first one would surely stun McClelland, who sees in Canetti's rich typology of crowds (of which only some are evil) the book's strongest point. Stern continues:

> What precisely is the relationship between all those many, often very lengthy episodes and myths he quotes from the papers and journals of anthropologists and explorers, on the one hand, and our modern Western experience, on the other? Are these episodes to serve as parallels to and illustrations of our conduct, or as accounts of its origins, or again as rudimentary prefigurations of it? Why is power seen always in its relationship to the crowd? Why is all power whatever seen as evil, concerned only with dealing death to others in order to ensure survival of the self? Why is survival always an outliving that entails the death of others? And what is the ontological status of Canetti's *Masse*—when does it cease to be an actual crowd and become a metaphor?[45]

Adorno asked Canetti a version of this last question in a radio interview in 1962, but it is doubtful that he was satisfied with Canetti's response, mostly consisting of more examples, and of the claim that "the events of the last 50 years" were on his mind while he wrote the book.[46]

If there is one thing that can be lifted from the morass of critical opinions, or, to use an image that Canetti was attached to, from the Babel tower of critics who seem to talk past one another, it is that he was right to fear his contemporaries' incomprehension or misunderstanding. Posterity asked difficult, important questions and reassessed his work in ways he probably could not have anticipated. How did he defend himself, and what work does the autobiography do?

A "Different Accent"?

In discerning the "accent" that Canetti might have given his ideas in the autobiographical volumes, which is an emphasis on the crowd as the countermodel to a defective sociality characterized by "distances," I will show that Canetti's interest in power was not primarily political, but social. The crowd was important to him as a redemptive experience, as a reminder of how equal and connected people feel when they are a crowd, traversed by the same consciousness-altering energies. The magnitude and ambition of Canetti's project are in my view comparable to those of Nietzsche's *Genealogy of Morals*; just as one does not take literally the latter's mystifying genealogy of a morality of the slaves, which he counters with an aristocratic morality of the strong, because one understands all along that Nietzsche needs these hyperbolic accounts in order to lay the foundations of his project, which is nothing less than the abolition of institutions that perpetuate a herd mentality and the prefiguration of a free individual who would live his life in style, one should regard Canetti as the reformer of a social field permeated by a Nietzscheanism gone astray, where everyone wants to dominate everyone else, suffering from an inability and unwillingness to communicate. Where Nietzsche praised the "pathos of distances" inherent to every strong age, Canetti deplores the often-perceived fact that "all life . . . is laid out in distances." Where Nietzsche wanted to hammer out the perceived herd mentality of his contemporaries, Canetti the exile moralizes the separateness of individuals in "a world of banished people." Following the claim that it is only for the sake of the abolition of these distances that individuals desire the crowd, his book is filled with crowds to the brim, overflowing this casual-looking frame (of distances) with the nonchalance of a baroque trompe l'oeil, and obscuring it to a degree where its relevance is lost from view. It is possible to see the second discrete instance of "distance" in the second half of the book as the bridge between its two halves; here distance appears as the privilege of the ruler, but this is quickly qualified: first by the claim that everyone likes to give commands, from parents to dictators, and that the stings of command account, at least in part, for the distances of everyday life; and second, by Canetti's emphasis on the mistaken exclusive focus of historiography on rulers to the detriment of those whose equally paranoid ambitions have not materialized.

To spell out the "accent" that I detect in light of the autobiography: power permeates not just all historical epochs as the privilege of omnipotent rulers, but also, in Canetti's account, all spheres of social life. As we shall see in the following section where I will dwell on some relevant passages from his memoirs, the ideas of *Crowds and Power* are not only enriched and embodied—the conductor-as-ruler turns out to have a real model in the larger-than-life Hermann Scherchen, whom Canetti knew closely, or the meat eater acquires a model in Veza Canetti's stepfather, a "figure from hell" who could only be appeased with a daily supply of meat, and so on—but the moralistic stance that I am highlighting here is contoured in all its complexity and ambiguities, from the formative years of his youth to the moment when Canetti and his wife fled Vienna for England in 1938. Significantly, this context gives greater prominence to his comments on the early novel *Auto-da-fé*, which already bore the mark of his conviction that the writer had to reform society. His retrospective contextualization of *Auto-da-fé* thus not only helps us understand the lifelong task that Canetti gave himself but is also instrumental in clarifying the relationship between his novel and the later work.

Die Blendung, *or The End of Babel Tower*

Originally named Kant and fated to end up burning in the midst of his precious library, Peter Kien, one of the main characters of *Die Blendung*, was the embodiment of Book-Man, the type of the isolated intellectual incapable of meaningful communication with his fellow human beings. He marries his housekeeper Therese because she dusts his beloved books really well,[47] but he is utterly incapable of understanding her materialistic ambitions, or the cruel selfishness, narrow-mindedness, and solipsism revealed to the reader by her repetitive monologues. Eventually she kicks him out of his own apartment and sets out to pawn his library with the help of the building concierge Pfaff, a brutal proto-Nazi who murdered his wife and daughter. Meanwhile, the disturbed sinologist is carrying an imaginary version of his library through the city, loading and unloading it daily from and back into his head, seconded by a hunchbacked Jew; Fischerle's own delusion is that he is a chess champion on his way to America, where his dreams of recognition will come true. To cut the five-hundred-page story short, Kien's dignified existence amidst his books is momentarily restored with the intervention of his brother Georg, a gynecologist turned psychiatrist—this is Canetti's ironic treatment of psychoanalysis—who takes some time off from his dubious work with the mentally deranged in Paris in order to diagnose Kien and send Therese and Pfaff away. However, the cunning of the mad Kien is far greater than his brother's professional acumen: left to his own devices, the sinologist inadvertently sets fire to the library and burns to death among his treasured books.

The later work encouraged some of Canetti's readers to understand the novel as foreshadowing the book on crowds: the voices that speak past one another in *Die Blendung*, the fortress-library in which Peter Kien addresses his twenty-five thousand books like the commander-in-chief of an army, the crowds vociferating in his confused mind, no less disturbingly than the curious assemblage of maniacs treated by Georg in his Paris clinic—all seemed to indicate that in the early 1930s, when Canetti wrote his novel, the ideas that he would formulate more explicitly in *Crowds and Power* were already there in symbolic form.[48] William Donahue, however, cautions against such hasty interpretations: in *The End of Modernism: Elias Canetti's "Auto-da-fé,"* he cogently shows that one does an injustice to the novel's richness, complexity, specific agenda (which Donahue calls "analytic modernism"), and, most importantly, novelistic genre, when one allows *Crowds and Power* to guide one's reading of the novel.[49] Indeed, Canetti himself made it quite clear in his memoirs that, while his interest in crowds had been piqued in the early 1920s and persisted throughout his life, the novel was conceived as part of a very ambitious project, the *Human Comedy of Madmen*, which would include novels featuring protagonists driven each in one direction, such as Man of Truth, the Religious Fanatic, the Collector, the Spendthrift, the Enemy of Death, the Actor (who could only live in rapid metamorphoses), and Book Man.[50] As Donahue compellingly shows, *Die Blendung* is a novel concerned with "the diminution of the social sphere," in many ways reflecting the Vienna of its time. Crowds were surely on Canetti's mind when he wrote *Auto-da-fé*, but to mention that does not give us the whole picture. What is the relationship between Canetti's early novel and the magnum opus of 1960, between the disturbing vision of a world torn asunder that eventually consumes itself in a conflagration, and the imperative need, apparently, to redeem the crowd, compromised for everyone but Canetti by their acquiescence in fascism? The autobiography is helpful in determining this relationship.

In the passages that bridge *The Torch in My Ear* and *The Play of the Eyes*, Canetti dwells on his own malaise after he set fire to Kien's library, a symbolic and definitive condemnation of contemporary civilization. He links this malaise to a sense of doom he experienced in the early 1930s for which he held his contemporaries responsible. They "had taken the most extraordinary pains to be the kind of person who deserve their ruin. Every pair of interlocutors I listened to seemed to me as guilty as I had been when I kindled that fire" (*MEC*, 590). A testimony to the seriousness he accords to the fate of a fictional character, and thus to the place of literature in diagnosing the ills of the world, his words also point to the role he assumed in dealing with those problems. Deeply disturbed by the gravity of his implicit allegations, he recalls that his room had nothing soothing to offer either: he had covered the walls with reproductions of Grünewald's altarpiece, images of the crucifixion that had struck him in Kolmar as a synecdoche for suffering inflicted by fellow human beings.[51] It was "a memory of the dreadful things that people do to one another" (*MEC*, 473) which mercilessly "penetrated [his] flesh and blood." This was a necessary experience, he admits, while he was writing his novel:

> my prints seemed to be in the right place, they spurred me on in one and the same direction, a merciless goad. I *wanted* the suffering they

> gave me, I got used to them, I never let them out of my sight, they became converted into something which, apparently, had nothing to do with them; for who would have been presumptuous or foolish enough to liken the sinologist's sufferings to those of Christ? And yet a kind of connection had established itself between the prints on my walls and the chapters of my book. I needed the pictures so badly that I would never have put anything else in their place. (*MEC*, 591)

The tribulations of the mad sinologist Peter Kien, a modern Christ figure, then, paint, in Herman Broch's words, "a picture of hell in this life." The dialogue that Canetti reproduced—whether the accent is on *re-* or on *produced* matters less—between Broch and himself in the autobiography serves to justify the indictment of humankind as part of his perceived role as a writer: "What repelled Broch was my zealotic, dogmatic way of making the improvement of mankind dependent on chastisement and without hesitation appointing myself executor of this chastisement" (*MEC*, 603). Acknowledging the influence of Karl Kraus, since "a good part of his being had gone into mine, especially . . . his rage," Canetti goes as far as to take pride in Broch's questioning of his motives as worthy:

> "What you have done in your novel and in *The Wedding* as well is to heighten fear. You rub people's noses in their wickedness, as though to punish them for it. I know your underlying purpose is to make them repent. You make me think of a Lenten sermon. But you don't threaten people with hell, you paint a picture of hell in this life. You don't picture it objectively, so as to give people a clearer consciousness of it; you picture it in such a way as to make people feel they are in it and scare them out of their wits. Is it the writer's function to bring more fear into the world? Is that a worthy intention?" (*MEC*, 615)

Asked more explicitly if he wanted to terrify people, Canetti confirmed, showing that a terrifying reality calls for extreme measures: "'Yes. Everything around us is terrifying. There is no longer a common language. No one understands anyone else. I believe no one *wants* to understand'" (*MEC*, 614). The "lovelessness" that Canetti imputes to his contemporaries will permeate the later work to an even larger degree.

In *Crowds and Power* Canetti remains concerned by the destruction that *Auto-da-fé* left behind, all the more so since Kien's *Brand* proved prophetic in the conflagration of World War II. Suggested by the recurrent emphasis on distances, the "diminution of the social sphere" is the original cause of modernity's most tragic episodes; the realm in which change is necessary in order to "master power" is the social. The autobiographical volumes give disquieting depth both to his apparently rhetorical notion of "distances" and to his understanding of power: ultimately the crowd's importance lies in its capacity to correct, to offer a countermodel to the discontents of everyday sociality. Various measures of this "distance" proliferate, in Weimar Berlin, the Vienna of the 1930s, England during the Blitz and after, all pointing to Canetti's conviction that power, far from being the exclusive privilege of rulers and dictators, as history used to teach us, or what circulates in the resonance chambers of institutions (as Foucault would have it), permeates in fact the sphere of everyday interaction, indeed all interpersonal relations. It is *this* kind of power, Canetti argues, that can degenerate into the oppressive power of rulers, of a Hitler; a power that all help perpetuate by living the way they do, that they petrify in, and that they attempt to dissolve in the crowd.

The impetus that traverses Canetti's lifework, then, beyond redeeming the crowd in the wake of fascism, writing its fascinating memoirs and inventing a new vocabulary to describe its incarnations or symbolic avatars, is a renewed chastisement and entreatment to change. The silence that Canetti imposed on himself between the publication of *Die Blendung* in 1935 and that of *Crowds and Power* in 1960 was a time of intense reflection on the role of the writer, a time when mere fiction seemed innocuous in the face of world-scale disasters. But I disagree with Honneth's claim that the two books should be read differently because they were written by the novelist, and the writer, respectively: if anything, Canetti only hardened his conviction that the world had to be changed. This is a significant link between the two books. "What makes the author Canetti so 'demanding,'" says Werlen, "are not experimental narratives, complex language, or esoteric erudition but rather an uncompromising understanding of his art, an understanding that demands from the readers, like Rilke's 'Apollonian Torso,' that they change their lives."[52] In a diary entry from 1975, Canetti muses on his role in the third person: "More and more often he catches himself thinking that there is no way to save humanity. // Is that an attempt to rid himself of responsibility?"[53] Five years later, the conviction that the moral imperative lies within him, as obvious as the reality of his repeated displacements and most likely determined by them, is affirmed with more assurance than ever: "Morality is narrow if one *knocks* against it. The real morality has become one's skeletal structure."[54] This is a statement that encapsulates *Crowds and Power*, contemplated in light of the autobiography: as one begins to suspect, the "real morality" comes from what he called the crowd *in his bones*.

Varieties of Distance, Redemptive Crowds

The peculiar ideation that materialized in the book *Crowds and Power* is retrospectively chronicled in Canetti's memoirs as a process of departure from Freud under the influence of an intense preoccupation with the perceived separateness and antagonism of people in everyday life, from which he took asylum in the inspiriting memory of crowd-immersion early in his youth. Canetti was most likely aware of the two strands concurrently running through his writings: the insistence with which he emphasizes the enduring influence certain experiences had on him can hardly be missed, making apparent his effort to "emplot" his life around these two major concerns.[55] "The thing that *impressed me most*," the formulation of the first one runs, "the thing that *determined the rest of my life, even today*, was the incompatibility of all the things that broke in on me" (*MEC*, 527, my italics). A few pages later it becomes clear that these conflicting "things" are not just heterogeneous aspects of life experience, but the diversity and incompatibility of people: "*I felt*," Canetti elaborates on his apprehension, "how pitiless life was: everything, racing by, nothing really dealing with anything else. It was obvious not only that no one understood anyone else, but also that no one *wanted* to understand anyone else" (*MEC*, 545, italics in the original). Yet the same claim to the enduring effects of an experience is made repeatedly with regard to the crowd experience, dating back to his immersion in a large mass of demonstrators in Vienna. This is the second, parallel strand, enunciated in the note with which Canetti prefaces the report of this encounter: "Something occurred that had the deepest influence on my subsequent life" (*MEC*, 484). He describes it as still present within him as he writes:

> Fifty-three years have passed, and the agitation of that day is still in my bones. It was the closest thing to a revolution that I have physically experienced. Since then, I have known quite precisely that I would not have to read a single word about the storming of the Bastille. I became a part of the crowd, I fully dissolved in it, I did not feel the slightest resistance to what the crowd was doing. (*MEC*, 484–485)

The crowd, one understands, offers the overwhelming intimacy that social life is lacking and that he is craving; while the general disease among his contemporaries is a lack of communication, a certain social aphasia, Canetti remembers his identification with the crowd, and eventually, as we shall see, goes as far as to identify something like a private language with the crowd seeping into his writings.

Following these two strands in the autobiography is crucial for understanding the tension running through *Crowds and Power* between the "distances" permeated by power in everyday life and the liberating energies carried by crowds throughout human history. In this light, *Crowds and Power* appears as an intensely personal book, bearing to an astounding degree the stigma of an exile in the mid-twentieth century. The paradox that his writings court, however, is that while analyzing varieties of distance and their implicit transactions of power, he seems to be, by inclination and training, as much of a distance-builder as he would like to be a redeemer.

Power and Distances: The Making of a Moralist

> A conscientious investigation of power must ignore success. We must look for its attributes and their perversions wherever they appear, and then compare them.
>
> —Canetti, *Crowds and Power*

The portrait Canetti draws of himself is that of a young man particularly sensitive to the difficulties of living in a Babel Tower–like world: "What I grasped," he tells us of the last six months spent in Frankfurt before he started university in Vienna, "was the separateness of opinions, the hard cores of convictions; it was a witches' cauldron, steaming and bubbling, but all the ingredients floating in it had their specific smell and could be recognized" (*MEC*, 330). There is much to ponder in this passage, a brief reformulation of the ideas so powerfully expressed by his characters in *Die Blendung*, not least because it recalls the so-called method of "acoustic masks" Canetti developed in his early novel and the play *Comedy of Vanity*: it is based on exaggerating the ineradicable peculiarities of the characters' idiolects, turning them into caricatures, hardening the core of opinions into convictions and thus enacting the extreme removal from the human community, the latter becoming increasingly centrifugal. Suggestively, the image of the witches' cauldron bears a hint that wickedness was being concocted, that the world would be as if cast under an evil spell during which unthinkable things would happen for which no one would assume responsibility. The memoirs also intimate, however, that wickedness, distances, and power are as much in Canetti's world as they are in the eyes of the beholder: the tremendous life-view of *Crowds and Power*, as we shall presently see, is to a large degree the outcome of the particular way of seeing and hearing he developed in his childhood and youth, through circumstances partly imposed, partly of his own making.

Adolescence is unsurprisingly remembered as a time of personal defiance, when he is accused, notably by his mother, of blinding himself to real experience. His retrospective defense is that he was blinding himself to the "imitative knowledge" of bourgeois morality, countering the pitiful clichés that were besetting the world around him with inspiring paintings like Samson's blinding or Brueghel's *The Triumph of Death*: these paintings were his blinders, repositories of wisdom to which he would return over and over again. Canetti, a self-made moralist? Well, not quite: on reading about his formative years, spent to a large degree reading intensely, one is struck by how vivid the presence of long-dead authors and ideas are to him, as if they had been his contemporaries and contributing actively to his self-cultivation.

Separation, miscommunication, distance are decidedly leitmotifs of the early years. In an episode whose humor does not escape the older narrator, the young Elias, frustrated by his mother's refusal to let him go on a hiking trip on grounds of their insufficient financial resources, generates a symbolic inflation by filling the pages of a notebook with the words "Money, money and money again," only to be diagnosed by a family doctor with a "too obvious" Oedipus complex, hence magnanimously sent hiking with a friend as a way of getting some distance from the worshipped-hated parent. To be sure, this is exactly what he does in an angry outburst of resentment that he documents in his diary; reading it many years later, Canetti confesses his shock at such precocious violence. Incidentally, this is also the trip on which he reads more closely Freud's *Group Psychology* and becomes vehemently determined to do away, once and for all, with the famous author's supposedly misguided theories. In the insightful study *La folie Canetti*, psychoanalyst Roger Gentis articulates these two disavowals—of Matilde Canetti and of "father" Freud—as one major event of emancipation, cautioning, however, against giving too much importance to the Oedipal motif. Canetti, he believes, was well aware that his story yielded itself to psychoanalytic interpretations and therefore set some traps in anticipation so that he could mock his critics better: "Who wouldn't recognize Freud," Gentis asks rhetorically, referencing an episode involving the possibility of tonsil removal, "in the man at whom he is sticking his tongue out?"[56] What cannot be missed here, in the way Canetti evokes the "Money, money and money again" incident, is that his gesture of protest, symbolically expressed in the grammar of the later crowd project (*Crowds and Power* lists inflation among crowd phenomena), is misunderstood by the doctor and reduced to the most hated of clichés, the Oedipus complex.

Another imposing figure took over, "enslaving," as Canetti puts it, the young Elias: the relentless critic of Viennese society Karl Kraus, editor of *Die Fackel* (*The Torch*) and author of *The Last Days of Mankind*.[57] Canetti remembers he missed none of the satirist's public readings between 1924 and 1928.[58] A scuttling mind, Kraus is portrayed as "a master of accusing people with their own words." He stands out as the towering figure of Canetti's Viennese youth, who instilled in his impressionable apprentice an unforgiving critical attitude that he would carry as a burden throughout his life. Is this the cross of the future redeemer? The passage below suggests as much:

> The reader must bear in mind the profound effect Karl Kraus's perpetual accusations had had on me. They took possession of one and never let one go (to this day I detect wounds they left me with, not all of which have healed), they had the full force of *commands*. Since I accepted them in advance and never tried to evade them, I might have been better off if they had had the stringency of commands; then it would have been possible to carry them out and they would not have become *thorns* in my flesh. But as it was, Karl Kraus's periods, as solidly built as fortresses, lay heavy and unwieldy on my chest, *a*

> *crippling burden* that I carried around with me, and though I had thrown off a good part of it while slaving over my novel and later while my play was erupting, there was still a danger that my rebellion would fail and end in serious psychic enslavement. (*MEC*, 698)

In this assessment of Kraus's influence, Canetti makes a curious use of the theory of command he would expound in *Crowds and Power*. The burden he inherited—the thorns of Kraus's implicit command to see the world in a certain way—was partly thrown off while writing *Die Blendung*. Yet thorns, *Crowds and Power* teaches us, can only be passed on, never transformed into something socially acceptable.[59] In light of this theory, *Die Blendung* is meant to be an affecting novel, to enact a kind of revenge on a guilty mankind. As the passage above suggests, however, Canetti hardly managed to subtract himself from Kraus's powerful influence. One suspects that if the people Canetti met throughout his life were beset by distances and separateness, their affliction might have been as much a reality as the effect of the way Canetti listened to them, with at least one ear still scorched by the fire of Karl Kraus's *Fackel*.

The account of his trip to Weimar Berlin in 1928 is an opportunity to articulate the moral outlook on society that would bear his signature, shaped by Kraus and given a more humane turn following the encounter with the Russian writer Isaac Babel. Weimar Berlin offers itself as a spectacle of vanity. Canetti is quick to identify the two artistic representations of it that best unveil its core: George Grosz's collection of caricatures *Ecce Homo* and Bertolt Brecht's *The Threepenny Opera*. Coming from Vienna, Canetti himself was to despise this society dominated by superficiality, a certain brand of American pragmatism, and greed:

> I myself, after four years under Karl Kraus's influence, was filled with all his contempt and condemnation and acknowledging nothing that was determined by greed, selfishness, or frivolity. All objects to condemn were prescribed by Kraus. You were not even allowed to look at them; he had already taken care of that for you and made the decision. It was a sterilized intellectual life that we led in Vienna, a special kind of hygiene prohibiting any intermingling whatsoever. No sooner was something universal, no sooner had it gotten into the newspapers, than it was taboo and untouchable. (*MEC*, 502)

The society Canetti describes in this chapter is that of bohemian artists, many foreigners, who made a name for themselves in Berlin, an avant-garde that Peter Gay describes as formed by "outsiders as insiders"[60] and that he is introduced to as a young aspiring writer who so far can base his self-esteem only on the unfailing kindness with which Veza, his wife-to-be, received his poems back in Vienna. The Austrian capital now appears sterile and austere, compared to the "hotbed of vice" that is Berlin: *Ecce Homo*, Canetti has to admit with George Grosz, whose drawings had struck him with their "strength and recklessness . . . , ruthlessness and dreadfulness. Since they were extreme, I regarded them as Truth. A truth that mediated, that weakened, that explained, that excused was no Truth for me. I knew that Grosz's characters really existed" (*MEC*, 511). Later on he understands more precisely his feelings as "an odd mixture of horror and approval. These were dreadful creatures of Berlin's night life that you saw here, but they were here because they were viewed as dreadful" (*MEC*, 513). *Viewed as*: the perspective, the framework, already matters a lot. Comically, the discovery that the graphic artist actually enjoyed as much as he despised the corrupted world he was sketching in his caricatures only brings Canetti's disgust to new depths.[61]

Suggestively titled "An Invitation to Emptiness," the chapter describes in great detail how the social promiscuity of avant-garde circles offends his sensibility: "Everything was equally close in Berlin, every kind of effect was permitted: no one was prohibited from making himself noticeable if he didn't mind the strain" (*MEC*, 526). Having indulged the language of closeness, Canetti is quick to dismiss the appearance of intimacy as "feigned," since "its goal was to surpass some other intimacy" (*MEC*, 527). Rather than the authenticity of human connections, what matters here is the authenticity and force of one's striving to be acknowledged by others; his portrayal of the avant-garde artist is a rather comic version of Trilling's aggressive, potentially murderous *authentes*, concerned, in Canetti's view, only with achieving recognition:

> Every individual who was something—and many people were something—struck away at the others with himself. It was questionable whether they understood him; he made them listen. It didn't seem to bother him that others made people listen in a different way. He had validity as soon as he was heard. And now he had to continue striking away with himself to keep being supplanted in the ears of the public. (*MEC*, 527)

Even after acknowledging, with hindsight, that the period was artistically prolific, Canetti returns to the human cost of such agonistic effervescence, claiming that one could only endure "that harsh existence" only through association with a group or a clique.

Helmut Lethen's *Cool Conduct: The Culture of Distance in Weimar Germany* is one of the most fascinating analyses of Weimar sociability, offering a compelling review of codes of conduct that proliferated after the First World War. It begins with Helmuth Plessner's *Limits of Community*, and follows up with texts by Ernst Jünger, Bertolt Brecht, Walter Benjamin (in correspondence with Carl Schmitt), Werner Krauss, and Walter Serner.[62] These authors have in common the rediscovery of Baltasar Gracián's *Art of*

Worldly Wisdom (1647), which inspired critiques of the oppressive warmth of the traditional community (*Gemeinschaft*) and privileged a cool hygiene of calculated interpersonal distance. The "sincerity" paradigm, the critique went, was an ethic of tactlessness: it obscured aggressiveness and offered no reliable code of behavior among strangers. By contrast, society (*Gesellschaft*) can only exist through the preservation of space, indeterminacy, and pockets of mistrust—all regulated by codes of conduct that teach strategies of face-saving, diplomacy, and tact.[63] One must read these texts to understand Canetti's evocation of Weimar Berlin as that of an outsider excluded from the unspoken rules of cool sociability. "Perhaps no one had the leisure to wonder where all this was leading to," he muses, a hint of unintended irony coloring his regret that "no transparent life came about in this way" (*MEC*, 527). Ultimately, he remains critical of the way fame was inextricably bound up with aggressive self-assertion and obliteration of others: "By acknowledging as little as possible, by hitting out in all directions, you yourself became somebody. Anyone who didn't know how to hit out in all directions was doomed and could simply hit the road: Berlin was nothing for him" (*MEC*, 528).

There are a few individuals who detach themselves from this background, and the way Canetti presents them is most often also a self-portrayal, revealing his critical inclinations: Wieland Hertzfelde, the owner of the Malik publishing house, for whom he worked on the Upton Sinclair project;[64] his brother John Heartfield, who "learned only from things that he regarded as attacks; and in order to experience something new, he had to see it as an attack" (*MEC*, 504); Bertolt Brecht, who stood for everything Canetti hated ("an Anglo-Saxon practicality of the American variety": he "had written a poem about Steyr Automobiles and been given a car for it. For me, these were words from the devil's own mouth" [*MEC*, 508]) and in whose presence his moralistic outlook becomes conspicuous even to himself: "Morality was one thing and matter was another, and when I dealt with this man, who cared only about matter, then nothing but morality counted for me" (*MEC*, 508). His distaste for the individual prevents him from expressing his admiration for the poet, whose *Manual of Piety* "shattered at one blow" his own hopes of becoming a writer. But most of all, his critical spirit is struck by Brecht's success in capturing the essence of a self-complacent society in *The Threepenny Opera*. It was, Canetti says,

> the most accurate expression of this Berlin. The people cheered for themselves: this was they and they liked themselves. First they fed their faces. Then they spoke of right and wrong. No one could have put it better about them. They took these words literally. Now it had been spoken, they felt as snug as a bug in a rug. Penalty had been abolished: the royal messenger rode in on a real horse. The shrill and naked self-complacence that this performance emanated can be believed only by the people who witnessed it. (*MEC*, 532)

Probably the most significant encounter in Berlin is with Isaac Babel, who seems to trigger a personal *Kehre* of sorts in Canetti the moralist. No wonder this meeting is narrated as an episode in his "school of hearing": his apprenticeship with Babel comes as a corrective to the previous one, under Kraus, inflecting his tendency to absorb the world with a more humane purpose. "I learned something," he confesses, "which may have seemed even more important after my lengthy apprenticeship with *Die Fackel*: I learned how wretched judging and condemning are as ends in themselves" (*MEC*, 536–537). As a remedy, Babel modeled for him an exemplary way of observing people, characterized by slowness, restraint, and muteness.

The moving portrait he makes of the Russian writer is probably equaled in tenderness only by his later characterization of Dr. Sonne, the poet Avraham ben Yitzhak, whom he would meet in Vienna. Babel is portrayed as both a kindred spirit and as a model, someone who brought to self-consciousness his own aims as a writer, his intention to turn to people with a very specific expectation—"I wanted people, including myself, to become *better*, and so I had to know absolutely everything about every single human being" (*MEC*, 537).

Just to what extent the experience of reckless self-assertion in Berlin affected the young Canetti appears more explicitly in the last chapter of *The Torch in My Ear*, where the forced name-feeding, as he now describes his encounter with Weimar artists, is set in contrast with the spectacle of unassuming ordinary people that he enjoys listening to in taverns late at night, anonymously: "I opposed this united affliction and harassment by names, I resisted it by means of every person who had no name, everyone who was poor in name" (*MEC*, 577).[65] It is easy to imagine Canetti unobtrusively listening to people in taverns, even turning to the wall or shutting his eyes in order to allow his ears get their fill of the "variety, and . . . the poverty, banality, the misuse of words"—more meaningful, however, than "the braggadocio and bumptiousness of writers" (*MEC*, 578). One readily recognizes interwoven here a set of themes that Canetti's writings take up in various guises: language and its power (*Macht*), the world as a stage populated with acoustic masks conversing to the rhythm of speaking and replying, people's unselfconscious inability to transcend their subjectivity and reach others through language. "Whether achieving their effect or not, the scenes recurred—or perhaps it would be more accurate to say that the purview of their calculation was so narrow that they were bound to appear unsuccessful to the listener, and hence futile and innocent" (*MEC*, 578). It matters, of course, that the listener should be Canetti, well initiated by Karl Kraus in the power of language; for it is this aspect that Canetti brings here to the fore, in the contrast between the deft, annihilating, rhetoric of the "shriek" in Berlin, and the derisory stakes of Everyman's crude use of words. A hint of irony cannot be missed in Canetti's self-congratulatory attentiveness "without disrespect" to these individuals' speech, in the consolation he draws from their inoffensive chatter: "I liked these people, even the most hateful among them, because they were not given the power of speech [weil ihnen die Macht der Rede nicht gegeben war]":[66] it is Canetti himself, schooled by Kraus, the "master of accusing people with their own words," who deprives these people of power by describing them as such, and by the same token claiming the power of understanding as his exclusive privilege. Their portrayal looks very much like a caricature: "They made themselves ridiculous in words, they struggled with words. They gazed into a distorting mirror when they spoke; they demonstrated themselves in the distortion of words, which distortion had become their alleged likeness. They made themselves vulnerable when they courted understanding; they accused one another so unsuccessfully that insult sounded like praise and praise like insult" (*MEC*, 578). Canetti acknowledges that these people's "powerlessness," which reminds him of his own insignificance in Berlin, has a therapeutic effect:

> *It seized hold of me, I was thankful to it; I was unable to sate myself with it*, and it was not the openly declared powerlessness with which others like to operate selfishly: it was the hidden, dyed-in-the-wool powerlessness of individuals who remained apart, who couldn't get together, least of all in speech, which separated them instead of binding them. (*MEC*, 578, my italics)

Canetti never mentions any attempt to participate in the sociability of the tavern, in the "scenes that took shape in the ebb and flow," remaining aside from them in order to dissect better their presumed separateness. Do they really remain apart, as Canetti sees them, night after night? One has reasons to doubt it: perhaps their community only gives off the impression of failed communication, while relying on a foundation of long-term familiarity, complicity, double-entendre, ambiguous interpellation that remains opaque to outsiders. Might Canetti remain oblivious to the private dynamic of communities he simply observes as an outsider, unsuspecting that his cultivated distance might actually preclude closeness? On reading the passage above, one sees the world transforming itself into a novel in front of Canetti's eyes; and not just any novel, but one that is as disturbing as *Auto-da-fé*, where precisely the disconnect between the ways in which characters use language and how it echoes outside, how it is misunderstood by others, causes them to move in parallel worlds. However far from the Berlin cafés, Vienna's taverns do not offer Canetti a more appealing model of human interaction: in one place as well as in the other, he is equally struck by the separateness of people, both when caused by their too-skilled use of language—penetrating like "a shriek"—and by their perceived deprivation of this "power."

Canetti's catalog of distances includes one most sophisticated sample: the British variety, described in *Party in the Blitz*. This late autobiographical volume, published posthumously, resembles in very few respects the thoughtful, often poetic, previous tomes; rather than an autobiography, it reads like a collection of portraits: Herbert Read, Kathleen Raine, Aymer Maxwell, Lord David Stewart, Bertrand Russell, Franz Steiner, Enoch Powell, Veronica Wedgwood, T. S. Eliot, Iris Murdoch, Oscar Kokoschka, Ralph Vaughan Williams, and others. Canetti sketches them with hardly any concern for propriety, political correctness, or even objectivity, as an old man who can afford to be blunt and show no restraint in the making public of his antipathies. In place of a self-portrait, the early essay "No-one in England or the Silence of Contempt" casts light on the anonymity of exile, and on how the distances encoded and prescribed in British social norms prevent genuine human contact. Yet again, the claim to be "no-one," or at best the object of silent contempt, might suggest some of the feelings that colored these evocations. "You could describe it," Canetti says ironically about the typical English party, "as an advanced social training." This time, his writing sounds like the bitter parody of a code of conduct:

> You're brought together into a small space, very close, but without touching. It looks as though there might be a curse, but there isn't. Freedom consists in the distance from your opposite number, even if it's only a hair's breadth. You move smartly past others who are crowding in on you from all sides without brushing any of them. You remain untouched and pure. It would be accounted a fault, a stain, if you permitted yourself the least contact with anyone else. . . . The riddle of mystery and distance mustn't shrivel, otherwise the party would collapse like a punctured balloon.[67]

The party here is to be taken literally and metaphorically, for he identifies its main characteristic, distance, with a national trait. In "On the Nearness and Distance of the English," he sets out on a brief ethnographic excursus that resonates with the beginning of *Crowds and Power*: "Distance is a principal gift of the English. They do not come too near. They may not, they cannot come too near. For their own protection, the person sheathes itself in ice. To the outside, everything is patted back. Inside, you're left to freeze."[68] This is the opposite of the agonistic mode of interaction in Berlin: while there everyone hits at everyone else with themselves, everything being permeable, unbearably close, in England everyone is shielded in ice, everything is distant. But in both cases, intimacy is missing. The ironic passages that follow mimic, by way of a multiplicity of impersonal pronouns and nouns, this absence: between "the person," "he," "you," "anyone," and "him," between implicit questions and passive voices, an elaborate strategy of evasion is constructed:

> Social life consists of futile efforts at proximity. These are as hesitant as *the person* making them is brave. *He* really is, because he knows how alone he truly is.

> Basically, *you* shrink back from *anyone* new: you fear in *him* the worst, someone who will leap over the distance you set up. He may give every *appearance* of reserve, but *you* do not trust him, and keep him off with elaborate politeness: the silent, but searching question with which you investigate him, "How high? How low?" is as existentially important as it is implacable.
>
> The urge to climb in society is always alive, it is fuelled by reverence for the very highest echelons, but tamed by the difficulty of approaching them, and, even if an approach has been successfully made, then by the difficulty of touching them. This is something only learned in closest proximity of others.[69]

Canetti's social apprenticeship in England, where he lived for thirty years, obviously worked its way into the outlook on everyday interactions that permeates *Crowds and Power*: not only is "distance" the experience of the foreigner who is tolerated, yet never absorbed by the new community; society itself is structured in hierarchies that maintain (vertical) distances between individuals. From the volume as a whole one gathers that Canetti's sidelong glances at the English, traversing these distances they seem so good at maintaining, bespeak a frustration that is the mirror image of the "being nobody" in Weimar Berlin: whereas there, as an unpublished author, he had felt threatened with annihilation by aggressive "names," abroad again, he feels rendered invisible by the lack of recognition he would now feel entitled to, owing to the fame of his tremendous novel. *Party in the Blitz* is permeated with the frustration, and often the resentment, felt by the writer who cannot relate meaningfully, who cannot make sense of others, to others.[70] Or perhaps that picture is a distortion. Canetti, so deeply affected by the "witches' cauldron of opinions," the Babel Tower that is the human world with its diversity of idiolects, finds in England renewed opportunities for his talents of dissecting separateness and distances, of detecting the fine, invisible filigrees of power that traverse them. In contrast to the unselfconscious powerlessness of the tavern men in late-night Vienna, here power is tactfully dissolved in silence, all the more insidious because suspected to be present, as a strategy of maintaining distance. Or at least this is Canetti's interpretation of it:

> It is taken for admirable modesty if very prominent persons mingle with others and succeed in distinguishing themselves so little that they remain unrecognized. They wear no masks, but nor do they introduce themselves. You can have a conversation with someone, without having a clue who he is. He can walk away from you, without having the least sense of obligation to you. Nothing has been promised, nothing transacted, it was an innocent exercise in espionage, that suppressed any thought of . . . The one mustn't sense how

> deeply he is despised, and the other mustn't let on how much power he would have—anywhere but here.
>
> Because, of course, power has accrued, but it has been distributed as well, and . . . its limits by being concealed in the midst of so many others.[71]

Again Canetti cultivates his outsider's stance—could he not take the initiative to introduce himself, even at the risk of advertising his foreignness?—and suspects the presence of power. In light of all these examples, the idiosyncratic language of *Crowds and Power* appears less surprising: to Canetti, the eternally displaced, the world presents itself under the guise of a conspiracy, as a play of masked characters who are either in retreat, because, self-sufficient, they care for no genuine human interaction, or else expected to reveal something unpleasant, something concealing a death threat, hence the apprehensive step back, the fear, the awe.

Canetti was struck by a similar aspect in Kafka's letters: "He says that fear and indifference combined make up his deepest feeling toward human beings."[72] This insight would explain, Canetti believes, the uniqueness of Kafka's work, "in which emotions hardly appear. . . . If one thinks about it with a little courage, our world has indeed become one in which fear and indifference predominate. Expressing his own reality without indulgence, Kafka was the first to present the image of *this* world."[73] "Fear and indifference . . . *this* world": Kafka's and Canetti's. In these locales populated by variously separated people—Frankfurt, Vienna, Weimar Berlin, London—which turn out to be typical of the times (as the comment on Kafka suggests), Canetti often dwells on discrete instances of serious miscommunication, of people trying to wrench themselves free from under the influence of others because the others either aggress them with their forceful speech, or else fail to speak to them. A few examples, which must be accompanied by the acknowledgment that *this* world of Canetti's indeed weighs more and more heavily, should give us a sense of the full picture. I will not dwell on the deeply problematic relationship with the mother, whose admonitions Canetti perceived as imperious commands,[74] except to note that the autobiography reads like an elaborate farewell; unsurprisingly, *The Play of the Eyes* ends with her burial, which is supposed to seal their sundering. Whether this was the case remains an open question: his wife, Veza, who in a certain sense replaced her, was subsequently no less affected by Canetti's apparent efforts not to become excessively attached, perhaps even dependent on her; at one point he moves away from her apartment on Ferdinand Street—which was too close to where he lived—deciding that it was "best if distance was created, if the whole of Vienna lay between [them] . . . voices . . . voices" (*MEC*, 406). Another example of distance is equally striking: while he was working on his chemistry degree, which was "barely grazing the skin of [his] head," he was having daily conversations with a female friend about a foreign colleague.

One day this colleague committed suicide, for which, strangely, Canetti takes some responsibility: "Instead of toying with her, I should have talked her into loving him" (*MEC*, 442). Canetti, usually so reserved about love, reproaches himself for not having thought of it as an antidote to distance. A last example features his old friend Hans, who accompanies him on the liberating trip to the mountains after he is released from the maternal enclosure. The separation from Hans after a week together is one of the uncanniest moments in the memoirs: Canetti recalls the wordless look, presumably filled with hatred, that his friend cast on him one day with no apparent reason—indeed, the reader is taken completely by surprise here—and realized, he claims, that Hans, this longtime family friend, wanted to kill him. With no explanation they parted ways; a few hundred pages later we find out that Hans committed suicide. "Not until later," Canetti adds without dispelling the mystery, "did I realize that his personal misfortune was to create the distances separating him from people he was close to. He was a distance builder; this was his talent, and he built distances so well that it was impossible for others and for him to leap across them" (*MEC*, 406). It is probably inconsequential whether these words are a reliable characterization of Hans; but it is at this point in the memoirs apparent that they apply to Canetti himself, the *Dichter*, a "distance builder": at least some of the distances he so keenly maps in the memoirs are likely of his own—rhetorical—making. And what is the role that he assumes in this life performance? It is curious that Canetti noted in the book about his kindred spirit "the distance without which he—Kafka—could not write."[75]

Distances, *Crowds and Power* shows, are created by the stings of command. Yet in the autobiography, Canetti uses this image repeatedly with reference to himself: Karl Kraus's words and rage poured into him, and he carried them along like thorns in his flesh; his mother filled him with anger and resentment, and he carried all these feelings with him, perhaps all his life; while writing *Auto-da-fé*, he describes his need for the suffering exuding from the crucifixion represented on the Isenheim prints, showing how it "entered his own flesh and blood." Is this a clue? What is the crucifixion, that "memory of the dreadful things that people do to one another," if not the image of a man with thorns in his flesh? "Who would have been so presumptuous or foolish enough to liken the sinologist's sufferings to those of Christ?" Canetti asks rhetorically, but surely the preterition cannot be missed. And how can one not see that Canetti himself is filled to the brim with the distances—and the stings—of others, stung into the consciousness of a world torn asunder; and that something in the way of a redemption is not only needed, but impossible to avoid? One "cannot fall outside of the world,"[76] however often the stateless exile has to contend with the burden of his stings and take refuge elsewhere. But before this point can be pressed further, we need to look at Canetti in the midst of the crowd.

The Crowd: Vision and Private Language

"I had been *moved* by the crowd," Canetti remembers in *The Torch in My Ear*:

> It was an intoxication; you were lost, you forgot yourself; you felt tremendously remote yet fulfilled; whatever you felt, you didn't feel it for yourself; it was the most selfless thing you knew; and since selfishness was shown, talked, and threatened on all sides, you needed this experience of thunderous unselfishness *like the blast of the trumpet at the Last Judgment*, and you made sure not to belittle or denigrate this experience. At the same time, however, you felt you had no control over yourself, you weren't free, something uncanny was happening to you, it was half delirium, half paralysis. How could all this happen together? What was it? (*MEC*, 364, my italics)

This crucial passage might well serve as an epigraph to any reading of *Crowds and Power*, since there is no clearer statement of the function of the crowd in Canetti's book: the equalizing immersion in a multitude of people is the moment of redemption, the glimmer of hope in a world beset with distances. The apocalyptic image returns in a later description of the crowd, which resonates with the echo of the trumpet of the Last Judgment mentioned in the passage above:

> You felt the fire, its presence was overwhelming; even if you did not see it, you nevertheless had it in your mind, its attraction and the attraction exerted by the crowd were one and the same. . . . Your connection with others (an open or secret connection, depending on the place) remained in effect. And you were drawn back into the province of the fire—circuitously, since there was no other possible way. (*MEC*, 488)

This urgent redemptive function of the crowd experience, incomprehensibly missed by others—"you made sure not to belittle or denigrate this experience" is obviously a gesture toward his crowd-theorist predecessors—appears throughout the memoirs in frequent evocations bearing a tinge of the ineffable, the ungraspable, the sublime: "It was the physical attraction that I couldn't forget," "as if this were what is known in physics as gravitation" (*MEC*, 353). For Canetti the *Dichter* such an overwhelming experience cannot be explained away once and for all with a theory; his interest is in mapping out, rather than restricting to a clear-cut explanation, the symbolism of the crowd, hence the images of fire, music, wave, rhythm, gravitation, resonant wind; all these are reiterations of the crowd symbols to which an entire chapter is dedicated in *Crowds and Power*: "You heard something everywhere: there was something rhythmic in the air, an evil music. You could call it music; you felt elevated by it. I did not feel as if I were moving on my own legs. I felt as if I were in a resonant wind" (*MEC*, 487). And then Canetti multiplies the examples of crowds, his effort amounting to no less than a re-presentation of human experience—his book is like a Noah's ark in which all manner of crowds have to be sampled, or like a large city in which ancient streets coexist with more recent ones: this is indeed reminiscent of Wittgenstein's picture of language.[77] It is possible to situate Canetti in proximity of ordinary language philosophers who care about illustrations rather than definitions, showing thus that one does not need the precision of definitions when we have such a disquieting variety of examples: it is after all Canetti's ambition to find and describe elements of crowd behavior in all the human civilizations as well as in all realms of human experience that makes the effort of understanding *Crowds and Power* so frustrating.[78] Just as Wittgenstein in the first part of the *Philosophical Investigations* is subtly hinting at mistaken ways of doing philosophy before him, in order to later show a better way, Canetti quietly brackets the work of his predecessors, aiming to offer an alternative way of dealing with crowds, a different way of thinking about human experience. The "method," to the extent that there is one, is to build a new picture by way of many examples, to intimate various ways out, in his case transformation, sting removal, goodness (as we shall soon see), and so on; from the proliferation of examples of crowds ultimately transpires a Wittgensteinian question: "Do you see what I see?" What he offers is a new way of seeing, a new vision, rather than an explanation. Canetti is a kind of poet of the ordinary, who finds his elemental condition not in language, but in the crowd. For besides this "nostalgia for the particular"—the words belong to Iris Murdoch, but they apply to Canetti's attachment to so many examples—there is also the insistence on the irreducibility of bodily experience as that which is absolutely reliable and exemplary. Canetti's *recognition* of the crowd phenomenon is insistently expressed in terms of an overwhelming firsthand experience: "I returned over and over and watched; and even today, I sense how hard it is for me to tear myself away, since I have managed to achieve only the tiniest portion of my goal: to understand what a crowd is" (*MEC*, 490). From the first encounter with a crowd, the latter challenges him as something defying understanding, akin to the experience of the sublime: "The riddle wouldn't stop haunting me; it has stuck to me for the better part of my life. And if I did ultimately hit upon a few things, I was still as puzzled as ever" (*MEC*, 353). By the time Canetti wrote his memoirs, his accomplishment seemed of less significance than what he had expressed in the letter to his brother on completion of the manuscript. "During the following year [after the manifestations he took part in on July 15, 1927, in Vienna] and then again and again later on, I tried to grasp the wave, but I have never succeeded. I could not succeed, for nothing is more mysterious and more incomprehensible than a crowd. Had I fully understood it, I would not have wrestled with the problem of a crowd for thirty years, trying to puzzle it out and trying to depict it and reconstruct it as thoroughly as possible, like other human phenomena" (*MEC*, 488). To be sure, it is not *a picture* that holds him captive, to use here Wittgenstein's words, but something that Alain Badiou might call *fidelity to an event*: an experience to which he often returns, which has become part of himself, as if following a transubstantiation. "Fifty-three years have passed," he reflects in *The Torch in My Ear*, "and the agitation of that day is still *in my bones*" (*MEC*, 484, my italics). The original experience was one of complete identification: he had "fully dissolved in [the crowd]"; he had felt the crowd outside, but also within himself: "even today I sense how hard it is to *tear myself away*" (*MEC*, 490, my italics). This unforgettable immersion is Canetti's encounter with the ordinary, both within and outside himself, the experience of a porous body traversed by the crowd.

There is no doubt something paradoxical about the connection with Wittgenstein, since the people Canetti evokes do not find a community in language: as we have seen, he believes language keeps them apart. Is it that the events separating Wittgenstein and Canetti have compromised language irremediably? Is Karl Kraus's rage, his habit of using people's words against themselves, which have seeped into Canetti's way of seeing the world, too . . . deconstructionist?[79] In any case, Canetti seems to want to retrieve something that precedes even the commonality of language, a dimension of experience that is also present in Wittgenstein's *Philosophical Investigations*: something like the shared experience of living in a body, but which becomes with him a shared substance, transpiring in an *intoxication*, feeling like a *higher unity*. This is no metaphysical, sublime beyond; on the contrary, this is Canetti's version of the *ordinary*: it foregrounds the body as a pathway to human truth.

Language is not obliterated from the picture altogether; it appears in an unexpected guise as a medium of intimacy with the stentorian voice of a crowd, that he hears from his room cheering during a game played on a stadium nearby. "I could hear the crowd, and it alone, as though everything were taking place right near me," he remembers. He shares the excitement of the crowd, although he did not root for either side, both indifferent to him. "There were two crowds, that was all I knew; both equally excitable and speaking the same language" (*MEC*, 492). The proximity of this language is sufficient for him to identify fully with the emotions of the crowd, every single sound affecting him: "Reading through manuscripts of those days, I believe even today that I can discern every point at which such a sound was heard, as though it was marked by a secret notation" (*MEC*, 493). In a remarkable passage, Canetti intimates an aural space within which a communion with the various emotions of the crowd takes place, one whose perfection is impervious to the passage of time. Those "effects" have trickled into his writing as if in the form of "a secret notation," recalling the private language whose existence Wittgenstein contested.[80] One might not have a private language of one's own, but as an "autobiographer of the crowd," Canetti also thought himself in possession of, or at least receptive to, its private language.[81]

What is the crowd to Canetti, then? If we allow the memoirs to shed light on *Crowds and Power*, it appears as a multitude of individuals who carry stings in their flesh. The stings of command usually create distances between them, but these distances disappear in the crowd. Redemption then is not the work of one individual, the Christ with his crown of thorns, but is enacted collectively, in a happening that would seem nothing short of miraculous if the metaphysical weren't precisely the ordinary: the ordinary raised at the level of a redemptive—that is, consciousness-altering, and "thunderousl[y]" unselfish—experience. Contemplating Canetti's world, Emil Cioran's picture of society from *Traité de décomposition* inevitably comes to mind: it is *an inferno of saviors*.

Having said this, we need to emphasize that with Canetti, we should always speak of the crowd in the plural. Canetti looks at crowds in history, ultimately intimating a human community that transcends the historical. The importance of this point can be best illuminated by highlighting this ideal character of community in the thought of other thinkers, such as Franz Rosenzweig and Giorgio Agamben. In *The Star of Redemption* (1921), Rosenzweig contrasts the community of religion with that of politics. Two features are significant in a discussion of *Crowds and Power*: the shared equality at the heart of the community, and its eternal, transcendental character. For Rosenzweig, the community of equals emerges from the silent listening to the reading of the Text, the affirmation of shared bodily equality in the communal eating, and the bow (to God) as a form of greeting. Canetti would obviously not dispute the equality of the members, but he would be bothered by the vertical relation to God. This fundamental difference helps articulate a commonality, however: where Rosenzweig shows that the eternal God transcends the fate of the historical leader or state, thus making the community transhistorical, Canetti turns the crowd itself into a transhistorical category, by pointing to its omnipresence in human experience. One can speculate that a utopian dimension ensues: just as with Christianity, the nature of the present is a preparation for the redemptive community, the process of forming a universal society, the countless types of crowds in the 1960 tome and the memories of crowd immersion recounted in the memoirs might harbor the image of a community that individuals must learn to belong to.[82] This might bring into focus Agamben's "coming community," except that Canetti does not seem to be interested in the singularity of each individual member: as we have seen, it is precisely against the claims to singularity made by his contemporaries that he developed his hope in the redemptive potential of the crowd experience.[83]

Two last questions remain to be addressed: What is missing from Canetti's world? And why is his outlook so bleak?

The Avoidance of Love

Once we understand that the "accent" Canetti gave his ideas by writing the memoirs is a moralistic one, his refusal to engage previous theories seems less surprising: Canetti's aims were simply incommensurable with those of his predecessors.[84] Already at twenty he was determined to remove all "scribblings" about crowds, "to have the crowd before [him] as a pure, untouched mountain, which [he] would be the first to climb without prejudices." A passage resonant with Karl Kraus's biting sarcasm claims that previous theorists

> closed themselves off against masses, crowds; they found them alien or seemed to fear them; and when they set about investigating them, they gestured: Keep ten feet away from me! A crowd seemed something leprous to them, it was like a disease. They were supposed to find the symptoms and describe them. It was crucial for them, when confronted with a crowd, to keep their heads, not be seduced by the crowd, not melt into it. (*MEC*, 407)

Not so with Canetti, who finds that the real disease is the power inherent to social life and that the antidote to it is the crowd: a shared experience of embodiment, a powerful reminder of the capacity to have common purposes, to be traversed forcefully by the same energies. Canetti elevates the ordinary to a transcendental reality and conveys this experience of the sublime as a powerful vision: hence the hyperbolic presentation of history as crowds, and of power as raw violence.[85] As a writer, Canetti's intent is not to offer a rational explanation of historical events or new philosophical concepts to understand them; this would mean yielding to the lures of an Enlightenment rationality that failed to prevent them—indeed, Adorno and Horkheimer would say, that *led* to them. Rather, he pursues a visceral reaction in his readers, a desire for change.[86]

The memoirs qualify the image of Canetti as an iconoclast with respect to previously held beliefs about the crowd, shedding new light on his relationship with Freud. First, he shows himself adamant about psychoanalysis, whose results "struck even the unschooled reader of twenty as dissatisfying and incongruent. . . . What I missed most in Freud's discussion was *recognition* of the phenomenon" (*MEC*, 407, italics in the original).[87] The crowd phenomenon, he adds, renewing the effort to put distance between himself and Freud,

> *struck* me as no less elementary than the libido or hunger. I didn't set out to get rid of this phenomenon by tracing it back to special constellations of the libido. On the contrary, the point was to focus on it squarely, as something that had always existed, and that existed now more than ever, as a given phenomenon to be thoroughly investigated,

> namely to be first experienced and then described. (*MEC*, 407–408, my italics)

It is hard to miss the epiphanic quality of Canetti's ideation about the crowd: he repeats that he was *struck*, later he speaks of an *illumination*, and in general the crowd experience is described in terms that harbor the etymological sense of enthusiasm (*enthusiasmos*—immersion in, but also possession by the crowd). The crowd is elementary, the relationship with it is almost mystical, and its understanding cannot be mediated by the "special constellations of the libido" laid out by Freud. Clearly, Canetti stakes a lot on this difference. In a radio interview from 1962, Adorno invited Canetti to elaborate on his relationship with Freud, soliciting a form of acknowledgment that is absent from *Crowds and Power*. At first Canetti was succinct and reserved.[88] Prodded again by Adorno, he acknowledges that he was critical of Freud's reliance on the figure of the leader in theorizing the crowd, as well as on two models, the church and the army, that Canetti excludes from the category of "crowds" because they are hierarchical. There is much more than these aspects in *Group Psychology and the Analysis of the Ego*, and Freud's attentive readers are justified in suspecting Canetti of evasion. Their discomfort is alleviated, if also teased, by a passage in the memoirs that brings to light the beginning of a revised attitude toward Freud:

> At the time, I was unaware of how much the manner of my enterprise owed to the fact that there was someone like Freud in Vienna, . . . I was sincerely, if naively, convinced that I was undertaking something different, something totally independent of me. It was clear to me that *I needed him as an adversary*. But the fact that *he served as a kind of model for me*—this was something that no one could have made me see at that time. (*MEC*, 387)

This rather puzzling passage—unique in its acknowledgment of Freud, since Canetti does not go on to explain his indebtedness, or how he understands the notion of "a model"—invites a renewed analysis of this relationship. How exactly is *Crowds and Power* modeled on Freud's work?

"Each detail exists in itself, memorable and discernible, and yet each one also forms a part of the tremendous wave, without which everything seems hollow and absurd. The thing to be grasped is the wave, not these details" (*MEC*, 488). This description echoes Freud's *Civilization and Its Discontents*, which begins with a discussion of the "oceanic feeling" brought to the author's attention by Romain Roland, a feeling that Freud confesses not being able to discover in himself.[89] However, he acknowledges that it probably occurs in other people, and wonders if it might be explained as the *fons et origo* of religions (his previous book was *The Future of an Illusion*, published in 1927). In Freud's account, the "oceanic feeling" is possibly a reminiscence of an ego-feeling left behind through socialization. Some of Canetti's descriptions of the psychological sensations experienced in the crowd chime in with Freud's hypothesis: he speaks of "a total alteration of consciousness, . . . both drastic and dramatic," of "an intoxication, an intensification of possibilities for experience, an increase of the person, who leaves his confines, comes to other persons leaving their confines, and forms a higher unity with them" (*MEC*, 353). But this is in the memoirs, not in the 1960 book. Ostensibly there is nothing personal throughout *Crowds and Power*, no mention of Canetti's own immersion experience, so often invoked in his more explicitly intimate writing, yet we have seen just how amply the echo of the first pages reverberates throughout the memoirs.

The beginning of *Crowds and Power* is evocative of Freud's *Group Psychology* as well:

> All life, so far as [man] knows it, is laid out in distances—the house in which he shuts himself and his property, the positions he holds, the rank he desires—all these serve to create distances, to confirm and extend them. Any free or large gesture of approach towards another human being is inhibited. Impulse and counter impulse ooze away in the desert. No man can get near another, nor reach his height. In every sphere of life, firmly established hierarchies prevent him touching anyone more exalted than himself, or descending, except in appearance, to anyone lower. In different societies the distances are differently balanced against each other, the stress in some lying on birth, in others on occupation or property. . . .
>
> Only together can men free themselves from their burdens of distance; and this, precisely, is what happens in a crowd. (*CP*, 18)

Canetti accounts for the origin of crowd-formation in terms of a collective desire for equality, the effacing of all differences, of all social markers. Individuals becoming masses through an experience of discharge (*Entladung*) that creates a bond among them, is an idea familiar from Freud's *Group Psychology*, published "long before the danger of German fascism appeared to be acute," as Adorno pointed out. But while in Canetti's view, equality is the otherwise utopian desire that leads to the crowd, in Freud's account it is the effect of the identification with the leader as the idealized superego. Adorno's analysis of the Freudian model, which he saw as instrumental in explaining fascism, helps situate Canetti's ideas both with respect to his illustrious predecessor and to contemporary critical thinkers of totalitarianism:

> in accordance with general psychoanalytic theory, Freud believes that the bond which integrates individuals into a mass, is of a libidinal nature. . . . [Freud explains] the coherence of the masses altogether in terms of the pleasure principle, that is to say, the actual or the vicarious

> gratifications individuals obtain from surrendering to a mass. Hitler, by the way, was well aware of the libidinal source of mass formation through surrender when he attributed specifically female, passive features to the participants of his meetings, and thus also hinted at the role of unconscious homosexuality in mass psychology.[90]

Nothing could be further removed from Canetti's conviction that the crowd is autonomous. A priori, Canetti has no use of the figure of the leader, central to Freudian group psychology: his equality is that of a freedom from distances, that is, from all hierarchies, not the equality of a collective dependence. Adorno's further comments on Freud shed even more light on essential differences from Canetti:

> by making the leader his ideal [the individual] loves himself, as it were, but gets rid of the stains of frustration and discontent which mar his picture of his own empirical self. This pattern of identification through idealization, the caricature of true conscious solidarity, is, however, a collective one. It is effective in vast numbers of people with similar characterological dispositions and libidinal leanings. The fascist community of the people corresponds exactly to Freud's definition of a group as being "a number of individuals who have substituted one and the same object for their ego ideal and have consequently identified themselves with one another in their ego." The leader image, in turn, borrows as it were its primal father-like omnipotence from collective strength.[91]

Had Canetti read this, he might have nodded in agreement with Adorno's lucid characterization of identification in the Freudian scenario as a "caricature of true conscious solidarity." As the two passages from *Crowds and Power* quoted above suggest, for Canetti the crowd has precisely the appeal of a collective attempt to cancel out social distances, following a longing that turns out to be shared:

> Man petrifies and darkens in the distances he has created. He drags at the burden of them, but cannot move. But how, alone, can he free himself? Whatever he does, and however determined he is, he will always find himself among others who thwart his efforts. So long as they hold fast to *their* distances, he can never come any nearer to them.

On the one hand, one might recall here Peter Kien and Therese in *Auto-da-fé:* Kien at first isolated in his library—Canetti describes it as a fortress-belt (*Festungsgürtel*)—and then married to Therese, whose rigid starched skirt discourages however all effort at proximity, "whatever he does, and however determined he is"; she does come closer, not with her body but with her furniture, taking up more and more space in the apartment, so that he tries to avoid her by "turning into stone," his body "petrified," eyes closed. On the other hand, the pages in *Party in the Blitz* describing English parties single out Canetti himself as the one who tried to "come nearer to them," while they were "hold[ing] fast to *their* distances."

The picture of the one confronting the many precedes the vision of equality embodied in the crowd, with its joyful contradiction of social arrangements:

> Only together can men free themselves from their burdens of distance, and this, precisely, is what happens in a crowd. During the discharge distinctions are thrown off and all feel equal. In that density, where there is scarcely any space between, and body presses against body, each man is as near the other as he is to himself; and an immense feeling of relief ensues. It is for the sake of this blessed moment, when no-one is greater or better than another, that people become a crowd. (*CP*, 18)

Since the memoirs fill these "distances" with echoes from Frankfurt, Vienna, England, suggesting that Canetti, a stateless person for most of his life, did not necessarily have one particular societal model in mind, it is possible to rewrite these autobiographical examples in more general terms: thus *distance* appears not just as the antidote to the archaic "fear of being touched" (which the title of the opening chapter gestures toward, and is what Canetti's readers usually notice), but also as the dominant principle of the layout of social life in cultures based on orders of rank commonly accepted, like the English one, illustrative for Trilling of the sincerity paradigm, and the necessary attribute of the avant-garde striving for authenticity (tipping the scale toward narcissism during so-called postmodernism).[92] To sum up, living with others burdens one with distances that affect one's freedom. Freud however had said as much in *Civilization and Its Discontents*: "The liberty of the individual is no gift of civilization. It was greatest before there was any civilization, though then, it is true, it had for the most part no value, since the individual was scarcely in a position to defend it."[93] But he also reminds that relinquishing part of the original freedom is the price to be paid for security and equal treatment: "The development of civilization imposes restrictions on it, and justice demands that no one shall escape those restrictions." Canetti, on the other hand, credits this process with nothing positive: the incontrovertible statement grounding his theory is that freedom is to be gained only in the experience of the crowd, where all distances are abolished.

This is how "distance" comes to be invested with different meanings by Freud and Canetti. *Group Psychology and the Analysis of the Ego* quotes Schopenhauer's story of the porcupines as a parable for the civilizing process: it is an illustration of how one learns to repress one's irritation with the other members of the group for the sake of a social, mutually beneficial, coexistence.[94] In Freud's account, no one can stand a too-intimate relationship with another because there is "a sediment of aversion and hostility, which only escapes perception as a result of repression" (he is anticipating here what he will later call the superego, absolutely central to civilization). What Nietzsche heralds as a "pathos of distances" appears in Freud in mutated form as a "narcissism of minor differences." The theory of the libido unfolds here, first in a discussion of narcissism, and then of identification: while narcissism "works for the preservation of the individual," identification helps to form libidinal bonds with other people. Freud understands narcissism as either ambivalence of feelings or as undisguised antipathy and aversion, a "readiness for hatred, an aggressiveness, the source of which is unknown, and to which one is tempted to ascribe an elementary character"; *but*, he continues, "when a group is formed the whole of this intolerance vanishes, temporarily or permanently, within the group."[95] Freud and Canetti are teasingly close here: what does Canetti accomplish by changing Freud's dialectic into one that so closely resembles it? In the memoirs he writes, "There is such a thing as a crowd instinct, which is always in conflict with the personality instinct, and that the struggle between the two of them can explain the course of human history. This couldn't have been a new idea; but it was new to me, for it struck me with tremendous force. Everything now happening in the world could, it seemed to me, be traced back to that struggle" (*MEC*, 387). Indeed, what Canetti calls "personality" can be easily understood in terms of Freudian narcissism and aggressiveness, and the crowd is a form of being with others, where all are equal, oblivious of their differences. He could not have disagreed when he read in *Group Psychology*: "So long as the group formation persists or so far as it extends, individuals in the group behave as though they were uniform, tolerate the peculiarities of its other members, equate themselves with them, and have no feeling of aversion toward them."[96]

At this point, however, Canetti might have become impatient with Freud: "Such a limitation of narcissism can, according to our theoretical views, only be produced by one factor, a libidinal tie with other people. Love for oneself knows only one barrier—love for others, love for objects."[97] This last statement finds no referent in the universe of *Auto-da-fé*, in the world Canetti chronicles in his memoirs, or the *Weltanschauung* that permeates *Crowds and Power*. Where Freud speaks of Eros as the mysterious moving principle of civilization, Canetti cannot follow him; in fact, he goes as far as to disavow familiarity with psychoanalysis. There is no love, Canetti showed in 1931 already as he wrote *Auto-da-fé*, and civilization was a myth, as the "dreadful things that people [did] to one another" in the following years demonstrated: all was barbarism. Canetti's discomfort with Freud's theory of the instincts, predicated on the opposition between Eros and the death drive, between libidinal ties (sexual relationships and aim-inhibited affection or friendship) and instinctual aggressiveness which threatens civilization, has not only a personal justification, but also a historical one. The implication is that, since Canetti rejects the whole of Freud's libidinal economy, he has to dispense with the superego, the internalization of authority; his is a world of self-perpetuating violence, populated by egoless vessels loaded with stings that are carried and passed on to others.[98] "A picture of hell in this life," one might be inclined to say, echoing Broch's dismay after reading *Auto-da-fé*, but obviously Canetti felt even more entitled to "rub people's noses in their wickedness" after the Second World War.

The implicit dialogue with Freud inevitably brings to the forefront *Civilization and Its Discontents*. In this book, finished in 1930 and slightly revised in 1931, Freud developed his dialectical view of human history, a permanent conflict between Eros and the death drive. Making a compelling case for aggressiveness as an instinct that threatens civilization, Freud describes it in great detail, with a rhetorical force that equals Canetti's descriptions of the "entrails of power." Critics who were appalled by the physiology of power detailed in *Crowds and Power* most likely did not have Freud's long ruminations about aggressiveness at hand:

> The element of truth . . . which people are so ready to disavow, is that men are not gentle creatures who want to be loved, and who at the most can defend themselves if they are attacked; they are, on the contrary, creatures among whose instinctual endowments is to be reckoned a powerful share of aggressiveness. As a result, their neighbour is for them not only a potential helper or sexual object, but also someone who tempts them to satisfy their aggressiveness on him, to exploit his capacity for work without compensation, to use him sexually without his consent, to seize his possessions, to humiliate him, to cause him pain, to torture and to kill him. *Homo homini lupus*.[99] Who, in the face of all his experience of life and of history, will have the courage to dispute this assertion? . . . In circumstances that are favorable to it, when the mental counter-forces which ordinarily inhibit it are out of action, it also manifests itself spontaneously and reveals man as a savage beast to whom consideration towards its own kind is something alien. Anyone who calls to mind the atrocities committed during the racial migrations or the invasions of the Huns, or by the people known as Mongols under Jenghiz Khan and Tamerlane, or at the capture of Jerusalem by the pious Crusaders, or even, indeed, the horrors of the recent World War—anyone who calls these things to mind will have to bow humbly before the truth of this view.[100]

Canetti not only bows to the "truth" of Freud's view, he goes to great lengths to illustrate it with examples of his own, such as the terrifying Muhammad Tuglak, the Sultan of Delhi, African kings, and mindless meat-eaters.

It is well known that, under the influence of the rise of Nazism, Freud added a quizzical last sentence to *Civilization and Its Discontents* in 1931; whereas the 1930 edition ended on a note of cautious hope—"And now it is to be expected that the other of the two 'Heavenly Powers,' eternal Eros, will make an effort to assert himself in the struggle with his equally immortal adversary [Death]"—a year later doubt looms large: "But who can foresee with what success and with what result?"[101] That in the same year Canetti was already far more pessimistic is clear from the ending of *Auto-da-fé*: whereas Freud had only decided that there was something uncanny about culture (his original title was *Das Unbehagene in der Kultur*) and questioned its chances of survival in the face of looming disaster, Canetti set fire, symbolically, to its best intellectual accomplishments as if to suggest the irrelevance of *Kultur*. By the time Canetti wrote and finished *Crowds and Power*, the verdict had been given quite eloquently, permeating his *Weltanschauung* irremediably: what Freud called Eros might as well have never existed; to talk about civilization was a form of self-flattery. The section about African kings, for instance, begins with a warning that resonates with other postwar diagnoses:

> Everything about these [African] Kings seems so strange and unfamiliar that one is at first tempted to dismiss them as exotic curiosities, or, if one lingers over accounts of them such as those which follow, to give way to a feeling of superiority. But one is well advised to show a little patience and humility and wait until one knows more about them. *It is not for a European of the 20th century to regard himself as above savagery*. His despots may use more effective means, but their ends often differ in nothing from those of these African Kings. (*CP*, 411)[102]

In other words, where Freud saw history as a dialectic of Eros/civilization and the death-drive/aggressiveness, Canetti—in 1931 already, with his novel—depicts a world of lovelessness, mercilessly goaded by the "memory of the dreadful things people do to one another"; in the wake of World War II, he could only be hardened in this view of human nature. As we have seen, instead of scapegoating Hitler, Canetti opens up the vista of the whole of humankind as a crowd of "survivors": that is, of potential despotic rulers, who only isolate themselves because they have a desire to overpower others. Canetti renews the indictment of *Auto-da-fé*, this time by way of a critique of historiography which leads the way to an interpellation of his readers:

> One should not allow oneself to be confused by the fact that, in a case such as Schreber's, the paranoiac never actually attained the monstrous position he hungered for. Others *have* attained it. Some of them have succeeded in covering the traces of their rise and keeping their perfected system secret. Others have been less fortunate or had

> too little time. Here, as in other things, success depends entirely on accidents. The attempt to reconstruct these accidents under the illusion that they are governed by laws calls itself history. For every great name in history a hundred others might have been substituted. There is never any dearth of men who are both talented and wicked. Nor can we deny that we all eat and that each of us has grown strong on the bodies of innumerable animals. Here each of us is king in a field of corpses. (*CP*, 448)

This is a most disturbing image, which one could cite as yet another example of Canetti's hyperbolically graphic style. Yet such images are no rarity in the literature of the past century, in which the metaphor of war as a slaughterhouse is recurrent: from Döblin's *Berlin Alexanderplatz*, with its crude imagery and "Menschen sind Schweine" leitmotif; Kurt Vonnegut's *Slaughterhouse-Five*; the propaganda film *Der ewige Jude*; J. M. Coetzee's "The Lives of Animals" in *Elizabeth Costello*, and so on. In this last text, the parallel between the Holocaust and the animal industry is given a new turn when Elizabeth has the vision of being surrounded by objects made of Jewish skin: "I return one last time to the places of death all around us, the places of slaughter to which, in a huge communal effort, we close our hearts. Each day, a fresh holocaust, yet, as far as I can see, our moral being is untouched." Like Coetzee's character Costello, Canetti is disturbed by the recurrence of unethical practices and gestures, which he links to the fabric of our moral life: "A conscientious investigation of power must ignore success. We must look for its attributes and their perversions wherever they appear, and then compare them" (*CP*, 448). *Wherever they appear*: that is, at all levels of human experience, including, most importantly, in the realm of everyday social interaction.

Toward a Reassessment of *Crowds and Power*

This chapter's subtitle, "Notes in the Margin of Elias Canetti's Lifework," refers to my indirect approach to *Crowds and Power*, Canetti's *Lebenswerk*, by way of the memoirs, in which he provided "a different accent" to his ideas by highlighting his deeply moralistic persona. Emphasizing this aspect does not invalidate critical readings that establish links with other theories of crowds and totalitarianism, but it does set such questions and critiques on a different footing. If we understand Canetti's conviction that his role was to scourge his contemporaries with the means at the disposal of the *Dichter*, questions about the "truth-value" of his Weltanschauung have a different bearing on how we read him. His view of the world is bleak, and much is left out of the picture that might offer atonement. But as an exiled Jew writing in German, he clearly found that something was amiss in the 1940s and 1950s: a deep understanding and a sense of responsibility for what had happened. His theory of command and the survivor suggests that he was not as much intrigued by the support of so many for Hitler the Führer, as he was disturbed that a Hitler, who could have been almost anyone, was the symptom of a defective sociality in need of radical transformation. His task was to show how the stings of command cause the suffering that shapes such an individual. Whereas Freud had identified two psychologies, of the ruled and of the idealized ruler, Canetti stated emphatically that there was only one: the psychology of human beings carrying thorns in their flesh.

It is ironic that while some critical thinkers dismissed his book for failing to explain Nazism, historians like Veronica Wedgwood or Pierre Nora praised the book for its insights in this regard. Moreover, Canetti's critique of historiography as the apotheosis of rulers and power-figures resonated with the "history from below" approach of the Annales school; unsurprisingly, *Crowds and Power* appealed to Pierre Nora, the leader of the "nouvelle histoire," who published the French translation in his new collection at Gallimard (*Bibliothèque des sciences humaines*, 1966), where texts by Raymond Aron, Georges Dumézil, and Michel Foucault were also to appear.

It only became possible in the 1980s to understand that Canetti's ideas about the rise of Nazism were by no means off the mark; indeed, that they were well ahead of his time. The influential *Sonderweg* thesis regarded German history from a deep historical perspective and highlighted its peculiarities: the lack of a bourgeois revolution, late unification, persistence of preindustrial, precapitalist traditions. As late as 1980, Jürgen Kocka reaffirmed, in his "Ursachen des Nationalsozialismus" ("Causes of National-Socialism"), the famous argument put forward by Ralf Dahrendorf in *Society and Democracy in Germany* (1965) about the specific backwardness of German political culture. Adapting Max Horkheimer's famous saying, Kocka decreed: "Whoever does not want to talk about pre-industrial, pre-capitalist and pre-bourgeois traditions should keep quiet about fascism."[103] The *Sonderweg* thesis was challenged by Geoff Eley and David Blackbourn, in *Mythen deutscher Geschichtschreibung*[104] and, it seems, definitively refuted in the expanded and revised English edition, *The Peculiarities of German History: Bourgeois Society and Politics in Nineteenth-Century Germany*, where they demonstrate that the causes of National Socialism should be looked for in the crises immediately following World War I.[105] This is exactly the perspective Canetti adopts, albeit in the symbolic manner we can now recognize as the signature of *Crowds and Power*.

Canetti identifies two major causes of the rise and success of National Socialism: the Versailles Treaty and economic inflation. He begins with the German national symbol: the forest, which he explains as an image of the army. "The crowd symbol of the united German nation which formed after the Franco-Prussian War of 1870–71 was, and remained, the army" (*CP*, 179). The Versailles Treaty negotiated at the end of World War I disbanded the German army and prohibited universal military service, thus depriving the Germans of their "closed crowd." This was the direct cause, Canetti demonstrates, of the adherence in such overwhelming numbers to National Socialism:

> The activities they were denied, the exercises, the receiving and passing on of orders, became something which they had to procure for themselves at all costs. The prohibition on universal military service was the *birth* of National Socialism. Every closed crowd which is dissolved by force transforms itself into an open crowd to which it imparts all its own characteristics. The party came to the rescue of the army, and the party had no limits set to its recruitment from within the nation. Every single German—man, woman or child, soldier or civilian—could become a National Socialist. He was probably even more anxious to become one if he had not been a soldier before, because, by doing so, he achieved participation in activities hitherto denied him. (*CP*, 181)

It is no surprise, Canetti shows later, that Hitler used the slogan *The Diktat of Versailles* so successfully: "*Diktat* belongs to the sphere of command. A single alien *command*, a command coming from the enemy and therefore dubbed *diktat* had put an end to the whole virile activity of command amongst Germans themselves, that is within the army" (*CP*, 181–182). Inflation was the second determinant factor. The Germans perceived the devaluation of the mark as a diminution of their identity: millions became available to many overnight, yet they were valueless. Canetti shows that the Germans felt they had to inflict the same treatment on the Jews, who were the obvious choice since they were "on good terms with money when others did not know how to manage it"; their numbers were made to "increase" through excessive visibility (by singling them out, both in Germany and in the territories the Germans occupied for the expansion of the *Lebensraum*), and then reduced to worthlessness, through "a dynamic process of humiliation" (*CP*, 187). By tracing the causes of Nazism and the Holocaust to the context immediately following World War I, Canetti anticipated the elaborate analyses that Eley and Blackbourn were to put forward in the 1980s, even if these historians did not couch their explanations in the peculiar language and symbolism of the crowd.

However, Canetti considered the Nazi crowds only one episode in the multifarious history of crowd phenomena. In heralding the crowd's equality and lack of distance among bodies, he was affirming a model that most of his contemporaries associated with the oppressive lack of distance imposed by totalitarian regimes, and that had spawned his own longing for space and freedom of movement, eventually leading him into his British exile. Hannah Arendt's spatial metaphors in *The Origins of Totalitarianism* provide a suggestive contrast. She explains that while the First World War was already a radicalizing and equalizing experience that brought about the "transvaluation of values" proclaimed by Nietzsche—the breakdown of classes and their transformation into masses[106]—the experience of totalitarianism meant an oppressive radicalization of these tendencies, leading to the complete regimentation of everyday life and the reduction to the point of obliteration of personal space. In Arendt's words, total terror

> substitutes for the boundaries and channels of communication between individual men a band of iron which holds them so tightly together that it is as though their plurality had disappeared into One Man of gigantic dimensions. To abolish the fences of laws between men—as tyranny does—means to take away man's liberties and destroy freedom as a living political reality; for the space between men as it is hedged in by laws, is the living space of freedom.[107]

A few lines down, she elaborates:

> By pressing men against each other, total terror destroys the space between them; compared to the condition within its iron band, even the desert of tyranny, insofar as it is still some kind of space, appears like a guarantee of freedom. Totalitarian government does not just curtail liberties or abolish essential freedoms; nor does it, at least to our limited knowledge, succeed in eradicating the love for freedom from the hearts of man. It destroys the one essential prerequisite of all freedom which is simply the capacity of motion which cannot exist without space.[108]

Admittedly, Canetti's defining experiences of the crowd predate the Nazi period, but the book was written mostly after the flight from Vienna to England in 1938 and finished in 1959; which also means that he had little firsthand experience of life under a totalitarian regime. Clearly, then, while Nazism occupies a central place, and carries a heavy symbolic weight in the book, his ideas and concerns have a much larger scope. The imposed equality and the "band of iron" that squeezes individuals together in Arendt's account of totalitarianism does not resonate with Canetti; it is by contrast of some significance that the metaphor of a surrounding, isolating band is present in *Auto-da-fé*: Peter Kien surrounds himself with his library like with a *Festungsguertel* (a fortress *belt*); this extreme isolation, characteristic of modern life more generally, is countered with the crowd experience, even if *some* crowds happened to have cheered the fateful leader of Germany.

Crowds and Power was ahead of its time not only with its account of the causes of Nazism, but also in the way it dealt with it after the fact. In the late 1950s when Canetti brought his book to a close, the Germans were not yet ready to "deal with the past"; they were still in denial, involved in the economic miracle of rebuilding Germany. Family chronicles documenting the past and assuming responsibility for the acquiescence in the Nazi extermination of the Jews began to be published only in the 1960s, and Alexander and Margarete Mitscherlich's work *The Inability to Mourn*, grounded in Freudian psychoanalysis, appeared in 1967. Canetti's move, in the 1950s already, is to deflect attention from the demonized figure of Hitler and to diffuse responsibility among his European contemporaries, showing that to blame was ultimately the way people live. Conversely, the survivor is not only the Jew who, guilty for being alive, mourns his or her dead kin.[109] The way Canetti rewrites the figure of the survivor draws attention, rather, to the potential violence engendered by violence, driven by a desire for revenge.[110] The *Dichter* has obviously made his point: the *hypocrite lecteur* is *semblable* to the banished Jew (Canetti was himself a Sephardic Jew), both victim and potential perpetrator. As part of the crowd of "survivors" pilloried by the author, they—the readers—must find ways of removing the stings of command and learn the lessons of metamorphosis.

But *how is command to be humanized*? This question, that many ponder on turning the last page of *Crowds and Power*, puzzled Iris Murdoch as well. Her review notes the absence of a psychology that would help us picture the humanization of command, which makes the book vulnerable to critiques coming from science and from morality. "How strictly is one to understand the imagery of the 'stings'? . . . Also, cannot the pain of stings be removed by love and compassion without any 'reversal'? How are we here to conceive the 'free' man?"[111] On the terms of *Crowds and Power*, love is not of this world, and it would be too comforting an idea to consider in a text that so keenly chastises its readers. Responding perhaps to Murdoch's remark that "no theory of human nature can place itself beyond the attack of purely moral concepts,"[112] Canetti's memoirs do offer goodness in the memorable, if elusive, figure of the poet Avraham ben Yitzhak, as an exemplary way to ward off the discontents of the world. However, the readers of the 1960 tome can only turn to Murdoch herself for a serious engagement with the question how to live with others in a more humane way. To Canetti's insistent reminders that the crowd, where bodies press against one another, symbolically annuls the distances of everyday life, she responds with a patient, finely wrought reflection on the difficult-to-achieve balance between distances outside, among members of the human community, and distances within oneself, often imponderable.

If Canetti and Murdoch seem worlds apart in their views on human nature, they are surprisingly close in the glimpses they give us into the rarefied realm of human delicacy. The auratic figure of Dr. Sonne, the quiet guest that Canetti would often spy on at the Café Museum in Vienna, and who later became a venerated intellectual companion, ideally marks the threshold between the wretched world canvassed by Canetti and the community of *délicatesse* envisioned by Barthes and Murdoch: "For one thing, he was so utterly impersonal. He never talked about himself. He never made use of the first person. And he seldom addressed me directly. By speaking in the third person, he distanced himself from his surroundings" (*MEC*, 686).[113] Implicitly acknowledging that the crowd is no viable model for everyday interaction, Canetti is touched by Dr. Sonne's "respect for the dividing lines between individuals" (*MEC*, 689), and alert to his tactful discernment: "He spoke with the authority of one passing judgment, but managed, with a simple wave of the hand, to exclude his interlocutor from that judgment. In this there was something more than kindness, there was delicacy, and I am amazed to this day by this combination and extreme rigor" (*MEC*, 695). *Something more than kindness . . . delicacy*: to examine these virtues in more detail, we need to turn to the lectures of Roland Barthes in conversation with the philosophical and literary work of Iris Murdoch.

Chapter 3

A Socialism of Distances, or On the Difficulties of Wise Love

Iris Murdoch's Secular Community

> Any artist knows what it is to look at the world, and the distance and otherness thereof is his primary problem.
>
> —Iris Murdoch, interview with Bryan Magee

> So long as the gaze is directed upon the ideal the exact formulation will be a matter of history and dogma, and understanding of the ideal will be partial in any case. Where virtue is concerned we often apprehend more than we clearly understand and grow by looking.
>
> —Iris Murdoch, "The Idea of Perfection"

> "All is vanity" is the beginning and the end of ethics.
>
> —Iris Murdoch, "On 'God' and 'Good' "

In *Comment vivre ensemble*, Roland Barthes anticipated the emergence of a new vision of home in the world, one that he hoped would come alive in a novel about a community of individuals committed to rethinking and living a meaningful life together. Had he indeed given novelistic form to his "phantasm" of the *vivre-ensemble*, it might have read like an estranged younger sibling of *The Bell* (1958), the fourth published novel of Iris Murdoch. Like Barthes's community, Murdoch's is imagined on the basis of a religious model: whereas Barthes felt an enduring fascination with the cenobites on Mount Athos and emphasized in his course the rebellious character of any retreat from the world, in Murdoch's novel, the lay community at Imber Court, a group of "unhappy souls to which the world offers no home" (*B*, 71) lives in proximity of an enclosed abbey whose authority they respect. Committed to "inventing" their rules, they combine individual pursuits and communal activities, and debate how the community should run and define itself. The deliberation of everyday rules and principles is for these self-governing communities a *diaita*, a life-diet (Barthes's word), a discipline of resistance to the established sociopolitical frameworks, to the regimentations, constrictions, and repressions characteristic of the "bureaucratic society of controlled consumption." The author of *Mythologies* (1957) was in agreement with Lefebvre's diagnosis in *Critique of Everyday Life*; Murdoch had sketched this society, too, in the background of her earlier fiction, most notably in her debut novel *Under the Net* (1954).[1] In *The Bell*, it is mostly an outside, a form of exteriority, with which the members of the community have an ambivalent relationship at best. It is an interesting coincidence that Barthes's first book, *Writing Degree Zero*, and Murdoch's own first book, *Sartre: Romantic Rationalist*, were published in the same year—1953—and that their subsequent writing careers bore the mark both of Sartre's influence, and of their critical detachment from his notion of *engagement*.

The preoccupation with the elusive (right) distance does not simply originate in the reaction to Sartre, however. In what follows, I will show that Murdoch, a trained philosopher, gave philosophical depth to the question that guided Barthes's reflections on the ideal community—"at what distance should I keep myself from others in order to build with them a sociability without alienation and a solitude without exile?"—furthermore, that her notion of love as a moral ideal can be placed, as will be suggested by way of reading *The Bell*, on a continuum with Barthes's *délicatesse*. The intricate plot of Murdoch's novel recasts the aporias of *Comment vivre ensemble*, partially resolving them in the poetic mode. With literature, one thus moves in the realm of the ethical, which, Barthes appreciates, is "everywhere . . . inescapable" (*N*, 33). Murdoch could not have agreed more with such a pronouncement: She pointed to this idea explicitly in her critique of Sartre's commitment, and illustrated it in her long career as a novelist invested in exploring the encounter between the everyday life of ordinary individuals and the neatly drawn principles of moral discourse. That both the late Barthes and the young Murdoch took an interest in rethinking community speaks to their shared notion that the ethical questions attending the project of living with other people fall out of the picture of a world driven, on the one hand, by individualism and, on the other, by ideological or moral frameworks that obliterate the individual.

At first sight, the related communities imagined by Barthes and Murdoch recall the sociopolitical projects mentioned by MacIntyre in *After Virtue*, communities created with the purpose of fashioning a complete framework of values in accord with which the pursuit of a fulfilling life becomes possible. What remains alive from the community that MacIntyre takes for a model, the polis presupposed by Aristotle in the *Nicomachean Ethics*, is the spirit of deliberation characteristic of *phronêsis*: the virtue that stands both before and beyond all others, since it involves an intelligent grasp of particulars and the "decision" concerning the application of the means to achieve an end. Insofar as Barthes and Murdoch propose something in the way of a "virtue," it represents something far less ambitious—or perhaps more challenging—than a positive choice, than the endorsement of an already existing alternative; rather, the attitude they foreground is one of lucidity, or "neutrality" (as we have seen with Barthes), and attention (as we are about to see in Murdoch's moral philosophy). In a different parlance, *délicatesse* and love.

How does a community fare, equipped with such elusive ideals? This question prompts a return to an aspect I briefly touched on in the introduction, concerning Barthes's use of "distance" in the plural, and with reference to concrete, lived experience. Both Barthes and Murdoch were concerned with the everyday, aware that, even as their communities cherish some ideals or sense of purposeful life, they still have to navigate contingency. In *The Powers of Distance* and the *The Way We Argue Now*, Amanda Anderson has isolated the notion of distance as a hermeneutic category, confirming its close association, in the British tradition and more generally in that of Western Enlightenment, with objective rationality enabling detachment. The Victorians cherished such ideals of distance, Anderson shows in her first book, but they were also ambivalent about them; our contemporary "cultures of theory," Anderson enjoins in the last chapters of her second book, should however still rely on the ideals of distance implicit in, for example, Habermas's communicative ethics.[2] In short, distance is for Anderson an epistemological category with moral valences in the Victorian era, with political—that is, liberal—stakes today. To use "distance" in the plural is to shift emphasis: a "socialism of distances"—the notion comes from Nietzsche, but Barthes does not unpack its original use—accommodates more modes of relating than one, and the question at the heart of his lectures suggests that a community might be just the space where various modes of interaction have to come together and coexist, in permanent (re)negotiation. Pluralism is here brought back to the rough ground of everyday life, to the field of practical experience, and distance, given the obsolescence of absolutes, no longer acknowledged as an ideal; rather, a *mise-en-commun des distances* (a conjoining of distances) keeps alive the necessity to resume deliberation, if perhaps not always in explicit fashion.

That Barthes and Murdoch's ideas about community remain tethered to the practical experience of everyday life—both in the sense of *Erlebnisse*, random, unexpected occurrences, and of *Erfahrung*, the accumulated and sharable wisdom derived from them—suggests the alignment with *phronêsis* to be meaningful both by way of a positive characterization of "distances" and as a way to illuminate the challenges and discontents of such a notion, perhaps even its impossibility. In the *Nichomachean Ethics*, *phronêsis* is integrated into a coherent system of the virtues, where it has the privileged position of a capacity to grasp intelligently the particulars of a situation and to determine the application of (the other) virtues in conformity with the demands of that particular context: it presupposes acuity of perception, knowledge of the good, deliberation of the means leading to decision or choice (for lack of a more suitable contemporary notion). Translated most commonly as prudence, *phronêsis* is vital for the well-being of the individual, with the proviso that *well-being* as a rendering of *eudaimonia* is of course misleading, since the state of fulfillment, of happiness that the good life pursues in and through the cultivation of virtues (that is, both as a telos and, most importantly, as a way of life) is determined by, and in accordance with, considerations about the harmonious life in, and of, the polis. Thus for Aristotle, morality and politics famously converge; the polis includes both the social and the political, without discriminating between them. As MacIntyre, among others, has unequivocally shown, such an all-inclusive framework is foreign to the denizens of late modernity:

> This notion of the political community as a common project is alien to the modern liberal individualist world. This is how we sometimes at least think of schools, hospitals or philanthropic organizations; but we have no conception of such a form of community concerned, as Aristotle says the polis is concerned, with the whole of life, not with this or that good, but with man's good as such.[3]

The communities imagined by Barthes and Murdoch, both reliant on models of monastic life, are in retreat from the world and its alienating social arrangements. The challenge lies in constructing a new framework of existence, central to the endeavors of the community. In *The Bell*, Catherine introduces Dora, a visitor at Imber Court, to the life of the community: "It's difficult, you know, for a lay community where nothing's ordained. It all has to be invented as you go along" (125). What is the meaning of "invent" here? Surely, values are not just made up: old ones have to be reevaluated, and configured in a new arrangement through constant deliberation among the members of the community, as a response to the needs that appear as they "go along." It is this aspect of *phronêsis* that I am retaining here: the imperative to evaluate a context, a state of affairs, lucidly, with sensitivity, and to deliberate what the best way of addressing a situation might be, in light of the common good. Barthes insists however that his community has no telos, and that its success is in the practice itself, which is a life-diet. Murdoch's community is equally open on both temporal ends: it brings together individuals disappointed with life outside and sharing a rather vaguely articulated spiritual aspiration, but no founding moral principles other than a loose Christian background, and it has no stated or commonly acknowledged understanding of its finality. If deliberation occurs, Murdoch suggests, it does not go hand in hand with the expectation of stable consensus; nor does it imply an idealization of rationality, of objective detachment—hence the plural of distances.

On the other hand, both Barthes and Murdoch find problematic romantic love, or the model of the couple, in their attempts to rethink community; this exclusion brings them in proximity of the philosophical reflection on friendship in the Western tradition, which draws a line between friendship and love based on the absence or presence of teleology. In *Interrupting Derrida*, Geoffrey Bennington begins the chapter "Forever Friends" with a brief reminder of this basic distinction:

> Friendship, unlike love, does not tend towards a fusion of the parties to it. If I love you, I want to become one with you, or so the tradition would have it, to fuse with you to the point of death; but if I am your friend, such a clear *telos* is absent, or such a *telos* is not really clear. The point of loving seems clear enough, even if we might think it absurd, irrational or unhealthy; the point of friendship is harder to grasp, and perhaps that makes it more attractive still. Love is something we can't do much about, it takes us over and sweeps us on and away, maybe into disaster; friendship seems cooler, more calculated, involves a salutary distance that, in principle at least, prevents it being such a mess.[4]

Derrida's *Politics of Friendship* translates the lack of telos in friendship as the necessary maintenance of distance: "There is no respect, as its name connotes, without the vision and distance of a spacing. . . . The co-implication of responsibility and respect can be felt at the heart of friendship, one of the enigmas of which would stem from this distance, this concern in what concerns the other: a respectful separation seems to distinguish friendship from love."[5] Bennington and Derrida share a view of love as fusional—that is, as lacking distance—which is the very reason, as we shall see, why Barthes and Murdoch exclude it from their respective communities.[6] Living-together then becomes the challenge of expanding the framework of friendship—typically limited to two individuals who thus are unconditionally available to each other—to several persons. Although excluded, erotic love provides both Barthes and Murdoch with the principle of delicacy and the inclination to regard others in a certain way, that friendship alone, when cultivated in community, seems to lack. And this has a bearing, as we shall see, on the way one comes to understand not only being with others, but one's notion of self.

Let us first tease out the principles that drive Barthes's community, which in turn will help us focus on the complex interplay of "distances" in the communal setting in Murdoch's novel. My aim here will be to show that although both Barthes and Murdoch start with what appear to be small, closed "communities of work," to use Jean-Luc Nancy's term, the attention both authors pay to interpersonal distance—to the ways individuals / characters approach, interact with, or avoid one another—unworks these communities from the inside, exposing their flaws and their necessary impossibility.

Comment vivre ensemble: The Community of *Délicatesse*

"A somewhat provocative word today," says Barthes about *délicatesse*; no less intriguing is its source in a passage featuring the Marquis de Sade from his previous book, *Sade Fourier Loyola*. Writing that text, Barthes was well aware that the perverse libertine de Sade would seem out of place in the venerable company of the other two figures; but what did bring them together, he claimed, was their incontestable merits as "logothetes," founders of language. In the spirit bequeathed by de Sade, part of the freedom Barthes arrogates himself in the lectures is to ground each course in a personal fantasy (*phantasme*), and to imagine himself "mining it in the open, like a quarry." In *Comment vivre ensemble* and *Le neutre*, the idea of fantasy itself relates to the capacity to distinguish fine nuances, making and savoring them in the slippery alleys of language. The original passage from *Sade Fourier Loyola*, which made its way into *Comment vivre ensemble* and *Le neutre*, reads:

> La marquise de Sade ayant demandé au marquis prisonnier de lui faire remettre son linge sale (connaissant la marquise: à quelle autre fin sinon le faire laver?), Sade feint d'y voir un tout autre motif, proprement sadien: "Charmante créature, vous voulez mon linge sale, mon vieux linge? Savez-vous que c'est d'une délicatesse achevée? Vous voyez comme je sens le prix des choses. Ecoutez, mon ange, j'ai toute l'envie du monde de vous satisfaire cela, car vous savez que je respecte les goûts, les fantaisies: quelques baroques qu'elles soient, je les trouve toutes respectables, et parce qu'on n'en est pas le maître, et parce que la plus singulière et la plus bizarre de toutes, bien analysée, remonte toujours à un principe de délicatesse."[7]

> The marquise de Sade had asked the imprisoned marquis to hand her his dirty linen (knowing the marquise: obviously to wash it, what else?), but Sade pretends to see there a rather different reason, a typically Sadian one: "Charming creature, you want my dirty linen, my old underwear? Do you know it's of an exquisite delicacy? You see how I appreciate the value of things. Listen, my angel, by all means, I want to satisfy your desire; you know that I respect all tastes, all fantasies: however baroque, I find them all respectable, both because one cannot master them, and because even the strangest and most eccentric of all, well analyzed, has its origin in a principle of delicacy."

In Barthes's account, de Sade's enunciation is itself illustrative of the principle of *délicatesse*: "Delight (*jouissance*) of analysis, a verbal operation which frustrates the expectation (the dirty laundry that needs to be washed) and conveys that delicacy is a perversion relying on the useless detail" (*N*, 58). The image of de Sade imprisoned, yet incorrigible in his perverse delights, both explains and confuses, or at least complicates, the word that helped crystallize Barthes's own phantasm of living-with-others. And this is precisely the trouble, one might note in passing, with Barthes's refusal to pin down exact meanings and his preference for examples: Each of them goes beyond the limits of a possible definition, and thus leads astray the disciple/reader who focuses too closely (tactlessly?) on just one illustration. De Sade's example speaks eloquently, which is to say, disturbingly, to the logic of the residual supplement of *délicatesse*. Here is, first of all, what Barthes calls a *fantasy*: "un retour de désirs, d'images, qui rôdent, se cherchent en vous, parfois toute une vie, et souvent ne se cristallisent qu'à travers *un mot*" (a return of images, of desires, that prowl, wander about in yourself, sometimes a lifetime, and sometimes they only crystallize in the encounter with a word) (*CVE*, 36). The word that the image of the marquis complicates is *idiorrythmie*, a combination of *idio* (individual) and *rhutmos* (oppressive rhythms of society, of a group) that Barthes lifts from Jacques Lacarrière's *L'été grec* and refashions for his own purposes. Originally, *rhutmos* was linked to a personal rhythm, a supple, mobile form, a changing pattern: *idiorrythmie* would have been a pleonasm, Barthes explains, if rhythm had not acquired the oppressive connotations of power inherent to collective life (*CVE*, 36–39). (The de Sade case—his eccentricities in the boudoir, his confinement in the Bastille—incidentally illustrates both the initial excess of the juxtaposition *idio-rhutmos* and the frictions of *idiorrythmie*.) Barthes's thinking about the ideal community conjoins thus the spatial metaphor of distance with the dynamic qualities of rhythm, and the challenge to synchronize multiple rhythms. This can result in oppressive *dysrhythmie*: "Le pouvoir, sa subtilité—passe par la dysrythmie, l'hétérorythmie—c'est en mettant ensemble deux rythmes différents que l'on crée de profondes disturbances" (Power, its subtlety—goes through dysrythmie, heterorhythmy—it is by bringing together different rhythms that one generates great disturbances) (*CVE*, 69; Foucault is mentioned here). The opposite of *dysrhythmy* is the utopia of *idiorrhythmy*, which Barthes's reader might link, encouraged by the adverb "ensemble" in the original course title, to the attunement of music instruments and their performance as an ensemble. Barthes rather likes this word, I suspect, for its connotations with music and dance (he mentions its Latin etymology, *insimul*, "at the same time"), hence the use throughout his course notes of the capitalized hyphenated *Vivre-Ensemble* as a compound noun, which stresses precisely the dynamism (*vivre*) of collective life, the necessary attunement.[8]

Following the distinctions drawn by Lacarrière in his Greek travelogue, idiorrythmic communities were groups that compromised between eremitism (total seclusion) and coenobitism (integrative sociality).[9] Barthes thus found in *idiorrythmie* a signifier for his personal phantasm, the Sovereign Good (le Souverain Bien) of living with others in a way that allows the individual to insert himself harmoniously in the life of the group. Ultimately, as Claude Coste remarks, Barthes identified with this notion all enterprises that attempt to reconcile individual and collective life, the autonomy of a subject and the ties of sociability:[10] "quelque chose comme une solitude interrompue de façon réglée: le paradoxe, la contradiction, l'aporie d'une mise en commun des distances—l'utopie d'un socialisme des distances" (something like a solitude interrupted in a preset manner: the paradox, the contradiction, the aporia of a conjoining of distances—the utopia of a socialism of distances) (*CVE*, 40). Notably, Barthes thinks of *idiorrythmie* not only as a category of time (the challenge of synchronizing different rhythms), but also, as his subtitle suggests, one of space charged with symbolic meaning. His eclectic use of sources is here most unexpected: Ethology teaches us, he reminds for instance, that even the most gregarious species of animals regulate interindividual distance. "Ostensibly this is the most important problem of living-with-others: finding and regulating the critical distance, beyond or below which a crisis is imminent."[11] It is not, however, Schopenhauer's porcupines who inspire him most, but Nietzsche. The following excerpt, a lengthier one, but I think illuminating, is quite typical in its idiosyncratic sampling (musical, one might say) of ideas:

> La distance comme valeur. Cela ne doit pas être pris dans la perspective mesquine du simple quant-à-soi. Nietzsche fait de la distance une valeur forte—une valeur rare: "l'abîme entre homme et homme, entre une classe et une autre, la multiplicité des types, la volonté d'être soi, de se distinguer, ce que j'appelle le pathos des distances est le propre de toutes les époques fortes" (*Le crépuscule des idoles*, 107) La tension utopique—qui gît dans le fantasme idiorrythmique—vient de ceci: ce qui est désiré, c'est une distance qui ne casse pas l'affect ("pathos des distances": excellente expression). Quadrature du cercle, pierre philosophale, grande vision claire de l'utopie (*hupar*);[12] une distance pénétrée, irriguée de tendresse: un *pathos*[13] où entrerait de l'*Eros* et de la *Sophia*[14] (grand rêve clair). (*CVE*, 179–180)

> Distance as a value. That should not be taken in the petty perspective of self-containment. Nietzsche makes of distance a strong value, a rare value: "the abyss between man and man, class and class, the plurality of types, the will to be oneself, to stand out—what I call the pathos of distances, that is characteristic of every strong age" (*Twilight of the Idols*) The utopian tension—which lies in the phantasm of idiorrythmie—comes from the fact that what is desired is a distance that does not break the affect ("pathos of distances": excellent formulation). Squared circle, the philosopher's stone, grand luminous vision of utopia (hupar); a distance suffused with tenderness: a pathos conjoining Eros and Sophia (a transparent dream).

The short quote from Nietzsche's *Twilight of the Idols* takes us on a path that Barthes only vaguely gestures toward in *Comment vivre ensemble*, but that his 1975 autobiography allows us to explore further. The reader familiar with this text will suspect that there is more to the desire for distance than "a contemporary problem," as Barthes claims; doesn't there lurk, rather, or also, a more personal nostalgia? In *Roland Barthes par Roland Barthes*, another text organized around traits (*biographèmes*), he wonders ingenuously whether one might not be able to enjoy the charms of the *art de vivre* bourgeois in a socialist society, as one would enjoy an exoticism: This is what he would call a "contretemps" (64). This gaze backward brings him close to another nostalgic intellectual, Adorno, whose *Minima Moralia*, as we have seen in the introduction, lingers in the moment just before the bourgeoisie's presumed demise, in an unselfconscious attempt to lift from its *art de vivre* a certain sensitivity to the singularity of the individual.

Given the times, Barthes realizes the anachronism of his sympathetic understanding of the aristocratic desire for distance. In the middle of the passage above, just after the quote from Nietzsche, he therefore marks a leap—an arrow connects the two halves of the paragraph, not through logical deduction, but following blithely a more unexpected line of flight. Nietzsche serves here both as a model of interpretative freedom and as the source of an appealing formulation that Barthes rewrites by breaking the "pathos of distances" into affect and distance, and thus injecting something that is famously absent from the *Genealogy of Morals*, namely communal ties valued explicitly in a positive manner.[15] It is this reformulation that makes possible recasting Barthes's phantasm in close proximity to Murdoch's *The Bell*: the community that conjoins the distance respectful of distinction *and* a certain affect among its constitutive members is composed of a select number of individuals whose involvements are governed by the principles of *délicatesse*. As the passage quoted above suggests, *délicatesse* as distance suggests a field of tension between two poles: closeness (*Eros*) and remoteness/detachment (*Sophia*); the tension, as in a magnetic field, is felt at any given point between the two poles. All this, Barthes anticipated, ought to be not just the stuff of fantasy, but also that of a story, as the title of his later course, *La préparation du roman*, suggests.

Although every now and then Barthes encouraged the rumor that he entertained the project of writing a novel, and also took some distance from himself in the autobiography by prefacing it with the disclaimer that "everything should be read as if uttered by a character in a novel," he never wrote one. Toward the conclusion of *Comment vivre ensemble*, he acknowledges that he had often felt like writing a "domestic utopia" or, rather, "the figurative quest of the Sovereign Good concerning living [*l'habiter*]":

> le Souverain Bien—sa figuration—mobilise toute l'extension et la profondeur du sujet, dans son individuation, c'est-à-dire dans son histoire personnelle au complet. De cela, seule pourrait rendre compte une écriture—ou si l'on préfère un acte romanesque (sinon

> un roman). Seule l'écriture peut recueillir l'extrême subjectivité, car dans l'écriture il y a accord entre l'indirect de l'expression et la vérité du sujet—accord impossible au plan de la parole (donc du cours), qui est toujours, quoi qu'on veuille, à la fois directe et théâtrale. (*CVE*, 177–178)

> The Sovereign Good—its figuration—mobilizes the whole extension and depth of the subject in its individuation, that is, in its personal history. Only writing could render an account of that, or, if one prefers, a novelistic act (or even a novel). Only writing can take in extremes of subjectivity, because in writing there is accord between the indirectness of expression and the truth of the subject—an accord which is impossible in speech (therefore in class), because the latter is always direct and theatrical, whatever one does.

A novel requires a full display of subjectivity, since in writing—his first book suggests as much—there is full accord between the in-directness of expression and the truth of the subject. As the idiosyncratic autobiography of 1975 intimates however, full display of the self—be it in a mode of indirection—would be a failure of *délicatesse*. This is his excuse for now, there will be others; in fact, as we shall see, the last course, significantly titled *La préparation du roman*, is all about what gets in the way of writing a novel, what makes the writing of the novel impossible, from one's own predilection for the discontinuous, the epiphanic, the fragmentary, to the impossible desire for the absolute book—Mallarmé's *Livre*, Proust's novel of someone desiring to write—which is ultimately too overwhelming a passion for literature as the source of a desire for language and for an anchor in an intense present.

Roland Barthes, a character in search of a novel, already at the end of *Comment vivre ensemble*. Perhaps in the form Barthes had sketched it out in the 1976 course, it had already been written in England in 1958 by an uncommonly imaginative philosopher? The model he outlined in *Comment vivre ensemble*—a community navigating the everyday "in solitude with regular interruptions," cautious to live at the right distance from one another—sketches quite well the framework of Iris Murdoch's *The Bell*. And the passage that comes closest to a positive definition of *délicatesse* in his course would be a most suggestive epigraph to her novel:

> Délicatesse voudrait dire: distance et égard, absence de poids dans la relation, et, cependant, chaleur vive de cette relation. Le principe en serait: ne pas manier l'autre, les autres, ne pas manipuler, renoncer activement aux images (des uns, des autres), éviter tout ce qui peut alimenter l'imaginaire de la relation. = Utopie proprement dite, car forme du Souverain Bien. (*CVE*, 179–180)

> Delicacy would mean: distance and regard, absence of weight in the relationship, but also lively warmth of this relationship. Its principle would be: not to manipulate the other, the others, not to deceive, actively give up the imaginary of the relationship. = A utopia in the proper sense of the word, a form of the Sovereign Good.

Neither in the World nor Out of It: Moral Dilemmas in Iris Murdoch's *The Bell*

If the language of ethics is only one among many in Barthes's course—the more desires, the more languages one needs, he quips—it is the vocabulary of predilection in *The Bell*, a moral philosopher's novel. Like Barthes, who contrasts the indifference of a highly politicized society with the community respectful of its members' singularity, Murdoch has her characters form a community driven by a shared discontent with a world in which an ethical life is difficult to sustain. Their spiritual aspiration is at odds with the political subjects that are desirable in "present-day society, with its hurried pace and its mechanical and technical structure," the Abbess explains; they are "a kind of sick people whose desire for God makes them unsatisfactory citizens of ordinary life, but whose strength or temperament fails them to surrender the world completely."[16] If the causes of the discontent with society are rather vague in *The Bell*—the spiritual leader of Imber Abbey simply recognizes that the world "offers no home to these unhappy souls"—the philosophical *Zeitdiagnose* Murdoch formulates in her essays could not detail more aptly her characters' disenchantment. She writes, for instance, in "Against Dryness" (1961):

> We live in a scientific and anti-metaphysical age in which the dogmas, images, and precepts of religion have lost much of their power. We have not recovered from two wars and the experience of Hitler. We are also the heirs of the Enlightenment, Romanticism, and the Liberal tradition. These are the elements of our dilemma: whose chief feature, in my view, is that we have been left with far too shallow and flimsy an idea of human personality.[17]

It is significant that Murdoch sets out to think through a more complex notion of personality in a novel about community: the personality that she seeks to reimagine will not mark a return to the old notion of the subject, but will have to emerge from the difficult experience of socialization with others, from the practice of a communal life in which the right distance between oneself and others—as we shall see, Barthes's formulation is relevant here—will have to remain permanently open to (re)negotiation.

The choice of the community as an environment that would offer a corrective to the alienating life outside also speaks to the views Murdoch held about the indirect ways in which a good writer deals with social reality: alluding to Sartre, she emphasized her belief that a good novelist should "not worry about social commitment," because just "working well and honestly, and only saying what he knows and what he understands, will in fact tell a lot of important truths about his society."[18] In *The Bell*, it is the spiritual leader of Imber Abbey who initiates the project of the community: echoing the postwar leitmotif of the spiritual, and often physical, homelessness of many individuals, the Abbess welcomes them and encourages them to form "a permanent lay community attached to the Abbey, a 'buffer state' . . . between the Abbey and the world, a reflection, a benevolent and useful parasite, an intermediary form of life" (*B*, 71). The *life-diet* of the community—Barthes would characterize it as "a solitude interrupted in an organized manner"—combines collective activities such as prayer, meals, gardening, classical music concerts played on the gramophone, and time for individual pursuits. Their aim is stated by James as he introduces Toby, a young visitor, to the life of the community: to restore dignity to life and work through a semi-retired life of work and prayer. That the Abbess refers to the lay community as a "buffer *state*," and of its members as "unsatisfactory *citizens*" in the world outside, suggests that they are—albeit under the subtle guidance of the Abbess who remains invisible, yet omniscient, in the monastic enclosure across the lake—responsible for fashioning a more sustainable, spiritually fulfilling communal life. This is the farthest Murdoch goes in her fictional articulation of the problems that beleaguer her contemporaries, as well as in imagining a way out in the self-legislating community projected in *The Bell*. We find here an echo of Adorno's own diagnosis of the institutions of late modern society, which have espoused the logic of rationalization of capitalism and are therefore at odds with individual well-being and with the possibility of an ethical life. Once the idea of society is compromised, only a smaller community—Barthes suggests eight to ten members, and Murdoch seems to agree with this number—might be conceivable, a community that would negotiate its own mode of communal life. As MacIntyre has pointed out in *After Virtue*, such a sociopolitical community offers the opportunity to reiterate a question put forward by Australian philosopher John Anderson: not "What end or purpose does it serve?" but, rather, "Of what conflicts is it the scene?"[19] This means shifting attention from the teleology of the community (thus from the main plot, and relatedly, from action, whose centrality in moral philosophy Murdoch disputes) onto the tensions generated by the absence of a foundation of governing principles. The lack of a coherent moral system, MacIntyre explains, makes a question like Anderson's inevitable: the work of the contemporary philosopher is to analyze the configuration of (often conflicting) bribes of moral traditions that are preserved and coexist at a given moment in the moral fabric of social life. Murdoch, philosopher and novelist, understood her task in this sense—she offered a full-fledged critique of the philosophical traditions with which she was contemporary—and dramatized in *The Bell* the conflicts between opposed moral views in the community negotiating its daily existence at Imber Court.

MacIntyre's point about the anachronism of such a self-legislating community in a modern liberal individualist world is corroborated by the scant attention critics have paid to the centrality of the community in *The Bell*. Much of the critical literature on *The Bell* has analyzed the plot that drives the story of the eponymous bell and its symbolism, as well as the philosophical ideas underwriting it, but attention to the centrality of the community in the novel has been mostly dismissive of its efforts.[20] Obviously, it is impossible to speak about the community and its tribulations without looking at the dealings and interactions of its members, all the more so since, as A. S. Byatt pointed out in her nuanced reading of *The Bell* in *Degrees of Freedom*, "here we have a novel which has the solid life that Miss Murdoch praises in the great nineteenth-century novels":[21] the characters are both fully developed and free, they seem to be in possession of their destinies and we come to care about them, perhaps even wonder what their individual lives will be like after the community disbands. But it is important to approach them from some distance, and understand their situation in the larger framework. To go back to Anderson's question: it is useful in that it prompts an examination of the community as the scene of a threefold conflict: practical (economic and political), philosophical (moral), and interpersonal (ethical). The first two, Murdoch seems to suggest, can be discussed, negotiated, agreed upon, compromised on (the small size of the community and the commitment of its members to it are no doubt important); some issues are often taken up only to be suspended indefinitely or postponed yet again, proof that Murdoch does not idealize the capaciousness of open conversation (or what we might call the "public sphere" and its attending principle of rationality). What is truly difficult, it turns out, is maintaining an equilibrium in the realm of personal relationships and interactions, to practice what we have begun to call here, with Barthes, communal living as an art of distances. Murdoch ends up leaving in the background of the story the philosophical and practical disagreements in order to allow the aspects that really threaten the community's life-diet, its very texture, to reveal themselves in their complexity. And this speaks to Murdoch's conviction that even if moral philosophy broadens its field and vocabulary, it is literature that truly cultivates the "nostalgia for the particular" that enables us to explore the multifaceted reality of human experience.

If, from the perspective of the Abbey, the lay community acts as a "buffer state," this intermediary position is experienced by its members as perviousness both to the spiritual vibes emanating from the monastic enclosure, itself impenetrable, and to the intrusions (hence potential disturbances) of the outside world, typically occasioned by short- or long-term visitors or by some members' short trips. This position helps illustrate what her philosophical essays discuss explicitly, namely that in Iris Murdoch's moral framework there is room not only for general moral principles and rules, but also for belief, intuition, spiritual energy channeled by prayer, the contemplation of nature and art; and that she does not shy away from facing and trying to understand what occurs in the confrontation between different worldviews, conflicting positions, ideas, and habits, not only among various individuals but also within the personal world of a character. The community in *The Bell* is an ideal setting for such an investigation, especially because its members deliberate and make decisions about the kind of communal life they want to have in the absence of a founding dogma. While it is true that a Christian background is already in place and to some extent taken for granted as a basis for finding solutions to conflicts, discussions reveal that the members do not understand its principles in the same way; moreover, in their debates some blind spots of Christianity itself are brought to light. The community proves indeed to be the scene of difficult conflict: Is the shooting of animals acceptable in a community that prides itself on respecting creation and peaceful coexistence of all God's creatures, especially when the vegetarianism of some of the members implies a heartfelt protestation against the cruel treatment of animals? If the community's avowed aim is to "restore dignity to work," is technology a way of increasing productivity and thus to make more of what is already given, augment God's gifts, or is it an unwelcome interference, compromised by capitalist structures outside? How should the division of labor be optimally planned, and why are some of the members overworked while others have a less enthusiastic relationship to labor or a more leisurely attitude to a *vita activa*? But then how does one determine the roles of each member and make sure they are adequately fulfilled, without replicating the oppressive hierarchies and structures of retribution and punishment outside? And what should the relationship to the outside world be, especially when the community cannot (yet) support itself financially, but would like to become independent (how else, if not by increasing productivity, or by taking up crafts?), and eventually encourage other individuals to join in? In the weekly debates about various aspects of their life together, temporary, and often surprising, alliances are made and unmade in the process of voting: James, one of the characters who have internalized most profoundly the Christian ethos, is for instance on the same page with the otherwise problematic character Nick on the subject of shooting as a pastime, at odds with the rest of the community who would rather not have guns at Imber; yet, somewhat surprisingly, he is also against the acquisition of a mechanical cultivator which would compromise the desired simplicity of their life, but which, in Michael's view, would alleviate the unnecessary burden carried by the community in their attempt to produce their own food. Although such discussions, often tense, form a significant background to the plot of the novel (the richness of detail makes one wonder if to speak of plot is to do justice to the complex texture of Murdoch's narrative), they are the stuff of everyday life and thus ultimately negotiable: it goes through critical moments, but does not lead to irresolvable crisis.

Such a crisis comes rather from the realm of the ethical, of divergent moral views, and ultimately from the subtler distances that mark interpersonal relationships. The tensions to which the reader is made privy portray Imber Court as a scene of conflict between two major moral positions, the "faint appearance of two parties" disrupting the image of a "peaceful and reasonably efficient" arrangement (*B*, 75–76). The tension, explored in great detail by Murdoch, is between a morality of uncompromising rules (a Kantian morality, one might say), and an ethic informed by the complexity of human nature, by its fallen character. The clearest formulation of these two contradictory positions appears in the two sermons, James's (chapter 9) and Michael's (chapter 16), both putting forth the arch-theme of the novel: "the chief requirement of the good life . . ." As the object of a philosophical quest, this requirement hovers uncertainly between "liv[ing] with no image of oneself" (*B*, 119), as James proclaims, and "hav[ing] a clear knowledge of one's capacities" (*B*, 185), as Michael pleads. The former view requires one to do the best thing imaginable with no provisos, the latter, to do the second best thing, if that is what one's spiritual level realistically allows.

The student of Murdoch's moral philosophy will readily see in the significant differences between James's and Michael's perspectives the fictional treatment of a tension that she systematically analyzed in her essays between the two philosophical traditions that dominated the 1950s, linguistic analytic philosophy (to which she often refers as "the current view at Oxford") and Sartrian existentialism (which she took a serious interest in, as her early book *Sartre Romantic Rationalist* suggests).[22] Two terms encapsulate the charges she brings to these two traditions: *convention* (the loss of the individual in a larger social totality, the alienation, I might add, that Barthes feared in the experience of the social) and *neurosis* (the tendency to fabricate self-absorbed myths or fantasies that obscure the reality of others, or Barthes's solipsism).[23] In a very brief summary, Murdoch's critique rests on an opposition between the followers of Kant, whose typical hero is in her account Ordinary Language Man (in England, from Locke and Hume to linguistic analytic philosophy), and the followers of Hegel (all the way to Kierkegaard and Sartre) whose representative is Totalitarian Man. Thus the "contemporary view at Oxford," her essays suggest, provides a picture of man that she characterizes as conventional, behavioristic, and liberal: Ordinary Language Man is surrounded not by empirical others but by civilized society, subject to its rules and judgments, all part of the network of ordinary language, that is, of moral conceptual activity at its most universally accepted level; what matters is the reasoned choice, and actions are commendable and intelligible only on a background defined by staple notions such as the good, choice and will.[24] *On the current view*, she charges, "freedom is conceived as the freedom of overt choice, and there is a corresponding lack of interest in differences of belief. Moral language is taken closely related to choice—that it recommends to action is its defining characteristic—and all this can then be offered as an analysis of the meaning of the word "good." "This is good" equals 'choose this.' "[25] Cautiously setting apart Wittgenstein's *Philosophical Investigations*, marked by "a peculiar reticence" on the subject of the inner life, Murdoch aims her critique at other analytic philosophers like Hampshire, Hare, Ayer, Ryle, who "have hastened to draw further and more dubious moral and psychological conclusions," excluding the mental life from morality as irrelevant. To these, Murdoch opposes the view that "there are lots and lots of objects, more or less easily identified, in orbit as it were in inner space," that it is "not silent and dark within," and that such a rich dimension of human experience is surely most significant.[26]

On the other hand, the hero of existentialism is in Murdoch's account "a clear-cut piece of drama": modeled on Hegel's solitary consciousness, Sartre's man abhors the contingent or accidental, sees other individuals not as separate others but as menacing extensions of his own consciousness, and lives "like a neurotic who seeks to cure himself unfolding a myth about himself."[27] Sartrian existentialism, she charged both in her book on Sartre and in many of her essays, posits an empty notion of freedom from which the inner world of deliberation is absent, and offers no account of relations between the individual and his fellow human beings, suffering from a paucity of imagining meaningful forms of sociality and therefore falling into solipsism.

In sum then, "convention and neurosis, the two enemies of understanding, one might say the *enemies of love*; and how difficult it is in the modern world to escape from one without invoking the help of the other." Although set in opposition, the two traditions suffer ultimately from some of the same ills:

> Existentialism shares with empiricism a terror of anything which encloses the agent or threatens his supremacy as a centre of significance. In this sense both philosophies tend toward solipsism. Neither pictures virtue as concerned with anything real outside ourselves. Neither provides us with a standpoint for considering real human beings in their variety, and neither presents us with any technique for exploring and controlling our own spiritual energy. Ordinary Language Man is too abstract, too conventional: he incarnates the commonest and vaguest network of conventional moral thought; and Totalitarian Man is too concrete, too neurotic: he is simply the centre of extreme decision, man stripped and made anonymous by extremity.[28]

How does Murdoch propose to transcend such unsatisfying alternatives? First of all, she insists on broadening the field of moral investigation beyond a notion of freedom obsessed with choice and action, toward a richer understanding of experience that would have to include the mental life; as a corollary, the vocabulary of moral discourse would be expanded to include a variety of moral terms, descriptive and nuanced:

> Our freedom is not just a freedom to choose and act differently, it is also a freedom to think and believe differently, to see different configurations and describe them in different words. Moral differences can be differences of concept as well as differences of choice. A moral change shows in our vocabulary. How we see and describe the world is morals too—and the relation of this to our conduct may be complicated.[29]

Literature, Murdoch believed, was well equipped to take over some of the tasks formerly performed by philosophy: it had the means to delve into the psychology of characters, to show, for instance, the moral significance of the mental processes that precede decision; most significantly, to convey the reality of other persons, which was, she emphasized, the quintessential task of the novelist.

In this sense, the very first scenes in *The Bell* offer both a foreshadowing and a lesson in reading. We meet Dora Greenfield, who is returning to her husband. Happy neither with nor without him, she is torn between the image of herself as a spontaneous creature living in the moment and for whom "the past was never real," and a morality of rules, which dictates that she *ought to* stay with him and submit to his rigid impositions. But the novel is quick to discourage such facile philosophical diagnoses: after a momentary and dismayed realization that two fellow travelers were also going to Imber (they turn out to be James, one of the leaders, and Toby, a young visitor), Dora becomes oblivious to her surroundings and kneels down to rescue a butterfly, worried that someone in the crowded compartment might step on it on their way out. This distraction makes her forget her suitcases on the train, provoking her husband's anger: he had anticipated using in his research at the Abbey the notebooks that Dora was bringing from his London apartment, and he makes no effort to conceal his frustration, thus adding a note of bitterness to their already awkward reunion. Dora's delicacy is to him only irresponsible, foolish extravagance, and the ecstatic moment of the butterfly's release does nothing to atone for her inadequacies. The contrast between these two perspectives opens up the repertoire of *délicatesse* that Barthes explores in his thematic dictionary in *Comment vivre ensemble*, a repertoire that bears on the interpersonal relationships that the characters in *The Bell* navigate daily. Murdoch's rich exploration of the vagaries of thought and desire messing up the neatness of clearly articulated moral principles is thus inaugurated with a symbolic image: "holding the wrists together and opening the palms like a flower. The brilliantly coloured butterfly emerged. It circled round them for a moment and then fluttered across the sunlit platform and flew away into the distance" (*B*, 18). This inaugural moment, registering a movement away from one's concrete circumstances into undefined distance, anticipates, it seems to me, what the Imber community is about: pondering the separation between self and the endless difference of others. It also speaks to a rich cluster of themes that are central to Murdoch's thought, both dramatized in the novel and systematically explored in her philosophical essays: what happens when the strange, unexpected occurrences of everyday life, one's attachments and idiosyncratic hierarchies of value put ill at ease the "ought" of a morality of rules, when one takes seriously—in Murdoch's words—"the inexhaustible detail of the world, the endlessness of the task of understanding, the importance of not assuming that one has got individuals and situations 'taped,' the connection of knowledge with love and of spiritual insight with apprehension of the unique."[30] The flight of the butterfly is also a moment of beauty, which has everyone momentarily forget themselves and look outside, in an ecstatic contemplation of something other that has a reality of its own; a gesture that negates thoughts of possession, seizing, incorporation: this is, Murdoch points out in an essay, one of the lessons of beauty: the alterity of the world is there to be contemplated rather than destroyed. It is no coincidence that in this early scene already, Dora walks away from James, the upholder of the morality of rules. The other two points of view from which the story is narrated, Toby's and Michael's, suggest that Murdoch herself believes that such a morality does not adequately address the difficulties a community is likely to experience, the tensions inherent to living with others, the hesitations, dilemmas, desires, and apprehensions with which people approach one another. Significantly, the only time James gets a direct hearing is when he gives his sermon in chapter 9; but even then, his stern exhortations are in counterpoint with Dora's mental vagaries, as she keeps tuning out. It is as if Murdoch were intent on illustrating that his stern moral outlook, of which we do not get full hearing because we keep "tuning out" with Dora, simply does not apply to everyone. Similarly, Toby joins the community for the summer before going to Cambridge for his engineering studies, equipped with noble ideals of a simple, virtuous, hard-working life, ideals bearing the mark of what Murdoch would call a rather puritanical and austere, self-righteous liberal mentality. Both James and Toby will be challenged to broaden their understanding of human nature in the encounter with Michael, who at a certain point in the novel reflects:

> James was certainly no connoisseur of evil; a result perhaps of a considerable pureness of heart. Could one recognize refinements of good if one did not recognize refinements of evil, Michael asked himself. He concluded provisionally that what was required of one was to *be* good, a task which usually presented a singularly simple though steep face, and not to recognize its refinements. There he left the matter, having no time for philosophical speculation. (*B*, 104–105)

If James and Mrs. Mark pull the community, ideologically speaking, toward the sphere of uncompromising religious faith and rigid moral values, Michael and Dora come and go, remaining connected to the outside world: Dora goes to London (just for a dance, it turns out, and a short visit at the National Gallery of Art), while Michael takes young Toby on a trip to buy a mechanical cultivator (the acquisition of which is resisted by James, attached to the idea of manual work). The outside world of temptations becomes however more concrete, therefore potentially more disturbing, when Nick, a rather insolent young man (the brother of Catherine, a community member soon to enter the Abbey), comes to Imber and is offered a place to live indefinitely. To be sure, he does not become a full member of the community; he lives across the lake, and remains throughout the novel what we might call with Barthes an "integrated reject," the excluded that the community carefully includes as a way to inoculate itself against unexpected contamination.[31] The trouble is that by (begrudgingly) accepting to take Nick in because he is Catherine's sibling, the community also inadvertently lets in unresolved conflicts from the past.

The story of the past relationship between Michael and Nick remains unknown to the other members of the community: when Nick was a fourteen-year-old boy, an ambiguous relationship developed between him and his then-teacher, Michael; for undisclosed reasons, Nick brought their emotionally charged meetings to an abrupt end by confessing "everything," apparently more than actually happened, to the school principal, after which he disappeared from Michael's life, leaving him frustrated not only in his romantic, but also in his professional aspirations. After fourteen years: Michael has founded the community at Imber Court, in which, as Mrs. Mark emphasizes, the practice of "a little austerity" involves severing oneself from one's past, both the source of undesirable "images of oneself," and, when shared with others, the object of potentially malicious curiosity. Nick coming to Imber has the uncanny quality of a return of the repressed, evidence that the past, the self, contingency, cannot be bracketed out. For people like Michael, the importance James attaches to the idea of "a cloistered virtue" is unrealistic. Although still equally thrilled and obfuscated by the past episode with Nick, Michael avoids encounters and conversations with him, focusing his attention on Toby, the young visitor to whom he feels attracted, all the while convincing himself of his potential role as Toby's mentor, role which might provide a new "pattern" to his life. As James's foil, Michael is an "existentialist" hero, deeply engrossed in a myth about his life, pursuing a "pattern" which he rarely loses from view. This proves to be, as Murdoch shows in her philosophical essays, one of the "enemies of love."

Michael's attraction to young boys, homosociality threatening to become homoeroticism, the weight given by Murdoch to the emotional charge of gestures, amplified in the self-indulgences of the imagination—all these chime in with Barthes's elaborations on distance and *délicatesse*. If Barthes only lifted from various cultural and literary sources fascinating examples of distance, wishing he had been able to write a novel in which to explore its nuances, these examples make wonderful companions to moments in Murdoch's story, scintillating their insights onto the difficulties of an ethical community. The linchpin between *Comment vivre ensemble* and *The Bell* is the figure of the lover, capable of the most exquisite delicacy toward the object of his or her affection. In Murdoch's later philosophical essays, looking at someone else (as if) through the eyes of love is the epitome of ethical behavior, elevated to the rank of a moral ideal. Michael's story thus allows us to place love on a continuum with Barthes's *délicatesse*, and to show eventually how, in her scenario, this emotion gives depth to the elusive formulations under the heading *délicatesse* in *Comment vivre ensemble*. Michael's tribulations engage, from beginning to end, the theme of *délicatesse* in all its richness and contradictions—as a "social obscene" (*l'obscène social*, with which Barthes refers to its association with homosexuality, hence its provocative potential), as tact verging on, then sliding into avoidance and powerlessness, finally as erotic love confusing images of the self with wisdom. Juxtaposing a few brief excerpts from Barthes's and Murdoch's texts will shed light on this trajectory.

"Delicacy as a social obscene," writes Barthes, "falls under the indictement of preciosity: 1) condemnation, in the name of virility, of the delicate (*delicatus* = effeminate), of the effete, crisscrossed by a manly image of the empirical: what is futile is feminine 2) principle of delicacy—has to do with a kind of social erring, taking on the excessive margin" (*N*, 64). Such indictments occur in the novel twice, the first coming from Toby, who contrasts James's impressive "masculine vitality and Christian candour" (38) and Michael's disappointing appearance: "There was something tired and weedy about him, he lacked the conspicuously manly look of James, and was not so obviously a leader" (*B*, 40). The second is voiced by James, whose firm moral principles leave no room for such "deviations" as homosexuality or human frailty; unaware of Michael's sexual orientation, he indirectly condemns it by rehearsing the social stereotypes that Nick's persona inspires: "'He looks to me like a pansy,' [James] said to Michael, soon after Nick's arrival. 'I didn't like to say so before, but I had heard it about him in London. They're always trouble-makers, believe me. I've seen plenty of that type" (*B*, 104). Both Barthes and Murdoch are well aware that in each of these cases, the admiration or condemnation is a matter of perspective. Admiration, sympathy, love—they can illustrate the principle of delicacy only "if the social does not cast it abusively in a preciosity/coarseness paradigm: one can only speak of preciosity from the perspective of coarseness" (*N*, 65). This proviso recalls the moment in *The Bell* when Dora and Michael, walking through the forest, suddenly catch a glimpse of Toby bathing:

> Dora saw at once, saw sooner than her recognition, that except for his sun hat Toby was quite naked. (*B*, 66)

> Michael's face, as she now saw, was indeed troubled as he still looked upon the boy. Then he turned quietly about, and touching Dora's arm led her noiselessly back along the path by which they had come. Toby was not disturbed. All this seemed to Dora to show a foolish delicacy. (*B*, 67)

The most exquisite forms of delicacy are only intelligible from a perspective of openness to their possibility, from placing oneself—if one isn't already—within the field of vision of someone in love, proposes Murdoch.[32] The entry "délicatesse" in Barthes's *A Lover's Discourse*, where it is illustrated with an anecdote from Van Gulik's *La vie sexuelle dans la Chine ancienne*, suggestively intimates a similar idea:

> The last Han emperor (6–1 B.C.) had a number of young lovers, of which the most famous was a certain Tong Hsien. One day, as the emperor was sharing his bed with this Tong Hsien, the latter fell asleep laying on the emperor's sleeve. When the emperor was called for a public audience, he took his sword and cut his sleeve, lest he should trouble the sleep of his favorite. Hence the term *toan-hsieo*, "cutting the sleeve," which became the literary expression for masculine sexuality.[33]

Coincidentally, this anecdote has a suggestive echo in Murdoch's novel:

> [Toby] slumped quietly sideways and Michael could feel his weight against him. The boy's head descended gently on to his shoulder. Michael drove on in a dream. . . . He tried to breathe more quietly so as not to disturb the boy, and found that he was taking long deep breaths. . . . He was afraid his heart-beat alone might wake the sleeper. . . . That Toby should just go on sleeping seemed the most desirable thing in the world. Michael felt an ecstasy of protective joy. (*B*, 141)

This scene—suffused with tenderness—precedes the kiss that triggers the crisis of the novel. A kiss, that is, a momentary forgetting of the *critical* distance: "As Michael contemplated that tiny distance between the thought and the act it was like a most narrow crack which even as he watched it was opening into an abyss" (*B*, 149). And this occurred in a moment when his lucidity was weakened by the aggrandized image of himself, under the influence of Toby's confessed admiration for him.[34] In other words, Michael illustrates here the consequence of not following the "chief requirement of the good life" in James's formulation (that is, not living with an image of oneself), reiterated in *Comment vivre ensemble* as "not managing the other, the others, not manipulating, actively giving up images (of everyone involved)" (179).

The unwritten principles that Michael breaks here are what Barthes highlights as the "rules of distance" (*règles de distance*) specific to certain monastic communities, meant to prevent eroticism among monks. In scenes of overwhelming emotional intensity, first involving Michael and Nick, later Michael and Toby, Murdoch explores the minute gestures of desire and restraint that both disrupt and reinforce such unspoken principles. Barthes's understanding of delicacy as distance suffused with tenderness, Eros with Sophia, resonates with the difficult oscillation, in *The Bell*, between erotic impulse and a striving for wisdom. The lectures spell out memorably that "le Vivre-Ensemble, surtout idiorrythmique, emporte une éthique (ou une physique) de la distance des sujets cohabitant. C'est un redoutable problème—sans doute le problème fondamental du Vivre-Ensemble, et donc de ce cours" (the Living-Together, idiorrhythmy, involves an ethics (and a physics) of the distance among the participating subjects. This is a formidable problem—without a doubt, the fundamental problem of Living-Together, and therefore of this course) (*CVE*, "Distance," 110–113). A form of this problem, Barthes adds, is "the distance among bodies."[35] In *The Neutral*, he explains:

> Sujet en proie à la bienveillance—se trouve devant une aporie: . . . le bon dosage de l'émoi et de la distance: émoi, marque de l'Agapè, reconnaissance du désir, ancrage dans le corps (non refoulé) et distance, garantie qu'on n'écrase pas l'autre sous une demande poisseuse, qu'on ne lui fait aucun chantage à l'attendrissement en somme, un Eros bien conduit, "retenu," "réservé" (au sens de *coitus reservatus*). Rappelons que la retenue est un principe érotique du Tao. (*N*, 42)
>
> The subject of goodwill finds himself confronting an aporia: the good proportioning of emotion and distance: emotion, mark of Agapè, acknowledgment of desire, anchoring in the body (not repressed) and distance, a guarantee that one does not confound the other with a sticky demand, that one does not try to move the other by blackmailing him in short, a well-managed Eros, "self-possessed," "restrained" (in the sense of *coitus reservatus*). Let us remember that restraint is an erotic principle in Tao.

This passage parallels and spells out the meaning of two symmetrical moments in Murdoch's novel, where Michael and Toby reflect on the difficulty of maintaining distance:

> Looking at his darkened countenance Michael had suddenly a strange sense of *déjà vu*. Where had this scene, with its inevitable ending, happened before? And even as he spoke and moved he remembered the fading light in his room at school when he and the boy had sat for so long quite still and face to face. . . . No power on earth could have prevented him at that moment from touching Toby. He reached his hand out blindly toward the boy—and as if drawn magnetically Toby's hand met his in a strong grip. They stood silently together in the darkness. (*B*, 155)
>
> . . . What lingered chiefly in Toby's mind was the way in which Michael had seized his hand, and the long moment when they had

> stood with their hands tightly clasped. If only it hadn't been for that; for the fact was that Toby knew that he himself had been just as anxious for the contact as Michael had been. He too had been brimming with emotion. In spite of the words, it had been like a scene between lovers; and looking back, it seemed as if the words were merely straw, flying upward to destruction in the fierce heat of the encounter. (*B*, 157–158)

Destruction, a form of power, the opposite of delicacy: Murdoch, as her other novels also suggest, was fascinated with the form of personal power that manifests itself in the desire to protect others. Mischa Fox—perhaps the literary incarnation of Elias Canetti—suffers from it in *The Flight from the Enchanter*, and Michael himself, in *The Bell*, sublimates his homosexual inclinations by contemplating them under the guise of his presumed role to protect the young Nick, then the young Toby. Projected as the ultimate expression of tact, the fiction of mentorship is tactless because its foundation is in the imagination (it "feeds the imaginary of the relationship," as Barthes might say), not attuned to the particulars of the situation: "Nick, who was his lover, would become his son; and indeed already, with a tact and imagination which removed from their relationship any suggestion of crudeness, the boy was playing both parts" (*B*, 94). That protectiveness is a form of power appears unequivocal in Toby's musings as well: what he experienced, Murdoch's wise narrator says, "although he did not at the time recognize it as such, was a feeling of pleasure at being suddenly in a position of power vis-à-vis someone whom he had so unquestioningly accepted as his spiritual superior. . . . He found himself feeling, towards Michael, curiously protective" (*B*, 148).

Would it be sufficient to avoid power? Michael seems to hope so, while also dismayed by the awareness that his position of leader often requires the exercise of power. As Murdoch puts it, wisdom consists in making the fine distinction between power as the affirmation of one's will and power as the capacity to see the reality of a situation and act with great lucidity: "One of the most good people that he knew was also one of the most powerful: the Abbess. He lacked still the insight which would show him in what way exactly her exercise of power differed from his own. He felt himself compelled to remain in a region where power was evil, and where he could not honourably find the means to strip himself of it completely" (*B*, 75). An ominous note is struck quite early in the novel when the narrator quips: "Those who hope, by retiring from the world, to earn a holiday from human frailty, in themselves and in others, are usually disappointed" (*B*, 75). This comment refers to Michael, who, in trying to avoid power, ultimately turns delicacy into avoidance of responsibility (toward his former pupil Nick) and thus inadvertently provokes a catastrophe.[36]

Nick was presumably an invisible witness to the kiss Michael gave Toby, then to the latter's adolescent seduction of Dora: his "perfect" revenge is to talk Toby into the "machinery of sin and repentance," and thus force him to confess everything to James, "the only available saint"; then he—Nick—engineers the fall of the new bell into the lake during the ceremony of Catherine's entrance into the Abbey, and finally commits suicide. Many are affected by this course of events, and Murdoch is careful to show just how many layers of mediation there are between the complicated motivations of someone's actions and the only partial understanding—or complete misunderstanding—thereof by others: the legend of the old bell's fall into the lake in the Middle Ages (told by Paul to his wife Dora as a moral fable, who then conveyed it to Catherine) involved a nun who was cursed by a bishop for not disclosing the identity of her lover; this story troubled Catherine deeply, who saw in the fall of the new bell during its christening ceremony a sign of her own unworthiness (on account of her secret passion for Michael) so she unsuccessfully tries to drown. The repetition of yet another story insinuates itself when Toby is sent off to Cambridge before Michael has the chance to talk to him—years before, Nick, now Toby—so Michael is shattered. Why the community disbands is only implicitly understood: it appears that the series of misfortunes that befell the community in rapid succession have irremediably compromised it in the eyes of the world outside, not only turning into ridicule its spiritual aspirations with the bell falling into the lake, but, with Nick's suicide, suggesting a serious disunity, even a conflict of values among its members. The reader however is left wondering, What exactly is the nature of the transgression and what does Murdoch make of it? It is around Michael's effort to understand where he failed that Murdoch's views appear to crystallize: rather than an infatuation with someone else out of a deluded relationship with oneself, love has to be a way of seeing the other person in his or her difference from oneself; the caprice of attachment becomes in this scenario the moral imperative to take reality in a normative sense and to look at the other person(s) "as knowable by love."[37]

If the story with Toby suggests that too little distance can be destructive in a community, after Nick's death Michael realizes that avoidance—that is, too much distance—is also fatal: "Nick had needed love, and he ought to have given him what he had to offer," "he should have opened his heart: should impetuously and devotedly and beyond all reason have broken the alabaster cruse of very costly ointment" (*B*, 287). The image of love as a preciously safeguarded substance is suggestive here of a common understanding of exclusive love that Murdoch takes her distance from: in her moral universe, a loving gaze ought to be directed toward *all* beings, and only in this project of attention is it possible to gain a gradual understanding of the world around ourselves. "One day," Michael anticipates, "no doubt all this would seem charged with a vast significance, and he would try once more to find out the truth. One day, too, he would experience again, responding with his heart, that indefinitely extended requirement that one human being makes upon another" (*B*, 289).[38] These last words express Murdoch's ethics in a nutshell, her rewriting of Kant's sublime, replacing the spectacle of nature—in her account, a triviality—with the endless diversity of human nature.[39] This view has been compared to Levinas's ethics,[40] only for Murdoch—at least in the 1950s—the Other is no transcendental: as Michael's turn from religion to the requirement of another person symbolically suggests, she shifts her attention from God to the reality of other people, to the Good.[41] This does not mean that she rejects religious belief, only that she displaces the demand of a distant God in favor of the acknowledgment of the "extended requirement" of fellow human beings; that she is putting the resources of religious practice into the service of interpersonal relationships and a human(e) morality. Similarly, her philosophical framework is grounded not in a metaphysics of the Other, but in the reality of the other as a contingent person, who is, "to an extent one can never cease discovering, different from ourselves." It takes tremendous *délicatesse*, that is, wise love, to understand, and fully take in, the nuances of such difference. Or, to go back to the passage in *Comment vivre ensemble* that I suggested could be an epigraph to *The Bell*: "distance and respect, a weightless relationship . . . : not managing the other, the others, not manipulating, actively giving up images (of everyone involved)" (*CVE*, 179–180).

Murdoch goes even further than suggesting a new moral imperative, however nuanced: Dora, despised by some of the community members, is ironically the only one who survives unscathed, who, moreover, flourishes at the end of the novel and anticipates telling the story to her friend. Hers is a story of personal growth, which shows that moral concepts have varying meanings as individuals change as a result of their personal experiences and that, ultimately, these concepts push one increasingly toward intimacy and inward contemplation. The novel then is not just about love that includes unconditionally the others (the imperative of a sustained effort at proximity), but also about the inevitable increasing privacy of one's moral life, which justifies a necessary distance from others; these two aspects give Barthes's question about distances renewed justification. Thus her focus on Michael's private reflections after the community scatters parallels the emphasis she lays in her philosophical essays on the mental life as relevant to morality, perhaps even more so than decisions and actions. There is, for instance, some ambiguity surrounding the repetition that Michael is contemplating, perhaps a hint of the same delusional mechanism tinting the hope of a revelation of meaning: "One day no doubt all this would seem charged with a vast significance, and he would try once more to find out the truth" (*B*, 289). Is Murdoch suggesting that Michael is likely to relapse into the trap of his solipsistic search for a pattern, or that he is prepared to navigate the difficult waters of reality? And in either case, how would he determine the difference?

It seems to me that his focus on "the indefinitely extended requirement" of another person might point to the loss of a concern with his own dispositions: as Murdoch puts it in the essay "On 'God' and 'Good,'"

> In such a picture sincerity and self-knowledge, those popular merits, seem less important. It is *an attachment to what lies outside the fantasy mechanism*, and not a scrutiny of the mechanism itself, that liberates. Close scrutiny of the mechanism often merely strengthens its power. "Self-knowledge," in the sense of a minute understanding of one's own machinery, seems to me, except at a fairly simple level, usually a delusion.[42]

"An attachment to . . . the outside" amounts to a continuous process of attention, which is a condition, for Murdoch, of the moral life. But this is only half of the picture she provides. As a way of addressing the perceived failures of ordinary language philosophers, she also stresses the limited application of conventional moral evaluations to the particulars of one's situation and to the varying meanings of concepts in the course of one's life. This holds true for both Michael and Dora, whose stories are the clearest examples of the fact that moral concepts have, besides a commonly acknowledged meaning, a personal dimension determined by one's experience and growth: "The active 'reassessing' and 'redefining' which is a main characteristic of live personality often suggests and demands *a checking procedure which is a function of an individual history*."[43] Murdoch does not mention Wittgenstein here, but this intimate procedure speaks directly to the question raised by one of Wittgenstein's voices in the *Philosophical Investigations* in the argument about the possibility of a private language: referring to the scenario of one's private attempt to determine the identity of something felt at different moments in time, the voice asks: "What is this ceremony for?" with the implication that such a "ceremony" is irrelevant as long as it does not bear a witness (or presuppose a community of language) to confirm its veracity. Murdoch disagrees, pointing out that the use made of ordinary words, especially where moral concepts are concerned, is "partly a function of the user's history." This leads to the conclusion that Michael would be the only one able to tell the difference in meaning between past and future experiences as a result of his moral progress. Dora's story, too, sheds light on this point: dismissed by both Michael and James as "a bitch"—her contemporariness with the "angry young men" is striking especially in the first half of the novel—she undergoes a process of maturation and in the end is the one who will have a story to tell: "How wonderfully, Michael thought, Dora had survived. She had fed like a glutton upon the catastrophes at Imber and they had increased her substance. Because of all the dreadful things that had passed there was more of her. Michael looked with a slightly contemptuous envy upon this simple and robust nature" (*B*, 185). Symbolically, Dora is the last one to leave Imber, so even this last witness to her growth is rendered superfluous. The capacity to evaluate one's change without interference appears as the privilege of an individual who has become a responsible agent of one's own moral life. The relevant passage in "The Idea of Perfection" seems worth quoting in full:

> A deepening process, at any rate an altering and complicating process, takes place. There are two senses of "knowing what a word means," one connected with ordinary language and the other very much less so. Knowledge of a value concept is something to be understood, as it were, in depth, and not in terms of switching on to some given impersonal network. Moreover, if morality is essentially connected with change and progress, we cannot be as democratic about it as some philosophers would like to think. We do not simply, through being rational and knowing ordinary language, "know" the meaning of all necessary moral words. We may have to learn the meaning; and since we are human historical individuals the movement of understanding is onward into increasing privacy, in the direction of the ideal limit, and not back towards a genesis in the rulings of an impersonal public language.[44]

The novel ends with Dora's anticipation that she would tell the whole story to her friend, which not only emphasizes her newly won status of agent of her own life, liberated from the judgment of others which has so far shaped her every gesture and decision, but also makes one wonder what her own version of the story might sound like, how she makes sense of everything that has happened. This would mean replaying the story anew—which would replicate the notion that on Murdoch's account the moral process is always incomplete—and it would presumably confirm the intuition that there is more to her than meets the eye; that her hesitations, deliberations with herself, guilt feelings and unchecked impulses are all significant clues to the final denouement. "What is this ceremony for?" Murdoch the moralist points out, as we have seen, that it is for one's own private checking as part of one's moral growth. Murdoch the novelist might suggest yet a different response to Wittgenstein's query, changing the *what* for a *who*: it is for the reader.

To spell out the implications of the former answer: Murdoch's claim that "language is far more idiosyncratic than has been admitted" (i.e., by ordinary language philosophers), and therefore that "human beings are obscure to each other . . . unless they are mutual objects of attention or have common objects of attention" is, I take it, a plea for distance: alongside the community of language and shared values, she reclaims the private life; parallel to the acknowledgment of the other's difference and the necessary response to the "infinitely extended requirement" coming from the other person, she acknowledges the unavoidably idiosyncratic and therefore inaccessible (to others) reality of one's personal life in the complexity and detail of its progress. The way I understand her position to give philosophical weight to Barthes's quest of "a sociability without alienation and a solitude without exile" is by implicitly bringing together closeness and remoteness: the field of tension defined by Barthes's Eros and Sophia, might appear, thanks to Murdoch, traversed equally by Wittgenstein's repeated injunction not to flee the ordinary, to return to the rough ground (the approach of "no approach," as Richard Fleming might put it, referring to Wittgenstein's claim that we are always already within language, partaking of the condition of embodied individuals) and by a Levinasian insistence on the remoteness of the radically different Other. As we have seen, Iris Murdoch attempts to create a private space within Wittgenstein's communal world of language (not more, nor less than the space of one's body, of one's mental world and idiosyncrasy throughout the unique configuration of occurrences that add up to one's personal life), but this is a space that one is also ready to acknowledge unconditionally in the other person, who remains, importantly, an empirical Other, not Levinas's transcendental.[45] What seems to link the two aspects is her notion of attention, which is a continuous "effort to counteract states of illusion,"[46] both regarding oneself (Michael's existential "pattern") and with respect to others (in this picture, "reality" is a normative concept): it is "the fat relentless ego" that, she shows, comes in the way of love.

The ambiguous story of the bell paradoxically adds a light touch to the complexity of Murdoch's moral philosophy. Dora wants to surprise the community by substituting the long-lost bell that Toby and herself, unbeknownst to the rest, have found in the muddy lake—engraved with Nativity scenes, this bell comes from times that shared a Christian morality, before the disenchantment of the world—for the new one, simpler, that is about to be introduced into the Abbey. But Dora eventually realizes that such a "miraculous" apparition would be at odds with what the community represents; moreover, her witch-like gesture would seem to mock the ongoing efforts of the community to put into practice a new way of harmonious coexistence. The course of events takes a turn for the worst however when, thanks to Nick's vengeful devices, the new bell falls into the lake (as the old one had, according to the legend, centuries before), but the nuns remain unfazed, although the newspaper reports turn the occurrence into an object of ridicule in the eyes of the outside world. The nuns quietly close the gates of their enclosure, and when the bell is retrieved from the water, it is taken in without further ado. Even if the authenticity of the old bell would presumably make it more valuable, they seem to consider its symbolic weight obsolete so they send it to a museum; the new bell, although lacking the elaborate religious ornamentation of the old, introduces a meaning that seems more attuned to the spiritual aspirations of the contemporary world: it says simply "Gabriel vocor. Vox amoris sum—My name is Gabriel. I am the voice of Love"—which is, as we have seen, a no less demanding moral imperative. It is also suggestive that Murdoch's nuns are ethereal yet worldly wise creatures: they fascinate Toby with their relaxed laughter and their benevolent reassurance when he trespasses into their enclosure, surprise everyone when the "amphibious nun" saves Catherine from drowning, and in general give good advice without being self-righteous in conversations with members of the community. The nuns thus seem to be the happy few who can live effortlessly both up to James's moral standards (doing always the right thing) *and* in harmony with Michael's (this is what their spiritual level allows for), practicing naturally the art of *délicatesse*, a wise love.

Literature, the Only Successful *Idiorrythmie*?

When we pursue what appears to be a shared ideal of living-with-others in Barthes's course and in Murdoch's philosophical essays and fiction, the differences underwriting it are of course not negligible; what has the fascinating appearance of coincidence could also appear as mirror-play, the two objects facing each other from two different realms. For instance, critical of poststructuralism in general, Murdoch could not have disagreed more with Barthes's claim that "in the realm of the subject, there is no referent."[47] Her insistence on philosophy's task to rethink human personality, and on moral philosophy's interest in expanding its analysis to the inner life, speaks to this point. Yet this latter aspect also brings her close to Barthes, to his fascination with the sinuous ways the imaginary traverses the very fabric of our lives. Murdoch's stories have been called by critics "fables of unselfing," reflecting her critique of existentialism and the necessity to live, in that sense, without images of oneself. For Barthes, *délicatesse* also requires not indulging self-imagery, not primarily out of a concern not to obliterate the reality of other people, but as part of the ethos of depersonalization at the heart of a modernist version of the *souci de soi*, a paradoxical care of the self. The neutral, as we have seen, is a form of lucidity, a necessary skill to cultivate in an age of suspicion. Attention, on the other hand, is for Murdoch a moral category, originating in the work of Simone Weil. These two forms of engagement with the world (lucidity, attention) are characteristic of the writer who, both Barthes and Murdoch believe, tells a profound truth about the world, yet not in an explicitly *committed* way (à la Sartre, whose notion of engagement they both reject); on both accounts, the writer deals with language, a language saturated with value, hence the inescapability of the ethical. In Murdoch's words, "it is important to remember that language itself is a moral medium, almost all uses of language convey value. This is one reason why we are almost always morally active. Life is soaked in the moral, literature is soaked in the moral" (*EM*, 27). In his lectures at the Collège, Barthes often affirmed this same aspect. And he would certainly have agreed with Murdoch's claim that "the novelist is revealing his values by any sort of writing which he may do. He is particularly bound to make moral judgments in so far as his subject matter is the behaviour of human beings" (*EM*, 27). Barthes and Murdoch meet halfway between a hermeneutic of suspicion softened by a deeply ethical concern with the human person, and a moral philosophy whose interests and vocabulary Murdoch wants to expand: Their common ideal is thus to live "attuned to the nuance" (*N*, 37), to cultivate a "nostalgia for the particular" (*EM*, 43). Such nuance, such particulars, are not only those of empirical reality but also of literature, therefore the ideal can only be adumbrated while thinking the aesthetic (literature) and the ethical (morality) together. Barthes offered the intimation that literature might be the only successful *idiorrythmie*. Perhaps Murdoch would have nodded in agreement: After all, the dispersal at the end of *The Bell* concludes with the promise of a story. "Tonight," Dora anticipates, "she would be telling the whole story to Sally" (296).

Murdoch's moral outlook—paralleled by Barthes's fascinating repertoire of *délicatesse*—offers an interesting counterpoint to Canetti's worldview. In the review of *Crowds and Power*, Murdoch raised the issue of its "moral" (her quotation marks, as if realizing the incompatibility of their perspectives), asking "cannot the pain of stings be removed by love and compassion without any 'reversal'?"[48] As we have seen, both Barthes and Murdoch believe that love is essential to the well-being of the community: Barthes injects love into Nietzsche's "pathos of distances," changing it into pathos/affect and distance, Eros and Sophia, while Murdoch builds on a Christian framework (later adding Platonism) and speaks of love of another through attention.

Roland Barthes's ideal community is a beautiful utopia, but it remained hovering indeterminately, "in preparation" until the very end, perhaps because it is hard to imagine delicacy or tact when the aristocratic morality and ritual in which it might find an anchor is obsolete and can only be imagined as an anachronism. On the other hand, if love is not untimely, we might suspect with Freud that people are not able or willing to extend their love beyond their intimate circle, embracing everyone, indiscriminately. Is that what Murdoch demands? Perhaps not quite: rather, to approach the other "as knowable by love" in a process of continuous attention (which is precisely not indiscriminately). This casts light on the project of the community that interests us here: in it, love as Murdoch envisions it is "a small piecemeal business that goes on all the time and not a grandiose leaping about unimpeded at important moments"; superfluous to say, it fills in the "distances" in which life, in Canetti's world, is laid out.

It is the project of attention that brings the moral philosopher and the artist together, intimates Murdoch. The artist, who deals with the distance and otherness of the world, she says, also keeps looking, in "a process of deepening or complicating, a process of learning, a progress." This is art's own "ceremony," illustrated in *The Bell* by Dora visiting the National Gallery and learning to look by gazing at portraits (learning from painters looking at people looking at others). When Murdoch claims in an essay that art teaches us distance—art cannot be possessed, seized or incorporated—it is as if she were responding directly to Canetti; as she seems to do when she speaks of vision—as opposed to "the blinding" of Peter Kien, to so much blindness to others in the world he describes. To be sure, hers is a very different view of the role of art: rather than scourging one's contemporaries, showing them a model. Is Peter Kien the shadow that darkens the luminous view described in the passage below?

> I think good art is good for people precisely because it is not fantasy but imagination. It breaks the grip of our own dull fantasy life and stirs us to the effort of true vision. Most of the time we fail to see the big wide real world at all because we are blinded by obsession, anxiety, envy, resentment, fear. We make a small personal world in which we remain enclosed. Great art is liberating, it enables us to see and take pleasure in what is not ourselves.[49]

Barthes also remained loyal to the belief that literature was perhaps the only successful *idiorrythmie*, and the only reliable source for learning to live attuned to the rich nuances of the world, against reductive ideologies. Murdoch set literature in opposition to a rule-based morality which could not "secure us against the ambiguity of the world." And this is because "there are times when it is proper to stress, not the comprehensibility of the world, but its incomprehensibility. . . . Certain parables or stories undoubtedly owe their power to the fact that they incarnate a moral truth which is paradoxical, infinitely suggestive and open to continual reinterpretation."[50]

Part II

✦

"The World in Me"

The Distantiality of Everyday Life

> The great subject of the arts and philosophies of the twentieth century—the discovery of the ordinary—draws its energy from the dawn of the acrobats, which ensues in parallel with it.
>
> —Peter Sloterdijk, *You Must Change Your Life*

"I'm not sure," writes Fredric Jameson in a review of Günter Grass's novel *Ein weites Feld* (*Too Far Afield*), "that we can have a direct intuition of our own daily life: it is par excellence what others have, and what we acknowledge in a kind of productive and generous envy."[1] Jameson echoes here a thought of Heidegger's, who speaks of the common experience of a paradoxical closeness that makes one oblivious to the singular presence of all-too-familiar things: the glasses sitting on one's nose, the telephone receiver in one's hand, or the street one walks on. "One feels the touch of it at every step as one walks; it is seemingly the closest and realest of all that is ready-to-hand, and it slides itself, as it were, along certain portions of one's body—the soles of one's feet."[2] And yet, Heidegger adds, "it is farther remote than the acquaintance whom one encounters 'on the street' at a 'remoteness' of twenty paces when one is taking such a walk." The street is experienced in the circumspection characteristic of our involvements with objects we take for granted, which only become *conspicuous*, *obtrusive*, or *obstinate* when they are not working properly, when they are missing, or when they are in the way. Socially, we exist alongside others, without usually questioning the origin or logic of what we know, what we do, what we live for.

However, the acknowledgment of the everyday that Jameson describes as "a kind of productive and generous envy" is in Heidegger's view less dignified, since he sees everyday life as the realm of inauthenticity par excellence. Its subject is the public *das Man* (*they*), characterized in terms of publicness (*Offentlichkeit*), levelling down, irresponsibility and unaccountability (or in Heidegger's words, the disburdening of one's Being ["it was not me"]), and accommodation ("everyone is the other, and no one is himself," the 'who' of the everyday is the 'nobody' ").[3] *Sein und Zeit* describes everyday sociability in terms of a nagging *care as to the way one differs from Others*, "whether that difference is merely one that is to be evened out, whether one's own Dasein has lagged behind the Others and wants to catch up in relationship to them, or whether one's Dasein already has some priority over them and sets out to keep them suppressed." And such measuring up to other people, this "envy," not necessarily generous, is detrimental to community: "The care about this distance between them is disturbing to Being-with-one-another, though this disturbance is one that is hidden from it. If we may express this existentially, such Being-with-one-another has the character of distantiality [*Abständigkeit*]. The more inconspicuous this kind of Being is to everyday

Dasein itself, all the more stubbornly and primordially does it work itself out."[4] Heidegger insists on several occasions that his account of Dasein's everyday existence is part of a project concerned with the ontology of Being, and therefore that "it is far removed from any moralizing critique of everyday Dasein";[5] and yet, it would be hard to characterize as neutral passages like the following, shot through with the suspicion that everyday sociability conceals an unacknowledged antagonism:

> Everyone keeps his eye on the Other first and next, watching how he will comport himself and what he will say in reply. Being-with-one-another in the "they" is by no means an indifferent side-by-side-ness in which everything has been settled, but rather an intent, ambiguous watching of one another, a secret and reciprocal listening-in. Under the mask of "for-one-another," an "against-one-another" is in play.[6]

It is equally difficult to dispute that his dismissal of everyday practices—talking and conversing are described as gossiping and simply passing along baseless information, curiosity as distraction and entertainment, writing as scribbling, moving through life as groundlessness—paints a view of the everyday experiences of most people as superficial and meaningless. Dasein, he writes, "lets itself be carried along [*mitnehmen*] solely by the looks of the world; in this kind of Being, it concerns itself with becoming rid of itself as Being-in-the-world and rid of its Being alongside that which, in the closest everyday manner, is ready-to-hand."[7] Lived in a passive mode, everyday life not only fails to disclose anything essential about Being, it actually closes off the very possibility of such disclosure, lacking the awareness that it does so: "Everything looks as if it were genuinely understood, genuinely taken hold of, genuinely spoken, though at bottom it is not."[8] It would be difficult to imagine such an understanding of the everyday as the premise of an ethical life, all the more so when it remains, as both Jameson and Heidegger suggest, hidden from consciousness. No wonder that the "representation of a daily life is itself a complicated task, to be achieved only by indirection, as it were out of the corner of the eye."[9]

Heidegger concedes that "the extent to which [the dominion of *das Man*] becomes compelling and explicit may change in the course of history."[10] Indeed, Henri Lefebvre's claim, in 1947, that "l'homme sera quotidien ou ne sera pas" (man will have an everyday life or will not exist), corroborated with Maurice Blanchot's musings on the impersonal "parole quotidienne" bespeak Heidegger's point; where the latter speaks of *das Man*, Blanchot listens for the *on* (one). Who is this *one*? In the second half of the twentieth century, the everyday became an object of interest for sociologists, ethnographers, critical theorists who have variously identified the impersonal workings of this *one*. For some, like Lefebvre, the everyday was the site of oppression and bureaucratically controlled consumption; for others—Michel de Certeau,

Guy Debord, Raoul Vaneighem—speaking in the wake of May 1968 and keen to retrieve the revolutionary potential of quotidian practices, the everyday invented itself with "thousands way of poaching" of public systems, undermining them from the inside. The 1980s saw the ethnographic turn in anthropology, which meant a shift of attention to the proximity of local neighborhoods and their modes of life. As Michael Sheringham compellingly shows in his compendium of everyday life theories, the interest in everyday life is not the exclusive privilege of theorists; writers such as Baudelaire and the surrealists have captured the contradictory experiences of the modern metropolis, which exposes one to the lives of other people. The others can remain, of course, an undifferentiated, anonymous crowd; but for the *flâneur*, as Benjamin shows, they are wonderfully singular and endlessly fascinating. These theorists suggest that the everyday has become something to be reckoned with, to be apprehended not "out of the corner of the eye," as Jameson puts it, but as a self-conscious experience that consists not only of the ways we use economic, social and cultural systems, but also of our complex involvements with other people.

In this second part of the book, I want to turn my attention to autobiography, which over the course of the twentieth century has constituted a subjective counterpoint to theories of everyday life, and in so doing registered a process of "unselfing" in the very sense proposed by Iris Murdoch: under the normative imperative of the reality of other people, encountered in the experience of quotidian events, it seems to have yielded to "a nostalgia for the particular." Annie Ernaux, author of an unusual diary in which she focuses almost exclusively on "the outside," and Günter Grass, who penned a chronicle of the twentieth century told in the first person by almost one hundred different narrators, have radicalized experiments in self-writing that, roughly from midcentury onward, unsettled the centrality of the self characteristic of traditional autobiography in favor of an inclusion of other people, often, though not exclusively, family members, as part of a project to understand the formation of identity as shaped by larger factors, such as major historical events (world wars, displacement, exile) or class mobility. I have in mind, in France, Ernaux's own "family ethnography" (*La place*, *Une femme*), in Germany, family chronicles grappling with the Nazi past (*Vergangenheitsbewältigung*), such as Christa Wolf's *Kindheitsmuster* (*Childhood Patterns*) and Monika Maron's *Pawels Briefe* (*Pawel's Letters*), or even to some degree Peter Weiss's *Abschied von den Eltern* (*Leavetaking*) and *Fluchtpunkt* (*Vanishing Point*), and in Britain, autobiographies by writers of working-class origin like Carolyn Steedman's *Landscape for a Good Woman* and George Osborne's *A Better Class of Person*. In *Journal du dehors* (*Diary of the Outside*, published as *Exteriors*) and its sequel *La vie extérieure* (*Exterior Life*), Ernaux no longer focuses on her family but on the anonymous individuals she encounters in public places, who are thus part of her everyday experiences; and in *Mein Jahrhundert* (*My Century*), Grass lends his autobiographical "I" to various narrators, the so-called "little people" whose stories shed light on various aspects of lived experience in twentieth-century East and West Germany.[11] Although not formulated in ethical terms, the interest in the lives of others shared by Grass and Ernaux can be situated in the ethical sphere of the examined life—especially as they write, formally at least, in the framework of the autobiographical genre: the term proposed by Michael Sheringham to characterize Ernaux's writing, "project of attention," describes equally well Grass's tome. The authenticity of the self appears here as a function of the least personal aspects of their authors' personalities, pertaining to the social or the historical self.

By differentiating the anonymous subject of the everyday, the public *das Man* of averageness, irresponsibility and leveling down (to return briefly to Heidegger), and by making of it the singular-plural subject of autobiographical writing, Ernaux and Grass redefine the self in relation to other people. Jean-Luc Nancy's critique of Heidegger resonates here, with its insistence on "the differentiated singularity that the *everyday* already is by itself: each day, each time, day to day." The passage that follows is crucial and deserves quoting *in extenso*:

> One cannot affirm that the meaning of Being must express itself starting from everydayness and then begin by neglecting the general differentiation of the everyday, its constantly renewed rupture, its intimate discord, its polymorphy and its polyphony, its relief and its variety. A "day" is not simply a unit for counting; it is the turning of the world—each time singular. And days, indeed every day, could not be similar if they were not first different, difference itself.[12]

Nancy's ontology of spacing (*dis-position*) at the heart of his rethinking of the everyday as "the mode of a constantly renewed singularity" bears on the nature of the relationship with other people: the "others" are not in a relation of opposition or antagonism, as in Heidegger's *distantiality*, but in a rapport of nonclosure (an inclusion that remains open to different others). Incidentally, this corresponds to Heidegger's ontology of the self-other relationship, where the Others are not "everyone else but me—those over against whom the 'I' stands out. They are rather those from whom, for the most part, one does not distinguish oneself—those among whom one is too."[13] Heidegger is right, but his ontology of the *mit* (with), Nancy points out, is no more than a sketch; *Being Singular Plural* rewrites this insight as its premise: the lowercase other, he says, with an explicit allusion to Lacan and an unacknowledged reference to Levinas, "is 'one' among many insofar as they are many; it is each one, and it is each time one, one among them, one among all and one among us all."[14] Where Heidegger, critical of the philosophical tradition he inherited, claims that one cannot sever the subject from the Others and then glue it back, Ernaux aims to connect with other people by cultivating the very habits of tarrying, observing, examining that Heidegger sees as lacking in *das Man*'s mode of distracted existence. In his account, "curiosity is characterized by a specific way of not tarrying alongside what is closest," seeking "restlessness and the excitement of continual novelty and changing encounters"—that is, a "never dwelling anywhere [*Aufenthaltslosigkeit*]."[15] It is precisely the inconsistency of *das Man*'s curiosity [*Neugier*] that bothers Nancy as well: "For [Heidegger], curiosity is the frantic activity of passing from being to being in an insatiable sort of way, without ever being able to stop and think."[16] Discovering in "the other"—whether a newborn child, a face encountered on the street, an insect, a pebble—an access to the origin of the world, Nancy describes curiosity in terms of "being intrigued by the ever-renewed alterity of the origin and, if I may say so, in the sense of having an affair with it."[17] As a *flâneuse*, Ernaux does exactly that: she tarries, genuinely curious. She is intrigued. She has an affair with the world. She starts by removing her subjectivity from her writing, intent on capturing objectively the reality of other people's lives; she looks at them from a distance, they are *entfernt*, to use Heidegger's word, but she pursues, one might say, a kind of *deseverance* (*Entfernung*) that casts in a meaningful light the connection with them. Their experiences bring into focus episodes from her own life, thus revealing "the world in [her]" as shared vulnerability. In *My Century*, the author's autobiographical voice is indistinguishable from the other narrators that speak in the first person; they are "those among whom one is too."

The presiding figure of the second half of the book is Walter Benjamin: I read Ernaux's diaries and Grass's chronicles as apt responses from the end of the twentieth century to Benjamin's portrayal of his own century, the nineteenth, in the *Arcades*, and to his farewell to it in *Berlin Childhood around 1900*. This small book provides the model for the autobiographical portrait, from which the self emerges as from a cocoon protected by the family house, by the city itself, while *The Arcades* project offers the theoretical and imaginative tools for leaving behind the purely autobiographical diary or autobiography, making possible such hybrid, we might even say oxymoronic, genres as a diary of the outside, or a collective portrait of one's century. Ernaux and Grass inherit Benjamin's paradoxical legacy: Ernaux is a flâneuse who expands the autobiographical space to include the outside;[18] Grass takes the portrait and multiplies it indefinitely, giving temporal amplitude to the autobiography by covering the whole of the twentieth century. Benjamin, as we know, stepped into the past century looking back, nostalgic for increasingly obsolete forms of life and experience and therefore left behind. But his texts are invaluable compendiums of modernity, as well as, especially *Berlin Childhood*, illustrations of Adorno's aphorism on the morality of not feeling at home: written in exile while no longer having "a proper abode," this small book of miniatures is underwritten by a condition of displacement that the protagonists of Ernaux and Grass take as given. By focusing on stories of other lives, real or imagined, at the expense of the authorial self, Ernaux and Grass disrupt the autobiographical pact, speaking alongside a philosophical reflection of recent decades that has sought to rethink community not as something secondary to the self, but as constitutive of the self.

Damon Galgut's novel *In a Strange Room*, which will be the focus of the final chapter, is a most eloquent illustration of the "community of those without community" that thinkers like Jean-Luc Nancy, Giorgio Agamben, Roberto Esposito, and others derived, through critical engagement, from Heidegger's *Mitsein*. Alternating between the first and the third person, and thus straddling the boundary between memoir and fiction, Galgut's novel makes a compelling case for moving away from the notion of an autonomous subject toward singularity, finitude, exposure, and relationality. Whereas Ernaux's unusual diaries offer reminders of the full reality of other people's lives, which she tries to imagine, and Grass's collective portrait of the last century moves freely between autobiography and fiction, Galgut's novel blurs the self/others divide through a seamless shift from first, to third (impersonal), and back to first (singular plural) person. The importance that Ernaux, Grass, and Galgut attach to individual stories raises the question of representation, of relating to, and speaking in the name of others, which will be one of the threads woven throughout this second half of the book. Ultimately, the *distantiality* of the everyday turns into an ethical principle of willing exposure and receptivity to the singularity of other people. Echoes from the previous chapters come together here: Orwell's commitment to the ordinary man, Canetti's acerbic critique of individualism and his sympathy for the crowd, and, finally, Murdoch's attention to the endless difference of countless others. All these are crucial aspects to the rethinking of community under the auspices of an art of distances.

Chapter 4

✦

In Search of a Whole Self

Benjamin's Childhood Fragments

> I was distorted by similarity to all that surrounded me. Like a mollusk in its shell, I had my abode in the nineteenth century, which now lies hollow before me like an empty shell. I hold it to my ear. What do I hear?
>
> —Walter Benjamin

In the afterword to Walter Benjamin's *Berliner Kindheit um 1900* (*Berlin Childhood around 1900*), published posthumously in 1950, Theodor Adorno insightfully remarked that the book could be seen as the subjective counterpart to the *Arcades* project:

> This book belongs to the ensemble of the prehistory of modernity that Benjamin worked on during the last fifteen years of his life and forms a subjective counterpoint to the mass of documents that he collected for the projected work on the Parisian arcades. The historical archetypes that he wanted to develop in this work, based on their pragmatic, social, philosophical origin, were going to sparkle in the book on Berlin, triggered by the immediacy of the memory, with the violence of the pain caused by that which one will never see again and which, once lost, ends up coagulating in the allegory of its own ruin.[1]

Whereas the *Arcades* was an extensive collection of quotations and observations about nineteenth-century industrial culture and technological mediation, intended as a compendium of cultural, historical, and ideological features of an era and place to which Benjamin felt attached, *Berlin Childhood* was in a sense a way of grounding these experiences in a more personal setting, in a cryptic yet portentous catalog of things, small events, and places evoked in the form of fragmentary miniatures. Encapsulated in enigmatic titles like "Loggias," "Butterfly Hunt," "Tardy Arrival," "The Fever," "Peacock Island and Glienicke," "Crooked Street," "Mummerehlen," "Hiding

Places," "A Christmas Angel," "The Little Hunchback" are images of Berlin and of the parents' house in the West End district, of courtyards and streets, markets, zoo, ice-skating, and historical monuments: each one evoked in masterful prose poetry, the fragmentary character of the text making the reader dwell—literally and metaphorically—in and on each of these (textual) places. And this is where *Berliner Kindheit* rejoins the *Arcades* book: if the quotations in *Arcades* are strategically blown out of a fossilized past and placed in a new structure of dialectical juxtapositions and temporal discontinuities where they can be read more closely, in the same way the fragment privileged by *Berliner Kindheit* singles out and brings to the fore a place, a moment, a state of mind, on which both the narrator and the reader are brought to linger. Each fragment is a renewed attempt by the exiled Jew to reconnect with a world lost to National Socialism, and more generally to an advanced modernity alienated from itself.

The farewell represented by *Berlin Childhood* is thus twofold. The title suggests the image of the child playing at the threshold between centuries, a reminder that Benjamin, as Hannah Arendt suggested, was a man of the nineteenth century, for whom late modernity was an experience in alienation:

> His gestures and the way he held his head when listening and talking; the way he moved; his manners, but especially his style of speaking, down to his choice of words and the shape of his syntax; finally, his downright idiosyncratic tastes—all this seemed so old-fashioned, as though he had drifted out of the nineteenth century the way one is driven onto the coast of a strange land. Did he ever feel at home in the twentieth century? One has reason to doubt it.[2]

Indeed, throughout his writings, Benjamin deplores the loss of the auratic through mechanical reproduction and the modern incapacity to communicate experience.[3] In *Berliner Kindheit*, for instance, the telephone is portrayed as a symbol of inadequate communication that spoils established ways of living: "Not many of those who use the apparatus know what devastation it once wreaked in family circles. The sound with which it rang between two and four in the afternoon, when a schoolfriend wished to speak to me, was an alarm signal that menaced not only my parents' midday nap but the historical era that underwrote and enveloped this siesta" (*BC*, 49). More dramatically, however, Benjamin's is a farewell bid to a Berlin where all places were like so many dwellings, at a moment when the exiled writer had no proper abode. The *attempt*, then, to renew with the lost world of childhood in these fragments points, in more than one way, to the essay form, both in the sense of fragmentary writing that breaks the spell of beginnings and endings, as his friend Adorno put it in "The Essay as Form";[4] and as an always renewed rhetorical effort to convince an audience (i.e., readership) to follow a certain mental trajectory: Benjamin's own introduction to *Berliner Kindheit* could be read, in keeping with the consecrated practice of ancient rhetoric, as both *expositio*—the place where the author states his intentions—and as *captatio benevolentiae*, the gesture of modesty, in Benjamin's case, made toward the reader, to join and follow him:[5]

> Ich halte es für möglich, dass solchen Bildern ein eigenes Schicksal vorbehalten ist. Ihrer harren noch keine geprägten Formen. . . . Dagegen sind die Bilder meiner Grossstadtkindheit vielleicht befähigt, in ihrem Innern spätere geschichtliche Erfahrung zu präformieren. In diesen wenigstens, *hoffe ich*, *ist es wohl zu merken*, wie sehr der, von dem hier die Rede ist, später der Geborgenheit entriet, die seiner Kindheit beschieden gewesen war.[6]
>
> I think it is possible that such images are reserved a fate of their own. No fixed forms are stamped on them yet. . . . Perhaps the images of my childhood city are suitable for pre-forming, in their intimate core, later historical experience. I hope they reveal the extent to which the one who is here discussed was later deprived of the shelter he had enjoyed in his childhood.

The effort underwriting these fragments is that of measuring the deprivation of his exile against the meaningfulness of the childhood home and experiences, but also to decipher, in the keeping of childhood's surroundings, forebodings of a future to come. In more ways than one, though: the idea points to a Benjaminian locus, that of an everyday at best inchoate, which therefore cannot be approached as a fully conscious experience, hence the need to create poetic forms to articulate *Erlebnisse* and transmit them as *Erfahrung*.[7] Beyond that, however, *Berliner Kindheit* evokes the young man surrounded by things endowed with a prophetic quality he could only intimate, but never fully decipher, things with which the child appears to have had not an objective, but an existential relationship: his world is animistic; things have eyes and look back.[8] A child playing at the threshold between centuries, often lingering at the threshold between ignorance and knowledge, trying to seize the "fugitive knowledge" with which things seem to tease him: *Berliner Kindheit* reveals itself—this is how I will read it here—as a book about thresholds: between insides and outsides; the phenomenal and the symbolic; otherness from, and intimacy with, things. Above all, it contemplates the threshold between the experience of childhood (sutured around the self thrilled at its own emergence in language, and keen to explore the house and the city), and the disjointed present of exile, a wandering without abode.

The *Arcades* project was in many ways one about thresholds. Paris represented for Benjamin the capital of the nineteenth century, a city whose boulevards were formed by houses that "[did] not seem made to be lived in, but [were] like stones set for people to walk between."[9] In other words, Paris was a city in which *outside* was at the same time *inside*, a coincidence epitomized in the arcades, the city's "true nature in quintessential form." In Paris, Benjamin thought, "a stranger feels at home because he can inhabit the city the way he lives in his own four walls."[10] The Parisian arcades thus inspired in him the dream of an authentic *Schwellenkunde*, a science of thresholds: "The threshold," he mused, "is a zone. And in fact a zone of passage [*Űbergang*]. Transformation, passage, flux—all are contained in the word threshold. . . . We have become quite poor as far as threshold experiences go. Falling asleep is perhaps the only such experience that has remained to us."[11]

These reflections reverberate in *Berliner Kindheit*, to which Benjamin extends his meditation on thresholds. As an exile deprived of "a proper abode," he maps out nostalgically a social geography of intimacy and comfort protective of the child's emerging self, a geography best evoked by the idea of threshold (as transformation, passage, flux), in the relationality captured in objects and, retrospectively, in dialectical images. The threshold is the privileged space affording access to a "fugitive knowledge" that the adult is all the more eager to grasp, since his present is historically precarious. It is not clear, however, that *Berlin Childhood* offers solace, given the glimpses he catches at the social periphery of the lives of servants, beggars, basement dwellers, and so on, whose brief portrayal is all the more poignant given his own circumstances.

The very first section of the book gestures to the *Arcades*, with its evocation of the loggias, the liminal space where everything—the book, the city, childhood—begins. The last paragraph of the section cites (and thus resites) the passage from the foreword (quoted above), in which Benjamin designates himself in the third person:

> Seitdem ich Kind war, haben sich die Loggien weniger verändert als die anderen Räume. Sie sind mir nicht nur darum nahe. Es ist vielmehr des Trostes wegen, der in ihrer Unbewohnbarkeit fűr den liegt, der selber nicht mehr zum Wohnen kommt. An ihnen hat die Behausung des Berliners ihre Grenze. Berlin—der Stadtgott selber—beginnt in ihnen. Er bleibt sich dort so gegenwärtig, dass nichts Flűchtiges sich neben ihm behauptet. In seinem Schutze finden Ort und Zeit zu sich und zueinander. Beide lagern sich hier zu seinen Fűssen. Das Kind jedoch, das einmal mit im Bunde gewesen war, halt sich, von dieser Gruppe eingefasst, auf seiner Loggia wie in einem längst ihm zugedachten Mausoleum auf. (*S*, 387)

> In the years since I was a child, the loggias have changed less than other places. This is not the only reason they stay with me. It is much more on account of the solace that lies in their uninhabitability for one who himself no longer has a proper abode. Berlin—the city god

> itself—begins in them. The god remains such a presence there that nothing transitory can hold its ground beside him. In his safekeeping, space and time come into their own and find each other. Both of them lie at his feet here. The child who was once their confederate, however, dwells in his loggias, encompassed by his group, as in a mausoleum long intended just for him. (*BC*, 42)

This passage mentally zooms in on the loggias as a place meant to set limits (*Grenze*), not as one for dwelling, and the consolation they offer to the exile who has no proper abode (*der selber nicht mehr zum Wohnen kommt*) lies precisely in their uninhabitability (*Unbewohnbarkeit*). They suggest the idea of threshold as that which separates, which does not grant the comfort of a place; and if it is one, it can only be a mausoleum. However, throughout *Berliner Kindheit* the threshold is also valued as that which means passage, access to higher, esoteric knowledge—that is, as a privileged place. Although fragmentary, the text is not just a collection of disconnected fragments; rather, they relate through an exchange of relays (images, metaphors, motifs) that "fills in" the liminal space separating them.

Suggestively, the first section (*Loggien*) ends with a meditation on liminality and is followed by *Kaiserpanorama* (opening up a panoramic view onto the city), and *Die Siegessäule* (Victory Column), which symbolically elongates the "panorama" on a vertical plane, giving it historical perspective. Reading *Berliner Kindheit* appears rather like mental *flânerie*, a sort of losing one's way in the text like in a city, both advancing and tarrying; it is like following the flâneur's motto, "see everything, touch nothing" (that is, *attach yourself to nothing*), not even to what might occasionally look like the core of a fragment. Granted, each section, by virtue of being isolated graphically on the page, is singled out, and one therefore lingers on it as on a small whole, but the text also reads metaphorically like a constellation waiting to be reconfigured, motifs and images to be blown out and rearranged in new patterns. Importantly, thresholds in *Berliner Kindheit* are not (only) zones that separate, but also zones of passage, of connection, of transmission, in keeping with Benjamin's persistent interest in related ideas like the communicability of experience, the transmissibility of truth, the translatability of a text.

"We have become quite poor as far as threshold experiences go. *Falling asleep* is perhaps the only such experience that has remained to us," Benjamin says in the *Arcades* passage quoted earlier, to which he adds, later on, the symmetrical moment: "Can it be that *awakening* is the synthesis whose thesis is dream consciousness and whose antithesis is consciousness? Then the moment of awakening would be identical with the 'Now of recognizability,' on which things put on their true—surrealistic—face." This reflection, on which Benjamin elaborates poetically in *Der Mond* and *Wintermorgen*, casts the idea of threshold in terms of movement seized in almost static form, movement as a dialectical synthesis between *before* and *after*. Adorno pointed to this aspect in Benjamin's writing in the following terms: "To understand Benjamin properly, one must feel behind his every sentence the conversion of extreme agitation into something static, indeed, the static notion of movement itself."[12] As the above reflection on awakening suggests, movement as stasis is cast first of all in relation to the temporality of memory, understood by Benjamin not in the Bergsonian sense of a repository of images, but as a place of synthesis between past and present. The image—a *Denkbild*—is thus for Benjamin dialectical; it is dialectics at a standstill:

> What differentiates images from the "essences" of phenomenology is their historic index. . . . These images are to be thought of entirely apart from the categories of the "human sciences," from so-called habitus, from style, and the like. For the historical index of the images not only says that they belong to a particular time; it says above all that they attain to legibility only at a particular time. And indeed, this acceding "to legibility" constitutes a specific critical point in the movement at their interior. Every present day is determined by those images that are synchronic with it: each "now" is the now of a specific recognizability. . . . It is not that what is past casts its light on what is present or what is present its light on what is past; rather, image is that wherin what has been comes together in a flash with the now to form a constellation. In other words: image is dialectics at a standstill.[13]

The image, then, is a gathering of moments awakened to consciousness; but it is also a thing—understood as gathering[14]—which captures a luminous meaning (*eine Bedeutung*), a prophecy awakened from slumber: a revelation. The notion of image is significant here because this is how Benjamin introduces *Berliner Kindheit,* as "*Bilder*, die im Exil das Heimweh am stärksten zu wecken pflegen—die der Kindheit—mit Absicht in mir hervor" (*S*, 385, my italics). Writing *Berlin Childhood* becomes a question of *recognizing* those privileged moments from childhood which, *legible* in the present of the writing, become enlightened moments of awakening; moments which, like monads, encapsulate everything else. In his 1929 essay "On the Image of Proust," Benjamin made this remark: "A remembered event is infinite, because it is merely a key to everything that happened before it and after it."[15]

The fragment as image, the image as monad: Benjamin's writings—and *Berliner Kindheit* is no exception—document a fascination with the miniature, the infinitesimally small; as Arendt points out, "For him the size of an object was in an inverse ratio to its significance—the smaller the object, the more likely it seemed that it could contain in the most concentrated form everything else."[16] *Reading* the meanings of things in retrospect, *writing* them as a form of longing: both of these gestures have at their core the idea of movement which Benjamin attempted to grasp in almost static form (as Adorno said), as an essence, as a metaphor. The following passage from "The Reading Box" is remarkable in that it brings together all these elements: writing and reading, but also two other instantiations of the idea of movement, grasping and walking, as well as the suggestion of a monad, of something that potentially contains everything else.[17] Everyone, muses Benjamin in this passage,

> has encountered certain things which occasioned more lasting habits than other things. Through them, each person developed those capabilities which helped to determine the course of his life. And because—so far as my own life is concerned—it was reading and writing that were decisive, none of the things that surrounded me in my early years arouses greater longing than the reading box. It contained, on little tablets, the various letters of the alphabet inscribed in cursive, which made them seem younger and more virginal than they would have been in roman style. . . . The longing which the reading box arouses in me proves how thoroughly bound up it was with my childhood. Indeed, what I seek is just that: my entire childhood, as concentrated in the movement [*Griff*] by which my hand slid the letters into the groove, where they would be arranged to form words. My hand can still dream of this movement, but it can no longer awaken so as actually to perform it. By the same token, I can dream of the way I once learned to walk. But that doesn't help. I now know how to walk; there is no more learning to walk. (*BC*, 140–142)

The reading box appears here like a monad: the recipient, virtually, of all possible words, hence of all possible writing, and anticipating the later passion for naming. Symbolically, the childhood is concentrated in the movement of the hand, the *Griff* (literally, the grasp), the gesture with which the child would relate to the world of things, would take it into possession—the most intimate relationship one can have with objects, thought Benjamin—would define it as a space of intimacy, in other words, of *proxemics*. This last word in itself aptly gives access to the manifold relationship to space and objects in which the child delights in *Berliner Kindheit*, therefore it seems worth dwelling on.

Borrowed by Roland Barthes from Edward T. Hall in his inspiring *Comment vivre ensemble*, it applies here to the space which surrounds closely the subject: the space of the familiar gaze, of objects one can grasp with the hand ("presque à l'aveuglette" [almost groping], says Barthes), the sphere of the immediate gesture, in short, a microspace of gestures.[18] It belongs to a whole typology of ways to relate to subjective spaces, like dwelling, hiding, recoiling, reaching not only with the hand but also with the gaze, the smell, the ear.

Returning to *Berliner Kindheit* mindful of Barthes's elaborations, the book seems a poetic reflection on proxemics, understood as an affective realm of desire for what surrounds the child: a desire for things, which sometimes takes the form of imaginary immersion, even identification with them; in the "Mummerehlen" fragment, for instance, the chameleonic transformation of the self ends with the image of the body "distorted by similarity" with the surrounding things, like the Chinese artist absorbed by the landscape in his own painting.[19] Suggestively, the narrator remembers he used to disguise himself (*sich mummen*) in words as if they were clouds. These two acts of immersion—in the world of things, in words—echo the ambiguity of the gesture of grasping letters from the reading box to form words: the word that is made conjures up an object and gives it reality; the word is a piecemeal re-creation of the world. Grasping, in the "Reading Box" section, is thus the essential gesture of proxemics, of the taking in possession of the interior (i.e., of creating an *interior* in the others' world).

Significantly, the other movement Benjamin dreams of in this passage is walking: "My hand can still dream of this movement, but it can no longer awaken so as actually to perform it. By the same token, I can dream of the way I once learned to walk." If grasping is taking in possession the space of proxemics, walking is nothing if not a way of broadening an interior space of intimacy with things toward the outer space of the city: the microspace of proxemics becomes the broader space of flânerie. These two notions presuppose familiarity, intimacy even, with the spaces explored: for is not the grasping *presque à l'aveuglette* the small-sized version of the famous "losing one's way in a city," which, as Benjamin puts it, requires some schooling? "Sich in einer Stadt nicht zurechtzufinden heisst nicht viel. In einer Stadt sich aber zu verirren, wie man in einem Walde sich verirrt, braucht Schulung" (Not to find your way in a city does not mean much. But to lose your way in a city, like one loses one's way in a forest, needs schooling) (*S*, 393). If in the Paris of the *Arcades*, the houses are there not to be inhabited, not designed for an inner life, but rather to hollow out the streets, and thus create the city and its continual movement, in the Berlin of Benjamin's childhood the outside seems an expansion of the inside, an extended proxemics where the walk, the wandering in a familiar space replaces the gesture of grasping. *Familiar*, meaning personal, for just as grasping objects/naming them is bringing them to life, re-creating them anew each time, the city's paths are drawn anew with every walk; just as the child has his own objects and places in the house (his obscure hiding places), he creates a city of his own in the real-world one, privileging corners, thresholds, peripheral spaces where most people would rarely stop. It is with his own body—through the grasp, the walk—that the child takes the measure of both the inside and the outside.

Another section, "Das Fieber," adds more echoes to these gestures, as it sketches the image of the sick child in bed, waiting for the world to come to him.[20] As Barthes shows in the same lecture, the bed is the very essence of proxemics, it is the body's prosthesis, like a fifth member: "foyer de l'expansion fantasmatique du sujet: par la lecture; par la fenêtre; par l'élaboration fantasmatique" (the hearth of the fantasmatic expansion of the subject: through reading; through the window; through the fantasmatic elaboration). Benjamin's evocation of the child lying in bed and fantasizing his relationship with the world is very suggestive in this sense: the bed, he remembers, was ordinarily "the site of his quietest and most retiring existence [der Ort des eingezogensten und stillsten Daseins]," "the precinct of secret enterprises in the evening—leafing through a story or playing with his candles [das Revier heimlicher Unternehmungen am Abend: des Schmökerns und meines Kerzenspiels]." But when he was sick, it became much more than that:

> Ich bin viel krank gewesen. Daher stammt vielleicht, was andere als Geduld ans mir bezeichnen, in Wahrheit aber keener Tugend ähnelt: die Neigung, alles, woran mir liegt, von weitem sich mir nahen zu sehen wie meinem Krankenbett die Stunden. So kommt es, dass an einer Reise mir die beste Freude fehlt, wenn ich den Zug nicht lange auf dem Bahnhof erwartet konnte, und ebenfalls rührt daher, dass Beschenken zur Leidenschaft bei mir geworden ist; denn was den andern überrascht, das sehe ich, der geber, von langer Hand voraus. Ja, das Bedürfnis, durch die Wartezeit so wie ein Kranker durch die Kissen, die er im Rücken hat, gestützt, dem Kommendem entgegenzusehen, hat bewirkt, dass späterhin mir Frauen um so schöner schienen, je getroster und länger ich auf sie zu warten hatte. (*S*, 403)

> I was often sick. This circumstance perhaps accounts for something that others call my patience but that actually bears no resemblance to a virtue: the predilection for seeing everything I care about approach me from a distance, the way the hours approached my sickbed. Thus, when I am traveling, I lose the best part of my pleasure if I cannot wait a long time in the station for my train. And this likewise explains why giving presents has become a passion with me: as the giver, I foresee long in advance what surprises the recipient. In fact, my need to look forward to what is coming—all the while sustained by a period of waiting, as a sick person is supported by pillows at his back—ensured that, later on, women appeared more beautiful to me the longer and more consolingly I had to wait for them. (*BC*, 72–73)

If grasping (creating, confirming the space of proxemics) and walking (wandering in the city) are acts of movement *toward* the world, symbolic gestures of appropriation, waiting in anticipation (imagining, expecting) is a way to project the contemporaneity of things present in the same space onto time, an attempt to bring the future closer to the present: a back-and-forth movement between future and present, belonging to the realm of dialectical images. The "Fieber" section conjures up the recurrent motifs of the gaze and of the gift, which, as Gerhard Richter aptly suggests in his reading of *Berliner Kindheit*, forge relays in the text between sending and receiving. More importantly, waiting is not a passive act but keen, active anticipation, an attempt to imagine and grasp the traces of a coming event: or, in Benjamin's words, a way to preform later (historical) experience, to challenge the history of an event to begin. Imaginative anticipation, then, triggers not only lived experience but also narrative, which initiates the process from the other end of time, in retrospect: as Szondi famously suggested, Benjamin seeks the future in the past, in every place that harbors *das Kommende*, that bears "the features of what is to come."[21]

This is the most poignant aspect of *Berlin Childhood*: the quest of a promise concerning the future—Benjamin's present at the time of writing, a present of rootlessness—in the past. The intensity with which the exile distends the present moment to find in it the "now of recognizability" has its corollary in the patience with which, as a child, he would wait indeterminately for a sign that would open up a discrete passageway into the future. As the section titled "Der Fischotter / The Otter" suggests, a precondition to finding an auspicious place for such waiting is to lose one's way first.

One such place is nested among the alleys of the zoological garden, where the child likes to visit the least-admired animals and to dwell in the least frequented spots. The "Fischotter" section maps time spatially, with the suggestion that while the present is the most populated region, the future is like an esoteric place accessible only to those who have the capacity to recognize it at the periphery of things. Strikingly, the narrator suggests a comparison here between the geography of the zoo and a social one that valorizes the center at the expense of the outskirts, on which it nevertheless relies for its existence: "One forms an image of a person's nature and character according to his place of residence and the neighborhood he inhabits, and that is exactly what I did with the animals at the Zoological Garden" (*BC*, 78). Passing the ostriches that "marshaled before a background of sphinxes and pyramids," and the hippopotamus that "dwelt in its pagoda like a tribal sorcerer," he first gets lost, then eventually comes in proximity of a "threshold dweller" whose appearance can never be waited for too long. The passage speaks more explicitly than any other to Benjamin's longing for a prophetic insight into *das Kommende*, the "what is to come":

> Seltner waren die [Tiere] unter ihnen, die schon durch die Lage des Hauses etwas Besonderes hatten—meist Insassen des Weichbilds: jener Teile, mit denen der Zoologische Garten an die Kaffeeschenken oder das Ausstellungsgelände anstiess. Vor allen andern Bewohnern solcher Gegenden was aber der Fischotter bemerkenswert. Unter den drei Portalen war ihm das an der Lichtensteinbrücke zunächst gelegen.

> Es war bei weitem das wenigste benutzte, führte auch in die abgestorbenste Region des Gartens. . . . Dieser Winkel des Zoologischen Gartens [trug] die Züge des Kommenden. Es war ein prophetischer Winkel. Denn wie es Pflanzen gibt, von denen man erzählt, dass sie die Kraft besitzen, in die Zukunft sehen zu lassen, so gibt es Orte, die die gleiche Gabe haben. Verlassene sind es meist, auch Wipfel, die gegen Mauern stehn, Sackgassen oder Vorgärten, wo kein Mensch sich jemals aufhält. An solchen Orten scheint es, als sei alles, was eigentlich uns bevorsteht, ein Vergangenes. In diesem Teile des Zoologischen Gartens also war es, wo immer, wenn ich mich dahin verirrte, ein Blick mir über den Brunnenrand vergönnt war, welcher hier wie in der Mitte eines Kurparks auftieg. Das war der Zwinger des Fischotters. (*S*, 407)

> Rarer were those [animals] which, by the location of their housing alone, already had something particular about them: inhabitants of the outskirts, mainly—of those sections where the Zoological Garden borders on coffeehouses or the exhibition hall. Among all the denizens of these regions, however, the most remarkable was the otter. Of the three main entry gates, the one by Lichtenstein Bridge was closest to the otter's enclosure; it was by far the last used entranceway, and it led into the most neglected part of the garden. . . . This corner of the Zoological Garden bore traces of what was to come. It was a prophetic corner. For just as there are plants that are said to confer the power to see into the future, so there are places that possess such a virtue. For the most part, they are deserted places—treetops that lean against walls, blind alleys or front gardens where no one ever stops. In such places, it seems as if all that lies in store for us has become the past. Thus, it was always in this part of the Zoological Garden, when I had lost my way and strayed into it, that I was granted a look over the edge of the pool that welled up here, as in the middle of a spa. This was the cage of the otter. (*BC*, 78–79)

The otter, dweller of a privileged place, is, in its emergence from the water, like one of Benjamin's "similarities" that "flash up fleetingly from the stream of things only in order to become immediately engulfed again," enacting what Benjamin calls in Baudelaire's poetry a rhetoric of emergence: "the particular beauty of the openings of so many of Baudelaire's poems: the emergence from the abyss."[22] This emergence, however, is only granted to those who know how to recognize it, since the image is a question of recognizability and legibility. A *question*, that is, a dilemma: Benjamin recalls waiting by the otter's cage, hinting at the child's identification with the otter because of its presumed privileged position—a position which, in retrospect, the narrator has reasons to be suspicious of. He reminisces:

> And so time and again I would remain, endlessly waiting, before those black and impenetrable depths, in order somewhere to catch sight of the otter. If I finally succeeded, it was certainly just for an instant, for in the blink of an eye the glistening inmate of the cistern would disappear once more into the wet night. Of course, the otter was not actually kept in a cistern. Nevertheless, when I gazed into the water, it always seemed *as though the rain poured down into all the street drains of the city only to end up in this one basin and nourish its inhabitant*. For this was the abode of a pampered animal whose empty, damp grotto was *more a temple* than a refuge. It was *the sacred animal of the rainwater*. But whether it was formed in this runoff of the rains, or only fed from arriving streams and rivulets, is something I could not have decided. Always it was occupied to the utmost, as if its presence in the deep were indispensable. (*BC*, 80, my italics)

This passage is a rare instance in *Berlin Childhood* where the narrator discreetly, if still sympathetically, reaches out to explain the fascination of the child. For the aura with which he used to surround the otter—the sacred animal, dwelling in a temple that all the street drains of the city converge toward to nourish him—is also the aura of a privileged child around whom the world revolves, who therefore can feel secure and content: "In a good rain, I was securely hidden away. And it would whisper to me of my future, as one sings a lullaby beside the cradle. How well I understood that it nurtures growth. In such hours passed behind the gray-gloomed window, I was at home with the otter" (*BC*, 81). It is only the narrator who, in the "now of recognizability," identifies fissures in the perfection of that dream: whether he was right to think of the otter—and of himself—as at the center of such convergence, he "could not have decided." In search of a reassuring younger self that used to find a home while losing himself both in proxemics and in flânerie, Benjamin suspects that the "convergence" of all things toward himself might have been a delightful illusion, whose recollection, in *Berliner Kindheit*, might be only a projection.

This *now* of exile also makes to him palpable the predicament of other marginal individuals, of whose lives he caught vague glimpses as a child. The landscape of Benjamin's childhood is one of peripheries recuperated in the playful re-creation of a world of his own at the heart of the others' world: but in addition to "hiding places [*Verstecke*] in the house, and rarely visited spots in the Zoological Garden, it contains the world of the poor on which the young boy casts curious gazes. Like Kafka, about whom Benjamin said that it was "little so emblematic . . . as the suspicious gaze that he casts time and again on what is bad, disturbing, discarded as though it were something inconvenient but long familiar," the child is suspicious of the bourgeois milieu of his parents' and grandmothers' apartments—in which there was no place for misery or death—and of the social and familial strategies to mask them.[23] The poor, Benjamin remembered, "for the rich children of my age . . . existed only as beggars. And it was a great advance in my understanding when for the first time poverty dawned on me in the ignominy of poorly paid work."[24] In *Berliner Kindheit*, they make their presence visible at Christmas, when the young man also guesses the presence of old age and sickness behind the dark windows in his neighborhood:

> Mit den Tannenbäumen begann es. . . . Dann barst sie eines schönen Tages und Spielzeug, Nüsse, Stroh und Baumschmuck quollen aus ihrem Innern: der Weihnachtsmarkt. Mit ihnen quoll noch etwas anderes hervor: die Armut. Wie Apfel und Nüsse mite in wenig Schaumgold neben dem Marzipan sich auf dem Weihnachtsteller zeigen durften, so auch die armen Leute mit Lametta und bunten Kerzen in den bessern Vierteln. Die Reichen schickten ihre Kinder vor, um jenen der Armen wollene Schäfchen abzukaufen oder Almosen auszuteilen, die sie selbst vor Scham nicht über ihre Hände brachten.[25]

> It began with the firtrees. . . . Then one fine day they burst, spilling out toys, nuts, straw, and tree ornaments: the Christmas market. With these things, something else came to the fore: poverty. Just as apples and nuts might appear on the Christmas platter with a bit of gold foil next to the marzipan, so the poor people were allowed, with their tinsel and colored candles, into the better neighborhoods. The rich would send their children out to buy woolen lambkins from the children of the poor, or to distribute the alms which they themselves were ashamed to put into their hands. (*BC*, 103)

In the bourgeois world of Benjamin's family, political truths can only be seen, the narrator suggests, from the lower perspective of the child's small stature: the two vassals on the Victory Column, the poor dwellers in basement rooms, gazed at through shaft openings in the pavement, the miners encased in the large glass cube offered for entertainment by Tante Lehmann (a toy, the narrator remarks, dating from an era that did not yet begrudge even the child of a wealthy bourgeois household a view of workplaces and machines), the servants without whose presence he would be unable to imagine the gloomy apartment of his aunt.[26] From the perspective of the estranged adult, these threshold dwellers appear like protective spirits. Their evocation, therefore, is both poignant and consoling:

> Sie waren meist massiver als die Gebieterinnen, und es kam vor, dass der Salon da drinnen, trotz Bergwerk und Schokolade, mir nicht so viel zu sagen hatte wie das Vestibül, in dem die alte Stütze, wenn ich kam, mir das Mäntelchen wie eine Last abnahm und, wenn ich ging,

> die Mütze, als wenn sie mich segnen wollte, mir in die Stirn drückte. (*S*, 400)
>
> [The old servants] were generally more massive than their mistresses, and, as it happened, the drawing room within, despite the mine and the chocolate, had less to say to me than the vestibule where the old servant woman, when I arrived, would take my coat from me as if it were a burden and, on my departure, press my cap back down on my forehead *as though to bless me*. (*BC*, 66, my italics)

In the theater of the past that is awakened here, summoned from the destitution and loneliness of exile, these characters of ambiguous power seem to possess the secret of endurance. Would these in-between spaces, if only evoked powerfully enough, yield a usable wisdom? Can the adult still benefit from their blessing by way of his telepathic writing? Do these threshold dwellers still keep vigil, across time, over his fate?

The answer is perhaps less than hopeful, since the image of the towering, benevolent servant morphs, by the end of *Berlin Childhood*, into the more ominous appearance of the hunchback. This last fragment symbolically recapitulates the textual trajectory followed by Benjamin's marginal figures; in the subtle unfolding of *The Little Hunchback*, the silhouette of the narrator himself has by the end of the text mysteriously become one of them. Stepping down from a child's nightmare into the ambiguity of superstition, the hunchback, Benjamin recalls, is the creature who can cause mischief just by looking: "Whoever is looked at by this little man pays no attention. Either to himself or to the little man. He stands dazed before a heap of fragments" (*BC*, 121). *Berliner Kindheit* ends on a note of ambiguous disappointment, with this representative of the subterranean world of basement dwellers, but also of the mythology of childhood. The hunchback, *das bucklichte Männlein*, is the last of Benjamin's dialectical images in *Berliner Kindheit* and an epitome thereof: it is never sure, not even for the grown-up narrator, whether it is the hunchback who causes trouble by looking, or whether the one who stands dazed before a heap of fragments—one's childhood, one's life—invokes the hunchback as a way to find solace, and exact oblivion. This figure is familiar to Benjamin's reader from the essay on Kafka, which dwells so insistently on forgetting, and on the distortion things assume in oblivion. It is significant that Benjamin should be so attached to Odradek, Kafka's character without a "fixed abode," whom he sees as the prototype of distortion, the hunchback: "Among the images in Kafka's stories, none is more frequent than that of the man who bows his head far down on his chest: . . . quite palpably, being loaded down is here equated with forgetting, the forgetting of a sleeping man."[27]

The section ends, and with it *Berliner Kindheit*, with the evocation of the folksong "The Little Hunchback," a little man who is "at home in distorted life."[28] Kafka's hunchbacks precede Benjamin's, just as the hunchback precedes the child (or is it the adult?) in search of meaning: it is not the child who looks back, but the hunchback that had been looking at him all along. Where Benjamin had said (in "On Hashish") that he wanted to write "something that comes from things the way wine comes from grapes," at the end of *Berliner Kindheit*—ostensibly the book meant to tease out wisdom from the keeping of things—he writes:

> Where the hunchback appeared, I could only look on uselessly. It was a look from which things receded—until in a year's time, the garden had become a little garden, my room a little room, and the bench a little bench. They shrank, and they grew a little hump, which made them the little man's own. The little man preceded me everywhere. Coming before, he barred the way. . . . Only I never saw him. It was he who always saw me. (*BC*, 121–122)

The text ends on a note of ambivalence: as a figure of chance accompanying the child, "it has long since abdicated"; but as a figure of fate accompanying the exiled writer in search of meaning, it is there, mute, like Kafka's Odradek: "He does no harm to anyone that one can see; but the idea that he is likely to survive me I find most painful," muses Kafka's narrator.[29]

After Benjamin's death, in the 1940s, Adorno wrote *Minima Moralia: Reflections from Damaged Life*; is his subtitle a response to Benjamin's "distorted life"? Perhaps; all the more reason to take seriously his aphorism in "Refuge for the Homeless": "Today . . . it is part of morality not to be at home in one's home" (*MM*, frag. 18, p. 39). If Benjamin stood, as Hannah Arendt memorably put it, on the threshold of the Last Judgment, it will be only fitting to ponder his situation from afar—the other end of the twentieth century—through the lens of literary texts that echo some of his tribulations: those of Annie Ernaux, Günter Grass, and Damon Galgut.

Chapter 5

✦

Annie Ernaux's Diaries of the Outside

Flâneuse, Transfuge de Classe, Sympathetic User

> The flâneur is still on the threshold, of the city as of the bourgeois class. Neither has yet engulfed him; in neither is he at home.
>
> —Walter Benjamin, "Baudelaire, or the Streets of Paris"

Well-known for an extended family ethnography evoking the lives of her petit-bourgeois parents from the perspective of the highly educated, successful writer she became, over the course of almost fifteen years Annie Ernaux kept an unusual diary, published as *Journal du dehors* (1993) and *La vie extérieure* (1999).[1] Speaking of her urge, after moving to the new town of Cergy-Pontoise, "to transcribe scenes, words, gestures of strangers one never meets again, graffiti no sooner scribbled on walls than erased," she conceived her project as "an attempt to convey the reality of an epoch—that acute yet indefinable feeling of modernity associated with a new town—through a series of snapshots of everyday life" (*JD*, 8). This early passage situates her in a long tradition of writers keen on capturing the specificity of modern urban experience: more than a century after Baudelaire, she sees herself no longer as a "*painter* of modern life," but as the author of a "*photographic* writing of the real" from which her subjectivity should be as if evacuated.[2] At first sight, the challenges facing such a project are radically different from similar endeavors a century before: they are not about coping with the intense nervous stimulation of the metropolitan personality, "the maelstrom of perpetual disintegration and renewal, of struggle and contradiction, of ambiguity and anguish."[3] Rather, if we take for granted the views of Henri Lefebvre or Guy Debord, the *villes nouvelles* present the inhabitant with the prospect of "unredeemable boredom," an effect of the pure functionalism that governed their planning: "historicity has disappeared," notes Lefebvre, "the historic city too only survives as a vague regret, as something quaint and picturesque or as commercialized, organized trade value for sightseers."[4] Indeed, some early entries in Ernaux's diary, in which she records the schizophrenic experience of living without attachments, echo such views: "To find myself in a place suddenly sprung up from nowhere, a place bereft of memories, where the buildings are scattered over a huge area, a place with undefined boundaries, proved to be an overwhelming experience" (*JD*, 7). The diary is instrumental in mapping out a place with "no density, just shadows and light . . . the white and remote dream of a schizophrenic" (*JD*, 41), a place that, twelve years after moving in it, eludes her still: "I still don't know what it looks like. I am unable to describe it, unaware where it begins or ends" (*JD*, 64). The lack of bearings is compounded by the experience of losing her mother to Alzheimer's disease, a loss that puts a personal spin on Debord's claim that in the *villes nouvelles*, temporality becomes a category of space. During the progressive loss of her connection to the past embodied by her mother, Ernaux directs her attention to the improvised sociality of everyday spaces—the street, the shopping mall, the metro—of which she becomes the attentive observer: a flâneuse.[5]

Other readers see in Ernaux a female counterpart to the type that Benjamin consecrated in his readings of Baudelaire. Janet Wolff argues that in Baudelaire's poems, female city dwellers such as the prostitute, the widow, the old lady, the lesbian, the murder victim, and the passing unknown woman do appear, but "none of these women meet the poet as his equal. They are subjects of his gaze, objects of his 'botanizing.'"[6] Indeed, a traditional separation of the private and the public that relegates women to the domestic sphere would confirm the category of the flâneur as exclusively male, with some notable exceptions that only reinforce the rule.[7] The nearest Baudelaire comes to a direct encounter with a woman who is not either marginal or debased is in the poem "À une passante," about which Benjamin famously said: "The delight of the city-dweller is love—not at first sight, but at last sight."[8] What is missing, Wolff concludes, is "any account of life outside the public realm, of the experience of 'the modern' in its private manifestations, and also of the very different nature of the experience of those women who did appear in the public arena: a poem written by 'la femme passante' about her encounter with Baudelaire, perhaps."[9]

In *Streetwalking the Metropolis: Women, the City and Modernity*, however, Deborah Parsons shows that in the Paris and London of 1880–1940, women's relationship with the urban space was actually highly diverse, as the work of writers like Virginia Woolf, Amy Levy, Dorothy Richardson, Jean Rhys, Janet Flanner, Djuna Barnes, Anaïs Nin, Rosamond Lehmann, and Elizabeth Bowen suggests; in her postscript, Parsons turns to Doris Lessing's character Martha Quest, opening up possibilities for postwar women to inhabit, explore, and identify in creative ways with the public spaces of the modern metropolis.[10] Responding directly to Wolff, Parsons establishes "that women's fiction does provide such accounts [of life outside the public realm], and that in the modern city of multiplicity, reflection, and indistinction, la *femme passante* is herself a *flâneuse*, just as the 'man of the crowd' is also a *flâneur*."[11] Is there any notable difference between the two? Parsons believes so, pointing out that, while the flâneur keeps his distance from the crowd, even as he knows himself colored by it (as Benjamin puts it in *Illuminations*), female walkers tend to immerse themselves in the crowd, or in any case have a more porous rapport with it. Virginia Woolf's essay "Street Haunting" is an illustrative example: her narrator empathizes "to the point of identification with strangers glimpsed in passing in the city, and becom[es] 'an enormous eye' that can 'put on briefly for a few minutes the bodies and minds of others.'"[12]

True to her experience of everyday life, Annie Ernaux does not aestheticize it by turning it into a poem (as in Baudelaire's "À une passante"), preferring instead uneven diary entries that capture various moments and encounters in their raw reality. Situated in the tradition outlined by Parsons, Ernaux's work sheds an ironic light on Lefebvre's claim that women, "because of their position in everyday life—which is specifically part of everyday life and modernity—are incapable of understanding it."[13] Her diaries reflect a most intimate understanding of the everyday, which she experiences not with the detached, critical distance of a theorist, but with the ambivalence of a self-conscious user. This ambivalence, it bears noting, is an effect of her social position as a *transfuge de classe*. In "Baudelaire, or the Streets of Paris," Benjamin already insists that "the *flâneur* is still on the threshold, of the city as of the bourgeois class. Neither has yet engulfed him; in neither is he at home. He seeks refuge in the crowd."[14] Ernaux, then, is in a precarious position vis-à-vis the already marginal figure of the flâneur. Living in a *ville nouvelle*, describing what she sees in the metro, RER, and underground stations, she is definitely on the threshold of the city; but she is also someone who moves between social classes and thus has a perspective across a social threshold—the double view afforded by her knowledge of her family's social class and by her familiarity with the upper middle class, to which she had access through education and marriage.[15] Whereas the flâneur feels restless both in the city and among the bourgeois, Ernaux feels uncomfortable in a city that is no longer a historical city, but a *ville nouvelle*, and in a class which she can neither fully embrace nor reject, but which she confronts, within herself, with mental habits and references that characterize her original social milieu—in the terms proposed by Pierre Bourdieu, whose sociological analyses played a major role in Ernaux's intellectual life, with an *habitus clivé*.[16]

The whole project of the family ethnography, Ernaux has explained in interviews, was "authorized" by the publication of *Distinction*, which validated her experience by providing tools for examining and bringing it to light: indeed, "not just the authorization, more than that, the injunction to write about all that, dare not only think, but dare to write."[17] This experience of social dislocation, which involves a split self and the negotiation between contradictory experiences and feelings, requires a particular kind of writing that Ernaux calls "une écriture de la distance" (a writing of distance):

> Through the analysis of painful sensations, I have come to the certainty that the only viable narrative position was to adopt a "writing of distance" corresponding to my situation: distance from my parents, distance between my old and my current self, distance between the past and the present, between the original culture and the one that enables me to write. This phrase, "writing of distance" designated to my mind both the style, the voice, deprived of affective markers, and the method.[18]

Distance from self and others; distance both as affective detachment with regard to style, and as a method of approaching her subject; with the hindsight, Ernaux continues, she came close to what she later discovered Bourdieu called in his sociological work an "objectifying distance [*la distance objectivante*]."[19] A passage she borrows from his *Méditations pascaliennes* could serve as an epigraph (a second one, after the one from Rousseau) to her diaries: "I shall speak very little about myself, the singular self, in any case, that Pascal calls 'hateful.' And if I nonetheless never cease to speak about myself, it will be the impersonal self that the most personal confessions pass over in silence, or refuse, on account of its very impersonality."[20] Similar to Adorno in *Minima Moralia*, the real subject of interest is here that of social substantiality, which Ernaux seeks in her encounters with others. Despite her original intention to be an objective observer, her selection of scenes and incidents, as well as her reactions to them, are clearly determined by her story of social mobility. Diary entries featuring working-class people, beggars, petty humiliations of disempowered individuals, commuters who ignore or avoid looking at the poor, are informed by a solidarity with and sympathy for the less privileged: she is certainly not "dépaysée" (uprooted, alienated) in the metro, as she reports historian Jacques LeGoff as saying (*JD*, 41), and there is no condescension in her writing, such as she sees in President Jacques Chirac's formulation "les petites gens" (the little people), broadcast on television (*JD*, 35).

Yet Ernaux, although unambiguously critical, is not a moralist. As Benjamin already noted about the flâneur, his "botanizing on the asphalt" precludes the moralistic stance that Engels, for instance, took on the busy streets of London.[21] By contrast, for a Parisian flâneur, Benjamin muses, "to move in this crowd was natural. . . . No matter how great the distance that an individual cared to keep from it, he still was colored by it and, unlike Engels, was not able to view it from without."[22] One must amend the last sentence when referring to Ernaux: as a *transfuge de classe*, she is colored by the others, but, as an educated woman empowered by her reading of Bourdieu, she can also view it from without. Her detailed, insightful view of the variegated forms of experience that characterize urban life in the late 1980s and 1990s[23] are often in agreement with Lefebvre's and Debord's critique of consumption, manipulation, control, illusions of rationality, separation, and abstraction. But her awareness of the multitude of ways of living (such as Perec playfully illustrated in *La vie mode d'emploi*),[24] of the ingenuity with which individuals negotiate their identities and lifestyles, does not lead her to celebrate the *inventiveness of the quotidian*, like Benjamin (following certain readings) or de Certeau; the latter's jubilant "le quotidien s'invente avec mille façons de braconner" (the everyday invents itself in thousands ways of poaching)—echoing Benjamin's politics of the residual, perhaps the last gesture of a utopian consciousness—speaks to his faith, which she does not share indiscriminately, in the resourcefulness of "users" of systems to find their own original, even subversive, ways of poaching that which is publicly shared.[25] Her aims also differ from those of Lefebvre, who wanted to apply a revolutionary politics to the everyday, and her attitude—from his condescension vis-à-vis (what he saw as) pathetic aspirations toward a bourgeois lifestyle: Ernaux acknowledges, both in herself and in others, the vulnerability, ambiguity of desire, deprivation, insecurity—in other words, the socially marked affects—that tinge the self-presentation, behavior, and decisions made in the sphere of the everyday; also, the occasional cynicism, avoidance of others, or reactions that do not cohere with one's beliefs.

Ernaux's unique position as a flâneuse and *transfuge de classe*, which combines a critical awareness and a user's ambivalence, affords insight into the complex ways in which individuals relate to systems. Departing from both Lefebvre and de Certeau, and echoing Bourdieu, she notices, for instance, how symbolic violence operates in the social sphere, with many of the victims aware of it "like something in [their] flesh and blood [comme une chose de chair et de sang]."[26] By recognizing her own ambivalence and vulnerability, and by acknowledging that other people evoke in her episodes from her past, she intimates a continuum of humanity that links her to the lives of others. "Que faire de notre vulnérabilité?" (What to do about/with our vulnerability?) asks Guillaume le Blanc in a recent book that resonates with Ernaux's position. As we shall see in what follows, she answers by turning shared vulnerability into a platform for restoring the excluded their humanity; and this can only happen, her diaries suggest, by narrating their lives and thus by looking at them (again) as persons worthy of empathy and consideration.

The Distantiality of the Everyday: Fiction, Ambivalent Desire, Examined Life

The context from which *Journal du dehors* and *La vie extérieure* emerged puts Heidegger's notion of *distantiality* in perspective. As she revealed, Ernaux began her diary because she needed to map out her *ville nouvelle*, and in order to "keep in touch with the world" that her mother—and in a certain way, herself—was losing; these two circumstances are no doubt related: the vanishing link to the past and to her grounded self is, through diary-writing, replaced by a sustained attention to the lives of other people. The project, however, is hardly about measuring herself against them; rather, her position as a flâneuse, *transfuge de classe*, and "user" of the everyday uniquely qualifies her to chronicle other lives sympathetically, yet with a critical eye. Most importantly, she points to the various narratives that frame our everyday experiences, including her own, which often create contradictory impulses, ambivalence, desires, or unresolved confusion. *Distantiality*, then, or that all-too-human tendency to compare one's life with the lives of others, becomes a more complex affair as soon as, rather than look at the lives of others "from the corner of the eye," one takes a step back to really look, with that "enormous eye" that Woolf speaks of. A few diary entries convey the many uses to which such distantiality can be put and point us unmistakably to what Ernaux chooses to do in her diary of the outside.

Journal du dehors, it bears noting, does include a few entries about Paris, one of which casts light on the figure of the flâneuse. In this fragment, Ernaux engages in a stroll in the footsteps of a mythical figure, Breton's Nadja, seeking to revive the practice of surrealist *dérive*: "tapping into the unrealized possibilities harboured by the ordinary life we lead rather than rejecting it for another life," not "losing one's reason, but wanting what reason made them lose" and therefore rejecting "all fixed canons of taste, logic, and representation," championing instead "hysteria, dreams, the irrational, chance, 'amour fou,' 'humour noir,' revolution, and convulsive beauty."[27] How would such ideals fare at the end of the twentieth century? Ernaux's reenactment of Nadja's stroll offers an ambiguous answer:

> Then I turned into the Boulevard Magenta, looking for number 106, Hôtel de Suède, which used to be called the Sphinx Hôtel. The façade was sheathed in a tarpaulin; the whole of the interior was being demolished. One of the workers leaned out of a window; he looked at me with amusement and said something to the others. I was standing motionless on the opposite sidewalk, gazing up at the hotel (which they may be converting into private apartments). He thought I was returning to a place that held memories for me, as a lover or a whore. In fact I am reliving the memories of another woman, Nadja, the Nadja associated with André Breton, who lived in this hotel around 1927. Displayed in the window where I was standing were outmoded pairs of shoes, of a single color, black, and slippers, also black. It looked like a store for mourning shoes or ecclesiastical footwear. I continued down the Boulevard Magenta and turned into a small alleyway, the Ruelle de la Ferme-Saint-Lazare; it was deserted. A man was sitting on his doorstep. Bloody remains soiled the cobblestones. Then I turned back into the Rue La Fayette and walked on until I got to the café "La Nouvelle France," with its ancient-looking curtains. Framed in the entrance, a boy was waving to an Eurasian girl on the

> other side of the street. I continued to follow in Nadja's footsteps in the sort of daze that gives one the impression of an intense life. (*JD*, 70–71, translation modified)

Ernaux's attempt to conjure the memory of Nadja proves more elusive than the woman portrayed in Breton's novel. Her mystery is irretrievable from the debris of the Sphinx Hotel, a building that appears to be efficiently transformed from a space of lightness, travel, or promiscuity into one of settled routine; the old-fashioned shoes mourn vanished times, the bloody residue adds an uncanny touch to a reality that advertises its novelty ("la Nouvelle France"), in spite of the ancient-looking curtains that frame it. And is the man sitting on his doorstep, in this surrealist film, Benjamin himself? Ernaux plays a double game here: she mimics nostalgically a surrealist engagement with the real, while also denouncing the superficiality and anachronism of her gesture. Why, she asks in a different entry, does she look for the signs of literature in real life? And why cling to the past, in an age no longer committed to the historical?

As Lefebvre put it, in the contemporary age, history can only be a vague regret—or perhaps a parody? Certain entries hint at this possibility, juxtaposing texts or cultural references that enter in a subversive rapport with one another: Ernaux notes, for instance, that on the walls of a classroom at Nanterre University where a professor teaches Proust lingers, ironically, the memory of 1968 slogans:

> Unrestricted pleasure
> Free sexuality
> Free love
> Student you're sleeping
> You're wasting your life
> Let's impose economic equality
>
> (*JD*, 58, translation modified)

And in a different register, she points out two coexisting modes of belief and of writing, a capitalist one that gambles on rational efficiency, and an archaic one that taps into the irrational:

> A free sheet with classifieds is slipped into my mailbox every week. "PROFESSOR SOLO-DRAMA. THE GREAT MARABOUT is among us at last. He offers to solve all our problems: unhappy love life, loss of affection, adultery, spells, poor academic results, bad sporting performances, departure of the loved one. If you want to be happy, don't waste any time: come and see me. Quick, professional service. Results guaranteed. 131B, Avenue de Clichy. 3rd floor. Right-hand door." (The photograph in the box shows a good-looking African.) In a few

> lines, a panorama of man's desires, a narrative written in the third person, then in the first. A character with a mysterious identity—a sage, maybe a magician—whose name conjures up poetry and drama. Two modes of writing, relying on psychology and marketing respectively. A sample of fiction. (*JD*, 26–27)

Ernaux's comment is insightful, if elliptical and seemingly offhand: she traces a connection between the "panorama of man's desires" and "fiction," a diagnosis that situates her response within more ambiguous parameters than Lefebvre's critical reaction to the social aspect foregrounded by the classifieds she quotes here. Here is Lefebvre's unequivocal unveiling of the paradox of irrationality that thrives in everyday life:

> If we probe into the private lives of the members of this society we find that they are, in many cases, fortune-tellers, witches, quacks, star-gazers . . . Indeed, one has only to read the papers; it is as though people had nothing in their daily lives to give them a meaning, a direction, apart from publicity, so they fall back on magic and witchcraft. Perhaps they hope in this roundabout way to adapt their desires, discover and orientate them. Thus the rationality of economism and technicity produces its opposite as their "structural" complement and reveals its limitations as restricted rationalism and irrationalism pervade everyday life, confront and reflect one another.[28]

Although Ernaux would partially agree with Lefebvre's critique, she is less dismissive of the desire for meaning, for a direction. A diary entry, for instance, engages the register of superstition, Ernaux looking at herself perform the role of a "featherbrained schoolgirl": "I bought a copy of *Marie-Claire* at the station in the New Town. This month's horoscope: 'You will meet a wonderful man.' Throughout the day I wondered several times if the man I was talking to was the one they meant" (*JD*, 17, translation modified). This passage does not provide any indication of a possibly ironic performance of the role in which the horoscope casts her: there seems to be no critical self-awareness. But the aside that follows, in brackets, draws attention to a gap between an acceptable public stance (a rational, therefore unambiguously critical approach to the everyday, à la Lefebvre) and the more complex ways in which one chooses to experience—in the mode of performance—the everyday:

> (By choosing to write in the first person, I am laying myself open to criticism, which would not have been the case had I written "she wondered if the man she was talking to was the one they meant." The third person—he/she—is always somebody else, free to do whatever they choose. "I" refers to oneself, the reader, and it is inconceivable,

> or unthinkable, for me to read my own horoscope and behave like some mushy schoolgirl. "I" shames the reader.) (*JD*, 17)

By opening a parenthesis in her diary, Ernaux sheds light on a niche in the public discourse that bans the acknowledgment of superstition: as a writer who addresses herself to a reader, she is not "supposed" to confess that she indulged the empty fantasies encouraged by "la presse feminine."[29] But what if, as a "user" of public systems, as de Certeau might put it, the feminine press being one such system, she *chose* to behave like a *midinette*, perhaps because it amuses her, or because it reminds her of a youthful naïveté with which she might have read the horoscope as a schoolgirl, or because she finds it ironic that the possibility of running into "un homme merveilleux" would be an irruption of the miraculous ("le merveilleux," just as for the surrealists) in her life? Ernaux brings to light here the risks she is aware to be courting by writing such an unusual diary: words like "je m'expose" and "inadmissible" suggest that a photographic transcription of everyday occurrences, which involve various self-performances, must by necessity relinquish the benefits of the anonymity which protects one in everyday life. The third person of fiction is also the deixis of anonymous public everyday existence, which the use of the first person, one that also interpellates the reader, disrupts. With this aside, she steps out of what might appear as innocuous transcription of random occurrences: the very choice of aspects that she writes about, as well as their juxtaposition, adds to her scattered metacommentaries.

The entry I have just discussed, for instance, follows after the evocation of a shopping experience, or rather, it turns out in the last sentence, the debunking of the fictions and ideologies that determine and shape mass consumption:

> For ages now, at La Samaritaine, in the Trois-Fontaines shopping mall, we have been hearing a man's voice urging us to buy up the whole store in various tones: quizzical, merry, threatening, playful: "It will soon be winter; you'll be needing thick, warm gloves and scarves. Come and see our new range of woolen accessories," or "Madame, has it ever occurred to you that the virtues of a perfect hostess are reflected in the choice of her tableware? In our china department . . ." A young, coaxing voice. Today the man belonging to that voice was surrounded by toys, a microphone in one hand. He's a redhead, half-bald, with huge, thick spectacles and small, greasy hands. (*JD*, 16–17, suspension points in the original)

This entry reads like a nod to Benjamin's remark that "the department store puts even *flânerie* to use for commodity circulation. The department store is the *flâneur*'s last practical joke."[30] It is the joke of consumer capitalism that Ernaux swiftly spells out in this "temple of frenetic consumption" (Debord), in the disconnect between the oracular, chameleonic voice attaching urgency to the satisfaction of the customers' presumed needs and the unglamorous person who has become only its function. If in this case Ernaux points to the man's alienation from his own voice—he has become "l'homme de la voix," in a preposterous relation of ownership—and to the insidious ways the desires of consumers are made to coincide with "buying the whole store," by contrast, in other instances she dwells on the subtle ways in which one's personal history, anxieties, precarious social identity, and deprivations of various sorts determine one's relationship to things, to the very idea of ownership. "Vague desire for clothes," she acknowledges at a certain point: "I see myself dressed in a twirling of coats and blouses. . . . I succumb to a strange condition in which I want all sorts of clothes for myself, regardless of shape or color, in which I am seized with an overriding compulsion to buy a coat or a handbag" (*JD*, 28, 48), only to walk out into the street, relieved that she has left the pressure to get something behind. Yet later she shows understanding for a woman in the metro who admires the things she has just bought: "It's a common enough scene: happiness at possessing something beautiful, at seeing one's longing for beauty satisfied. Our relationship to things is so moving" (*JD*, 77–78).

One can imagine a different situation where Ernaux might wonder why the woman unpacks her purchase in public, the way she notices, at the butcher's, on the street, in the metro, that certain conversations or gestures are meant for "the gallery"—that is, for the other people present, as a form of what Erving Goffman called "impression management."[31] And yet not all of these entries sound ironic because she sees such behaviors as part of a desire to take the measure of one's life under the gaze of others, in imaginary relationship to their existences. This brings us back to Heidegger's distantiality, of which Ernaux offers an eloquent illustration in the following entry:

> A man is questioning a young woman on the train to Paris: "How many hours a week do you work?" "What time do you start work?" "Can you choose when you take your vacation?" We all need to assess the advantages and constraints of a profession, the material side of life. Not out of harmless curiosity, or to make polite conversation, but to learn about other people's lives so that we can learn about our own life or the life we might have chosen. (*JD*, 49)

Ernaux is no stranger to the selfish reasons or perfunctory politeness that can motivate one's interest in other people's lives; and yet she does not see distantiality as the purely negative phenomenon that Heidegger sees as detrimental to being-with-others: on one hand, she understands its necessary dimension ("assessing . . . the material side of life"); on the other, her own focus on other people's lives shows that one's reasons and aims can be vastly different. Thus as a *transfuge de classe*, she tends to look not down on, but down at individuals whose lives she might have had. She could have been, occasionally she tells herself, the cashier that no one cares about beyond the commercial transaction, in which she is "only a hand that is permitted no mistakes"; had she been very poor, an entry rhetorically pursues, would she have preferred to be a beggar, or a prostitute? This extreme form of identification introduces the aspect where she most disagrees with theorists of everyday life like Benjamin and de Certeau, who emphasize the disruptive, possibly revolutionary, potential of the everyday; Ernaux, for her part, looks at the excluded and sees shared vulnerability, as well as the possibility for us to expand the notion of humanity we live by. It is this larger aim of Ernaux's writing that qualifies—to the point of contradicting—Heidegger's view of "distantiality": asking questions about other people's lives is not simply about examining one's relation to a social script (that attaches social and cultural capital, for example, to various activities and accomplishments, establishing hierarchies of what counts as success); it can be an opportunity for comparison (one's own life with other people's lives) with the purpose of learning "about our own life or the life we might have chosen"—in other words, a way to realize one's own highest potential for being: perhaps not exactly in the hard-to-achieve way of Heidegger's authenticity, but in the sense of a life in which being—with others—is an issue: an examined life.

The "Enormous Eye" of the *Transfuge*: Disposability, Exclusion, Vulnerability

"Photographers, like painters, can teach us to see specific things, or to see them in a specific way," writes Alfred Döblin, prefacing a photo album by August Sander. Ernaux's diaries, with their ambition to be nothing more than "photographic snapshots of reality," create indeed a specific way of seeing, even when the author contents herself with simply recording or sketching out scenes that she witnesses. As we have just seen, her diaries invite conversation with other well-known observers of everyday life, such as Benjamin, de Certeau, Lefebvre, or Debord; her attitude, however, brings her in close proximity to the insights of a contemporary thinker, Guillaume le Blanc, author of *Vies ordinaries, vies précaires* and *Que faire de notre vulnérabilité?* Le Blanc's work seems to me a particularly apt companion to Ernaux's diaries because it helps articulate their contribution to a rethinking of community, which I take to be at stake in her autobiographical experiment.

Journal du dehors contains some descriptions of the New Town, in which the "reality of [her] epoch, this modernity impossible to define" appears in images of disintegration or wearing out, of detritus, residue, leftovers, disposable materials and individuals. Previous writers invested in the project of defining modernity hinted at an apparent affinity between the everyday, waste, and creativity: Benjamin's *Lumpensammler*, Baudelaire's *chiffonnier*, de Certeau's every(day) man—all use productively the residues of modernity.

Not so in the landscape of Cergy-Pontoise that Ernaux describes in an early diary entry:

> Opposite the rows of neat, tidy suburban houses, pin, cream-coloured, with green shutters . . . , separated from the urbanized area by a street bordered with lawns, starts an area of wasteland, with copses, a few derelict houses and a footpath with potholes filled with water. There are discarded objects everywhere, in the brambles and along the edges of the path. A wrapper of Dutch cookies Spirits, a broken Coca-Cola bottle, cardboard packaging for a six-pack, a copy of the local gazette, a length of iron-piping, flattened plastic bottles and a white substance with blisters—maybe sodden cardboard—suggesting a cluster of Sahara roses. . . . Metamorphoses of all these objects, twice broken, rumpled and flattened—first by those who leave them behind, then by the bad weather. Combining two forms of wear and tear. (*JD*, 24, modified translation)

The layers of litter take the place of a historical sedimentation felt to be missing among the disconnected existences of the new town; but these residues of consumerism and human encounters, or the grafittis exuding youthful defiance, are less unsettling than the social detritus of disposable individuals who make appearance repeatedly in the pages of *Journal du dehors* and *La vie extérieure*: beggars, down-and-outs, tramps, people in retirement homes, working-class individuals whose bodies visibly bear the burden of everyday life.

Just as, in the passage above, "the rows of neat, tidy suburban houses," where presumably a well-ordered life of plentiful consumption unfolds, contrast with the derelict houses and the discarded objects, a logic of symmetry applies in the social realm: the validation and inclusion of some individuals calls for the exclusion of others. An entry about layoffs at Renault is part of a cluster of notes in the diaries that expose a phenomenon Guillaume le Blanc also discusses extensively in his work, "the production of disposable people":[32]

> The closing down of the Renault factories at Vilvorde, in Belgium, triggers the first European strike. At the same time, the stocks continue to "soar" (the image itself is charming, light, while the words for the workers weigh down, they are "struck," "threatened"). Bluntly put, that means that some people are struck off so that others, the share holders, get rich. Ultimately, the death of some might be acceptable so that others can take advantage. We are shown the laid-off workers, never the share-holders, invisible like money. (*LVE*, 89)

In "Reflexionen zur Klassentheorie" ("Reflections on Class Theory," published posthumously in 1975), Adorno identified the logic illustrated in this diary entry, pointing out the "immanence of the oppressed to the system." Le Blanc takes up Adorno's idea, explaining, in line with Ernaux's own insight: "Exclusion maintains the excluded within the system, since exclusion is symmetrical, not contrary, to inclusion. 'Symmetrical' means here that the inclusion of some calls forth the exclusion of others."[33] As Ernaux also notes in several of her entries, le Blanc shows that the "accreditation of lives is not complete. Moreover, it can only be established economically, juridically, politically, it seems, on condition that it does not concern everyone, that it leaves aside, like an indeterminate reserve that it will be able to dip into whenever necessary, disqualified lives as superfluous lives."[34] Illustrative of this principle, Ernaux's entry about the fired Renault workers is prefaced by a sequence of two others, which put into social, economic, and historical context the impact of unemployment on those affected, as well as the ways in which the system legitimates certain voices while delegitimizing others:

> A voice in the RER. "Today I'm not selling newspapers, I would but no one cares anymore." The man follows up mentioning all these people who took to the streets against the Debré law, but no one marches against unemployment, "we can as well continue to sleep in the street and starve." Once again, the voice from below speaks the truth. "In 89 they cut off the king's head, people today would be too scared to do it." During this time, I grade papers on Dom Juan. The man talking is poorer and unhappier than a peasant in Molière's time. [She doesn't give this man anything, but she is moved enough by a musician's familiar songs to reward him with a coin.] (*JD*, 85–86)
>
> 4 March
>
> On the radio, Alain Madelin was answering the questions of listeners, who were saying: "Salaries go down, my pension goes down, I have no work, Renault has just got rid of jobs.' To each Madelin responded invariably, "you should create an enterprise!" He pronounced "cre-eate": you should cre-eate! Cre-eate! With the tone of voice of someone talking to half-wits. Berating triumphantly his interlocutor: "I can hear the fright in your words, sir!" Indeed, one must be the last coward not to create an enterprise when one is unemployed, two rents behind and fearing foreclosure.
>
> At some point, Madelin brandishes his origins, "my father was a skilled worker, I know pay slips." As if he had been the same as the little boy of long ago, in a working-class town.
>
> This discourse, an insult to people and reason, was held by a former minister, without anyone intervening to denounce the disdain and imposture. The listeners couldn't "insult" him back—the danger that the micro would be cut off—by asking him how much he earned

> every month, where he lived, what enterprise he had "cre-eated" himself. Once again, the media legitimized the propositions, however absurd, of an authorized voice. I felt hatred (which is why I am writing these lines). (*JD*, 86–87)

There is much happening in these two entries, and in their juxtaposition: the laid-off workers express their discontent on the radio, but by listening—or, rather, being forced to listen—to a cynical former minister, they only participate in a symbolic violence that perpetuates itself through the mediatization of his advice, and that Ernaux angrily dismisses as "absurd": coming from a place of social and economic privilege, it is oblivious of the vulnerability of their position. These workers' unemployment is on a continuum with the precarious situation of the beggar in the preceding entry, who denounces not only the preposterous compromise of a politics of care—selling useless newspapers—but also the unwillingness of those still "included" to listen to the impoverished. The person addressing himself to the metro passengers—about whose situation Ernaux notes that it is worse than in the seventeenth century, presumably despite contemporary narratives of progress—points out that unemployment is no longer interesting enough to protest against; those whose voices still matter are reacting to a more recent development, the Debré anti-immigration law. The unemployed man's voice, to put it in le Blanc's words, "is lost not because it ceases to speak, but because it is no longer heard, and it is no longer heard because it is not considered from a social point of view to fulfill the normative expectations of official channels of listening."[35] By juxtaposing the "voice from below [that] speaks the truth" and the "discourse" smacking of disdain and imposture of the former minister, Ernaux shows, like le Blanc, that "voices are not democratically heard. They are constituted as audible voices by the social labels that give them credit, or, on the contrary, that discredit them."[36] Many of Ernaux's diary entries invite a sustained reflection on the possibility of representing the excluded, people who fall out of the sanctioned frameworks of social, juridical, political recognition of society and are thus denied, or are about to lose, their right to citizenship.

The question of representation is all the more important since she voices criticism of intellectual pretense, snobbery, and obliviousness, of the smug enjoyment of the "mirage of social interiority."[37] Those in the system, Ernaux notes, protect themselves not only by othering, but by dehumanizing the disposable individuals maintained on the fringe, outside yet still inside.[38] On a cold November day, for instance, Ernaux writes about the information broadcast on the media that an SDF woman died from the cold in Toulouse and three SDFs died in Paris; this makes her note that to use the term SDF, the French acronym for the homeless (*sans domicile fixe*), "is to designate a sexless species that wears bags and ragged clothes, whose steps go nowhere, without a past and without a future. That is to say they do not belong to the category of normal people" (*LVE*, 123). Le Blanc uses the same words: "To be excluded is to be deprived at the same time of social qualities and of future. That means discovering oneself without a present because one does not have a future. The excluded is therefore potentially nowhere because he has no share in the common world."[39] This situation, Ernaux and le Blanc agree, leads to a loss of humanity:

> There are in France thirty million dogs and cats that one would never leave outside in such cold weather. But we do let die men and women on the street, perhaps precisely because they are our fellow human beings, with the same desires and needs as ourselves. It is too difficult to bear this part of ourselves, dirty, dazed by the lack of everything. The Germans who were living close to the concentration camps didn't believe that the Jews in lousy rags were human. (*LVE*, 123)

Le Blanc spells out the logic of Ernaux's last sentence:

> The decision to no longer see the excluded as a man or as a woman unravels the figure of exclusion and underlines vigorously that to be excluded is not only to lose one's place in a class or a particular classifying system, but it is to risk, at the same time, to lose all place, to no longer be anywhere, potentially to become nobody. What does nobody mean here? That one is no longer retained by the slightest reference.[40]

This takes us very far from Benjamin's and de Certeau's politics of the disposable; every now and then, Ernaux's entries recall de Certeau's notion of "poaching the system" only to cast doubt on the efficacy of such forms of subversion. Of the numerous entries that record encounters with beggars, the following one comes closest to acknowledging creativity: "A new form of 'begging' over the past few weeks: 'Would you spare two francs so I can get pissed?' A young man with an earring. Cynicism has replaced the appeal to pity. Endless creativity of people" (*JD*, 77, translation modified). Surely, as Ernaux notes, this man does not conform to the social script of humbly asking for money in order to fulfill a basic need; rather, he chooses to imply that such a plea would fall on deaf ears, and performs instead the negative stereotype of beggars as shameless drunkards. But we are not told if such an ironic appropriation disrupts in any way the status quo; most likely, it only reinforces it. The following entry points convincingly to this likelihood: "In a corridor, on the ground, in an area marked out by chalk, someone had scribbled: 'For food. I have no family.' But the man or woman who had written that had gone, the chalk circle was empty. People avoided to step in it" (*JD*, 20, translation modified). Ernaux's last remark points to the irony of a literal othering through disidentification with the public space appropriated by a beggar, and thus the consolidation of a "distribution of the sensible" (places and visibility) that works through exclusion.[41] The chalk circle is the visible index of an existence under the sign of deprivation, and its emptiness ominously points to the possibility of its occupant's disappearance: what starts with unemployment, Ernaux's juxtaposed entries suggest, is on a continuum with selling newspapers, begging, and more desperate efforts to cling to survival; finally, with disappearance.[42] At the end of the spectrum of precariousness is the *fait divers* of the death of a person reduced to the anonymity of three letters: SDF.

The diaries do the difficult work of bridging the gap between the social perception and handling of poverty, on one hand, and a more humane understanding of it, on the other. Where one might see creativity or provocation, she sees—to adapt a word used by Simone Weil and Anne Carson—a decreation of the social self. This phenomenon, however, is not inevitable:

> At the Charles-de-Gaulle-Etoile station, a man in his thirties gets into a subway car and sits down on a folding seat. . . . Later on, he stands up. Leans against the wall, undoes his jacket and lifts his tee-shirt. He scrutinizes his stomach for some time, then pulls down his tee-shirt. Clearly, his actions are not intended to provoke; they are the ultimate manifestation of loneliness—true loneliness—in the midst of the crowd. Beside him, there's a plastic bag, the trademark of the homeless. When someone loses their home and their job, how long does it take before the presence of other people no longer prevents them from doing in public things that are perfectly normal, but in our culture unacceptable in public? Where starts the indifference to the "good manners" we were once taught at school and at home, over the dining-room table, when *we* used to fall asleep dreaming of the big bright future? He got off at Auber. (*JD*, 90, translation modified, my italics)

Unlike other destitute individuals who engage in some way with the other users of public systems, the young man in this entry adopts the same attitude as fellow travelers on the metro who pretend not to see: he acts as if they were not present. Ernaux points out that, once detached from the forms of social accreditation of employment and fixed lodging, he feels exempt from social conventions. The sociality of the metro is to him no "system" that he might use provocatively or creatively—his gesture is a step in unlearning proprieties, the savoir faire acquired as a child, at school, or at home. Striking, in Ernaux's comments, is the use of the plural pronoun *nous* as she conjures up a time of youthful hopes in everyone's life, but at the same time, this *we* includes her, and her readers, in the contemplation of the varying degrees to which those hopes materialized.[43] And with this, she recasts the episode within the context of a human life, rather than seeing the man merely as the silhouette of "a beggar." *A life is being excluded*, le Blanc would say, *that has not always been excluded, and that could have been otherwise. The exclusion happens to a life that has been lived, that existed as a life without exclusion*[44]—like ours.[45] Ernaux is aware of a possible alternative reading that would understand the man's baring of his belly as a gesture of provocation; and she does not avoid spelling out the significance of such gestures, as for instance in a situation where a clochard exposes not his stomach, but his sex. Stripped of almost all signs of social framing, he exposes the only form of identification left to him: "forme déchirante de la dignité: montrer qu'on est un homme" (a heartbreaking form of dignity: showing that one is a male). Ernaux comments on this mute, but radical, disruption not only of social proprieties, but of the status quo: one cannot give him money, she notes, just pretend not to see him. "It is a gesture that ruins everything—the vanity of women in fur coats, the determined stride of market conquerors, the humbleness of musicians and beggars to whom one gives the odd coin" (*JD*, 32, modified translation). The gesture does not comfort the status quo, like the submissiveness of beggars who accept the charity of passers-by; it disrupts the comfortable anonymity of a public space, creating an anomalous zone—like the white circle traced with chalk—that everyone avoids to confront. Ernaux would no doubt agree here with le Blanc's analysis: the rant of the clochard, inaudible as it may be, or postures judged indecent, are disruptions of an unspoken social contract, most often provoked by the loss of social bearings: "the rage that inhabits these postures represents a way of being decidedly turned against society."[46]

If on a personal level, the reaction to poverty is avoidance or mercy delivered in the form of small change, the bureaucratic response to it is, in Ernaux's fragmentary account, a politics of care that others, controls and humiliates the impoverished. In an entry dated June 9, 1998, she visits the office of social welfare of the City of Paris in the Tenth Arrondissement, where she is struck by the attitude of an assistant "who barks at everybody." She looks at the small separated desks where people are called to talk about their circumstances—Ernaux calls the place "the confessional of the poor"—and takes note of the assistant's eagerness to make the newcomers "feel his power and their indignity" (*LVE*, 110). She concludes: "This is a place where only the impoverished come, where the possibility of the presence of other people is not considered" (110). This last remark aptly summarizes a host of phenomena: the prompt labeling of anyone who enters such an office as lacking financial means, hence power, autonomy, and the right to privacy; soliciting support equals loss of dignity, a diminished condition that warrants diminished (or no) respect. The assistant's attitude corroborates a suggestion that remains implicit in Ernaux's diaries, that exclusion affects not only those excluded, but also those who accept its logic; in other words, the dehumanization affects everyone involved—the excluded because they are deprived of their life, of their voice; the included because they deny the others their humanity, which entitles them to behave in inhumane ways.

The danger of a politics of care is to silence completely the persons affected and to recast them in alienating scenarios, while the system pats itself on the back. Ernaux's entry about the Maison de Nanterre, an institution for the homeless and the retired, is mediated by a television documentary in which a man is shown collecting the stones in the courtyard and disposing them meticulously around the trees. "He says it's bad to leave the stones lying around. It's the last image of the film, accompanied by a voice-over: 'This may be seen as a metaphor for the Maison de Nanterre—an establishment where order reigns supreme, where order is preserved' " (*JD*, 42). The man's futile gesture might be reminiscent for Samuel Beckett's readers of the eponymous character in the novel *Molloy*, who, not yet confined but equally humble, collects pebbles and tries to find the best possible way to distribute them among his pockets; but unlike Molloy, who decides to throw his pebbles up in the air, unable to find a satisfying solution to his conundrum, the man here participates in the mechanisms of his social containment, offering a convenient aesthetic gesture that comforts the viewers. He is no "schizo out for a stroll" subverting the system, as Deleuze and Guattari describe Molloy, but a well-disciplined individual whose existence is reduced to the rituals of order.[47] Ernaux's comment insists again on the erasure of the real life in this process, as well as on the erasure of the possibility of using one's imagination to bring it back into focus: "To find a fitting conclusion, they single out the gestures of one man—a chunk of his existence—and turn these into a symbol, a stylistic device. *It stops you wondering why that man is there*" (*JD*, 42, my italics).

How to bridge this "emotional distance" that takes the form of the proposition "That is not me" that Ernaux notices prevails in most situations of exposure to destitution and social exclusion?[48] How to amend the official script that is often superimposed and substituted for the stories of the excluded, like in the case of the man at the Maison de Nanterre? The diaries are remarkable through a quality—or one had better say, with Pierre Zaoui, a *practice*—of discretion: Ernaux removes herself from the scene of encounter, letting the others be, live, express themselves, react, interact, without any intervention. Many of the entries are simple notations, "photographic snapshots of reality," as the author calls them, without as much as a caption. This affective absence or minimalism, which solicits the reader's emotion, is most interesting when considered in relation to the sequence of entries, and the effects—of contrast, elaboration, echo, or imagined relation—that the different scenes produce. In yet other cases, Ernaux fails to remain a silent photographer, commenting on an incident by articulating that which the destitute fail to see or express, the violence done to them, the mechanisms of exclusion. The reader's experience thus oscillates between shock or surprise, sympathy ("I feel what the other is feeling") and volunteered passion (the text produces "a blank spot where the reader . . . [steps] in to supply the missing fear, grief, shame or anger").[49] Most importantly, Ernaux prompts the reader to supply an imaginative dimension typically withheld in the encounter with the destitute, and this by repeatedly suturing the continuum of humanity as one of vulnerability. In the following sequence of four entries, for instance, she zooms in on different kinds of vulnerability, and in each she supplies the missing context, deplores its obliteration, or gestures toward the oblivion that can engulf victims who remain anonymous. Given the randomness of the violence, however, they could be anyone:

> Early July . . .
>
> First mayoral decree forbidding begging and the "lying position" of certain persons in public places. One saw this one coming. Let us finally hide these beings who expose their slouching bodies . . . that offend the view of tourists sitting on café terraces.
>
> The "lying position," that of love, of sleep, and of death. Of abandonment and of arrested time. A vision that negates civilization and progress. Temptation.
>
> The Serbs have taken back Srebrenica, Zepa. Since no one is capable of imagining a *real* war any longer, or *actual* concentration camps, everyone shows revolt and doesn't give a dime.
>
> 26 July
>
> Yesterday a bomb exploded in the RER at the Saint-Michel station. It was half past five in the evening. Seven dead, several wounded whose legs were blown up. . . . We do not know yet all the names of those who died at Saint-Michel. In a week, in a month, waiting on this platform where bodies were pulverized as if nothing had happened. (*LVE*, 66–67, italics in the original)

In this succession of entries, a concatenation of forms of suffering, the intervention of Ernaux diminishes progressively. In the first one, she supplies the meaning of the "position allongée" denied to beggars in public spaces, after ironically feigning to adhere to the official justification for the decree. The cryptic enumeration of love, sleep and death, abandonment, and "arrested time" circumscribes an experience of human vulnerability usually cherished as private, the withdrawal of which from the public is usually perceived as the very index of civilized life. The disruption of this narrative of progress by the poor who lie down in public is what justifies the official decree, Ernaux seems to concede. Yet by supplying these very contexts—love, sleep, death—that define a shared humanity, Ernaux also surreptitiously makes a point about the violence of depriving people of a private life where such basic human experiences can be had; having to supply these reminders, which are obliterated from the public discourse that defends the right to leisure of the tourists and the comfort of grand narratives of progress is a reminder of the cost of preserving the latter intact. The second entry, about the war in Yugoslavia, spells out the capacity that diminishes in the modern world to "imagine" the real, even as a display of emotion offers reassurance as to the capacity for empathy. It does not make a difference if the war victims are geographically distant, or, as in the last entry, if the dead and wounded in a bomb explosion could be any of the underground passengers: this sequence of entries situates on a continuum the oblivion to the humanity of beggars, the erasure of the suffering of war, and the forgetting of victims, that is—potentially—of ourselves as singular human beings.

One of the most remarkable fragments in *Journal du dehors*, the record of a conversation between two clochards, brings us even closer to articulating Ernaux's position. On the one hand, like the man who collects stones at the Nanterre retirement home, this entry might remind readers of Beckett's characters. More generally, the recurrent images of disposable objects, texts, and people in *Journal du dehors* register with Beckett's representation of the human condition as regulated by waste;[50] the decreative acts she records align with the disintegrating bodies in Beckett's novels and plays, with Molloy's unlearning proprieties, his regression to the fetus, and then to the egg, by the third volume of the trilogy, *The Unnamable*. Decreation in Ernaux's *Journal du dehors* echoes Beckett's "experiment in diminution," both sketching out, one in the mode of reportage, the other in the aesthetic of minimalist drama, the stages and details of a dehumanization that, in Beckett's work at least, is never done ending. One must acknowledge, however, that by entertaining the comparison with Beckett's characters, one risks aestheticizing the clochards in Ernaux's diary, thus doing them an injustice.[51] But then, inspired by le Blanc, another possibility presents itself: isn't, rather, their capacity to speak like characters in a play, referring to the stories they imagine about their own lives, their frustrated ambitions, their missed opportunities, precisely that which could steer us to look at them differently, to see in them something other than *just* clochards?

> Tonight, at les Halles, just as the RER doors were about to snap shut, two tramps entered noisily and sat down on opposite seats. Two shaggy, unkempt men in tattered clothes. The younger of the two, aged between thirty and forty, lays an empty bottle down on the floor and opens Libération. The other one, around fifty, maybe younger, starts to bawl the French national anthem. He spits into a rag and says: "Who cares about the army? Look at that gob of spittle, you won't see another one like that, not even in the army." Then, trying to engage his companion in conversation, he asks: "Why d'you look like a fag?" The other ignores the trite insult, delivered with friendly intent, and exclaims: "You've got the Serbs! You've got the Croats! It's a good thing we got newspapers, otherwise I'd be stupid." He rustles the paper. "See that? Some people make it to Gabon and we

> only end up in Sartrouville." A short silence. "It's just not fair." Then: "I want to go back into my egg, it was nice and cozy."
>
> The man reading *Libération* goes on muttering "it's just not fair," while taking an interest in this imaginary subject: "Did you have a shell over your head?"
>
> —No, it was skin. I may not be a gynecologist, but I'm not a moron!
>
> —I don't want to leave! It's a great squat—real warm!
>
> —I wanted to stay so badly my mom had to have a Caesarian.
>
> —At the time, they used chainsaws to do Caesarians.
>
> —She suffered a lot. That's why she never acknowledged me.
>
> —Mine didn't either. (*JD*, 92–93)

Ernaux refrains from commenting on the humor of the clochards' exchanges, and does not draw attention to the symbolic dimension of the older man's desire to return to "his egg." The scene is fit for a play in the theater of the absurd, and there is nothing for Ernaux to add, except to remind the readers that this is *not* a stage performance, and that before becoming characters in her diary, the two clochards performed themselves—in theatrical fashion, indeed, the only one they know in a society that refuses to hear them otherwise. The clochards expose the negative truth of the everyday, and their theatricality paradoxically conveys the absurd authenticity of their existence. If one chooses to listen to their conversation (rather than overhear it)—and by writing it down, Ernaux compels the reader to pay attention—one is struck by the aspects in these individuals' lives that do not conform to the stereotypical silhouettes of beggars, meager not only in their physical appearance but also through the absence of a life story that would maintain them in the sphere of humanity. "Toutes les allures de vie de l'exclu ne se ramènent pas à l'exclusion. Plus encore, parmi ces allures de vie de l'exclu, certaines sont des contestations explicites de l'exclusion elle-même" (All the contours of the life of the reject do not come down to exclusion. Moreover, among these aspects of the reject's life, some are explicit contestations of exclusion itself).[52] They are not simply destitute people and nothing else: they read newspapers, interested in events from remote parts of the world; quip ironically about the negative identities imposed on them ("Why do you look like a fag?"); imagine themselves in other situations; ponder the affecting episodes of their lives; articulate the sense of injustice that pervades their experience of the world. And these are the very aspects, as Cora Diamond and Guillaume le Blanc emphasize, that constitute the human quality of a life:

> What constitutes the human quality of a life is the possibility to see imaginatively its variables: a life might be excluded, but it is retained as a fully human life as long as "I" notice under the features of the clochard in rags the silhouette of a young woman and I imagine her

> for example when she was a child or even baby pushed by her mother in a stroller. It is when this capacity to imagine is lacking that a reject becomes a life excluded from humanity, a dehumanized life, because it is then considered unhinged from our life and even from the group of humans to which we feel we legitimately belong. Then it is because this dehumanization that begins with the refusal to imagine the other life as fully human is completed in the dismissal of the other's imagination . . . [that] we refuse to consider [the other] as a fully imaginative subject, capable of constructing a fiction of their life, of their life and of the life of others. These two refusals are linked.[53]

The double refusal that le Blanc elaborates on—that of imagining the lives of others as human, and that of taking the others for humans endowed with an imagination that makes their life meaningful—can only be understood and challenged if the frameworks through which the lives of the destitute are apprehended change; le Blanc emphasizes that the social sciences, literature, philosophy, and cinema, among others, can contribute to this change. How? By following, he suggests, an imperative of nonclosure; by broadening our notion of "humanity" through the recognition of the link that exists between all lives, not only, as Judith Butler suggests, because we share the world with the excluded, but because we might ourselves become excluded.

Some of the entries in Ernaux's diaries intimate that such an ethical stance is easier imagined than adopted in everyday life. On the eve of Christmas 1995, for instance, she notes that on her way back from grocery shopping, she gave a ten-franc bill to a man who was sitting by some trash bags. "A face ravaged by poverty and alcohol. He smelled very badly" (*LVE*, 67). No sooner does she reciprocate his wishes of "Merry Christmas" with the perfunctory "You, too" than she realizes the symbolic violence in which both of them participate with this exchange: "Then I feel so disgusted that, to efface shame, I feel like rolling in his coat, kiss his hands, smell his breath" (68). Three years later, again around Christmas time, she registers a similar empathetic reaction, this time trying to imagine what it feels like to be a beggar or a prostitute: "Sitting on the concrete floor of the metro [station], lowering one's head and putting out one's hand. Hearing steps, seeing legs walk by, those that slow down, the hope. What would I prefer, that or prostitution, the public or the private shame?" (*LVE*, 124). Differently put: what is more affecting, the experience of humiliation witnessed by other people, or the solitary one? "The need to imagine myself in the most extreme forms of dereliction, as if in the name of a truth otherwise inaccessible" (*LVE*, 125). But what would this truth be? Through the fragmentary record of other people's lives, by imagining what they must feel like, by echoing words usually no sooner spoken than ignored, so they have a new power to reach others, Ernaux includes herself (and her readers) in a collective "we" whose shared condition, she emphasizes, is vulnerability. In this context, writing about other people's lives becomes speaking in their name, which means, as le Blanc puts it, not "speaking for others" or "in their place" but, rather, participating in a "we" generated by the conjoining of vulnerability and subalternity.[54]

The World in Me: Toward a Community of Transpersonal Selves

"I don't speak to them. I only watch them and listen to them. Yet the emotions they arouse in me are real," Ernaux writes, self-consciously spelling out the guiding principle of her practice (*JD*, 32). These brief notations also read like a definition of discretion, that Pierre Zaoui dwells on at some length in *La discrétion, ou l'art de disparaître*: "discretely enjoying the presence or the existence of others, that is, literally enjoying separately their apparition without having to show up oneself and maintain a posture."[55] Depersonalization, withdrawal from the "game of perpetual projections and introjections that usually link us to others" (extricating oneself from distantiality): this is an ethical stance to which Zaoui attaches political value in a world of visibility and surveillance.[56] To Warhol's "fifteen minutes of fame" would correspond, in this scenario, fifteen minutes of (desirable) anonymity.

Zaoui's reflection resonates with Ernaux's project, all the more so since Benjamin's flâneur is the provider of the conditions of the material and political possibility of such an experience of discretion. Zaoui identifies five such conditions that account for the secularization of discretion, an experience that he originally traces to a religious disposition. First of all, because the city is the condition of discretion, the flâneur gives a different meaning to Gracián's ideal of an "homme du monde," since the world here is not a small circle where everyone knows everyone else (which is also the sociability of rural communities, where discretion is impossible); rather, it is someone "who goes into the world as in a realm to traverse, not as in new territory to conquer."[57] The city is also the place where the flâneur develops his love of the crowds, in the middle of which a "populated solitude [*une solitude peuplée*]" is possible: "a dissymmetrical state of communication in which one sees without seeing and is seen without seeing: only the crowd, the undifferentiated mass for the one who cannot see and unbelievably differentiated for the one who can, is the community of those without community to which one can alternately give oneself and refuse oneself."[58] From this derives the third condition of discretion, the "passion of anonymity," the "love of the incognito" of the one who "is self-sufficient and does not seek approval," as Baudelaire says of Constantin Guys. "The passion of no longer being someone, just a mere electron without a name thrown at top speed into the immense crowd."[59] And then there is the flânerie itself, both always available and always in movement, the very image of the circulation of commodities in capitalism; as Baudelaire puts it, the experience of a free perambulation among the reified forms of life. Finally, concludes Zaoui, there is, in discretion, "the more subtle political exigency not to yield to the reification of all life and to invent new forms of subjectivity, visible or sublime."[60] The second and fifth conditions articulate the stakes of discretion that are most relevant to Ernaux's diaries: the elaboration of a new form of subjectivity and, through it, the intimation of a new understanding of community. Let us unpack these intertwined threads.

As we have seen, Ernaux starts from the premise of a neutral, "photographic" writing, a mere collection of "snapshots of reality" from which her subjectivity would be evacuated. As such, she would conform entirely to Zaoui's description of discretion: entering in this mode is unlike "entering religion or a monastery, but rather like when one enters furtively into other people's houses, people we do not know, not out of curiosity or to break in, but simply in order to see how they live and to let oneself be moved by the neutral beauty of things, that is, without a personal subject and without a specific object."[61] Presumably, the absence of a personal subject would leave her in a social, or even presocial state of being, but Ernaux readily acknowledges the impossibility, in the end, to separate the "profound self [*le moi profond*]" from the social self; both, as the diaries suggest, because the people, behaviors, and interactions she is most likely to notice are determined by her own experiences, by the configuration of distances within herself, and because the people she looks at bring her back to herself.[62] Such, for instance, is the case with an early scene she records in *Journal du dehors*, in which a woman scolds her teenage daughter vehemently, concluding: "I won't always be there! You're going to have to manage all by yourself in life" (*JD*, 88). She is struck by this interaction because she was once in the teenager's shoes: "I can still hear my father or mother saying: 'We won't always be there!' Their intonation. I see the severe expression on their face again . . . It was a threat from living people; now they're both dead. 'You'll see when we're not there anymore!' The sentence alone remains, absurd, atrocious, when said by others" (*JD*, 88, suspension points in the original). It is only now—in a present contemporary with her mother's recent passing—that she can measure the raw force of the parental warning: paradoxically, the sentence has to be uttered by a foreigner for its lesson of tough love and vulnerability to become an intimate knowledge. A lesson about not being at home in the world, yet having to make the world one's home—occasionally, Ernaux wonders about it:

> Why do I describe and detail this particular scene, like many others in the book? What is it I am desperately seeking in reality? Is it meaning? This may, sometimes, though not always, be true since I have acquired the mental habit not only of experiencing emotions but of "getting them into perspective." Also, committing to paper the movements, postures and words of the people I meet gives me the illusion that I am close to them. I don't speak to them, I only watch them and

> listen to them. Yet the emotions they arouse in me are real. I may also be trying to discover something about myself through them, their attitudes and their conversations. (Sitting opposite someone in a subway car, I often ask myself, "why am I not that woman?") (*JD*, 32)

The epigraph to *Journal du dehors*, borrowed from *Rousseau juge de Jean-Jacques*—"Notre vrai moi n'est pas tout entier en nous" (Our real self is not entirely within ourselves)—turns on its head the postulation of traditional autobiography (ironically, modeled on Rousseau's *Confessions*, to which, according to Michael Sheringham, Western autobiography is only footnotes) that the authenticity of the self has its sources in introspection.[63] The "outside" offers countless opportunities for the revelation of what Annie Ernaux has called in an essay about her family ethnography a "transpersonal I," all the more so given that these later diaries transcend the setting of the family and focus on anonymous strangers: such a self seeks not "to bolster an identity but to grasp, in the field of [Ernaux's] own experience, the signs of a wider collective reality."[64] Strikingly, by opening the autobiographical space to the outside, various moments of her past—or occasionally her future—are accessed in recollection or anticipation. The historicity missing from the *ville nouvelle* becomes accessible through responsive immersion in the experience of the everyday, in the existences of others:

> Both . . . the young man and the little boy take me back to moments in my life. On other occasions, a woman waiting at a check-out desk would remind me of my mother because of the way she moved or spoke. So it is outside my own life that my past existence lies: in passengers commuting on the subway or the RER; in shoppers glimpsed on escalators at Auchan or in the Galleries Lafayette; in complete strangers who cannot know that they possess part of my story; in faces and bodies that I shall never see again. In the same way, I myself, anonymous among the bustling crowds on streets and in department stores, must secretly play a role in the lives of others. (*JD*, 95)

"Porteuse de la vie des autres": the first volume of the diary concludes on the reciprocity of a relationship of partly overlapping life-stories. This amends Iris Murdoch's reflection that "the others are, to an extent one can never cease discovering, different from ourselves" by emphasizing that the others may also reveal to us differences, or distances within ourselves, about which we forgot they existed. And these have a transformative potential: "Si je poursuivais une telle expérience ma vision du monde et moi-même s'en trouveraient radicalement changée. Peut-être n'aurais-je plus de moi" (If I pursued such an experience [this form of observation and diary writing] my vision of the world and I myself would alter radically. Perhaps I would no longer have a self) (*LVE*, 26).

The transpersonal self that emerges from Ernaux's diaries, open to the currents that other people "send rippling through us" in the form of interest, anger, or shame (*JD*, 7), confirms Zaoui's intuition that the practice of discretion "surreptitiously slid[es] from beings and things towards the relationships they produce."[65] These new relationships, captured in her formulation "le monde en moi" (the world in me),[66] suggest a new sense of community, one that precedes, like in Heidegger's *Mitsein* or Nancy's com-pearance, a sense of self.

My Century, to which I will now turn, reads like the answer offered by a German novelist to Ernaux's entry dated August 5, 1997, in which she puzzles over the meaning of an unchronicled life:

> The 122-year old woman, dean of humanity, Jeanne Calment, has died. Almost national mourning. She leaves behind no testimony susceptible to be passed on universally, not even a diary. Her only work [*œuvre*] is a life continued beyond all hope. Jeanne Calment was just time, the very embodiment of time.
>
> The time we have not lived. Her existence reached where memory—our own, that of our parents or grand-parents—cannot go. Her eyes saw a world henceforth beyond representation. She was ten during Victor Hugo's burial, twenty during the Dreyfus affair, and a mature woman when soldiers of the Great War left [*la fleur au fusil*]. As they say, she could have known Maupassant, Verlaine, Zola and Proust, Colette, Ravel, Modigliani, all younger than herself, and dead a while ago. One could walk the figure of this little woman without history—all the more easily because she was without history—like a marker on all the pages of the century she had traversed. Unscathed, almost without memories, since the person credited with all the century's memory only remembered the assassination of the tsar's family in 1917. She was pure biological time, delivered of all the horrors and upheavals. (*LVE*, 92–93)

Chapter 6

Günter Grass's Century

In contrast to Ernaux's commitment to a photographic writing that would provide, in realistic vein, glimpses into the lives of other people, Grass's project reclaims the privilege of the writer, indeed, his inalienable right, to imagine the lives of others by lending his (autobiographical) "I" to a plurality of fictional narrators: "I, trading places with myself, was in the thick of things, year in and year out."[1] Thus begins his imaginative chronicle, modifying with the very first sentence the autobiographical pact, which stipulates, following Lejeune's definition, the author's identity with the narrator and the narrated self.

How do we read Arendt's premonition that Benjamin stood on the threshold of the Last Judgment, from the perspective offered by Günter Grass in 1999, when he published his chronicle of the twentieth century, *Mein Jahrhundert*? Interspersing the objective and the subjective, the everyday and the momentous, Grass's idiosyncratic chronicle offers a strange, and appropriately twentieth-century response to Walter Benjamin's farewell to the nineteenth century. If Benjamin's *Berlin Chronicle* was a long farewell to the "mausoleum designed especially for [him]," to his parents' Berlin house, and to the nineteenth century to which he felt he belonged, Grass's narratives read like so many frescoes on a monument to the twentieth century. The title of the book refers both to the century in which Grass was born and to his own version of it.[2] But whether he felt "at home" or not, is not a question one can answer; perhaps one that the text invites reformulating: was it possible to feel at home in the twentieth century? Striking, in this tome, is the relinquishing of the purely autobiographical in favor of an inclusion of voices of various people, all contributing perspectives on this question. As in Wim Wenders's *Der Himmel über Berlin*, where, with Benjaminian nostalgia, everyday details and historical events are blown out of the flow of time and given symbolic significance (the Olympic Games, a lovers' embrace, an old man reading the *Odyssey* to an unblinking child on a hill appear as equally revealing), in Grass's tome history is evoked from below, in a leveling out of events and objects, an interweaving of history and stories. I read Grass's text as a response both to the *Arcades*—Benjamin's quotes from famous writers are in Grass replaced by short narratives of fictional everyday lives of the more or less obscure—and to *Berlin Childhood*: while Benjamin's is a personal portrait, the city functioning as a broadening of the familiar space of the house, which is an extension of the child's own body, around 1900 (as evoked from the alienating perspective of exile), Grass's is the (hi)story/(auto)biography of the century written from the perspective of 1999: there is no "home," but rather an acknowledgment of the lives of other people; not an everyday in its inchoate form as in Benjamin, but an everyday projected onto the larger perspective of the century.[3]

Like Ernaux, who claims that there is no hierarchy in our experiences of the world, and that the most trivial occurrences contain a human truth, Grass seems to level down the significance of major historical events that have marked the past century by providing one hundred stories of equal length corresponding to each year from 1900 to 1999. He thus seems to give equal attention to various aspects of everyday life: wearing a straw hat or the use of zeppelins appear to be as important as the popularity of record players or the prospect of cloning; November 9, 1938 (*Kristallnacht*), as crucial to remember as November 9, 1989 (the fall of the Berlin Wall); the meetings between Heidegger and Celan in the late 1940s as memorable as the love parades of the 1990s. In thirteen of the vignettes, Grass briefly reminisces over his own past, in a meditation on the coincidence between his birth-year and the publication of Heidegger's *Sein und Zeit*, for instance, or on various episodes of his life as a politically invested citizen or as a public intellectual. But his own existence appears as one among many, they are all interconnected and part of the texture of history, woven, from the beginning to the end, in the first person. As a chronicle grafted onto an autobiography—or is it the other way?—*My Century* courts an interesting paradox: on the one hand, by constantly shifting perspective in an accumulation of voices that are meant to give a variety of inflections to the tenor of the century, it suggests that history is a collective experience and that no one life story could possibly provide a full picture of it.[4] On the other hand, it attaches importance to each individual story, taking seriously its exemplary value, the singularity of its historicity.

My interest in Grass's tome will here be limited to questions that relate directly to the displacement of the autobiographical self through attention to other lives, real or imagined. *My Century* is, as many critics have remarked, a very German book, and as such it does not serve my philosophical argument about the intimation of a nonexclusionary notion of community that distances itself from a "project" or from a commonality (Germanness, for instance). What Grass's book does contribute to our discussion, however, through its expansion of the temporal framework to the whole century and the inclusion of so many (characters') lives is an interesting problematization of the very idea of representation and exemplarity that add perspective to the transformation of the autobiographical, completing Ernaux's. My aim is to show how his "project of attention" to the lives of others—I am reusing a formulation with which Sheringham characterizes Ernaux's diary—situates Grass in proximity of German historians of the everyday (a group around Alf Lüdtke), but also within the more recent framework of "memory contests" after reunification, a cultural paradigm that acknowledges the plurality of views on the legacy of the past. A brief review of the literature will provide a departure point for these elaborations, grounding them in the critiques that have been brought to Grass's tome. The criticisms leveled at *My Century* are important as symptomatic of the tensions with which the very notion of representation is fraught; as Grass himself put it in a speech in 1994, in the postmodern media age, "the newly published book is not itself the event: the response to it is."[5]

The book was published in July 1999, a little less than three months before the Stockholm Nobel Prize Committee announced that Grass, a candidate in waiting since the publication of *Die Blechtrommel* (*The Tin Drum*, 1959), was to receive the award. Compared to other books by him, *My Century* received much less, and more ambivalent, attention; and after the award, it was mentioned in passing, overshadowed by more prominent works like *The Tin Drum*, the other two novels in the Danzig Trilogy, *Cat and Mouse* and *Dog Years*, *Diary of a Snail*, all the way to *Too Far Afield* and later *Crabwalk*, not to mention *Peeling the Onion* (2006) which caused a heated controversy with implications that transcended the public persona of Günter Grass, and that bore on the legacy of National Socialism and the question of German national identity, the autonomy of the institution of literature and of literary prizes including the Nobel. Evaluated against Grass's own previous writing, *My Century* appeared as an oddity and hardly any aspect of it was consensually praised.[6] In *The Literary Quartet* (*Das literarische Quartet*), the ZDF show that made the critic Marcel Reich-Ranicki a household name in Germany, he expressed reservations—in agreement with the other participants in the discussion—about the structural device of the book of devoting one story to each year of the twentieth century, which he found flawed. Although many critics did appreciate the diversity of the stories and topics, some bemoaned the "Grass sound" which allegedly permeated them: while Ingo Arend, for instance, praised Grass's strategy of making the century come alive in a mosaic displaying the sophistication of a colored Neuruppin broadsheet, especially in the (exclusively German) view from below; and Helmut Böttinger appreciated Grass's research, use of folklore and, occasionally, dialect, which gave an air of authenticity to his stories; Bruno Preisendörfer characterized *Mein Jahrhundert* as a notable work of contemporary literature, but estimated that the first-person narratives sounded too much like Grass and lacked variety, and Fritz Raddatz praised the pastiche feature of the stories, but also critiqued the author's voice, which to his ears sounded like a dogmatic Cassandra.[7] Others found problematic precisely the diversity of topics, on grounds that they remain obscurely German—that is, unintelligible to readers who are not deeply familiar with German history and social life from the earliest days of the century to its end.[8] Other critics had mixed feelings about the claims they thought were implicit in the title of the work: Ulrich Greiner claimed that Grass had already written a compelling book about the twentieth century, and that had been *Die Blechtrommel*; Volker Hage thought the title was rather presumptuous, since the author is present in only thirteen of the one hundred chapters, and because the selection of episodes featuring historical events was rather arbitrary; moreover, some critics bemoaned the lack of a more explicit rapport between human actions, social relations, and the forces of history.[9] Iring Fetscher defended the book against critics who claimed that the perspective of the little people predominated to the detriment of other viewpoints, citing the entry for 1994, featuring the unnamed Birgit Breuel, identifiable as the chief of the *Treuhand*, and the 1960s meeting between Erich Maria Remarque, author of the well-known antiwar novel *Im Western nichts Neues* (*All Quiet on the Western Front*, 1929) and Ernst Jünger, whose *Im Stahlgewittern* (*Storm of Steel*, 1929) was criticized as a glorification of war.[10] However, Fetscher is not always in agreement with Grass's choice of consequential episodes or moments: for instance, instead of the fictional encounter that Grass stages between Gottfried Benn and Bertolt Brecht in the year of their deaths (1956), Fetscher would have found more compelling the evocation of Soviet leader's Nikita Khrushchev's secret speech about Stalin's crimes, which marked the beginning of de-Stalinization and thus had epochal significance. In the same critical vein, hinting with the interrogative title "My Century?" at the idiosyncratic choice of events in Grass's tome, Wolfgang Weber enumerates the significant moments in the history of the past century that Grass did not recall, such as the October 1917 revolution in Russia, the November 1918 revolution in Germany, the 1929 collapse of the world economy, and so on.[11]

On the other side of the Atlantic—the English translation was available only after the Nobel Prize was announced, which gave a more celebratory tone to the reviews, although many were reticent—critics also raised the question whether the text is "inclusive and shared enough, whether *My Century* is bigger, more truly universal, than the sum of its parts."[12] Additionally, cultural historian Peter Gay and Richard Bernstein agreed that the book does not form a coherent whole: it is a "collection of fragments that fail to cohere" (Gay), and although it exhibits "flashes of brilliance," and is in part "gripping and uniformly intelligent," it consists of "mostly forgettable fragments" that do not offer a "coherent, gripping or illuminating whole" (Bernstein).[13] Furthermore, writer and academic Ian Buruma critiqued the book's political undertones, coinciding with Grass's well-known political positions, for instance in the ambivalent or negative way it portrays the nationalist aspirations of the GDR population. As is well known, Grass was critical of the project of reunification—he repeatedly invoked the disastrous consequences of former dreams of national greatness during Germany's Nazi past, and claimed that after two dictatorships, East Germany had no experience of democracy—which, according to Buruma, "represents a colossal failure of imagination . . . [in one of] the most celebrated writers of the twentieth century."[14]

While it is beyond the scope of this chapter to address all these critiques, many will be put in perspective by considering *My Century* in the broad framework of an analysis of the representation of the everyday, the sphere of experience shared with other people. To begin with, Bernstein's characterization of the book as providing "unsatisfactorily fragmentary glances at people and events that disappear almost as soon as they are seen" finds an apt rebuttal in Ernaux's description of her project, to transcribe "scenes, words, gestures of anonymous people that one will never see again, graffiti on walls, no sooner scribbled than erased" (*JD*, 8) and by this token places Grass in the position of a retrospective chronicler of everyday life. There are several immediate consequences that ensue from this: the stories cannot form a coherent whole, because the everyday is notoriously a space of heterogeneity; furthermore, by staging stories of a great variety of characters, often around a conflictual situation triggered by a historical event, Grass challenged the view of a unified German history, striking a note that has become more familiar in Germany in recent years in the numerous "memory contests" occasioned by various public events (not least by the publication of *Peeling the Onion*). The charge that the one hundred stories are permeated by the same, recognizable Grassian sound loses its force in confrontation with the opposite view, of critics who praise the diversity of topics and genres, including monologues, dialogues, letters, short stories, reminiscences, and confessions. Grass's novels have typically been praised for the complexity of his characters, presented in their "flaws and dross"; do shorter sketches, necessarily less thick portrayals, become excessively "Grassian" through accumulation? This question also touches on the question of how "representative" *Mein Jahrhundert* is or can be, since it necessarily bears Grass's signature: is it inclusive enough? Is not the title arrogant, as one critic said, with its implicit claim that its author, even someone of Grass's stature, could represent everyone who lived in the twentieth century? "Should the emphasis be placed on 'my' or on 'century'?" Decidedly, on both: *My Century* plays on the double register of autobiography and chronicle, reclaiming the writer's right to artistic idiosyncrasy, be it expressed in the form of imaginative forays into the fraught territories of history.[15] To illustrate this point, let us consider some of the criticisms that challenge the notion of representation (of events and people) in Grass's account of the twentieth century.

Thirteen of the hundred episodes in *My Century* feature Grass himself, covering each decade of his life (with the exception of the 1940s, a silence filled in 2006 with the publication of *Peeling the Onion*). The image of Grass that emerges is less of the private individual than of the involved citizen and intellectual. However, one can hardly confine the "autobiographical" to the concrete entries evoking events of his life; the very choice of events that he recalled and the kinds of narrators he delegated for this task, the stylistic features of the vignettes, the political views that Grass otherwise expressed and defended in the public arena—all make *My Century* the book that it is. Although Grass's project is to "represent" the century in which he lived (the historical twentieth century), he is a historical individual and the choices he made can only be subjective—"his" century (i.e., the representation thereof) cannot possibly coincide entirely with someone else's, therefore critiques that highlight events Grass "did not recall," or claim that in a particular year, a different moment proved to have epochal consequences, are indicative of their authors' preferences or agendas (rather than of Grass's failures or omissions), and suggest what *their* "century" would have looked like, had they chosen to undertake a version of the project conceived by Grass. Or is the implication that out there, there is an "objective" chronicle of the century, and that in each given year, there is one event that detaches itself with absolute clarity, as *the* most significant, both in that particular context and in retrospect? Who is part of the tribunal that determines such a hierarchy of events? Even if we were to grant the possibility of such an objective view, what notion of literature is implied in the critique that a text does not align itself with that objectivity? And how to respond to the charge that Grass's text might not be inclusive, or representative enough? Since Grass called his book *My Century*—not *Our Century*—his writer's imaginative testimony should be a compelling enough account, no more, but also no less than an *example*, of what it was like to live (and imagine living) in the past century. Two examples will serve to show that to determine what counts as "representative" in this tome is not an easy task, since Grass's century does not progress in straightforward fashion, or at a uniform pace, toward its own completion (or exhaustion), despite the appearance of stories equal in length corresponding to each chronological year. "Representation," in Grass's writing, typically works by way of indirection, irony and allusion, as readers of his previous novels are well aware; it is negotiated, in other words, in unquantifiable variables. And there is often, in these modes of indirection, more than what is explicitly said.

Let us consider, for instance, Iring Fletcher's point that in some cases Grass might have chosen events whose impact was more lasting than the ones that do appear in *My Century*. To the fictional encounter that Grass stages between Gottfried Benn and Bertolt Brecht in the year of their deaths (1956), for example, Fletcher would have preferred the evocation of Nikita Khrushchev's secret speech about Stalin's crimes, which marked the beginning of de-Stalinization. I would contend that Grass's 1956 story is arguably richer in suggestions and subtler than a direct engagement with Khrushchev's secret speech might have been. First of all, Grass's *century* is German, so a story featuring this speech, delivered confidentially to the Twentieth Party Congress on February 25, 1956, would not have been coherent with his project. In the imaginary meeting between Benn and Brecht, however, there is an explicit mention of Stalin and a cautious intimation of a new era. One might go as far as to argue that Grass might have had this particular speech in mind, and that his story is a response—a writer's response, and featuring writers—to it. The beginning of Khrushchev's speech should suffice to illustrate this point:

> We have to consider seriously and analyze correctly [the crimes of the Stalin era] in order that we may preclude any possibility of a repetition in any form whatever of what took place during the life of Stalin, who absolutely did not tolerate collegiality in leadership and in work, and who practiced brutal violence, not only toward everything which opposed him, but also toward that which seemed to his capricious and despotic character, contrary to his concepts.[16]

The imaginary meeting between Benn and Brecht foregrounds the spontaneous collegiality between two writers who delight in quoting from memory from each other's work. With this imagined encounter, Grass makes a strong case for the community in spirit that art creates, and, with the specific choice of two politically involved authors, for art's forceful ways of articulating the ills of Western civilization: "Nothing in their wanderings or at least in the bits and pieces I put together betrayed any sense of enmity. Each quoted from the other's works rather than from his own and took pleasure in the ambiguity of the selection process" (MC, 144). Stalin is mentioned in passing when Benn quotes mockingly from Brecht's poem:

> Their own political sins they dealt with rather cursorily: one gave a mocking reading from a hymn to the party written by the other (". . . the great reaper-leader of the Soviet land, / Joseph Stalin, / Spoke of millet, spoke of dung and arid wind . . ."), whereupon the latter pointed out the connection between the former's onetime enthusiasm for the Nazi propaganda organ *Dorische Welt* and a speech he once gave in honor of the Fascist Futurist Marinetti. (*MC*, 145)

In these exchanges Grass foregrounds not only the misguided political allegiances that these writers subsequently distanced themselves from, but also the sympathy, even complicity, with which each of them points to the other's "political sins." Is this Grass's own reclamation of the right to be occasionally wrong, his plea for distance? Brecht's testament-poem "An die Nachgeborenen" ("The Coming Generation / To Those Born Later"), quoted by Benn, seems to point in this direction, especially under the auspices of Kleist, by whose grave Grass imagines their meeting:

> Der hinwiederum lobte "Die Massnahme" des anderen ironisch als "Ausdruckswelt eines wahren Ptolemäers," um sogleich beide an Kleistsgrab versammelten Sünder mit einem Zitat aus dem grossen Gedicht "An die Nachgeborenen" zu entlasten.

> "Ihr, die ihr auftauchen werdet aus der Flut
> In der wir untergegangen sind
> Gedenkt
> Wenn ihr von unseren Schwächen sprecht
> Auch der finsteren Zeit
> Der ihr entronnen seid." (*MJ*, 202)

> Then again one praised the other's *The Measures Taken* ironically as "the verbal universe of a true Ptolemean" only to exonerate both sinners gathered at Kleist's grave with a quote from the great poem *To Those Born Later*:

> "You who shall emerge from the flood
> We have drowned in
> Recall
> When you think on our frailties
> The dark times
> You have escaped." (*MC*, 145, translation modified)[17]

It is, of course, a matter open to the reader's interpretation what *Kleistsgrab*, Kleist's grave, stands for here: I would surmise that Brecht's address to posterity might harbor echoes of Kleist's ironic rebuff of all theories of human perfection. Grass sets up a fascinating game here: the picture of man torn apart by conflicting forces, of a split created by consciousness that renders humans neither animals nor gods, emerges from a dialogue that Kleist staged between two interlocutors who often speak rather ironically, entitled "On the Marionette Theater." Without going into the elaborate (and often slippery) details of Kleist's simulated dialogue, the idea that might be relevant here, central to their discussion, is that marionettes have a natural, single-minded grace that cannot be equaled by humans who are weighed down by self-consciousness and doubts, the result of their having eaten from the tree of knowledge. Kleist's dialogue has been interpreted as an ironic play on the ideals of classicism and romanticism, but in this context it sets the stage, with its allusion to the Fall of Man, for the Flood—which Brecht's poem references—that human failures caused later. "You who shall emerge from the flood / We have drowned in." Brecht and Benn are the two interlocutors in the dialogue staged by Grass, but also his puppets (in the sense reminiscent from Kleist's dialogue): they mimic single-mindedly and thus with grace an ideal of communication that contradicts the narrator's expectation of enmity, while also providing, by way of Brecht's art, the perfect plea for leniency on the part of the coming generations. In the opening paragraph of this 1956 entry, the narrator, who is a student of literature and aspiring poet, hints at Grass's own reasons for embedding the quiet nod at a new epoch:

> In March of that morbid-mournful year, when one died in July, shortly after his seventieth birthday, and the other, not yet sixty, died in August, when the world I had known seemed a wasteland to me, the stage a void, I, a student of German literature making his own first attempts at poetry in the shadow of two giants, encountered them both in Berlin at the grave of Heinrich von Kleist, a remote spot with a view of the Wannsee, the site of many an uncommon encounter both fortuitous and contrived. . . . At times they stood so close they might have been on a single pediment, but they also moved apart, concerned to maintain the presumed gap between them. (*MC*, 143)

Closeness and distance: Grass, weary of ideologies, whether Left or Right, also suspicious of promises, however discreet, of grand political changes, finds his own way of negotiating the rapprochement between the East and the West, in this encounter between two influential literary figures, "the one famed in the western sector of the city as literary—and consequently uncrowned—king, the other the readily quotable authority of the eastern sector" (*MC*, 143–144). Benn's ironic jab at Brecht's poem featuring Stalin is perhaps also Grass's way of gesturing toward the writers' much earlier realization—albeit after a period of misguided enthusiasm, but preceding by decades the beginning of de-Stalinization initiated by Khrushchev—of what Stalinism meant. Yet, to deflate the far-reaching symbolic implications of this imagined meeting, denying its oblique relevance to the year's epochal event (Khrushchev's speech) and giving a reason for his pessimism, Grass/the narrator concludes: "Nothing about the political situation. *Not a word about rearmament in East or West.* And still quipping over the quick and the dead, they left the grave of the immortal Kleist without ever having quoted or so much as mentioned him" (*MC*, 146, my italics). The bitter irony of the last sentence cannot be missed: towering over Kleist's work is an ideal of perfection achievable in art, and the belief that life was bearable only if approached with a life-plan.[18] The narrator of Grass's story alludes to the "wasteland" that the world seemed to him, and to the frustrated hope of gaining some insight into the present from the conversation between his literary idols: "The 'you' [in Brecht's poem] I took to refer to me, a member of the 'coming generation' currently listening in on them in the shadows. I had to be content with this admonition: I had expected my idols to give me more insight into their pioneering errors, but none was forthcoming" (*MC*, 145). The story concludes with his decision to give up literature and to turn to mechanical engineering, which adds yet another critical layer to the grim *Zeitdiagnose* that this story adumbrates so deftly.

The second example of a critical stance toward the issue of representation in *My Century*—this time also capturing the political sense of representing various groups suggested by the German word *Vertretung*—bears on Grass's attention to the lives of women. In the essay "'Gezz will ich ma erzählen' Narrative and History in Günter Grass's *Mein Jahrhundert*," Monika Shafi asserts that Grass undertook in his 1999 tome a "monumental task": "entering the stories and memories of nameless citizens into Germany's historical records can . . . not only save some of them from oblivion but also mobilize resistance and critical knowledge." Responding to reviewers who dismissed the book as "neither (literary) fish nor (historic) fowl," she commends precisely Grass's refusal to confine his text to one genre: "Grass turns his attention from the bios of the self to the bios of the collective, requiring him to perform multiple balancing acts between fact and fiction, literature and history, autobiography and biography."[19] Grass's account however falls short of this promising agenda, she notes, because women are underrepresented and no foreigner gets unmediated hearing. Some twenty episodes, Shafi grants, are narrated by women, while others are mediated by female figures, and some do tackle critically xenophobia in Germany. Furthermore, women in *My Century* "often comment critically on ideologies and corruption or advocate on behalf of their husbands," and "one could argue that Grass pictured how the majority of women lived in the first half of the century."[20] But, she continues, "without taking into account women's views and without a critique of this situation, such depictions reveal an unabashedly male perspective."[21] In other words, Grass did try to offer a sympathetic representation of women's lives, but his perspective is not feminist. What would that mean?

> Even when such issues as the campaign for abortion rights ("1971") or the students' movement ("1966," "1967," "1968") are discussed, in which gender played a pivotal role, women either perceive them as purely personal—her best friend suffering the consequences of a butchered abortion—or as party politics. Suffrage, access to institutions of higher learning, the West German women's movement of the seventies, East and West German women's struggle to balance career and family—none of this concerns Grass's female or male protagonists.

While these issues are no quibbles, and certainly not negligible landmarks in the history of women's liberation movement, Shafi's critique suggests how a feminist would have presented the twentieth century, the problem being that Grass, whose agenda Shafi characterizes as empowering the "little people" (i.e., the individuals whose lives and rights are not acknowledged by the dominant narratives) is not sufficiently sensitive to the perspective of a feminist historian. Even when he does portray women allowing them to speak in their own voice—that is, in episodes narrated by women—Shafi expresses reservations with respect to how the "message" is skewed by the setting in which these women are represented. To illustrate this point, it seems worth quoting in full her analysis of the episode corresponding to the year 1980. This is a particularly significant story because it actually portrays a woman from the perspective of a male narrator:

> A young woman, a housewife and mother of three young children, organizes a highly successful support of the so-called "boat people," refugees in the Southern Seas in China. The woman and her friends jeopardize the official German politics of non-involvement, prompting a visit by a high-ranking member of the German Foreign Service. This "Leiter des Zuständigen Referats" (298) is the story's narrator, informing his supervisor that the woman laughs at his references to the maritime law of 1910 while cooking stew and tending young children. Not surprisingly, the entire encounter takes place in the woman's kitchen, where the visitor sits uncomfortably on the laundry basket and is even asked to stir the stew. Ironically undermining the narrator's arguments (who in his heart sides with his opponent), "1980" supports the woman's point of view, applauding not only her political causes but also the easy manner in which she handles such diverse agendas as international politics and mundane domestic responsibilities. "'Mit links' mache sie das" (298), declares the protagonist, truly a superwoman, who is not only having it all but also doing it all. This story's numerous juxtapositions, grassroots activism versus governmental restraint, humanitarian support versus bureaucratic indifference, housewife/mother versus male diplomat, and official discourse versus common-sense talk, all center on the gendered opposition between the private and the public realm. Although the female figure represents an alternative to traditional politics and gender norms, her political empowerment is at the same time so overlaid with the conventions of female domesticity, empathy, and caring that it confirms rather than challenges the rules it purports to upset. Infusing her traditional woman's skills into high-powered politics makes her the better politician and the better human being, but her gender-based superiority offers primarily an up-dated version of standard patriarchal assumptions. A sympathetic interpretation might serve to highlight her irony, self-confidence, and common sense, which make for a powerful and inspiring depiction of female strength, but these qualities remain anchored in maternity and domesticity. They are summoned to make the world a better place, appealing to traditional femininity to provide alternative political scenarios.[22]

One way of evaluating Shafi's critique would be to note that she appreciates Grass's complex depiction of the female character in this story, which—to spell out some of its implications—in the spirit of third-wave feminism suggests allegiances between various forms of disempowerment (the plight of refugees in China and the predicament of women in the West), but she defends a brand of feminism which postulates that domesticity cannot be a choice and that a powerful woman cannot be cast in what is coded as patriarchal roles, such as motherhood and domesticity. But this kind of criticism, it is worth pointing out, was contested even among feminists of the second wave, who insisted that empowerment could be derived from a variety of experiences as long as they were chosen, and who supported motherhood and domesticity as viable options. To say that Grass's character is a powerful one, but that her strength is diminished by the setting in which she is presented, is to fault the author for not subscribing to the same brand of feminism. And even if Shafi's critique was left unquestioned, it would mean evaluating Grass's work against a standard of absolute political correctness; or, shifting to the sphere of moral discourse, against a Levinasian ethics, in which the writer is held accountable for all the *other* Others, and critiqued for not making the effort to relinquish completely his own subjectivity and espouse absolutely, indefinitely, the perspective of *all* others. Superfluous to point out that the title ***My** Century*—and in this instance I would stress the first word slightly—would be unsuitable to such an endeavor.

To contemplate singularity from a slightly different angle, let us turn briefly to a text with the same title as Grass's, Aleksander Wat's autobiographical memoir *My Century*.[23] In this book, the Polish poet Wat converses with his countryman the poet Czeslaw Milosz about life in midcentury Eastern Europe seen through the lens of his own spiritual struggle, imprisonment, and conversion from Judaism to Christianity after the night in which the sound of laughter brought to his Soviet cell the vision of "the devil in history."[24] There is no question of comparing the two accounts of "the century," they are incommensurable in tenor, scope, emotional intensity. What I wish to suggest is that, while Wat's life-shattering experiences, memories, and soul-searching give a very particular insight into the history of the past century, Grass's first-person narrators give a different picture of it, but that neither can be discounted as accounts of "the century" on grounds of the subjectivity of their authors. Wat reflects:

> Memories. What they say about the dying seeing their whole lives pass before their eyes like a movie in their last few minutes of life isn't true. But in prison it is. Not in a few minutes, but over the course of time—time that grows incredibly distended and loses its substance. Time has to be endowed with substance; in prison, time is empty and has to be filled. And you fill it with the movie of your life, which is sometimes vivid, sometimes not so vivid.[25]

How does "my life" become "my century"? And what happens when the life is "not so vivid," when memories lack the clarity of lived experience? "Endow time with substance," says Wat, describing the different ways this substance takes shape: soul searching (the pangs of conscience), what he calls a more vulgar form of inner life, "if-onlying," and pure memories, "unaccompanied by pangs and that make no distinction between good and evil. Visual, or rather artistic, memories, free of morality."[26] Wat is very much aware that his testimony of the century is not based on raw facts. On the one hand, his life is exemplary because it is traversed by the fractures of history, by war and deportation, and his memories, populated by many individuals (more or less vivid in his recollection) and embedded in the life of a community, add up to a narrative that appears as a synecdoche of the century. On the other hand, he is very much aware of the imaginative dimension of the process of recollection, and that the "substance" spawned by his memory is a mixture of wishful thinking, moral evaluation, and "artistic" memories—that is, images transfigured by time. These do not compromise the testimonial relevance of the narrative, however, which is given by the unity of his experience. Differently put, the reader trusts Wat's intention to testify.

How is this relevant to Grass, who invents most of his stories? Surely, one might say, there is a significant difference between an account that purports to be a reconstruction of the past, the most accurate possible to the best of the author's knowledge, and a collection of stories, be they anchored in real events, with the occasional autobiographical reminiscence often impossible to disentangle, however, from the web of the fictionalized or the purely fictional? The difference is one of degree of imaginative investment, and Grass's point, it seems to me, is precisely to question the claims to historical accuracy of historical narratives—the official historical records—that purport to provide an objective representation of things as they happened. This is not just a version of the distrust of "grand narratives" characteristic of late modernity, as Lyotard famously pointed out. In the German context, it speaks to two developments in the discourse about history: the emergence of a group of historians of the everyday in the 1980s and 1990s (*Alltagsgeschichte*) whose work still appears more legitimate abroad than in Germany, and the "memory contests" that have shown, especially since reunification, the plurality of historical perspectives and the imaginative mediation intervening in the reconstruction of the past.

In a study of German culture at the turn of the century suggestively entitled *Phantoms of War*, Anne Fuchs amends the traditional definition of autobiography as a representation of someone's life as it happened: "While autobiography has a strong mimetic appeal, it should not be defined by its enhanced referentiality, but rather by its preoccupation with modern identity discourses."[27] And she goes on to note that in recent years the notion of life-writing has emphasized the performance of identity through storytelling, especially in the form of family narratives about the inheritance of the past, involving the often contradictory perspectives of multiple generations that imagine community and collective identity in very different ways. To convey this cultural complex, Fuchs and Mary Cosgrove have proposed the notion of "memory contests," which denotes "retrospective imaginings that simultaneously articulate, question and investigate the normative self-image of groups of people," generating a pluralistic memory culture that does not enshrine a normative narrative and that acknowledges the intersection of history with personal experience.[28] This might seem a paradox, given that the Nazi era has become increasingly distant. But this is precisely the problem: Germans are registering a shift of paradigm from communicative memory (based on the firsthand experience of the war generation) to so-called postmemory (when members of this generation have passed away, memory relies increasingly on repositories of the past and is thus mediated, self-conscious, often ironic, and potentially more sensitive to contestation because of its imaginative, affective investment).[29] These issues have gained even more relevance after the German reunification, which gave renewed urgency to the question of reimagining national identity.

Susan Sontag's contestation of the notion of collective memory strikes a note that is often present in the world of Grass's characters. "What is called collective memory," Fuchs and Cosgrove quote from *Regarding the Pain of Others*, is "not a remembering but a stipulating: that this is important, and this is the story about how it happened, with the pictures that lock the story in our minds."[30] Several episodes in Grass's tome stage situations in which different characters have different outlooks on, and relationships to, a past event: the story corresponding to the year 1964, for instance, is narrated by a woman who is accidentally present at the Auschwitz trials in Frankfurt. Although advancing into the late months of pregnancy, she exposes herself to the revelations of Nazi horrors, and we see her successively intrigued, incredulous, shocked, and outraged. Her family, however, does not welcome her interest and provocations to share memories, especially her male relatives who rebuff her curtly:

> "Lay off, will you? I was four, maybe five at the time. And you'd just been born."
>
> Right, but Heiner's father and his uncle Kurt, who's this real nice guy, they were both soldiers and in Russia too. Heiner's mother once told me. But when the family finally all got together . . . , all they would say was, "We didn't know a thing about that. When did you say it was? 'Forty-three? All we could think about then was retreat." And Uncle Kurt said, "When we had to get out of the Crimea and could finally go home on furlough, what did we find but our houses in ruins. What do you hear about the Yanks and the Brits and their terrorist bombings? Not a word. And why? Because they won, and the losers are always to blame. So lay off, will you, Heidi?" (*MC*, 165–166)

But Heidi does not "lay off," and eventually talks her husband Heiner into organizing a trip to Auschwitz. The family appears here as a site where two generations enter into conflict, one standing behind an apologist victim discourse, the other assuming responsibility for the past. This story is most likely one in which the Grass "sound" makes itself heard in the insistence on the importance of assuming responsibility for the past. Similarly, the story corresponding to 1938, actually set in 1989, features a history teacher who instead of talking to his pupils about the importance of the fall of the Berlin Wall on November 9, insists on dwelling on the most gruesome details of another November 9, the *Kristallnacht* of 1938. The narrator is one of the children in the class, who admits, "It did start to get on our nerves hearing all those terrible things" (*MC*, 98). In response to the parents' suggestion to get over his "obsession with the past," the teacher insists in what might be Grass's own voice that "no child could understand the end of the wall without knowing when and where things started going wrong and what actually led to Germany being divided" (*MC*, 97). Grass himself, as one of the most vocal representatives of the Hitler Youth generation that dominated for decades the political and cultural scene in postwar Germany, was unabashedly skeptical of the reunification. This turning point in the history of Germany—*die Wende*—marked a clear shift in the formulation of national identity, from a negative image dominated by the cultural work of overcoming the past (*Vergangenheitsbewältigung*) to a more positive one supported by center-right intellectuals. The latter's dismissal of the discourse of contrition as in need of overcoming is articulated in Grass's story by the narrator's father: "'Of course I've got nothing against my daughter learning about the atrocities the SA hordes committed all over the place and unfortunately here in Esslingen too, but there's a time for everything. And that time is not now, when we finally have reason to rejoice and the whole world wishes us well'" (*MC*, 97).

The history teacher eventually gains the sympathy of the pupils through storytelling. This detail is significant, because it highlights Grass's own reliance on storytelling in his engagement with the history of the past century. Like Benjamin, who contrasted the news avalanche with storytelling, Grass remains attached to the figure of the storyteller, in whom the chronicler of earlier times has survived. Grass the chronicler mobilizes his storytellers in a concerted effort to disrupt the very idea of a *grand récit* (which the title might have encouraged some readers to expect), countering the latter with a proliferation of anecdotal stories that engage in a subversive relation to the idea of "representation" (both in the sense of *Darstellung*, objective rendering of events, of history, and of political *Vertretung*, as we have seen).[31] As Shafi usefully reminds us, new historicists like Joel Fineman, Catherine Gallagher, and Stephen Greenblatt emphasized the anecdotal in counterpoint to official historical discourses: anecdotes "would not, as in the old historicism, epitomize epochal truths, but would instead undermine them. The anecdotes would open history, or place it askew, so that literary texts could find new points of insertion. Perhaps texts would even shed their singular categorical identities, their division into 'literary' and 'historical.'"[32] A similar agenda was pursued by German historians of the everyday, a group including Alf Lüdtke, Hans Medick, and Lutz Niethammer, who were uncomfortable with the insistence on "big structures, large processes, huge comparisons" in the established West German profession.[33] In the way Geoff Eley describes the goal of *Alltagsgeschichte* in his foreword to *The History of Everyday Life*, one can easily recognize many of Grass's own topics of predilection in *My Century*:

> The goal was to develop a more qualitative understanding of ordinary people's lives, both by investigating the material circumstances of daily existence at work, at home, and at play ("the production and reproduction of immediate life," in Friedrich Engels's well-known phrase) and by entering the inner world of popular experience in the workplace, the family and household, the neighborhood, the school—in short, all those contexts normally assigned to the cultural domain. By exploring social history in its experiential or subjective dimensions, it was argued, conventional distinctions between the "public" and the "private" might also be transcended, and a more effective way of making the elusive connections between the political and cultural realism be found. Moreover, the new advocates argued, it was precisely these "insides" of the "structures, processes and patterns" of social analysis—"the daily experiences of people in their concrete life situations, which also stamp their needs" that had previously been left out.[34]

In keeping with the *Alltagshistoriker*'s perspective, skeptical of progress as the teleology of modernity, Grass's *My Century* also privileges "a social history of subjective meanings derived from highly concrete microhistorical settings," as if responding to Lüdtke's insistence on the "need for decentralization of analysis and interpretation" through the careful construction of historical "miniatures," especially featuring those individuals usually labeled the "little people," the *losers* of history. This project also brings Grass in proximity to Pierre Bourdieu, whose work he admired, and who declared himself "very much" touched by many episodes in *My Century*. In a conversation with the French sociologist titled "A Literature from Below," Grass speaks of the affinities that he sees between their work:

> When I think of your book *The Weight of the World* or of my last book, *My Century*, I see that our works have something in common: We are trying to retell History, as seen from below. We do not talk over society's head; we do not speak as conquerors of History; rather, in keeping with the nature of our profession, we are notoriously on the side of the losers, of those who are marginalized or excluded from society.[35]

Unsurprisingly, the result is that some of the stories that focus on details of the "prose" of life seem inconsequential and their choice unjustified, because they trump the importance of events that proved to be epochal in the larger German community. And yet, Grass seems to insist, such "details" reveal contradictions and discontinuities in the fabric of history itself, such as in the 1989 story narrating the fall of the Wall as the backdrop to someone's need to procure snow tires from an (apparently corrupted) acquaintance in East Berlin, well versed in the subtleties of the black market. Grass's reservations about reunification, to his mind unjustifiable only on economic grounds, are here obvious.

The Love Parade that Grass evokes in the entry corresponding to 1995 sweeps all individuality away, and the world seems to have turned into an enormous party:[36]

> What these young men and women want more than anything else is peace, peace on earth. But at the same time they want to show the world, "Hey, look, world! We are. And we are many. And we are different. We want to have fun. Fun, fun, and only fun." And when it comes to fun, they have no inhibitions. Because, as they themselves put it, they're different: they're no thugs, either skinhead or terrorist; they're no born-again sixty-eighters, always against one thing or the other but never quite clear about what they're for; they're no goody-goodies with candle-light processions and false alarms about the threat of war. No, the young people of the nineties—they're horses of many colors, so to speak. Just listen to their music, which some of you out there may think of as nothing but ear-splitting noise . . . , just listen to their music and you'll know these young people are in love with themselves and with chaos and all they really care about is boom-booming their way to ecstasy. (*MC*, 260)

And the reporter's comments continue:

> You won't be surprised to hear that name fashion designers are taking their lead, coming out with Love Parade lines, and the tobacco industry, Camel in particular, is featuring technodancers in its ads. By the way, nobody here bats an eyelid at all the advertising hoopla: this generation accepts capitalism hook, line, and sinker. The kids of the nineties are the kids of big business. They want to be the newest of the new and have the newest of the new. Which accounts in part for the popularity of the latest "high," the latest "dope"—ecstasy. A very mellow young man I talked to a few minutes ago had this to say: "The world's beyond saving, but it can still party." (*MC*, 261)

As distorted echoes of Hannah Arendt's premonition (that Benjamin stood on the threshold of the Last Judgment), such words could not sound more ironic. Grass is obviously not saluting or embracing all the developments of the twentieth century, and his writing about the reunification (a fait accompli), about the violence of xenophobic behaviors, or the prospect of a "fatherless future" reproducing itself through cloning does not imply a change of critical outlook on his part. But the "necromantic drama" he enacts in the 1999 episode, narrated by his resuscitated mother who recapitulates her life (and his), speaks to the awareness of one's inevitable untimeliness. The mother's acceptance that she is out of step with the times suggests the awareness that he, too, like the mother, and like everyone else, must have a unique perspective on the world, on his century. And if it is not sufficient that as a writer, he dealt with the stuff of the lives of others—the mother says: "I must say I like what he's come up with. Even his cock-and-bull stories, as my husband called them, showed consideration for others" (*MC*, 272)—he offers, voiced by the mother, the disclaimer that fiction is the realm, for him, of a paradoxical authenticity: "That's how he is. He gets the craziest ideas. Always exaggerating. You can't believe a word he writes" (*MC*, 276). As Rebecca Braun has compellingly shown in a study of authorship in Grass's work, this last entry is part of a concerted attempt on his part to undermine authorship: the author, she argues, "has mutated from fine representative of the power of imagination to a self-conscious liar whose grasp of reality is questionable. Collectively, the individual narratives undermine overblown notions of authorship, with Grass himself humorously presented as its most degenerate specimen at the end of the twentieth century."[37] The self-deprecatory gesture should, of course, not dupe us: it is still Grass staging the intervention of his mother, even as he seems to undermine his authorial position. What is highlighted with this last gesture is a century of imaginary portraits, of voices that, although they speak with Grass's inflections and cannot make claims to all-inclusive representation, nonetheless point insistently to the relentless pluralism and difference of perspectives; differently put, a distantiality redefined as the demand for recognition of the human community as constitutive of every one of us.

Introducing August Sander's 1929 gallery of portraits, titled *Face of Our Time*, Alfred Döblin articulates the significance of the singular, even as it forms an integral part of a composite whole: "Viewed from a certain distance," he writes echoing Walter Benjamin's reflections at the beginning of "The Storyteller," "distinctions vanish; viewed from a certain distance, individuals cease to exist, and only universals persist. The distinction between the individual and the collective (or the universal), then—with the wisdom of a Solomon—becomes a matter of varying degrees of distance."[38] Identifying the value of Sander's photographs in the achievement of a "scientific viewpoint" enabled through the juxtaposition of so many portraits, which leads to a comparison not unlike that of the anatomist, Döblin points out that the faces of these people coming from all walks of life inspire the desire for narrative: "Entire stories could be told about many of these photographs, they are asking for it, they are raw material for writers, material that is more stimulating and more productive than many a newspaper report."[39] Grass's tome does precisely this: it narrates stories, inchoate as they are, of everyday lives, composing a unique portrait—of the century, *our time*—of singular faces. How one measures the distance between self and others is the stuff not only of lived experience, but also—as reflection and exemplary practice—of literature.

In the last two chapters, my focus has been on Ernaux's and Grass's accounts of the myriad ways in which the time-fabric of one's life is intricately woven with the lives of others; these texts, I have argued, contribute to a reimagining not only of community, but also of the self. Having allowed these questions to emerge from the literary texts, and having highlighted how such preoccupations blur generic distinctions, particularly between personal writing such as diary or autobiography, and fiction, in the final chapter I will return more explicitly to the philosophical reflection on community and the plural self, which I will put in conversation with *In a Strange Room*, a novel by South African writer Damon Galgut. Like Ernaux's diary of the outside, where imagining the lives of others in the third person brings her back to herself, and like Grass's unusual (auto)biography of the century, where various characters, real and imagined, assume the first-person narrative voice, *In a Strange Room* is a literary experiment: Galgut pushes the confusion of interpersonal boundaries (self/other) even further, oscillating between the first person of memoir and the third person of fiction when referring to the same character, which might, or might not, refer to himself. I offer the reading of this novel, which also takes us out of Europe to distant places where Europeans sometimes go on holiday, as a corrective to Peter Sloterdijk's idiosyncratic account of everyday life as practice, an "acrobatics" driven by immunitary tendencies. As I will briefly indicate, the broader philosophical conversation here involves Jean-Luc Nancy and Roberto Esposito; but my aim is to show how, whereas Sloterdijk remains committed to a fashioning of the self, to a strong sense of self as the obvious premise of what he calls with a vague allusion to life in the Anthropocene "co-immunism," Galgut's literary experiment offers a piecemeal dramatization of depersonalization as crucial to reimagining an ethical community.

Chapter 7

✦

Damon Galgut on Emptying Oneself for Sleep

In the highly idiosyncratic book *You Must Change Your Life*, Peter Sloterdijk invokes Kafka "as a witness of the time" to testify to a shift to "a generalized acrobatics of existence," a shift he places at the beginning of the twentieth century.[1] One of the acrobats in question is Nietzsche's tightrope walker in *Thus Spoke Zarathustra*, the man pursuing an inevitable destination, the *Übermensch*, illustrating the endurance of a vertical tension previously reserved to religious practice directed to God. In Sloterdijk's reading, Kafka internalized the impulse toward the "de-spiritualization of asceticisms" to such a degree that he forgot its origin; and "he further developed the impulses in the direction of a progressive lowering of the heroic tone, while simultaneously reinforcing the awareness of the universal ascetic and acrobatic dimension of human existence."[2]

A passage from Kafka's *Betrachtungen über Sünde, Leid, Hoffnung und den wahren Weg* (*Observations on Sin, Suffering, Hope and the True Path*) serves to illustrate the shift: "The true path," Kafka writes, "is along a rope, not a rope suspended way up in the air, but rather only just over the ground. It seems more like a tripwire than a tightrope." The change in the position of the rope, Sloterdijk comments,

> seems to convey the message that the task of finding the true path is difficult enough already for one not to have to climb high in order to live dangerously. The rope is no longer meant to test the ability to keep your balance on the slimmest foundation; its function is more to prove that if you are too sure of yourself, you will fall if you simply walk forwards.

This change is key to understanding many of the historical and artistic developments witnessed by the past century:

> Existence as such is an acrobatic achievement, and no one can say with certainty what training provides the necessary skills to master this discipline. Hence the acrobat no longer knows what exercises

> keep him from falling—aside from constant vigilance. This fading level of artistedom by no means indicates a loss of this phenomenon's significance; on the contrary, it reveals how aspects of the artiste spread to affect all aspects of life. *The great subject of the arts and philosophies of the twentieth century—the discovery of the ordinary—draws its energy from the dawn of the acrobats, which ensues in parallel with it.*[3]

Sloterdijk refers here to a complex process of secularization, the "great unscrewing of the moderns from a system of religiously coded vertical tensions that had been in force for millennia," which has by no means rendered obsolete the search for meaning or for an ethical life: suggestively, Kafka and Nietzsche share the intuition that "the disappearance of the world above leaves behind the fastened rope." Yet in the absence of a system of values that would prescribe norms of behavior, such as Aristotle's *Nicomachean Ethics* or the Ten Commandments, it becomes difficult to know how to conduct the business of one's life. My suggestion, in a previous chapter, that we live as if all we had left of Aristotle's virtue system were *phronêsis*, a kind of practical intelligence, is echoed by Sloterdijk's mention of a "constant vigilance" in his reading of Kafka.

Community is one of the important, yet unacknowledged, aspects of life concerned by Sloterdijk's remarks; the "dawn of the acrobats" is also the dawn of powerful ideologies of community such as communism or fascism and of the "communities of work" inspired by them, as Jean-Luc Nancy might say. This dawn requires thinking community anew, a rethinking that needs to start from a more modest premise and to pursue a less grand finale, as Sloterdijk's reading of Kafka also confirms. In this spirit, philosophers like Jean-Luc Nancy and Roberto Esposito see the thought of community humbly return to finitude, mortality, and the ordinariness of human encounter. The "true path," then, to return to the passage from Kafka, denies itself the comforting script of existing relationships, the only commitment remaining that to "constant vigilance."

Evaluated side by side, the diagnoses that emerge from Esposito's and Sloterdijk's respective arguments look remarkably similar: Esposito sees the contemporary world dominated by an immunitary *dispositif* that has affected all spheres of experience to the detriment of community: "Everywhere we look, new walls, new blockades, and new dividing lines are erected against something that threatens, or at least seems to, our biological, social, and environmental identity. . . . The risk of contamination immediately liquidates contact, relationality, and being in common."[4] Although Sloterdijk does not work within the binary opposition of community-immunity and recognizes from the outset "the symbolic immune systems and ritual shells" in which life has always been carried out, today, he claims, we discover our narrow conception of immunity: "Protection always refers to a local self, and externalization to an anonymous environment for which no one takes responsibility; [historically,] . . . the victories of the own could only be bought with the defeat of the foreign."[5] Whereas Esposito suggests we should reverse the ways we think about community and immunity, associating community with difference and immunity with the impersonal, Sloterdijk concludes his long book with a few sketchy notes on "co-immunism": the realization, nowadays, that "the earth . . . is the limited shared site of human operations" requires imagining a coimmunitary system that extends beyond the traditional tribal, national, and imperial formatting, or more recently regional strategic alliances, to include the global. "The history of the own that is grasped on too small a scale and the foreign that is treated too badly reaches an end at the moment when a global co-immunity structure is born," when the earth is "conceived as the own," which would lead to the romanticism of brotherliness being replaced by a cooperative logic. "Humanity becomes a political concept."[6] Briefly, whereas Esposito sees "immunity" as the negative term of a binary, Sloterdijk sees it as inevitable, but recommends its expansion.

From the confrontation between these views emerges a striking difference, which concerns the notion of subject, or self, the two philosophers work with.[7] Like Maurice Blanchot and Nancy, who insist that there can be no subject prior to community, which is a *désoeuvrement*, or "unworking" (a term Nancy borrows from Blanchot), Esposito seeks to dismantle the autonomous subject and speaks of the *impersonal*.[8] Sloterdijk, by contrast, preserves the notion of a strong self intact and seeks its expansion into a sublime, all-encompassing *own*, in a coimmunism based on "the good habits of shared survival in daily exercises."[9] Whereas Blanchot and Nancy (and Esposito would agree) insist on "that which, before or beyond the work, withdraws from the work, and which, no longer having to do either with production or with completion, encounters interruption, fragmentation, suspension," Sloterdijk reminds his readers that asceticism means exercise and therefore gambles on "practice," on the strengthening of the self and of the own, indispensable in our secularized acrobatics of existence. It is all the more surprising then to understand, while reading the last pages of *You Must Change Your Life*, that Sloterdijk somehow takes it for granted that the "unconditional overtaxing" set up by his program can, or should be able to accomplish the "respectful inclusion of individual cultures, particular interests and local solidarities." He has shifted here from the realm of the ethical into that of the political ("humanity becomes a political concept"), but his denunciation of the "ship of fools that is abstract universalism" sounds ironic against his own sweeping oversight of the significant and painstaking work with difference that would be required here. How coimmunism is to be achieved with the expanded sense of *the own* he recommends remains a question; even if we do identify the right "good habits" and exercises, it is unclear how the "self," left intact, is going to fare under the pressures of a purely utilitarian perspective; and how will we negotiate our daily interactions with other people without "being too sure of ourselves," as Kafka cautions? Although Sloterdijk does take onboard Kafka's leaning toward humility, he leaves Kafka behind, manifesting explicitly and repeatedly his allegiance to the Nietzsche of "the doctrine of upward propagation."[10] There is no glance spared for the middle-period Nietzsche of modesty, or for the German philosopher's reflections on the multiplicity of the selves. Such modesty or humility would bring him closer to the finitude that Nancy and Esposito acknowledge as crucial to the ethics of community, and to the possibility of thinking through the subject and its relation to, and encounter with, the others (the respectful, inclusive being-with that he merely gestures toward).[11]

The Loss of Immunity in the Contemporary Novel: Damon Galgut's *In a Strange Room*

Such concerns have been central not only to the philosophical reflection of the past few decades, but also to the fiction of the same period. Indeed, to say that the contemporary novel offers a confirmation of the worldview canvassed by Esposito (blockades, dividing lines, risk of contamination) does not require too much elaboration: protagonists who surround themselves with walls, literal or figurative, and who consider themselves exempt from the economy of debt, gift, or exchange of community are in no shortage in the literature of the last hundred years, from the secluded sinologist Peter Kien in Elias Canetti's *Die Blendung* (*Auto-da-fé*, 1935) to the incorrigible drifters and suicides in Don DeLillo's *Cosmopolis* (2003), Damon Galgut's *In a Strange Room* (2010), A. D. Miller's *Snowdrops* (2011), Deborah Levy's *Swimming Home* (2011), or Alison Moore's *The Lighthouse* (2012), to name but a few recent novels. These characters illustrate that all too common contemporary tendency to disappear from the world and from oneself (to use David le Breton's formulation): vulnerability, a lack of attachments, and utter loneliness, whose causes are as much personal as they are social, are variously invoked; in other words, these characters are engulfed in the dark fold of liberal individualism.[12]

I have included "drifters and suicides" in one category based on their initial immunitary tendencies (in Esposito's sense of protection from, and exclusion of everyone who might disrupt through "contamination" one's sense of self, individual or collective), but their trajectories sharply set them apart: while some lose their immunity to find a community of those without community in life (thus intimating an ethical form of relationality with which I will be concerned in what follows), others join this community only in death, through suicide, voluntary or not. A paradigmatic example of the latter is Peter Kien, who at the end of Canetti's *Auto-da-fé* inadvertently sets fire to his precious library-fortress and to himself, in a delirium that is the utmost expression of the loss of connection with the human community. The reader might also remember the suicide of the poet at the end of Deborah Levy's *Swimming Home*, and the revelation that his public persona, fame, and carefree relationships were a deceiving façade that concealed his past as a victim in a Nazi camp. With their suicides, these characters do not offer the reader any form of poetic comfort; the abrupt, incomprehensible ending is anything but closure, soliciting hard and sustained work on the reader's part to figure out a way of suturing back the (fictional) world.

For similar reasons, the South African writer Damon Galgut has been called the "master of unease," and his 2010 novel *In a Strange Room: Three Journeys*, shortlisted for the Booker Prize, certainly does not contradict this characterization. His protagonist, also named Damon, finds the defining metaphor of his life in the happenstance of travel. Since anything can happen when one is unhinged from the constraints of community, Galgut's choice of travels could be regarded as a convenient plot strategy. But if we see travel as the premise of an unconditional openness to new relationships, *In a Strange Room* reads like a novelistic meditation on community—questioned, problematized, and imagined anew. This consideration has to be framed by taking seriously Galgut's preference for the three stories to be read together, as a novel, rather than as individual texts loosely connected by the theme of journeys. What is at stake in this preference, what difference does the generic labeling make?

Under the section titles "The Follower," "The Lover," and "The Guardian," the novel evokes three trips, which take place at three different moments in the character's life; at the center of each trip there is a relationship, each failed: one through separation, another through accidental death, the last through suicide. If we choose to follow these stories in their concatenation, Damon's existence appears as a rootless, footloose "wandering around from one spare room to another" (*ISR*, 67). The room is a recurrent motif in the three narratives; the "strange room" of the title comes from Faulkner, whose novel *As I Lay Dying* Damon is reading on one of his trips. The passage whose details he fondles in his thoughts is about the intimate connection between the content of one's mind, or self, and the room one sleeps in; ultimately, about the possibility of knowing who or what the self is: "In a strange room you must empty yourself for sleep. And before you are emptied for sleep, what are you. And when you are emptied for sleep, you are not. And when you are filled with sleep, you never were" (*ISR*, 47).[13]

The problem of the self would be philosophically banal but for its link to the room, to the home that Damon lacks. The epigraph Galgut has chosen for his novel, "He has no home," attributed to the artist Vojislav Jakiç, echoes Adorno's aphorism about the morality of not being at home in one's home. This, I will show in what follows, is also Galgut's *minima moralia*: by moving away, and repeatedly, from "home," his character opens himself to other forms of community, possibly negotiated around difference. More importantly, he opens himself to other forms of homelessness, more precarious and inevitable than his own. If we consider his repeated displacements together—and this "if" will be the explicit concern of the following section—they can be understood as a form of *anthropotechnics* in Sloterdijk's sense of the term, making of Damon an "acrobat": someone who repeats an experience, a practice. Yet, paradoxically, the self that emerges is not strengthened in its certainties, in its "selfhood"; rather, it is depersonalized, becoming a kind of dwelling for others. I will briefly elaborate on these two aspects.

Anthropotechnics as the Gamble of Plot

The beginning and ending of Galgut's novel, Chris Roper writes, "indicate a circular . . . experiential economy, a sense that life is something constantly lived, that the trite fact of having to keep living is perhaps the most important thing in the world."[14] This characterization captures well the affinity between Galgut's novel and Sloterdijk's *anthropotechnics*—if, and only if, we read the three stories as a novel. If so, much like Samuel Beckett's characters, Galgut's protagonist appears to live his life as a form of asceticism, which, Sloterdijk reminds us, is intimately related to exercise, to practice. The latter is defined as any "operation that provides or improves the actor's qualification for the next performance of the same operation, whether it is declared as practice or not."[15] This last precision is very important (that the actor's awareness of his or her engagement in a practice is irrelevant), since Damon would most likely consider himself a master of failed relationships.

The first story, "The Follower," evokes Damon's trip to Lesotho in the company of his German friend of recent date Reiner, with whom he shares "a certain humour related to an alienation from things" (*ISR*, 20). The delight at the prospect of shedding "the ballast of familiar life" in Reiner's company gradually wears off as a power dynamic develops between them, to a point where Damon finds it unbearable and returns to South Africa, abandoning his friend in a foreign land. The second story, "The Lover," spins again around travel, this time through Zambia, Malawi, Tanzania, and Zimbabwe, in the company of two Swiss twins, Jerome and Alice, and their French friend, Christian. Although their time together feels made of a liquid substance at the center of which the only solid object is Jerome, Damon cannot find it in himself to express his feelings or act on his affection, and, after an awkward visit and some correspondence, the news of Jerome's death marks the end of their relationship. The last episode, "The Guardian," is the most poignant and requires the most narrative tact: he is on the road again, this time in India, accompanied by a friend whom he is trying to help recover from a series of mental breakdowns and electroshocks. Self-destructive and resentful of his protection, Anna ends up attempting suicide and is saved only through Damon's superhuman efforts, supported by some acquaintances of recent date. She will kill herself once no longer in his care, while Damon finds himself in the company of his helper Caroline, an Englishwoman whose own experience of tragedy the novel withholds.

Formally then, we can speak of Damon's life as practice, or anthropotechnics, in the spirit of Sloterdijk's argument; the apparent progress registered by the succession of titles—follower, lover, guardian—would even confirm the logic of Nietzsche's "doctrine of upward propagation." But things are not so simple in Galgut's novel, because in each of the three stories, Damon's position is rather ambiguous: if it is true that Reiner is domineering and overbearing (vertical tension), it is in the end Damon who abandons him. This is not, however, an expression of strength; rather, it is the result of an emotional outburst, inevitable given his incapacity to express his discontent during their trip, and to negotiate better the power dynamic between them. Similarly, in the second story, the equality with Jerome (that one might presuppose on the basis of the title) is unsettled by their age difference and by Damon's refusal to settle in Switzerland with Jerome. Yet again, his refusal stems from his chronic inability to make and follow through with decisions; and in the end, what ends the relationship is not an act of will, but Jerome's unexpected death. And with Anna, since she is utterly unpredictable, abusive and ungrateful, it is often unclear who holds the power. Although he is her guardian, she accuses him of bullying her, an accusation that is so alien to his nature that it is sufficient to overpower him.

The recurrent image of the concentric circles in the three stories might tip the balance in favor of Sloterdijk's anthropotechnics, particularly the aspect of exercise *that prepares for future practice*; differently put, of a practice that has some identifiable meaning—if no teleology. When Damon and Reiner train for their expedition, for instance, they decide to walk in always broader concentric circles as a way to challenge themselves to become fitter; there are circles, as well, in the second and third stories. Yet Damon is often plagued by doubts whether there has been any progress: when he changes his mind about following Jerome, "he feels even less sure than before about the meaning of it all" (*ISR*, 117), and questions the logic of circularity: "He has already left, or perhaps he never arrived" (*ISR*, 117). Despite Damon's doubts and his unsuccessful relationships (which never endure, or even end tragically), Sloterdijk would encourage us to consider their effect on the practitioner: Damon's experiences could be regarded as a spiritual exercise, whose ethical significance would lie precisely in his reluctance to perform it (in the last part, he does what he feels is right, even as he resents it). If his acts are not part of a project, of an intended moral stance, they are however the direct expression of who he is most fundamentally, of who he becomes through them. Sloterdijk's passage on the effect of the practice on the practitioner strikes a meaningful note here:

> Being human means existing in an operatively curved space in which actions return to affect the actor, works the worker, communications

> the communicator, thoughts the thinker and feelings the feeler. All these forms of reaction, I would argue, have an ascetic, that is to say a practicing character—although . . . they largely belong to the undeclared and unnoticed asceticisms or the occulted training routines.[16]

A person who takes care of someone because he sees no alternative, as Damon does in "The Guardian," is (or becomes) a person who cares, a caring person. A wonderfully apt phrase that Sloterdijk uses for one of his exemplary "acrobats," the disabled violinist Unthan, strikes a chord here, too, capturing the contours of Damon's ethical life: he is a "reluctant virtuoso of existence."[17]

Whether we are convinced by this characterization hinges on our acceptance of Galgut's generic choice of the novel, favored over the collection of three individual stories.[18] In interviews, Galgut conceded that they could be read individually, but he found them "diminished by being read on their own. They're meant to resonate off of one another. One journey does reflect on the next one." Asked if it was difficult to decide on the order, he explicitly points out not only their autobiographical nature, but also the aspect that Sloterdijk's account of life as practice highlights, namely the emergence of who one is, an always more experienced self: "It's the order, firstly, in which they happened, and secondly, the order in which they were written. There's a certain integrity to the way it developed, so there was no point in fiddling with it. Damon ages as well and he doesn't learn much, but *he does learn a little as he goes along*."[19] At play here, in the slippage between the logic of chronology (this is merely the order in which they happened) and the logic of significance derived from these events ("he does learn a little") is a problem that modern fiction has wrestled with for the past century.

Jacques Rancière gives it eloquent expression in "The Thread of the Novel," an essay in which he distinguishes, in fine readings of Virginia Woolf and other modern novelists (also revisited by Erich Auerbach in *Mimesis* and by Paul Ricœur in *Temps et récit*), between the "tyranny of plot" and the "luminous halo" or the "semi-transparent envelope surrounding us from the beginning of consciousness to the end." Here Rancière extends Virginia Woolf's argument in "Modern Fiction," in which she borrows Joseph Conrad's phrase to distinguish between the realist writers of a previous generation, the "materialists," and her contemporaries, the "spiritualists." Rancière writes:

> The wandering thread is thus something different from the chance succession of atoms. It is the thread that links the atoms so as to make the light of the halo shine and let the spiritual texture of the envelope provide a new sense of the whole. Modern fiction is predicated on two principles: the radical exteriority of the atoms, which means the destruction of the usual modes of connection of causal action; and the living unity of the halo, which means the immanence of the whole manifested in the jump from one atom to another. How

> is the conjunction of those two principles thinkable? And how is its implementation workable?[20]

Rancière's questions reformulate the interrogations above, throwing into high relief the stakes in connecting the three parts of Galgut's novel into a meaningful whole, of examining the "luminous halo" or "transparent envelope" that surrounds his character from the beginning to the end. Referring to *In a Strange Room*, we can ask with Rancière: "What type of thread can at the same time be true to life and construct a concatenation of events that deserves the name of fiction," in other words, become a novel, rather than three disparate autobiographical stories evoking failed relationships? The answer he provides finds unexpected echoes in Galgut's novel:

> The success of "modern fiction" rests on a compromise. It rests on its capacity to construct a form of succession that fits the demands of a plot while making the "life of the soul"—the life of the impersonal or the infinite that denies the artificiality of all plots—appear. In order to make it appear or resound, one has to do two contradictory things: on one hand, one has to blur the edges, to dissolve the fragmented temporality of causes and effects, ends and means, thoughts and actions within the continuity of microsensory events succeeding one another just as an hour succeeds another hour; on the other hand, one has to create differences of intensity within this continuum.[21]

We have touched briefly on the recurrent image of rooms in the novel, which resonate not only intertextually with Faulkner's novel but also internally, between the seemingly endless succession of rooms Damon rents on a temporary basis, and the psychological space of his mind, emptied before sleep. The room of the title is "strange" precisely because it hovers between the physical and the psychological, paradoxically suturing the emotional space of the relentless alienation of travel; differently put, it is the always new, unfamiliar room in which he takes lodging that forges a certain continuity between all the other rooms in his life: that is, between happenings (the typical stuff of plot) and the myriad atoms of his mind that he empties before sleep—the life of his soul, his sense of self. This is the first "contradictory thing" that happens in the novel: the continuity between the two realms, of plot and of meaning, is enacted in the image of the room.

The second half of Rancière's formula, "one has to create differences of intensity within this continuum," also brings us into close proximity with Galgut's novel. In the work through which Rancière illustrates his idea, *Mrs. Dalloway*, the obvious "difference of intensity" comes from the "splitting of truth itself," enacted by the opposition of two characters, "the happy Clarissa and her sad double Septimus Smith." Rancière's explanation of the logic behind Septimus's suicide—a narrative necessity, as Woolf herself pointed out—likewise foregrounds the opposition between Damon and the characters who act as his doubles in each story (Reiner, Jerome, Anna). Highly illuminating, the passage is worth quoting in full:

> [Septimus throwing himself out of the window] is a condition for the fiction itself. Septimus, the insane double of the healthy Clarissa, must die. But on the other hand, Septimus, the martyr of the "life of the soul," must be there to contrast his unconditional faith with the idolatry of the pagan worshipper of the little miracles of the everyday. Or rather, the tragedy of Septimus must put a radical split in the heart of the story to prevent the "luminous halo" from being equated with the mere continuum of those miracles. There is no wandering thread allowing the luminous halo of life to dismiss the tyranny of the plot. The lyricism of truth cannot construct a fictional whole by itself. To break with the tyrannical logic of the plot, the expanded prose poem must be split by tragedy, by the fight against tyranny. Septimus thus appears as a new incarnation of a character that is crucial to modern fiction: the character who must be killed in order to secure the right relation between several plots.[22]

Such "splitting of truth" is present in Galgut's novel in each of the three episodes, each offering a negative characterization of Damon, the narrator and protagonist. In "The Follower," Reiner illustrates a kind of artistic morality, carrying himself as an athlete who exercises his body and mind, careless of the burden of rules and presence he imposes on others. Damon, by contrast, is an ascetic priest of self-denial who does not express his needs, but instead acts as an open receptacle in his relationships. Reiner thus represents the kind of "acrobat" that Damon is not. In the second episode, "The Lover," the tension between Damon and the younger Jerome reveals a split between the two of them, resolved—albeit without closure—in the terrible contingency of Jerome's fatal accident. Symbolically, we are told here again what Damon, against all appearance, is *not*: a victim of contingency. Damon's darkest double appears in the third episode in the utterly egocentric and capricious Anna. And unlike Jerome, whose death is accidental and the news of which falls out of an impersonal envelope, she kills herself, her repeated attempts to do so and finally succeeding adding up to a somber and perhaps ironic example of anthropotechnics. Reckless egocentrism, solipsistic despair, and finally suicide could also be the manifestations of Damon's solitude and lack of attachments; yet he does not fall into any of these.

However, this is no simple polarization; Galgut is too astute an observer of psychological complexity to intimate a picture of kindness by sentimentally aligning a predisposition to do the good, followed by a firm intention, which materializes into action (good deeds). There is no hint of tenderness in Damon's words, for instance, when Anna attempts suicide for the first time:

"I hope she wakes up so I can kill her." His frustrated anger is consuming and real. Most importantly, Anna does ultimately succeed in killing herself: this would probably not have taken place in a narrative keen to provide poetic justice, that is, to reward the protagonist for his care and efforts to prevent her suicide. The failure to do so complicates again the logic of the plot as anthropotechnics, that is, as a life practice from which one emerges wiser and better equipped for the future.

Although the traveling image of the room, which connects the realm of events and that of the inner life, as well as the "splitting of truth" between Damon and the three characters with whom he engages in relationships do have the effect of a "compromise" in Rancière's sense, I want to show that ultimately the decisive "splitting of truth" occurs in Galgut's novel at a different level. Taking a hint from Rancière's succinct formulation "the self becomes the plot," we return explicitly to the crucial problem discussed at the beginning of this chapter, as it emerged from the juxtaposition of Esposito's and Sloterdijk's arguments about the immunitary dispositif, and immunitary practice, respectively. But addressing the problem of the self in reading *In a Strange Room*, we are faced with a dilemma: which self? Is it the one retrospectively dramatized by the autobiographical Damon, or the one portrayed by Galgut, the writer of fiction?

Between Memoir and Fiction: The Ethical Import of Depersonalization

"When I started writing it wasn't with a conscious intent of splitting it between different voices," Galgut says of the recurrent switch between first and third person in the narrative perspective. On one hand, he had the revelation of the "ontological reality of that switch," corresponding, for instance, to the detachment one might feel even from one's own experience; on the other, Galgut was keen to explore this switch as "the chance to break out of the conventional approach to any kind of fiction," thus to find a fresh narrative strategy that would open up new possibilities: "If you lock into a mode of telling, into a first-person perspective or a third-person perspective, you commit yourself to what becomes the defining border of the genre. It takes on a certain authority, a truth. But if you switch between first and third it's very unsettling for the reader."[23] In Galgut's words, we witness the contemporary novel taking a stance not only against what Rancière called with Woolf the "tyranny of plot," but also against the constraints of a unique narrative perspective whose "authority" or "truth" the South African author denounces. What exactly are the literary possibilities unlocked by exploring the "ontological reality" of the switch between narrative perspectives, between first and third person, in particular?

As we have seen, there is a lot of indecision where the relationships of the main character are concerned. Torn between the impulse to act on his feelings and a chronic inability to do things for his own sake, he often surprises himself with his unpredictability, which paradoxically tends to take the shape of a pattern: typically, he moves as a substitute for thought, in a vacuum of emotion, when seemingly a decision forms itself in some inscrutable place within himself, or perhaps because of his procrastination, and then suddenly he sees himself rushing into the direction opposite to the one anticipated by his decision. For instance, when Jerome, Alice, and Christian are about to leave Africa, heading to Greece, he declines their invitation and apparently decides to avoid the awkwardness of taking farewell, walking aimlessly, clearly away from the bus station; "but then suddenly he is off, running the other way through the crowds. Where does this movement come from, it takes even him by surprise, he is looking for a taxi" (*ISR*, 104). At play in such situations is a tension between different selves within himself, variously inclined, of which one eventually gets (or fails) to make a decision, and if the latter, the lack of a decision determines the course of events.[24] Rather than a self—*one* self—then, one might speak of a landscape of subjectivity, or of personal experience, populated by various selves, not all of which are equally familiar even to Damon himself. This landscape is shaped by the various journeys he undertakes; in fact, a relationship between the inner landscape and the places he visits suggests itself: "The border is a line on a map, but also drawn inside himself somewhere" (*ISR*, 87). The motif of the border that needs to be negotiated, circumvented, or folded upon itself is thus not only a formal exploration of the possibilities of switching between narrative perspectives, as we have seen; it also translates into a fantasmatic reconfiguration of the map of the world and thus of subjectivity:

> In dreams he is constantly looking at maps, in which there are continents and countries, but they don't resemble the actual world. In these maps real countries are joined together in peculiar configurations, Mexico at the top of Africa, next to Borneo. Or else countries have mythical names and shapes which evoke a longing in him. He has always been drawn by the strangeness of places, by what he doesn't know instead of what he does. (*ISR*, 111)

This passage offers a reading lesson, intimating the possibility to transcend the established categories, borders, labels: against the conventional layout of the map, against what we believe we know about places (safely identified on maps and labeled once and for all), the longing to discover them otherwise, not in some essentializing truth, but through the experience of what one "doesn't know." There is an affirmation here of a radical openness to the revelation of the world as different, set free from the tyranny of convention. To this effect, Galgut compounds the use of shifting pronouns with another formal device, which often renders acute the emotional tension: in reported speech, questions maintain their interrogative structure but drop the question mark, as if the interrogation—and thus the openness created by the interrogative mode, the difficulty to know (a situation, the world, someone else)—were affirmed as a statement. The only certainty is the incertitude, the puzzling indecision, the hesitation, and thus the openness to multiple, even contradictory possibilities.

With the character Anna, Galgut shows himself aware that such self-division can be pathological and thus detrimental to the possibility of community with others:

> It's begun to feel to *him* as if a stranger has taken up residence in her, somebody dark and reckless that he doesn't trust, who wants to consume Anna completely. [Sometimes he can speak to her reasonably,] . . . enlist her on *his* side. But the dark stranger always appears again, peering slyly over her shoulder, doing something alarming, and the softer Anna shrinks away. At moments the pair of them are there together, the sister-Anna and her scary twin, and they jostle each other for the upper hand. It's an uneven battle, the stranger is certainly stronger, but *I* keep hoping the pills will vanquish her. (*ISR*, 137, my italics)

This passage is interesting for at least two reasons: it not only makes vivid Anna's division into a more malleable self and a reckless, scary "twin," but it also registers formally Damon's self-splitting in the switch between the third person and the first. Yet these are different phenomena: whereas in the case of self-centered, egoistic Anna, the "scary twin" is the outgrowth of solipsism, of an excessive ego, in his situation, the self-division, when not simply the index of distance between the narrating and the narrated self, is triggered by his identification with the plight of other people. A telling example is the scene with the local fisherman, who tells the tourists whom he is supposed to take back to their hotel that their departure is delayed by the loss of a flipper:

> The visitors sigh and chatter in the boat, while *I* get out to help him look. The price of the flipper is worth maybe a week or two of fishing to this man. *We* search in the shallow water, between the crevices in the rocks. Hurry up, one of the Swiss girls calls crossly, *we*'re waiting for you. But now the anger finally touches the surface of his tongue, you get out of there, *he* cries, his voice rising, get out of there and help us look. One of you has lost the flipper, *we*'re not going back till you find it again. There is muttering and resentment, let him buy a new one, but they all troop out onto the shore and pretend to cast around. In the end the flipper is found and everybody gets back into the boat and in a little while the frivolous conversation resumes, but *he* knows that his outburst has confirmed what they suspect, *he* is not the same as them, *he is a fucked-up South African*. (*ISR*, 77, my italics)

The use of the pronouns is telling: the scene is so vivid in his memory that the narrator assumes the first-person perspective to convey his detachment from the group of visitors. But the singular "I" swiftly morphs, in solidarity with the fisherman he helps, into the plural "we" ("we search") soon confronted by the collective "we" of the tourists ("we're waiting"). And here the narrator/character doubles into the detached stage director who observes his character, angered by the others' obliviousness, appealing to them by pointing out that the situation concerns them all ("we're not going back"), thus merging the two groups that had appeared in confrontation in the previous sentences.[25]

It is worth noting that the first switch from "I" to "we" (which includes the fisherman) passes through a sentence: "The price of the flipper is worth maybe a week or two of fishing to this man." Unlike the other visitors, concerned only with the inconvenience caused by the fisherman's tarrying, Damon sees beyond the instrumentalization the protagonist of a life, a life of precariousness vulnerable to the loss of a flipper. This moment builds on an increasing irritation with the other members of the group, complacent and oblivious in their pleasure-seeking and sense of entitlement: "They are completely content to sit around drinking beer for hours," the narrator remarks only a few pages earlier;

> they go out in search of loud music at night, and some of them show an unpleasant disdain for the poverty they encounter. The two young women in particular, who turn out to be Swedish, have stopped being silent and go on in loud voices about their terrible trip through Zambia. The rocks, oh, it was just horrible, and the bus-station, oh, it was so dirty, it smelled, oh, disgusting. The shortcomings and squalor of the continent have let them down personally, it never seems to occur to them that the conditions they found horrible and disgusting are not part of a set that will be struck when they have gone offstage. (*ISR*, 73)

"Drawn by the strangeness of places, by what he doesn't know instead of what he does," after the boat incident Damon steps out of the "set" (the "marina for wealthy expatriates, [where] expensive yachts lift their silken sails like standards") and goes into the village. What he discovers is extreme poverty: "the ragged clothes on the smiling children, the bare interiors of the smoky huts with their two or three pieces of broken furniture, the skeletal dogs slinking way at his approach" (*ISR*, 78). People in poverty, he learns, can hardly afford dignity: "For the first time he chooses to understand why people who live here, whose country this is, might want to run errands for these foreign visitors passing through, and catch fish and cook for them, and clean up after them" (*ISR*, 78).

The revelation of a different world is accompanied by an act of will—"he chooses to understand"—but this lucidity, which has the weight of a moral category (as with Adorno), by no means strengthens him in his certainties, or his sense of self. On the contrary, the follow-up to his stroll outside the touristic set leaves him psychologically disheveled: on returning to the hotel, a young woman solicits his sympathy, complaining in frustration about an incomplete service from an old local, who failed to fold the laundry he had washed for her. "He can't contain it any more, the anger that fuelled his little outburst yesterday is now a rage. . . . You ought to feel ashamed of yourself instead of being so certain that you're right," he tells her, pointing out her privilege and the local man's old age. And again, his taking a stance makes him uncomfortable because it reflects back to him his own privilege:

> He is as guilty as any of them, he too is passing through, he too has luck and money, all his self-righteousness will not absolve him. After she has gone scurrying off he sits in the twilight outside his room, while his anger cools into misery. . . . he knows that the spell is broken and he can't be one of the lotus-eaters any more, he has to move on, move on. . . . He'll travel north to some other town where nobody knows him. (*ISR*, 79)

Adorno could not have wished for a more unsettling illustration of the morality of willed discomfort, of an elected homelessness. The later scene, where Damon visits an art gallery, now reveals its full meaning: "He spends a day in a gallery of outsider art, paintings and sculptures made with the vision of the mad or the lost, and from this collection of fantastic and febrile images he retains a single line, a book by a Serbian artist whose name I forget, He Has No House" (*ISR*, 115). With this passage, we are back in the confidence of the "I," after a long detour through the story of a character identified in the third person. There are degrees of distance, still, between this narrating "I," who claims not to remember the name of the Serbian artist, and what would be the authorial "I," who attributes the epigraph of the novel (which reads "he has no home") to Vojislav Jakiç. Such an identity between the different markers of first-person selfhood would be the generic condition of the "autobiographical pact."[26] Yet Galgut blurred the generic conventions, making his intentions to this effect explicit in an interview. Acknowledging that much of the material in the novel *In A Strange Room* is autobiographical, he defends his preference for identifying the text as fiction:

> Memoir, as it happens, is a very popular form in South Africa right now, especially because there's this sense of unspoken history that's being reclaimed at the moment. It's not that I'm resistant to it. We think we know what these categories mean, you know? Memoir or nonfiction is supposed to be "the truth," whereas fiction, as we understand it, is "untruth." But, in fact, on closer scrutiny the borders between those different genres are really quite porous and sometimes meaningless.[27]

What brings fiction and autobiographical writing in close proximity, he argues, is the work of concentrating meaning in certain moments that are privileged over others (what he might call with Hayden White the work of "emplotment"). In the evocation of real experiences, for instance, "I'm going to forget all the irrelevant stuff and give it a core meaning, which is of my own construction. As a writer of fiction I contend that's what you do whenever you're constructing your own narrative."[28] Most intriguingly, Galgut claims that there is no difference between memory and consciousness: there is no such thing as a pure present, simply the memory of something that has just happened, which can be very different depending on which of the participants in an event one asks. The distance from the self who lives and the self who remembers is always there, and this is what *In a Strange Room* tries to capture: "So what I'm trying to do with the book—I haven't been very successful—but what I'm trying to do is go after the nature of consciousness itself, because if I had to distill this particular book to a sentence it would be that all consciousness is memory and memory is fiction."[29] This a remarkable insight, whose implications deserve to be spelled out more explicitly.

As Esposito points out, there is an ethical charge to the switch between the first person associated with autobiography and the third person of fictional narrative: if we manage to turn ourselves (as if) into fictional characters, to see ourselves in the third person (as others see us from the outside, the argument goes), and then return to ourselves, as Galgut's narrator does, a relativization of perspective ensues, an escape from solipsism. In the episode with the local fisherman, the switch from first to third person passes through the identification with someone else: "The price of the flipper is worth maybe a week or two of fishing to this man" represents a brief espousal of his perspective, a glance into his life, which turns him from a mere instrument into a man with a human life that Damon tries to imagine. Therein lies the key to the importance of the imaginative capacity at work in fiction. The thread of the novel—Kafka's rope—presents itself as a continuum of vulnerability: the precarious life of the fisherman, vulnerable to the loss of the flipper, the life of the old man who does the laundry for the rich tourist, the lives of the people who live in small houses that Damon discovers during his solitary walk in the village, his own difference, revealed to him through the imagined interpellation "he is a fucked-up South African." Once again, this recalls *Que faire de notre vulnérabilité?*, where Guillaume le Blanc enlists Cora Diamond to argue for the importance of seeing people as imaginative beings, living fully human lives and capable of telling themselves stories about their lives. It is by using his imagination in order to conjure up what the simple fisherman's life "maybe" looks like that Damon is aware of the humanity of someone usually invisible and therefore joins him in solidarity.

Before concluding, a few considerations on Galgut's gesturing toward the identification with a "fucked-up South African" are in order. In the interview with Hashemzadeh, he expresses a certain reservation vis-à-vis the label "South African writer" because he considers that as a white male his memories are not relevant to the ongoing project of giving voice to the marginalized, silenced voices of colonial history.[30] The plot of *In a Strange Room* is therefore not South African, and his intention was to leave the country in the background as much as possible.[31] If political events happen indeed in the background, doubled by a barely audible soundtrack of political commentary (we hear briefly of elections in Tanzania, violence on the train, corruption at the borders, inefficiency and disorganization in the Indian hospital where Anna is treated, corruption and violence of the police system), there is a yet subtler engagement with a South African theme in Damon's restlessness, a sense of exile in his own land. Referring to this aspect, Galgut comments: "I do know that some of the South African reviews have said, kind of to my surprise, that I'm expressing something essentially South African in this book. If anything, I was trying to do the opposite, but I guess if you are digging into the stuff of your own psyche you're going to be laying out whatever's in there, and I am South African." Yet he shies away from "speaking for" history, in a most tactful response to the demands of ethics in a postcolonial country, and in a global age where the happenstance of travel—encountering and becoming close with people whose lives unfold in places far away from us—becomes a metaphor for an ethics dependent on the dialectics of distance and closeness.

This is a move away from a notion of the self strengthened in one's beliefs, toward the impersonal, just as Esposito suggests, tracing a philosophical lineage that connects Simone Weil, Maurice Blanchot, and Deleuze and Guattari. It is a move that follows the trajectory of a paradoxical "decreation" (Weil's apt term in *La pesanteur et la grâce* redoubles its relevance), but which in Galgut's prose is indissociable from his grafting the genre of the novel onto that of the memoir. It is this circular move from first to third person, through the impersonal, and back to oneself that *In a Strange Room* puts forward, it seems to me, as a barely visible circle, its *minima moralia*.

How does Galgut's novel transform the vision of coimmunism canvassed by Sloterdijk in *You Must Change Your Life*? After his repeated encounters with others in experiences of following, falling in love, and taking care of other people—in short, by exposing himself to the world, and absorbing it—Damon has an experience of the sublime. But unlike the sublime that *You Must Change Your Life* concludes on, linked to the overtaxing of the imperative to make the earth one's own, Galgut seems to suggest that it is human suffering that, on the one hand, overwhelms us, and on the other, makes us realize our finitude, through exposure to the death of others: "It seems bizarre, to the point of bitter laughter, that a human being can be reduced to this" (179), Damon reflects while contemplating silently the bag of ash and bones that is left of his friend Anna. And on visiting the European cemetery in Morocco, where Caroline's husband was buried several decades before, "it seems unbearably sad that a life should come to rest here, on a sun-blasted hill above a foreign city, with the sea in the distance" (180). Moreover, in one of the most remarkable gestures of narrative tact that Galgut shows, Caroline's story is withheld from the reader: she tells it to Damon, and we have an inkling that it is devastating, but we never learn the details. On the one hand, given that we hardly know Caroline as a character, Galgut seems to suggest that we have not earned the right to learn her story, therefore its disturbing details would only respond to a certain need for sensationalism; but on the other, there is also an intimation that not only is our life limited, but so is our capacity to experience the pain of others, the endlessness of human suffering, which is the true sublime: "He finds himself suddenly, unexpectedly, sobbing. He tries to stop the tears, but they keep on coming. A huge emotion is welling up in him, unattached to the scene, he doesn't know either of these people, after all, and they died a long time ago. . . . Lives leak into each other, the past lays claim to the present" (*ISR*, 179). Strangely, this realization of finitude—human finitude, and finitude of the capacity to experience pain—has the contradictory effect of making him feel awful, but also relieved, "emptied out" (*ISR*, 180), the novel's last passage says. This is the *emptied out* of Faulkner's novel *As I Lay Dying*—"in a strange room, you must empty yourself out for sleep"—which thus leads us to understand Galgut's intimation of a notion of self that emerges out of repeated asceticisms (as Sloterdijk would put it), yet it could not be any less defined in terms of *the own*: coimmunism is not an expanded, strengthened sense of self, but rather, a profound realization of shared vulnerability, and thus of a self that becomes an absence of self, impersonal: Caroline's story "travels into him, his skin is very thin, there's no barrier between him and the world" (*ISR*, 175), and the only possible moral he can extract from it is that "it can happen to anyone, it can happen to you" (*ISR*, 176).[32]

The *strange room* of the title is the world of other people: the disquieting, unpredictable world in oneself.

CONCLUSION

When Barthes mused, in *Comment vivre ensemble*, that an age lacking shared moral norms demanded "a science, or perhaps an art, of distances," he echoed the realization of other intellectuals and writers in the aftermath of political, social, and cultural crises, when a desire to crystallize the tentative attunements of everyday interaction led to the proliferation of codes of conduct, as well as to a sustained reflection on living with other people. Perhaps not surprisingly, today's migration crisis—which, as Peter Sloterdijk points out in the closing chapter of *You Must Change Your Life*, is likely to become an ever more frequent occurrence in the Anthropocene—is often described in the language of distance and proximity: people whose lives once unfolded in faraway places are stranded in camps, hoping to settle in neighboring lands or in Western countries where they are met with explicit hostility, reluctant or apprehensive acceptance, or an unconditional welcome. How is such unexpected proximity experienced?

Peter Sloterdijk's 2006 essay "Warten auf den Islam," penned after the publication of the Muhammad cartoons in Denmark, strikes a relevant note with the description of "new proximities" emerging all of a sudden in the virtual infosphere, between distant countries, cultures, and systems of belief. Because these encounters are deregulated, Sloterdijk observes, "at first, more communication means, above all, more conflict." The virtual space becomes a "harmful density [*schädliche Dichte*]," a formulation that today strikes an ominous note, as Sloterdijk's description of virtual clashes recalls actual instances of physical violence: "Density is a measure of the probability of collisions—this increases dramatically when unwelcome strangers lead to deregulated interactions." As we have seen, the problem of *deregulated interactions* is hardly new; it takes us back to the work of Helmuth Plessner, which offers us important reminders about the value of distance.

More specifically, it is Sloterdijk's proposed solution that echoes Plessner's defense of distance:

> Risks of this kind [collusions] which follow from chronic overcommunication in an overwhelming milieu, can be reduced by civilization alone—for the loss of the physical distances between the new voluntary and involuntary neighbors can only be compensated for by a clever code of discretion. Discretion begins with the realization that getting-out-of-one-another's way is a satisfactory equivalent to understanding one another.[1]

While Plessner and Sloterdijk share a vocabulary of *civilization*, *discretion*, and *distance*, I am not sure that the author of *Grenzen der Gemeinschaft* would have agreed with the equivalence posited here; Slavoj Žižek's commentary on this passage from Sloterdijk's essay is symptomatic of an understanding of distance that Plessner, revisited and recontextualized, can help us rethink. Here is what Žižek has to say in "The Limits of Neighborhood," substituting "alienation" for "discretion" in the original text:

> One of the things alienation means is that distance is woven into the very social texture of everyday life: even if I live side by side with others, in my normal state I ignore them. I am allowed not to get too close to others. I move in a social space where I interact with others obeying certain external "mechanical" rules, without sharing their inner world. Perhaps the lesson to be learned is that, sometimes, a dose of alienation is indispensable for the peaceful coexistence of ways of life. Sometimes alienation is not a problem but a solution.[2]

While the gist of Žižek's idea might resonate with Plessner's insistence on distance, the impulses driving this practice could not be more different. Žižek speaks of alienation and ignoring others where Plessner referred to distance as that which preserves dignity—against, Barthes would add, a society of indifference, which pays no heed to human individuality. Rereading Plessner on this point pays off, and not only as an antidote to Žižek's hasty writing. From the vantage point of the early twenty-first century, with its specific global challenges, Plessner's ideas offer a welcome corrective to superficial engagements with distance, helping us imagine more thoughtful modes of social life. And from this confrontation with our time, Plessner's account, too, emerges differently accented.

Plessner made an early appearance in the introductory chapter, where I summarized briefly his defense of society: in counterpoint to the constraints and limitations of communal life, which interpellates one into a fixed identity, society is the space of unrealization (*Entrealisierung*), a conscious joining in the realm of appearances and games, where masks allow for the performance of various roles, and for the preservation of an inner life. Plessner gambles on his readers' willingness to avoid ridicule and conflict: tact, rituals, ceremonial, diplomacy, the cultivation of prestige are obviously preferable to "losing face" and to violence. Respect for distance comes then from an immunitary tendency; this is the mind-set, I take it, that accompanies Žižek's notion of "alienation." But Plessner took his ideas on society further, grounding them in a fully developed theory of human existence that represents a radical departure from Cartesian dualism.[3] He shows that this tradition, aligned with the Christian mind/body polarization, values interiority, morality, culture, and community against anything that is external: the life of the body, the sphere of civilization and society. In contrast, Plessner elaborates a theory of human experience that integrates the life of the soul with bodily existence, the inner and the outer, arguing that our life is a striving for both being (form) and becoming (transformation), and that whenever we are captive to a form (one can think here of the specific identity or roles into which our communities interpellate us), we have the capacity to deviate from it, in endless and unpredictable transformation; in short, we are never identical to ourselves. Put in the language I have used here, interpersonal distance is crucial to the preservation of inner distances, in which the partly mysterious life of "the soul" takes place.

Traversing a century in which community—with its attendant principle of sincerity, a certain understanding of the autonomous self, and bourgeois morality—has been the object of sustained critique, and a century that has seen a revalorization of the everyday (because it exposes one to the lives of others and thus brings home the awareness of vulnerability, hence a new sense of self), Plessner's ideas help us consolidate the realignment of social life and its cultivation of distance, with a broader understanding of morality (*pace* Murdoch), and a willingness to maintain human dignity. Dignity, following Plessner, equals the affordance of space for the soul to live its life of change, transformation, and multidirectionality, unperturbed by interpellation. Any label, Guillaume le Blanc has pointed out—"homeless," he says; "immigrant" or "refugee," we might add, with the awareness that the list could be very long—obscures the reality of a life that cannot be defined by the narrow contours of such profiling. In other words, what resonates in Plessner's account today is not only the value of distance in maintaining self-respect but also, crucially, in maintaining the dignity of other people.[4] It helps us rethink the value of distance not in terms of a mere externality, but in relation to the richness of human life.

A caveat that Žižek discusses in the chapter on the limits of neighborhood is worth addressing here, namely the risk of obscuring important differences. Žižek takes issue with the liberal Left's response to the migration crisis, premised on a flawed notion of human universality: refugees are victims of life-shattering, or, indeed, *world*-shattering circumstances, therefore we should extend them sympathy on ground of our shared humanity. Zooming in on a familiar trope, Žižek cautions that the "neighbor" might turn out to be aggressive, violent, or off-putting, and that sentimentality about refugees obscures the fact that "there is nothing redemptive in suffering: being a victim at the bottom of the social ladder does not make you some kind of privileged voice of morality and justice."[5] The universal dimension, therefore, should be sought "beyond sympathy and understanding, beyond the 'we're all human' level: at another level, which should be designated precisely as that of the inhuman Neighbor."[6] What does this mean?

Enlisting Robert Pippin's reading of John Ford's film *The Searchers*, Žižek offers a compelling argument which he ends with a typically provocative parenthesis that gives one reason to pause. It goes something like this: like

Ethan at the end of Ford's violent film (who surprisingly decides against killing his niece Debbie as he had long planned), and like ourselves, the neighbor is inhuman in that he or she does not fully know himself or herself; actions are not fully rational or predictable. This requires a rethinking of human universality, which is actually "a universality of 'strangers,' of individuals reduced to the abyss of impenetrability in relation not only to others but also to themselves." When dealing with foreigners, Žižek advises, "we should always bear in mind Hegel's concise formula: the secrets of the ancient Egyptians were secret also for the Egyptians themselves."[7] While I would not dispute this point—and Plessner, Murdoch, and Galgut probably wouldn't either—I can only pause when Žižek concludes: "That's why the privileged way to reach a Neighbor is not that of empathy, of trying to understand them, but a disrespectful laughter which makes fun of both of them and of us in our mutual lack of (self-)understanding (inclusive of 'racist' jokes)."[8] Empathy may be problematic in that it obscures judgment, as Paul Bloom compellingly argues in *Against Empathy*.[9] It can also turn out to be arrogant in its assumption that one can understand something that the other cannot fully know herself. But doesn't "disrespectful laughter" err along a similar path of assuming too much? To understand (or even have a nagging intuition of) my lack of self-understanding and decide that it is a laughing matter is certainly possible; but what if the other does not find such lack of self-understanding funny? What if the other in oneself is, rather than funny, perhaps unsettling, embarrassing, awe-inspiring, or has other unfathomable characteristics? And even assuming we can each laugh about our own lack of self-understanding, how can we be sure that in our shared laughter, we do not trivialize the important difference in understanding that one has—of one's self (limited), and of the other (even more limited than his or her own)? Shared laughter requires a basis of agreement—if only the distance necessary for maintaining the dignity of everyone involved—otherwise it might not take us very far.

When one follows the recurrence of the problematic of distance in the work of George Orwell, Paul Morand, Henry Miller, Elias Canetti, Iris Murdoch, Walter Benjamin, Annie Ernaux, Günter Grass, Damon Galgut, and others, the conditions, symbolic dimensions, and ethical underpinnings of encounters with other people are disclosed in disquieting complexity; these writers invite reflection on how the ethical and the political intersect and often conflict, on the roles that intellectuals might assume in the struggles of their time, and also on the generic forms that most adequately express such dilemmas. Something in the nature of this tireless quest of the ideal distance between oneself and others compels these authors to explore less-trodden territories between genres, such as journalism, novel, and autobiography; diary and sociological reportage; philosophical novel; memoir and fiction. Shifting from first to third person, and back, with the occasional use of a "you" (not accidentally interpellative), these writers participate in what appears to be a shared project of rethinking encounters and relationships with other people that turn out to be constitutive of the self. The art of distances is a matter of the affordances of form—in both social interaction and literary writing.

Why an *art* of distances, and in what sense can one speak of a *morality* for the everyday? What I have in mind is certainly not framed by an *ought*, or by the implication that these writers, from Orwell to Grass, might—or should—be taken for moral heroes. Reputations can lose luster or unravel following the publication of an unexpected letter (such as Orwell's list of "crypto-Communist writers," complete with jarring ethnic labeling and several variations on "Jewish") or of a late memoir (such as Grass's confession that, at seventeen, he was in the Waffen SS), which typically reframe the conversation about the significance of the literary work as well. Such debates have their legitimacy, rooted in the view of literature as a political act, a view that the authors of *Animal Farm* and *The Tin Drum* actively shaped. At the same time, literary works have a life of their own, especially when brought into conversation with other texts, with which they have affinities, correspondences, shared intensities of affect, unresolved but generative tensions, and with which they end up projecting a certain picture of life: How one sees that picture, and what one does with it, depends on each reader's proclivities. In *Comment vivre ensemble*, Barthes uses texts in a highly selective manner, handling them as a collector of scintillations, with which he furnishes his *fantasme*. It is as if he treated books with the *délicatesse* of an easy friendship, cultivating with them nonjudgmental relationships, teasing out in their company the things that strengthen one's resolve to live an examined life. Because this is, ultimately, the paradox we have explored here: how looking at, and listening to, other people, from a certain well-calibrated distance, appear to be the crucial gestures of an examined life, from which emerges a certain sense of self traversed by others.

An art of distances is an everyday practice, contextual, and therefore always to be resumed, born under the auspices of a humanity beckoning to be fully recognized. Such a notion detaches itself from the sphere of civilization, identified since Kant with formal codes of conduct and etiquette, joining that of culture, the realm of values.[10] But the latter are no longer attached to a rigid bourgeois morality; rather, they originate in the daily experience of embodied existence in a secular world. Orwell puts it memorably in "As I Please," where he warns that "man is not likely to salvage civilization unless he can evolve a system of good and evil which is independent of heaven and hell." Committed to the "full-bloodied drama of life," as a critic said, Orwell situates at the center of his system the reality of the body as a measure of truth, and the imperative that one should recognize that "one is ordinary 9/10 of the time." Canetti's interpellation in *Crowds and Power* is even less flattering: in his account, the twentieth century showed more than any other that humans are aggressive barbarians (the image of meat-eaters in a field of corpses is a post-Holocaust anthem), so he opposed to the distances of everyday life, in which he saw a desire to overpower others, the morality "in one's bones" revealed in the distance-annulling experience of the crowd. A multitude of touching bodies may represent the locus of a crucial reminder, the ideal of an undivided humanity, but it cannot be an everyday practice; the delicacy practiced by Dr. Sonne is the closest Canetti comes to intimating a considerate mode of interaction with other people. In this, Canetti is also close to Murdoch, whose novel *The Bell* is underwritten by a prolonged meditation on distance, not only among bodies—of amorous dispositions, of estranged individuals who avoid one another, or of ascetic monks—but also the distance within, that of inner growth, of openness to contingency, irrational impulses, moral deliberation, and competing selves. With an instinct for excruciating dilemmas, secrecy, and consuming relationships, Galgut's character Damon is no stranger to such distances; his body is also that of proxemics (as with Benjamin), flânerie (also Ernaux), and wandering abroad (like Orwell). With their "enormous eye" (Woolf) and a deep sense of the importance of a discreet regard, flâneurs and wanderers know that all those passersby are not just faces, collapsible into the abstract anonymity of numbers, but singular persons with stories to be discovered, imagined, and narrated—one at a time, Grass suggests, as one lives one's days. Zaoui would offer a reminder here: the link between discretion and discontinuity highlights the importance of the occasional step back, in a temporary self-removal from the mutual interpellations and roles of social interaction. This step back that creates space comes, le Blanc and Ernaux intimate, from the self-consciousness of vulnerability, of inner cleavages between different selves, of the distance between appearance and the complexity of inner life.

Barthes not only distances himself from bourgeois morality; he is also reserved about politeness, in search of that more elusive *délicatesse*—invoked, tongue-in-cheek, by the imprisoned marquis handing his dirty laundry to his wife, projecting onto her the fantasy (his own) of her perversion: he respects all tastes, he confesses, because they all come down to a principle of tact: that is, to a capacity to make fine distinctions. Hard to pin down, the latter finds its most eloquent defender in Plessner, who zooms in with careful precision on situations of tact. They can only arise, he writes, "under careful obedience to distance," through "the ability to perceive incalculable differences," "a feeling and touch for the distance of unremarkable, but information-rich things in the permanent oscillations of the situation of the social milieu," an "ability to respond to the subtlest vibrations of the environment."[11] Because the spheres of life are intricately intertwined, he cautions, this practice leads to subtle complications; as we have seen with the writers assembled in this book, dilemmas are bound to arise: "Where does sociability begin? Where does it end? Where does it become a transaction? Where begins the intimacy and trust of the communal circle? Where are we permitted to let down our guard and build towards goodness, love, understanding and insight? If tact cannot answer these questions, we are betrayed and sold out."[12] And yet, he insists, the value of tact is justified by "the vulnerability of psychological life and is tuned to the incalculability of individual differences"—not just within the social milieu, as for Plessner in Weimar Germany, but now inextricable from our contemporary context of conflict and the ensuing migration crisis, when the language of closeness and distance has become even more pertinent. The morality of homelessness—not feeling at home in one's home—is the only morality possible in the age of the Anthropocene. In Plessner's words, "Being ungrounded is an essential moment of tact. How else can one form the guidelines for one's conduct in the value-equivalent spheres of daily life?" Where no shared reasons and rules exist, one has to agree, *there remains to us no other ethical maxim.*[13]

Tethered to Barthes's "neutral," which is neither celebratory nor complacent, the art of distances demands a lucid, discerning and attentive stance, which, when the context requires it, might even translate into fulfilling an obligation of tactlessness. The way it differs from the notion of objective detachment implied in the notion of "distance" is by owning its subjective perspective: nondetached, self-consciously limited because positioned, and in that sense exemplary.[14] Orwell makes a compelling case for such commitment in "Reflections on Gandhi," an essay where, after praising "the deep earnestness, an attitude ethical rather than religious" in Gandhi's youth, he expresses strong disapproval of the Mahatma's doctrine of nonattachment. "The essence of being human," he writes, "is that one does not seek perfection, that one is sometimes willing to commit sins for the sake of loyalty, that one does not push asceticism to the point where it makes friendly intercourse impossible, and that one is prepared in the end to be defeated and broken up by life, which is the inevitable price of fastening one's love upon other human individuals."[15] A passionate defense of a full commitment to one's fellow human beings follows a few lines down:

> In this yogi-ridden age, it is too readily assumed that "non-attachment" is not only better than a full acceptance of earthly life, but that the ordinary man only rejects it because it is too difficult: in other words, that the average human being is a failed saint. It is doubtful whether this is true. Many people genuinely do not wish to be saints, and it is probable that some who achieve or aspire to sainthood have never felt much temptation to be human beings. If one could follow it to its psychological roots, one would, I believe, find that the main motive for "non-attachment" is a desire to escape from the pain of living, and above all from love, which, sexual or non-sexual, is hard work.[16]

One wonders what Orwell would have said about Murdoch's characters in *The Bell*: not only about Michael, who struggles with his attachments, or James, "no connoisseur of evil" and a living saint, but especially about the

Abbess, the ascetic sage who seems to be fully cognizant of the "pain of living" and of the hard work Orwell speaks of. In Murdoch's work resonates Orwell's insistence on the hard labor of love; this is where "morality" acquires the breadth formerly associated with the ethical life, once it has lost its bearings in the rigid grammar of the *ought* and in the outlines of deliberation leading to the right decision and action. To the gravitas of Orwell's passionate pronouncements, however, Murdoch the novelist counterpoints images of lightness: that of a nun walking with Toby in the peaceful cemetery, inviting him to try the swing (because "it would cheer the old swing up") and then reassuring him with a disarming confession: "We sometimes do it ourselves."

As a particular form of the abiding question of the one and the many, the art of distances is subtended by a rethinking of the notion of self, kindred to the philosophical problematic of the subject. Sympathetic to Jean-Luc Nancy's project of rethinking community, I would however not go so far as to suggest that something else must come *after* the subject.[17] As we have seen, attention to the sociopolitical and cultural dimensions of distance brings into discussion the place of the subject in relation to sociopolitical and cultural paradigms such as sincerity and authenticity: Adorno's and Barthes's respective reactions to Sartre's commitment put into question sincerity, as does the culture of distance that Lethen discusses with respect to Weimar Germany; and so does, with an interesting twist, Orwell's deep discomfort with the grand claims of empire (epitome of the subjugating self) and his passionate commitment to the "ordinary man." In a deeply moralizing mind-set, Canetti deplores the distances of rank and the self-aggrandizing gestures that he often equates with socializing, denouncing sincerity *and* authenticity as the modes of a self-interested desire to overpower others: in Canetti's account Nietzsche's "pathos of distance," though unacknowledged, intersects Freud's "narcissism of minor differences" and Heidegger's unfavorable view of distantiality. One wonders whether Benjamin's child, a *Denkbild* that emerges from his small book about Berlin, might offer a more serene alternative.

I follow Benjamin's quest for a whole self, that of the child emerging from the world of things and words, protected in equal measure by the parental house and the beloved city, in the central chapter of the book. This beautiful tome invites reflection on whether a "self of convergence" has ever been more than a fiction, here projected by the exiled Jew in search of a comforting dwelling; can a protected self be more than a cenotaph in the mausoleum of the childhood home? In highlighting the fictionality of otherness (the third person, *they*, endlessly different) as constitutive of the self, Ernaux, Grass, and Galgut make it difficult to answer such questions in the affirmative. Ernaux's diaries and Grass's idiosyncratic portrait of the past century register a revalorization of authenticity, but as socially mediated, in the experience of everyday life and collective history. Iris Murdoch's displacement, in her philosophical essays and fiction, of the "facile notions of sincerity or authenticity" onto the compelling reality of other people is a hinge in this shift. Inspired by her insistence, in the wake of World War II, on the need to elaborate a new notion of personality, one is likely to see it emerge from the texts of Ernaux, Grass, and Galgut: an understanding of personality growing out of examined relations between oneself and others, a new conception of the self as "one of them," or even as "the world within."[18]

This is surely not the fallenness into the anonymous, distracting, and irresponsible "they [*das Man*]" that Heidegger deplores in *Being and Time* on grounds of its inauthenticity ("constantly going wrong in its projects, as regards the genuine possibilities of Being").[19] When Ernaux recognizes with Rousseau that our real self is not entirely within, and writes that her experiment, continued, might result in her no longer having a self, or when "a huge emotion [wells] up" in Galgut's protagonist and is soon translated into the realization that "lives leak into each other"—such moments are nothing if not epiphanies of being-with, of *Mitsein*. To Heidegger's caveat that "the word 'I' is to be understood only in the sense of a non-committal formal indicator, indicating something which may perhaps reveal itself as its 'opposite,' "[20] these writers respond with an "I" pieced together of moving parts: living people, always on their way to, and away from, one; and narratives—diary entries, short stories, novellas—that resist suturing into a coherent whole, yet whose autonomy is belied by subtle connections. What Rancière calls the "thread of the novel"—that which connects and gives meaning to the separate existences of our days—reveals itself in the persistence to walk on Kafka's rope, a metaphor for the resilience demanded by the everyday, by the continuum of vulnerability that is human existence.

Had Barthes collected artworks, rather than literary *scintillations*, to flesh out his *fantasme*, what images might have haunted him? Perhaps Alberto Giacometti's *City Square*, populated by delicately elongated silhouettes?[21] Or M. C. Escher's lithograph *Relativity*, with its intricate staircases, the faceless characters who, whether climbing or descending, acquiesce in the knowledge that they cannot know exactly what the world looks like from where someone else stands, and that they can hardly know where the others are coming from, or going to, even as no one can fall out of the world?[22] Escher's was surely both a science, and an art, of distances. Closer to our time, the *fantasme* assumes the surrealist contours of Marian Simon's collection *Ființare*, mesmerized by an imposing brown-suited man wearing a clown's mask, his long legs seemingly chained in place by winding staircases, on which hasty individuals and monkeys on unicycles slide up and down.[23] What is the labyrinth of stairs unfurling from his head, and how far will the branches that protrude from his body extend? Isn't it strange how, even with a mask concealing his face, he seems quietly determined to carry on?

NOTES

Introduction

1. Roland Barthes, *Comment vivre ensemble: Simulations romanesques de quelques espaces quotidiens* (*How to Live Together: Novelistic Simulations of Some Everyday Spaces*), ed. Claude Coste, Cours et séminaires au Collège de France (1976–1977) (Paris: Seuil Imec, 2002). Hereafter cited parenthetically as *CVE*. All translations are mine.

2. Claude Coste, "Présentation," in *CVE*, 28.

3. I am referring to Mallarmé's "imaginaire trophée" in "The White Water Lily" (1897), published in *Divagations* (Paris: Fasquelle, 1943), where the reader leaves the text (*quitte le texte des yeux*), taking with him an imaginary trophy, a white water lily, barely picked (*un nénuphare blanc, à peine cueilli*).

4. See also "On the friend" in the first part of Friedrich Nietzsche's *Thus Spoke Zarathustra* (Cambridge: Cambridge University Press, 2006), 40–42.

5. Jacques Derrida, *Politics of Friendship*, trans. George Collins (London: Verso, 2005).

6. Aristotle, *The Nicomachean Ethics*, trans. Roger Crisp (Cambridge: Cambridge University Press, 2014).

7. See Jessica Berman's discussion of "communities of proximity" in "Cosmopolitan Communities," chapter 1 of *Modernist Fiction, Cosmopolitanism, and the Politics of Community* (New York: Cambridge University Press, 2001), 1–28.

8. In his misreading, to which I will return, resounds the Kantian distinction between respect and love, distance and fusion. Other writers have found Nietzsche's formulation equally seductive, using it in ways that the German philosopher would not have recognized. In 1913, for instance, James Huneker published a collection of essays titled *The Pathos of Distance: A Book of a Thousand and One Moments* (New York: C. Scribner's Sons, 1913), in which he uses Nietzsche's words with the meaning of idealizing the (distant) past. See, on Huneker, Jean-Michel Rabaté's essay "1913, or the 'Pathos of Distance,'" in *Die Tonkunst*, April 2013, 170–177, reprinted in his wonderful book of essays *The Pathos of Distance: Affects of the Moderns* (New York: Bloomsbury, 2016). For a different reading of Barthes's engagement with Nietzsche, see Rabaté's first chapter, "'Pathos of Distance': Huneker and Barthes Reading Nietzsche" (*The Pathos of Distance*, 15–37).

9. Martin Heidegger, *Being and Time*, trans. John Macquarrie and Edward Robinson, with a new foreword by Taylor Carman (New York: Harper Perennial, 2008), 142. In *Bubbles*, the first volume of his Spheres project, Peter Sloterdijk praises Heidegger for doing away with the spatial concepts of vulgar physics and metaphysics, which conceive of "being in" in terms of a recipient that preexists

the contained, such as the glass before the water, etc., in order to define being-in as a state of Dasein's Being; what Heidegger calls being-in-the-world, Sloterdijk recapitulates, "is nothing other than the world 'inside' in a verbal-transitive sense: living in it and benefiting from it already have been explored in prior acts of attunement and reaching out. Because existence is always a completed act of habitation—the result of a primal leap into inhabitation—spatiality is an essential part of it." Peter Sloterdijk, *Bubbles*, trans. Wieland Hoban (Los Angeles: Semiotext(e), 2011), 335. But Sloterdijk faults Heidegger for not following up on his opening on the spatiality of Dasein ("an embryonically revolutionary treatise on being and space" [340]): Heidegger has only "pulled out the beginning of a thread that is still mostly wound up. Had it been unraveled further, it would inevitably have opened up the multi-significant universes of existential spaciousness addressed here under the catchword 'spheres'" (340). In other words, as he explains in Excursus 4 (333–343), Sloterdijk's Spheres project is designed as complementary to Heidegger's work on the temporality of Dasein.

10. For an insightful discussion of these distinctions, see Simon Glendinning, *On Being with Others: Heidegger—Derrida—Wittgenstein* (New York: Routledge, 1998).

11. The horizon of intelligibility, or significance—the totality of involvements which make up the structure of the world—is what I take Wittgenstein to refer to as well, when he speaks of learning a language in terms of learning a form of life: not simply learning words for objects (as he reductively reads Augustine in the opening of the *Philosophical Investigations*; see also nos. 19, 23, 26), but training in the ways of living of a community. Ludwig Wittgenstein, *Philosophical Investigations: The German Text with a Revised English Translation: German Text, with a Revised English Translation*, trans. G. E. M. Anscombe, 3rd ed. (Malden: Wiley-Blackwell, 2001).

12. Heidegger, *Being and Time*, 158–159.

13. I am grateful to Chantal Bax for mapping out, with characteristic lucidity, Nancy's and Levinas's critiques of Heidegger sketched here. See her "Otherwise than Being-with: Levinas on Heidegger and Community," *Human Studies* 40, no. 3 (September 2017): 381–400.

14. See chapter 5, "Distances," in Emmanuel Levinas, *Difficult Freedom: Essays on Judaism*, trans. Séan Hand (Baltimore: Johns Hopkins University Press, 1997), especially "Heidegger, Gagarin and Us," 231–235.

15. Jean-Luc Nancy, *Being Singular Plural* (Stanford, Calif.: Stanford University Press, 2000), 11, my italics. "A single being is a contradiction in terms," writes Nancy, for reasons that recall why a private language is a contradiction in terms following Wittgenstein in *The Philosophical Investigations*. "Such a being, which would be its own foundation, origin, and intimacy, would be incapable of Being, in every sense that this expression can have here" (12). Nancy's critique of "community" in *The Inoperative Community* goes hand in hand with the critique of "philosophical politics" in *Being Singular Plural* on account of its "surreptitious appeal to a metaphysics of the one-origin," which turns it into "a politics of exclusivity and the correlative exclusion—of a class, of an order, of a 'community'—the point of which is to end up with a 'people,' in the 'base' sense of the term." *Being Singular Plural*, 24.

16. I will return to this term below.

17. Helmuth Plessner, *The Limits of Community: A Critique of Social Radicalism*, trans. and intro. Andrew Wallace (New York: Humanity Books, 1999).

18. Helmuth Lethen, *Cool Conduct: The Culture of Distance in Weimar Germany* (California Publishing Online, 2002), 54. I believe that Plessner's defense of distance has meaningful reverberations today: in my conclusion, I will show how it helps us to articulate its social and political stakes in the context of a migration crisis that is nowhere near its end.

19. Léon Wurmser, *Maske der Scham* (Berlin: Springer, 1990), 230, quoted in Lethen, *Cool Conduct*, 17.

20. The distinction between culture, associated with moral values, and civilization, the sphere of external behavior and etiquette, goes back to Immanuel Kant's *Idea for a Universal History from a Cosmopolitan Point of View* (1784); its classical account is Norbert Elias's *The Civilizing Process* (1939). For a more recent review of the literature on this distinction, see my essay "Visions of the End of Culture: Civilization, Barbarism, and the Place beyond Forgiveness," *Arcadia* 50, no. 1 (2015): 118–145.

21. Lethen, *Cool Conduct*, 50.

22. Ibid., 55. Barthes was also familiar with this parable from Schopenhauer's *Parerga and Paralipomena*, but apparently not with its use by other thinkers.

23. Plessner, quoted in Lethen, *Cool Conduct*, 60.

24. Taylor Ross, a graduate student in religious studies at Duke University, is currently writing a fascinating dissertation on the conceptual genealogy of "distantiality." He credits Plotinus with extending the Stoic reflections on the nature of time (particularly in the writings of Zeno and Chrysippus), and Augustine of Hippo with rendering and transforming the Plotinian concept διάστασις (variously translated as "extension" or "spacing") into the Latin *distentio*, which carries a certain pathos related to the entropy and dispersion of finite and temporal beings when separated from God. Heidegger's description of Dasein's everyday "they-self" in terms of a falling (*Verfallen*) and a dispersal or dissolution of the particular Dasein into "the they [*in das Man zerstreut*]" (*Being and Time*, 167) illustrates Heidegger's "de-theologization" of categories borrowed from St. Augustine's *Confessions*. On this, see Ryan Coyne, *Heidegger's Confessions: The Remains of Saint Augustine in "Being and Time" and Beyond* (Chicago: University of Chicago Press, 2015). I am grateful to Taylor for bringing this book to my attention.

25. Roberto Esposito, *Terms of the Political* (New York: Fordham University Press, 2013), 40–41.

26. Ibid., 59.

27. Pierre Zaoui, *La discrétion, ou l'art de disparaître* (Paris: Autrement, 2013), 44–45 (my translation).

28. Ibid., 45. As Helmut Lethen shows in *Cool Conduct*, the culture of distance in Weimar Germany grew from a profound antipathy for sincerity; here again, the problematic of distance, understood as discretion, intervenes against the paradigm of sincerity. In chapter 1 I engage with Trilling's account of sincerity and authenticity.

29. Ibid., 48.

30. Jean-Luc Nancy, *Being Singular Plural*, 18. Nancy continues: "A singularity is always a body, and all bodies are singularities (the bodies, their states,

their movements, their transformations)." This echoes Nancy's engagement with Heidegger's reflection on moods in *Being and Time* (172ff.): "As for singular differences, they are not only 'individual,' but infraindividual. It is never the case that I have met Pierre or Marie per se, but I have met him or her in such and such a 'form,' in such and such a 'state,' in such and such a 'mood,' and so on" (*Being Singular Plural*, 8).

31. See, for example, Jean-Luc Nancy, *Being Singular Plural*, 39–40, and *The Inoperative Community*, ed. Peter Connor, trans. Peter Connor, Lisa Garbus, Michael Holland, and Simona Sawhney (Minneapolis: University of Minnesota Press, 1991), 3–4.

32. Irving Goh, *The Reject: Community, Politics, and Religion after the Subject* (New York: Fordham University Press, 2015). For a critical engagement with Goh's argument, see my review in *Modern Language Notes* 130, no. 5 (2015): 1242–1247.

33. See Goh, *The Reject*, 246–248. As Goh's title suggests, he wrote the book as an answer to Jean-Luc Nancy's question "What comes after the subject?," sharing Nancy's conviction that the category of the subject was compromised. Although, in poststructuralist fashion, Barthes spoke of the subject as a fiction, he never really renounced it, preferring to speak of its plurality. Problematizing the notion, in the autobiographical *Roland Barthes par Roland Barthes (Paris: Seuil, 1975)*, he playfully refers to himself in the third person, as if speaking of a character in a novel.

34. "De qui suis-je le contemporain?" Barthes asks rhetorically, signaling that community needs to be understood not only in terms of a shared space, but also in relation to temporality. The way his notion of contemporariness plays out, however, echoes Agamben's Nietzschean understanding of "the contemporary" as a relationship of untimeliness to one's own time. See Giorgio Agamben, "What Is the Contemporary?," in *"What Is an Apparatus?" and Other Essays*, trans. David Kishik and Stefan Pedatella (Stanford, Calif.: Stanford University Press, 2009).

35. Stanley Cavell, *Little Did I Know: Excerpts from Memory* (Stanford, Calif.: Stanford University Press, 2010), 528.

36. Alain Robbe-Grillet, "[Impostor, Thinker, or Novelist?]," in *Critical Essays on Roland Barthes*, ed. Diana Knight (New York: G. K. Hall, 2000), 143, my italics. Robbe-Grillet is explicit about the view of objective truth that Barthes's position tries to circumvent: "Beautiful utopia, beautiful cheat illuminated the euphoric dawn of our bourgeois society, and one century later the dawn of scientific socialism. Alas, today we know where that science leads. Truth, in the final analysis, has only ever served oppression. Anyway, too many hopes, wretched disappointments and blood-soaked paradises teach us to be wary of it." (These essays were written in 1981, on the occasion of the anniversary of Barthes's death).

37. Roland Barthes, *Le degré zéro de l'écriture* (*Writing Degree Zero*), published by Seuil in 1953. The course following *Comment vivre ensemble*, *Le neutre* (*The Neutral*), cites *délicatesse* as an example of the neutral.

38. "On imagine mal aujourd'hui, dans ce monde dominé par la culture populaire . . . la *délicatesse* que revêt la force d'esprit d'un homme prenant la parole dans—pour et contre—la culture, pour affirmer que la culture existe et nous fait vivre, mais à la seule condition qu'on ne cesse de la déchiffrer, c'est-à-dire de la

critiquer pour la déplacer sans fin. Barthes s'est engagé dans cette voie avec une angoisse absolue et sereine." Julia Kristeva, *Sens et non-sens de la révolte, tome 1: Pouvoirs et limites de la psychanalyse* (Paris: Fayard, 1996), 391–392, my italics.

39. Ibid. (my translation). This "subtle distance" that only the sick know to preserve is surely that of Kafka, too, as Elias Canetti and Pierre Zaoui also point out. In *La discrétion*, the latter quotes from Kafka's diary an entry from December 8, 1917: "In your fight with the world, follow the world" and explains that the world forces Kafka to find "the right distance between himself and the others as well as the things outside: neither too close lest he should be devoured (that's why one has to fight it), nor too far lest one should feel too lonely and abandoned (which is why one has to follow it)." Zaoui, *La discrétion*, 19.

40. Tony Judt, *Un passé imparfait: Les intellectuels en France 1944–1956* (Paris: Fayard, 1994), 47–53 (my translation).

41. The Leninist-Stalinist doctrine, which heralded "the veridical and historically concrete presentation of reality in its revolutionary development" was introduced in France by Louis Aragon in 1935. See Jacqueline Bernard, *Le parti communiste français et la question littéraire de 1921 à 1939* (Grenoble: Presses Universitaires, 1972), 118.

42. Jean-Paul Sartre, *Situations, II: Qu'est-ce que la littérature?* (Paris: Gallimard, 1948), 288.

43. For an insightful analysis of the postwar French literary scene, see the first chapter of Manet van Montfrans, *Georges Perec—La Contrainte du réel* (Amsterdam: Rodopi, 1999).

44. Sartre, *Situations, II*, 305.

45. Roland Barthes, *Writing Degree Zero*, trans. Annette Lavers and Colin Smith (Boston: Beacon, 1953), 10–14.

46. For an analysis of the neutral in Blanchot's work, see Leslie Hill, *Blanchot: Extreme Contemporary* (London: Routledge, 1997), especially chapter 3, "Writing the Neuter," 103–158.

47. Barthes, *Writing Degree Zero*, 87.

48. Theodor Adorno, *Minima moralia: Reflexionen aus dem beschädigten Leben* (1944–1947, publ. 1951); Theodor W. Adorno, *Minima Moralia: Reflections from Damaged Life*, trans. Edmund Jephcott (London: Verso, 2005), 15. Hereafter cited parenthetically as *MM*.

49. See Amanda Anderson, *The Powers of Distance: Cosmopolitanism and the Cultivation of Detachment* (Princeton, N.J.: Princeton University Press, 2001), and *The Way We Argue Now: A Study in the Cultures of Theory* (Princeton, N.J.: Princeton University Press, 2006), to which I will return in due time.

50. That, for decades, in the dominant cultural narrative of postwar France modernity was equated with a great deception surely needs no extensive elaboration; Blanchot's review of *Mythologies* (1957) placed Barthes at the center of the project of denunciation, the last descendant in a tradition of demystification attempts counting Montaigne, Pascal, and Montesquieu, then Hegel, Marx, and Freud: "We owe our attention to *Mythologies* by Roland Barthes, if we are really concerned about the silent and perpetual hoax which is inside and outside us, which is the air we breathe and the breath of our words." Maurice Blanchot, "The Great Hoax," in *Critical Essays on Roland Barthes*, ed. Diana Knight, trans. Ann Smock (New York: G. K. Hall, 2000), 43–44.

51. J. M. Bernstein, *Adorno: Disenchantment and Ethics* (Cambridge: Cambridge University Press, 2001), 41. I readily acknowledge Bernstein's influence on my understanding of Adorno's thought.

52. Theodor W. Adorno, "Commitment," in *Aesthetics and Politics*, ed. Ernst Bloch (New York: Verso, 1995), 190.

53. Ibid.

54. Fredric Jameson: "Sartre's belief in the efficacy of the individual engagement seems much less questionable than a theory in which the production of 'autonomous' works of art is little less than magical." Jameson, "Presentation IV," in Bloch, *Aesthetics and Politics*, 147. Demystifying the thesis of modernist artistic autonomy, in *Temps et récit* (*Time and Narrative*) Paul Ricœur frames its problematic in terms of a shift in mimetic representation that does not really have anything revolutionary about it: "L'argument de vraisemblance a été simplement déplacé: autrefois, c'était la complexité sociale qui demandait l'abandon du paradigme classique; aujourd'hui, c'est l'incohérence presumée de la réalité qui requiert l'abadon de tout paradigme. Dès lors, la littérature, redoublant le chaos de la réalité par celui de la fiction, ramène la mimèsis à sa function la plus faible, celle de répliquer le réel en le copiant" (The argument of verisimilitude has simply shifted: before, it was social complexity that demanded the abandonment of the classical paradigm; today, it is the incoherence of reality that demands abandoning all paradigms. From now on, literature, reproducing the chaos of reality through the chaos of fiction, returns mimesis to its weakest function, that of replicating the real by mimicking it). Paul Ricœur, *Temps et récit*, vol. 2 (Paris: Seuil, 1984), 30 (my translation). Auerbach made a similar argument in his reading of Virginia Woolf's *To the Lighthouse* in *Mimesis*, suggesting that mimesis shifted, with modernism, into the realm of poiesis (reproducing, rather than copying, the real).

55. Adorno, "Commitment," 194.

56. On Adorno's critique that Hegel's narrative of history, although dialectical, is from the perspective of totality, see Bernstein, *Adorno*; Fredric Jameson, *Late Marxism: Adorno, or the Persistence of the Dialectic* (London: Verso, 1990).

57. Adorno, letter to Thomas Mann, December 1952, quoted in Gerhard Richter, *Thought-images: Frankfurt School Writers' Reflections from Damaged Life* (Stanford, Calif.: Stanford University Press, 2007), 153. In "Adorno's Advice: *Minima moralia* and the Critique of Liberalism" (*PMLA* 126, no. 2 [2011]: 398–412), Jakob Norberg emphasizes the paradoxical negativity that pervades Adorno's book. Showing that the latter enjoyed a degree of commercial success, which he attributes to its reception as a book meant to give advice at a time (post–World War II) of resurgence of interest in codes of conduct, Norberg argues that Adorno uses the genre only to demonstrate that advice has become impossible: it is a book for "the vanishing individual," since his or her agency is reduced to nothing by the "schemes of domination" of the total system; differently put, "a book of disempowerment" whose only aim can be to "fight the onset of stupidity as the ultimate way in which individuals participate in their own liquidation" (408). By situating Adorno's book in conversation with Barthes's lectures, and thus in a broader perspective, I hope to cast some light on his occasional moments of utopianism, manifest not least in the choice of a vocabulary of distance(s) that transcends its context.

58. See Jameson, *Late Marxism*, esp. chap. 5, "Benjamin and Constellations," 49–59.

59. If only in passing, it is worth noting in relation to this performance of the neutral that neither Adorno nor Barthes supported the students in 1968.

60. Roland Barthes, *Le neutre: Cours au collège de France* (Paris: Seuil, 2002), 33. Hereafter cited parenthetically as *N*.

61. "La méthode suppose toujours une bonne volonté de penseur, une 'décision préméditée.' La culture au contraire est une violence subie par la pensée sous l'action de forces sélectives, un dressage qui met en jeu tout l'inconscient du penseur" (Method always presupposes a thinker's will, a "premeditated decision." By contrast, culture is a violence suffered by thought under the action of selective forces, a taming that mobilizes the thinker's whole unconscious). Gilles Deleuze, *Nietzsche et la philosophie* (Paris: Presses universitaires de France, 1962), 123–124, my translation.

62. Barthes was the enthusiastic herald of the Nouveau Roman, notably of Robbe-Grillet's prose, and his essay on Sollers, "Drame, poème, roman," published in the collective volume *Théorie d'ensemble* in 1968, suggests that his appreciation of the avant-garde continued for at least another decade. In *Roland Barthes* (Paris: Seuil, 1975), however, the rather surprising question "Comment faire route avec l'avant-garde et ses parrains, lorsqu'on a le goût irénique de la dérive?" (106) anticipates an entry in his diary in 1979, another question posed with a certain gravity and full of implications for his contemporaries: "Et si les Modernes se trompaient? S'ils n'avaient pas de talent?" (What if the moderns were wrong? What if they lacked talent?). Roland Barthes, *Soirées de Paris*, posthumous text, *Œuvres complètes*, vol. 5 (Paris: Seuil, 2002), 980. Compagnon emphasizes that Barthes's choice of the fragment in the later texts and the course was a form of reclaiming the position of an *anti-moderne*: thus in an interview with *Magazine littéraire*, Barthes explained: "Le texte d'avant-garde, précise-t-il, texte de jouissance, texte scriptible, est aggressif, non vraisemblable sinon invraisemblable, non lisible sinon illisible, si bien qu'on manque de critères esthétiques pour en juger. Tout autre est le fragment, dont l'intention perverse—l'antimoderne est toujours pervers, installé dans la dénégation—est de 'feindre de rester à l'intérieur d'un code apparemment classique' et 'd'atteindre ainsi la dissociation du sens final à travers une forme qui n'est pas spectaculairement désordonnée, qui évite l'hystérie.' En somme, le texte moderne se situerait du côté de l'hystérie—ce qui n'est jamais un compliment—, tandis que le fragment antimoderne serait du côté de la perversion, suivant une autre opposition freudienne ou lacanienne familière à Barthes. Le fragment n'est pas dupe; il joue avec le classique, il parodie la dictée. Ainsi se définit l'antimoderne: 'Affinité carnavalesque du fragment et de la dictée.'" Quoted from Barthes's *Magazine Littéraire* interview in Antoine Compagnon, *Les antimodernes: De Joseph de Maistre à Roland Barthes* (Paris: Gallimard, 2005), 418. A last reminder is useful here: Barthes said in an interview with Jean Thibaudeau for *Archives du XXe siècle*, that his own theoretical position "est d'être à l'arrière-garde de l'avant-garde" (is to be at the rear guard of the avant-garde). Roland Barthes, "Réponses," in *Tel Quel*, fall 1971, quoted by Compagnon, *Les antimodernes*, 419.

63. The formulation with which Kristeva characterized the early Barthes's attitude, a rebellious delicacy, has probably by now lost its oxymoronic appearance.

64. I am referring here to the published record of *Comment vivre ensemble.* Antoine Compagnon, in *Les antimodernes*, did take note of Barthes's tiredness while giving the lectures, suggesting they might actually have been a chore.

65. Foucault proposed Barthes for the professorship at the Collège de France, and it is not surprising that some of their concerns should come close (his *Herméneutique du sujet* was delivered in 1981). Apparently, however, their lecturing styles could not have been more different: although discontinuity and fragmentation are major tropes in Foucault's work, his lectures were "terriblement efficace[s]" (extremely efficient) and "made no concession to improvisation." Foucault's perspective was less positive: "Il faudrait pouvoir discuter ce que j'ai proposé. . . . Mais cette question ne vient jamais. En France, l'effet de groupe rend toute discussion réelle impossible. Et comme il n'y a pas de canal de retour, le cours se théâtralise. J'ai un rapport d'acteur ou d'acrobate avec les gens qui sont là. Et lorsque j'ai fini de parler, une sensation de solitude totale." Gérard Petitjean, "Les Grands Prêtres de l'université française," *Le Nouvel Observateur*, April 7, 1975, in Michel Foucault, *L'herméneutique du sujet: Cours au Collège de France (1981–1982)*, ed. Frédéric Gros, François Ewald, and Alessandro Fontana (Paris: Gallimard, 2001), viii.

66. The notion of examples in these late lectures is to my mind very similar to the status of examples in Cavell. Since Barthes refuses to pin down meanings, he typically proceeds by giving illustrations, to the point that even the idea of illustration is suggested in the image—to which Barthes shows himself attached—put forward by Socrates, evoked by Bacon, that he was not showing his disciples how to make shoes, but rather displaying various pairs of shoes, of all shapes and kinds (*N*, 36). The "trouble" with this strategy is that each individual example introduces a supplement to what a definition would circumscribe, and thus leads astray the disciple/reader who focuses too closely—tactlessly?—on just one illustration.

67. I will return to Barthes and his discussion of de Sade in chapter 4, where I place *délicatesse* on a continuum with Iris Murdoch's notion of love as a moral ideal.

68. Barthes is quoting Friedrich Nietzsche, *Le crépuscule des idoles* (Paris: Denoël/Gonthier, 1980), 107.

69. Here I am using Duncan Large's translation of Friedrich Nietzsche, *The Twilight of the Idols, or How to Philosophize with a Hammer* (Oxford: Oxford University Press, 1998), 64.

70. Barthes, *Roland Barthes*, 64. For a closer engagement with Barthes's paradoxical relationship with the bourgeois art of living, see my "Roland Barthes's 'Domestiques,'" in *How to Live Together*, ed. Knut Stene-Johansen, Christian Refsum, and Johan Schimanski (Oslo: Scandinavian University Press, forthcoming).

71. "Non d'arrière-garde tout court, mais en retrait du moderne, à distance, en traînant les pieds, en louchant vers l'arrière, en exerçant un droit de regard ou un droit d'inventaire, comme Sartre disait de Baudelaire qu'il avançait l'œil fixé sur le rétroviseur." Compagnon, *Les antimodernes*, 419.

72. See, for instance, "More Haste, Less Speed," in which Adorno bemoans the modern estrangement from "bourgeois walking" in the process of adopting traffic regulations: "The body's habituation to walking as normal stems from the good old days. It was the bourgeois form of locomotion: physical demythologization,

free of the spell of hieratic pacing, roofless wandering, breathless flight. Human dignity insisted on the right to walk, a rhythm not extorted from the body by command or terror. The walk, the stroll, were private ways of passing time, the heritage of the feudal promenade in the nineteenth century. With the liberal era walking too is dying out, even where people do not go by car" (*MM*, frag. 102, p. 162). Surely Benjamin would have agreed, had he lived to read these reflections.

73. To this illusory closeness, Adorno opposes the knowing intimacy of nonconceptual art, despite its estrangement from the reality of lived experience: "The great works of art and philosophical constructions have remained uncomprehended not through their too great distance from the heart of human experience, but the opposite; and this incomprehension could itself be accounted for easily enough by too great comprehension: shame at involvement in universal injustice that would become overwhelming as soon as one allowed oneself to understand" (*MM*, frag. 96, pp. 146–147).

74. "But for all its aristocratic trappings, ritual falls into the late bourgeois habit of hypostasizing a performance in itself meaningless as meaning, of degrading mind to the duplication of what is there in any case. The norm followed is fictitious; its social preconditions, like its model, court ceremony, have ceased to exist, and it is acknowledged not because it is felt as binding, but in order to legitimize an order advantageously illegitimate" (*MM*, frag. 121, p. 189).

75. See here David Heyd, "Tact: Sense, Sensitivity, and Virtue," *Inquiry* 38, no. 3 (1995): 217–231.

76. Adorno's critique of the "tergiversations" of positivism also find echoes in Barthes's critique of realism, which is always an effect—an *effet de réel*—rather than the real it *uncritically* claims to represent.

77. The original passage from "Refuge for the Homeless" reads: "'Es gehört selbst zu meinem Glücke, kein Hausbesitzser zu sein,' schrieb Nietzsche bereits in *Der fröhlichen Wissenschaft*. Dem müsste man heute hinzufügen: es gehört zur Moral, nicht bei sich selber zu Hause zu sein" ("It is part of my good fortune not to be a houseowner," wrote Nietzsche in *The Gay Science*. To which we should add: today it is part of morality not to be at home in one's home) (*MM*, frag. 18).

Chapter 1

Abbreviated versions of parts of this chapter appeared in *Études britanniques contemporaines*, no. 49 (2015) and *English Studies* 97, no. 3 (2016): 298–316.

1. George Orwell, *The Road to Wigan Pier* (New York: Harcourt, Brace, 1958), 148. Hereafter cited parenthetically as *RWP*.

2. Sant Singh Bal, *George Orwell: The Ethical Imagination* (New Delhi: Arnold-Heinemann, 1981), 23.

3. Orwell evokes his trip to the economically depressed North in *The Road to Wigan Pier* (commissioned, by the same Andre Gollancz who had published *DOPL*, for the Left Book Club; the book—especially the second half, in which Orwell expressed unorthodox views about socialism—became an embarrassment to the club in 1937 when it was published, and Gollancz himself wrote an introduction in which he distanced himself from it) and his involvement with the anti-Stalinist Partido Obrero de Unificación Marxista (POUM, the Workers' Party of Marxist Unification) in the 1938 *Homage to Catalonia* (London: Penguin, 1988). Again, because of the perspective he gained in Spain on the internal

conflict of interests within communist circles, the critical views he expressed on his return to England—at a time when his contemporaries were convinced communists—were very much out of favor.

4. Raymond Williams's assessment of Orwell's early writing strikes me as one of the most accurate: "All of Orwell's writing until 1937 is, then, a series of works and experiments around a common problem. Instead of dividing them into 'fiction' and 'documentaries' we should see them as sketches toward the creation of his most successful character, 'Orwell.' This would not be so successful if it had not been so intensely and painfully lived. The exposure to poverty and suffering and filth and waste was as real as it was deliberate, and the record of the exposure is a remarkable enlargement of our literature." Raymond Williams, *George Orwell* (New York: Columbia University Press, 1971).

5. I am borrowing this apt phrase from Margery Sabin, "The Truths of Experience: Orwell's Nonfiction of the 1930s," in *The Cambridge Companion to George Orwell*, ed. John Rodden (Cambridge: Cambridge University Press, 2007), 45.

6. Kingsley Amis, quoted in John Rodden, "'The Rope That Connects Me Directly with You': John Wain and the Movement Writers' Orwell," *Albion: A Quarterly Journal Concerned with British Studies* 20, no. 1 (spring 1988): 64. Orwell's self-characterization was, repeatedly, as a democratic socialist.

7. Woodcock, "George Orwell, 19th Century Liberal," in *Politics* (1946), in Jeffrey Meyers (ed.), *George Orwell: The Critical Heritage* (London: Routledge and Kegan Paul, 1997), 235–247, 238.

8. As John Rodden points out, the case Orwell offers "not only a sociological but also *an ethical guide* to the contemporary relation of the intellectual and politics." Rodden, "'The Rope That Connects Me Directly with You,'" 64, my italics. Rodden endorses here the views expressed by V. S. Pritchett, "George Orwell," *New Statesman and Nation*, January 28, 1950, 96. See also George Woodcock, "Orwell and Conscience," *World Review*, April 1950, 28.

9. Meyers, *George Orwell*, 134.

10. Bal, *George Orwell*, 23.

11. Samuel Lynn Hynes, *Twentieth Century Interpretations of 1984; A Collection of Critical Essays* (Englewood Cliffs, N.J.: Prentice-Hall, 1971), 10.

12. See Wyndham Lewis, *The Writer and the Absolute* (London: Methuen, 1952).

13. George Orwell, "Inside the Whale," in *A Collection of Essays* (San Diego: Harcourt Brace Jovanovich, 1981), 210–252. Hereafter cited parenthetically as IW.

14. The essay "Mr Bennett and Mrs Brown" was first published in the *Literary Review* of the *New York Evening Post*, November 17, 1923, from which evolved a paper read to the Cambridge Heretics on May 18, 1924, and which turned into the more elaborated version titled "Character in Fiction" (hereafter cited parenthetically as CF), published in the *Criterion* in July 1924.

15. Virginia Woolf, "The Leaning Tower," in *The Moment and Other Essays* (New York: Harcourt Brace Jovanovich, 1948), 136–137.

16. Although the concern here is not with Woolf's merits as a chronicler of her own time per se, it is worth pointing out something resembling a rhetorical pattern in the two earlier essays and the one of interest to us here: in "Character in Fiction" and "Mr Bennett and Mrs Brown," she calls Eliot's and Joyce's work "a

season of failures and fragments," and, in the spirit of the metaphor of friendship that she associates with the institution of literature, she invites the reader to show patience with Joyce's "dull calculated indecency," with his "savagely broken windows," and with Eliot's obscurity. Implicit in Woolf's assessment, at stake in the 1920s was nothing less than an artistic revolution: it involved finding a form (she calls it a "convention" or, with Eliot, a "method") that would capture the "ordinary mind on an ordinary day," of the *real* Mrs. Brown, as she emerged out of the change in relations in evidence in 1910. Eventually, she promises, artists will "rescue" Mrs. Brown, even if by then she would be "a little pale and disheveled" (CF, 435). Such high stakes justified the "failures" that in Woolf's view were *Ulysses* and *The Waste Land*. Moving to the later essay, the 1930s witnessed "everywhere revolution": a different kind of revolution, to be sure. And if the 1920s artists had to be pardoned because they had no literary "convention" to rely on, only their desire to be true to their *reality*, to their *vision* (Woolf: "[Is] life really like that?") the following generation had "nothing steady to look at," no tranquility to recollect, to have a vision of.

17. In a similar move, in "Women and Fiction" and *A Room of One's Own* (both 1929), Woolf identifies autobiography, the literature of self-expression, as the first step in self-consciousness in the case of women writers, too; this initial stage is then followed by a less self-conscious stage, one in which it becomes possible to take an interest in the lives of others, and which allows the "impersonal" to emerge—a gesture we now identify as inaugurating a modernist ideal, the place where true art begins. By applying this pattern to the writers of the 1930s, she was led to believe in the possibility of a renaissance of literature once the war was over.

18. E. M. Forster, "Virginia Woolf," in *Two Cheers for Democracy* (London: Harcourt, Brace and Company, 1951), 242.

19. E. M. Forster, "English Prose between 1918 and 1939," in *Two Cheers for Democracy* (London: Harcourt, Brace and Company, 1951), 284.

20. Stephen Spender, *World within World* (London: H. Hamilton, 1951), 141.

21. Ibid., 142.

22. George Orwell, "Writers and Leviathan," in *The Collected Essays, Journalism, and Letters of George Orwell* (New York: Harcourt, Brace & World, 1968), 408–409.

23. Spender, *World within World*, 191.

24. Orwell, "Writers and Leviathan," 409. "No one, now, could devote himself to literature as single-mindedly as Joyce or Henry James."

25. Spender, *World within World*, 249.

26. Alan Swingewood, "Intellectuals and the Construction of Consensus in Postwar England," in *Intellectuals in Liberal Democracies: Political Influence and Social Involvement*, ed. Alain Gagnon (New York: Praeger, 1987), 87.

27. Noel Annan, "The Intellectual Aristocracy," in *Studies in Social History: A Tribute to G. M. Trevelyan*, ed. J. H. Plumb (London: Longmans, Green, 1955), 257–279.

28. I will return to Trilling shortly.

29. *The God That Failed* is the title of a collective volume originally published in 1950 by Arthur Koestler, Ignazio Silone, Richard Wright, André Gide, Louis Fischer, and Stephen Spender, all intellectuals who were drawn to communism

and then disillusioned by it after becoming familiar with the historical realities of Soviet Marxism under Lenin and Stalin. Richard H. Crossman, ed., *The God That Failed* (New York: Columbia University Press, 2001).

30. "These three were the only writers of real significance who did not at one time or another become deeply involved with the Communist Party and suffer a subsequent disillusionment which drove them back to an unrealistic social isolation." George Woodcock, "George Orwell, 19th Century Liberal," in *Politics* (1946), 235.

31. Stuart Samuels, "English Intellectuals and Politics in the 1930s," in *On Intellectuals: Theoretical Studies, Case Studies*, ed. Philip Rieff (Garden City, N.Y.: Doubleday, 1969), 247.

32. In "On the Political Sociology of Intellectuals," Rodden emphasizes the lifelong "outsider" stance toward the London intelligentsia: "Superficially his career does possess a comparable shape and sequence to other 1930s intellectuals: public school, travel abroad, return to teach, occasional journalism, a 'new signature' (in 1933 as Orwell), contact with the British unemployed, embrace of socialism, and off to Spain. But that narrative abstract masks and bleaches the very different experience that set Blair-Orwell apart from most intellectuals of his generation, at least after public school. The trajectory of his career suggests both the fallacy of linking mechanically class origins with political affiliation and the necessity of injecting a dynamic, historical dimension into an inquiry on the conditions for intellectuals' political radicalization." John Rodden, "On the Political Sociology of Intellectuals: George Orwell and the London Left Intelligentsia of the 1930s," *Canadian Journal of Sociology = Cahiers Canadiens de Sociologie* 15, no. 3 (summer 1990): 258–259.

33. Italics in the original. Although "Inside the Whale" makes no explicit reference to the literary or aesthetic merits of the works produced by the 1930s writers, Orwell seems to agree with Woolf that these merits were scant. In an essay on Arthur Koestler from 1944, he writes: "English writers, over the past dozen years, have poured forth an enormous spate of political literature, but they have produced almost nothing of aesthetic value, and very little of historical value either. . . . One result of this is that there exists in England almost no literature of disillusionment about the Soviet Union [as there is on the continent]. There is the attitude of ignorant disapproval, and there is the attitude of critical admiration, but very little in between." George Orwell, "Arthur Koestler," http://gutenberg.net.au/ebooks03/0300011h.html#part21, accessed August 20, 2017.

34. In a short review-essay, "From Bloomsbury to the Bowery," Orwell wrote: "England happens to be cursed with a class-system which, even as an expression of the economic structure, is hopelessly out-of-date, and which sees to it that nearly everyone's destiny is fixed for him at birth. The coal-miner, the naval officer, the grocer and the bank clerk simply can't meet and talk as they could in America; each of them lives from cradle to grave upon a single level, mixing only with his own sub-caste and cut-off from all the rest by dense walls of prejudice." George Orwell, "From Bloomsbury to the Bowery," *The Tribune*, April 12, 1940, 21–22.

35. Ibid., 20–21. This is a rare appraisal of Woolf by Orwell.

36. Presumably then, characters like Orlando, who not only upsets gender conventions, but also the boundaries between social classes, or Mrs. McNabb, the

maid whose body is set against "time pass[ing]" in the central section of *To the Lighthouse*, etc., would be lacking because they are grounded not in firsthand knowledge, but in acts of imagination.

37. For an eloquent elaboration of this point, see Rob Breton, "Crisis? Whose Crisis? George Orwell and Liberal Guilt," *College Literature* 29, no. 4 (fall 2002): 47–66.

38. In the essay "Max and the White Phagocytes," Miller comments on the whale in El Greco's painting *Dream of Philip II*, and then relates the imagery of the whale to the writing of Anaïs Nin. Orwell borrows the metaphor and radically politicizes its meaning: "The Whale's belly is simply a womb big enough for an adult. There you are, in the dark, cushioned space that exactly fits you, with years of blubber between yourself and reality, able to keep up an attitude of the completest indifference, no matter what happens. . . . Short of being dead, it is the final, unsurpassable stage of irresponsibility. And however it may be with Anaïs Nin, there is no question that Miller himself is inside the whale. All his best and most characteristic passages are written from the angle of Jonah, a willing Jonah. . . . Only he feels no impulse to alter or control the process that he is undergoing. He has performed the essential Jonah act of allowing himself to be swallowed, remaining passive, accepting" (IW, 245).

39. The theoretical analysis of this phenomenon offered by Pascale Casanova in "Literature as a World" casts this case in an interesting light: "We know that the US was subordinate in literary terms during the 1910s and 1920s, and that American writers came to Paris seeking literary resources and aesthetic models." Pascale Casanova, "Literature as a World," *New Left Review* (February 2005): 84, 86. Miller was one of the last of this large group, yet the "prestige" bestowed on his literary work by the French culture whose influence it bore (through his contacts with the surrealists, for instance) did not facilitate recognition and appreciation in Britain (if anything, perhaps quite the contrary). Orwell was ostensibly doing Miller a favor by writing about his novels in an English journal.

40. See my essay "A Passionate Misunderstanding: Orwell's Paris, Miller's China," *English Studies* 97, no. 3 (2016): 298–316. What follows in this section is a much abbreviated version of this article.

41. Lionel Trilling, *Sincerity and Authenticity* (Cambridge, Mass.: Harvard University Press, 1972), 26–27.

42. Ibid., 113–114, italics in the original.

43. Robert Pippin, *Modernism as a Philosophical Problem: On the Dissatisfactions of European High Culture*, 2nd ed. (Malden, Mass.: Blackwell, 1999), 61.

44. Ibid., 111.

45. Henry Miller, "Peace, It's Wonderful!," in *The Cosmological Eye* (New York: New Directions, 1939), 5.

46. Henry Miller, "Walking Up and Down in China," in *Americans in Paris: A Literary Anthology*, ed. Adam Gopnik (New York: Library of America, 2004), 391.

47. Trilling, *Sincerity and Authenticity*, 11.

48. Ibid., 131.

49. For a wonderful anthology of American texts about Paris, sketching the history of an enduring fascination with the French capital, see Gopnik, *Americans in Paris*.

50. George Orwell, *Down and Out in Paris and London* (London: Harcourt, 1961), 5–6. Hereafter cited parenthetically as *DOPL*.

51. Walter Benjamin, *The Arcades Project* (Cambridge, Mass.: Belknap Press of Harvard University Press, 1999).

52. See "The Thing" and "The Origin of the Work of Art" in Martin Heidegger, *Poetry, Language, Thought* (New York: HarperCollins, 2001).

53. In these words sound echoes of the avant-garde, especially the futurist and the surrealist manifestos, with which Miller was familiar, but from whose tenets Miller eventually strived to distance himself. See his "Letter to Surrealists Everywhere," in *The Cosmological Eye*, 151–197.

54. Miller's Whitman is quite obviously a rather idiosyncratic one, and Orwell models his own image of Whitman after Miller's. To state only an obvious point, "Whitman among the corpses" is an image that has its own autonomy and historical accuracy (with respect to the historical context of the Civil War that Whitman witnessed), which makes rather problematic the idealized "health"—be it only relative to contemporary, World War II events—of late nineteenth-century America.

55. Trilling, *Sincerity and Authenticity*, 132.

56. Orwell's first tramping expeditions to the East End of London occurred in October 1927; in the winter of 1928, he was tramping in the vicinity of London, after which, in 1928–1929, he lived in working-class district of Paris, where he began the early drafts of *Down and Out in Paris and London*. In 1929, between March 7 and 22, he was admitted to Hôpital Cochin, Paris, after coughing up blood (he wrote about the conditions he witnessed there in "How the Poor Die"). In 1930–1931 he used his parents' home in Southwold as a base, writing there but going off to tramp and live with down-and-outs in London. The book was published by Victor Gollancz in January 1933, under the signature "George Orwell." (See also his first letter about spending the night under the empty sky, and the installments in journals of his experiences as a tramp, hop-picker, etc., published in *The Collected Essays, Journalism, and Letters of George Orwell* (New York: Harcourt, Brace & World, 1968).

57. Orwell never uses the word "dishwasher." He is obviously fond of the word *plongeur*, most likely for its evocation of plunging, of going down (as in the statement of his intentions quoted early in the chapter, "to go down among the oppressed, be one of them," etc.). The idea of a hellish underworld is also explicitly present, for example in the evocation of a punishment one of the plongeurs was inflicted by a superior who locked him up in a hot oven.

58. Stephen Ingle, *The Social and Political Thought of George Orwell: A Reassessment* (London: Routledge, 2005), 50.

59. Unsurprisingly, Davies published an enthusiastic review of Orwell's first book in *New Statesman and Nation*, March 18, 1933.

60. Bal, *George Orwell*, 81.

61. See, typical of this gesture, Brian Finney, *The Inner I: British Literary Autobiography of the Twentieth Century* (New York: Oxford University Press, 1985).

62. Steven Marcus, "George Orwell," *Partisan Review* 60, no. 1 (1993).

63. George Steiner, *New Yorker*, March 1969, 139–151, in Meyers, *George Orwell*, 365.

64. Aaron Baker, "The Tramp: Down and Out in Chaplin and Orwell," *Literature/Film Quarterly* 17, no. 1 (1989): 27–32. Baker talks in general about

Orwell's experiences in *Down and Out* as tramping; it would be interesting, I think, to take into account in such a comparison not just the tramp, but also the figure of the worker in the context of production and consumption, that both Orwell's book (its first, Parisian, half) and *Modern Times* are concerned with.

65. Fifty years after the publication of Orwell's book, Penguin published a volume of photographs by Chris Schwarz meant to assess, half a century later, the conditions revealed by Orwell. See Sandy Craig and Chris Schwarz, *Down and Out: Orwell's Paris and London Revisited* (London: Penguin Putnam, 1984). Writing about Schwarz's exhibition at the Photographers' Gallery in 1984, William Bishop notes that "Schwarz doesn't make art out of suffering but uses his art to dramatize the facts of the situations that he sees." And quoting from Neil McIntosh's preface to the book: "'Dossers,' 'junkies,' 'down and outs,' 'queers,' 'delinquents,' the list of labels in English and in French is endless, and each label helps us to distance ourselves from the people we encounter. . . . The often eccentric and colorful personalities of the individuals who have chosen this way of life can also distract our attention from the reality of life without a home or job (Neil McIntosh quoted in Schwarz, "Preface," no page number).

66. One might ponder this combination as a logical possibility enabled by placing the two terms, "sincerity" and "authenticity," in opposition in Greimas's square.

67. The lure of India for this class is also explained by Orwell in terms of its snobbish attempts to keep up appearances: "The people who went there as soldiers and officials [like his father, and briefly himself] did not go there to make money, for a soldier or an official does not make money; they went there because in India, with cheap horses, free shooting, and hordes of black servants, it was so easy to play at being a gentleman" (*RWP*, 123–124).

68. Lewis: "Before [going to Spain], equally dramatically, he flung himself into the gutters and stinking cellars of Paris. . . . Verily, this man was determined to identify himself with the 'lowest of the low.' He wore his bug-bites with a grim smile. They were the equivalent of the hotel labels (Ritz-Carlton, Astoria-Grand) which we sometimes see upon the luggage of ardent travelers." Lewis, *The Writer and the Absolute*, 160–161. Also: "From the giddy heights of Eton, and the modest eminence upon which every sahib stood in India, or Burma, in the days of the British Raj, he flung himself with enthusiasm into the menial labyrinths of a great Paris hotel, into the bug-infested garrets where live the poorest of the poor, above the level—but just above—where the underworld of vagrants and beggars begins. It was a Stevensonian bourgeois romanticism" (ibid., 162).

69. Bal, *George Orwell*, 79.

70. Also relevant in this context is his memoir "Such, Such Were the Joys," in which he evokes the humiliations experienced as a young "scholarship boy" in a public school where most of the other pupils came from *better* families. See Orwell, "Such, Such Were the Joys," in *A Collection of Essays*, 1–48.

71. One example, among many, which also hints at a certain ethnographic dimension of his experiment: "Afterwards, when it was too late, I learned that it was wiser to go to a pawnshop in the afternoon. The clerks are French, and, like most French people, are in a bad temper till they have eaten their lunch" (*DOPL*, 20).

72. The fictional explanation for his tramping in London is that his arrangement to take care of a disabled person fell through, so he found himself penniless and without any job prospects.

73. Near the beginning of "The Lion and the Unicorn" (1940) and *The English People* (1944), for instance, Orwell introduces the viewpoint of someone arriving in England. "When you come back to England from any foreign country, you have immediately the sensation of breathing a different air." "It is worth trying for a moment to put oneself in the position of a foreign observer, new to England, but unprejudiced, and able because of his work to keep in touch with ordinary, useful, unspectacular people." Orwell, in *The Collected Essays, Journalism, and Letters of George Orwell* (New York: Harcourt, Brace & World, 1968), 57.

74. The parallel is hinted at in *Road to Wigan Pier*: "I now realized that there was no need to go as far as Burma to find tyranny and exploitation. Here in England, down under one's feet, were the submerged working class, suffering miseries which in their different way were as bad as any an oriental ever knows" (*RWP*, 148–149).

75. Post–World War II novels like *Brideshead Revisited*, *The Remains of the Day*, and *Waterland* explore this theme at some length. Evelyn Waugh, *Brideshead Revisited* (London: Chapman & Happ, 1945); Kazuo Ishiguro, *The Remains of the Day* (London: Faber and Faber, 1989); and Graham Swift, *Waterland* (London: William Heinemann, 1983).

76. In *Londres*, Paul Morand would ironically use an aristocratic vocabulary in designating this community the "down and out club." See Paul Morand, *Londres* (Paris: Plon, 1933).

77. In *The Road to Wigan Pier*, the dismissal of lower-class individuals appears as a childhood memory: "To me in my early boyhood, to nearly all children of families like mine, 'common' people seemed almost sub-human. They had coarse faces, hideous accents and gross manners, they hated everyone who was not like themselves, and if they got half a chance they would insult you in brutal ways. That was our view of them" (*RWP*, 126). Years later, he was still sharing the same views: "At the age of seventeen or eighteen, I was both a snob and a revolutionary. . . . I had not much grasp of what Socialism meant, and no notion that the working class were human beings. At a distance, and through the medium of books—Jack London's *People of the Abyss*, for instance—I could agonise over their sufferings, but I still hated them and despised them when I came anywhere near them. I was still revolted by their accents and infuriated by their habitual rudeness" (*RWP*, 140).

78. The term "anthropodenial," which Martha Nussbaum borrows from Frans de Waal, could be useful as a way to include the practice Orwell alludes to here into a larger class of complex sociological and historical phenomena that all share the negation of another individual or group's humanity, thus justifying to themselves and to the world aggressive treatment that is in usual circumstances deemed unacceptable. See Martha Nussbaum, *Political Emotions: Why Love Matters for Justice* (Cambridge, Mass.: Harvard University Press, 2013).

79. Adorno, quoted by Rolf Tiedemann in introduction to Theodor W. Adorno, *Can One Live after Auschwitz? A Philosophical Reader* (Stanford, Calif.: Stanford University Press, 2003), xxiv.

80. The kind that pushed Beckett to turn his work for the stage into "an experiment in diminution": shorter and shorter plays, just *dramaticules*. The scene described by Orwell (*DOPL*, 158–159) might well be such a playlet. (In fact, it was originally a short dramatic poem, now published in *The Collected Essays*, vol. 1.)

81. "Can one portray a city, just as one portrays a woman? Why not? A city is as easy to figure out, then to penetrate from the outside, as a human being. A foreigner might even do a better job than a native, because he is more detached." In the original, this passage reads: "Peut-on faire le portrait d'une ville comme on fait celui d'une femme? Pourquoi pas? Une ville est aussi facile à cerner, puis à pénétrer de l'extérieur qu'un être humain. Un étranger y réussit d'ailleurs mieux qu'un indigène car il a plus de recul." Paul Morand, *Le réveille-matin*, quoted by his biographer, Ginette Guitard-Auviste, *Paul Morand, 1888–1976: Légende et vérités* (Paris: Editions Balland, 1994), 183 (my translation).

82. "Combien en ai-je visité de ces pauvres logis londoniens, où les rats viennent manger sous les tables. C'est toujours le même décor, et presque toujours la même histoire. Trop d'enfants . . . mariage hâtif [. . .] C'est pourquoi la rue est pleine de joueurs de violon, de chanteurs ambulants, de marchands de pommes ou d'allumettes" (*L*, 83; first set of suspension points in the original).

83. Orwell despises and criticizes the form of Christian mercy that helps preserve the status quo; he does not "jump in" for the beggars (Heidegger's term *einspringen*, "leaping in for someone," comes in handy here), but rather confirms to them that they needn't be grateful and that they should revolt (a form of *vorausspringen*, of leaping ahead to clear the way and empower the person). "This kind of solicitude pertains essentially to authentic care—that is, to the existence of the Other, not to a 'what' with which he is concerned; it helps the Other to become transparent to himself in his care and to become free for it." Martin Heidegger, *Being and Time*, trans. John Macquarrie and Edward Robinson, with a new foreword by Taylor Carman (New York: Harper Perennial, 2008), 159. I will return to this point below.

84. In a passage evoking, then dismissing, his earlier "sentimentalism," the ideas of the younger Orwell come strangely close to Miller's: "In the end [he speaks here of the end of his experience 'in the East'] I worked out an anarchistic theory that all government is evil, that the punishment always does more harm than the crime and that people can be trusted to behave decently if only you will let them alone. This of course was sentimental nonsense. I see now as I did not see then, that it is always necessary to protect peaceful people from violence" (*RWP*, 146–147).

85. "What I profoundly wanted, at that time, was to find some way of getting out of the respectable world altogether" (*RWP*, 149).

86. I am relying here on Amanda Anderson's genealogy of the term "cosmopolitanism" in *The Way We Argue Now*, chaps. 3 and 4.

87. See Anderson, *The Powers of Distance*, 3–34.

88. Edward Twitchell Hall, *The Hidden Dimension* (Garden City, N.Y.: Doubleday, 1966).

89. This is a useful notion coined by Derek Attridge in *The Singularity of Literature* (London: Routledge, 2004).

90. George Eliot, "The Natural History of German Life," quoted in Anderson, *The Powers of Distance*, 15.

91. I am suggesting that there is interest in regarding Orwell's first book as an anticipation of the turn in 1980s ethnography toward an *ethnography of proximity*, which involved returning home to cast a trained-abroad gaze on everyday reality, and unearthing what was obscured by the overly familiar. See "Proximate

Ethnographies," in Michael Sheringham, *Everyday Life: Theories and Practices from Surrealism to the Present* (Oxford: Oxford University Press, 2006), 293–305.

92. George Steiner, *New Yorker*, March 1969, 139–151, reprinted in Meyers, *George Orwell*, 370.

93. Lionel Trilling, "George Orwell and the Politics of Truth," in *George Orwell: A Collection of Critical Essays*, ed. Raymond Williams (Englewood Cliffs, N.J.: Prentice-Hall, 1974), 72.

94. Steiner in Meyers, *George Orwell*, 367.

95. See Susan Sontag, *Fascinating Fascism*, in *New York Review of Books*, February 6, 1975, http://www.nybooks.com/articles/1975/02/06/fascinating-fascism, and Philippe Lacoue-Labarthe and Jean-Luc Nancy, "The Nazi Myth," *Critical Inquiry* 16, no. 2 (winter 1990): 291–312.

96. See, besides *Tropic of Cancer*, *The Cosmological Eye*.

97. "Je voudrais qu'après ma mort on fît de ma peau une valise," quoted in Guitard-Auviste, *Paul Morand, 1888–1976*, 118.

98. Steiner, in Meyers, *George Orwell*, 365.

99. That this is the case is suggested by his mention of Eliot's publication of *Prufrock* during the First World War, saluted by E. M. Forster because it "preserved a tiny drop of our self-respect, he carried on the human heritage." Orwell exclaims, in an indirect endorsement of Miller: "I should have felt, like Mr. Forster, that by simply standing aloof and keeping touch with pre-war emotions, Eliot was carrying on the human heritage. What a relief it would have been at such a time, to read about the hesitations of a middle-aged highbrow with a bald spot! So different from bayonet-drill! After the bombs and the food-queues and the recruiting-posters, a human voice! What a relief!" (IW, 248–249).

100. Rolf Tiedemann in Adorno, *Can One Live after Auschwitz? A Philosophical Reader* (Stanford, Calif.: Stanford University Press, 2003), xxiv.

101. Steiner: "I see no escape from Orwell's position and the obligations of untimeliness and tactlessness which it imposes." Meyers, *George Orwell*, 368.

102. I am referring to Stanley Cavell's attempt to define "tact" in the seminar he held at Duke University in the spring of 2010. I will return to this point below.

Chapter 2

First epigraph: Elias Canetti quoted in Friedrich Heer, *God's First Love; Christians and Jews over Two Thousand Years* (New York: Weybright and Talley, 1970), 507. Second epigraph: Canetti, *The Secret Heart of the Clock: Notes, Aphorisms, Fragments, 1973–1985*, trans. Joel Agee (New York: Farrar, Straus and Giroux, 1989), 67.

1. *Masse und Macht* was published in Germany by Claasen (Berlin) in 1960, and appeared in English translation as Elias Canetti, *Crowds and Power*, trans. Carol Stewart (1962; reprint, New York: Farrar, Straus and Giroux, 1984). Hereafter cited parenthetically as *CP*. The French translation came out in 1966.

2. Letter to Georges Canetti, July 3, 1959, in Veza Canetti, *"Dearest Georg": Love, Literature, and Power in Dark Times: The Letters of Elias, Veza, and Georges Canetti, 1933–1948*, ed. Karen Lauer and Kristian Wachinger, trans. David B. Dollenmayer (New York: Other Press, 2009), 367.

3. Elias Canetti, *Secret Heart of the Clock*, 41.

4. The original German titles are *Die gerettete Zunge: Geschichte einer Jugend*, *Die Fackel im Ohr: Lebensgeschichte 1921–1931*, and *Das Augenspiel: Lebensgeschichte 1931–1937*. The autobiography was originally published by Hanser (Munich) in 1977, 1980, and 1985 respectively. I am quoting here from Joachim Neugroschel's English translation, *The Memoirs of Elias Canetti: The Tongue Set Free, The Torch in My Ear, The Play of the Eyes* (New York: Farrar, Straus and Giroux, 2000), hereafter cited parenthetically as *MEC*.

5. Elias Canetti, *Party im Blitz: Die englischen Jahre* (Munich: Hanser, 2003).

6. Elias Canetti, *The Human Province*, trans. Joachim Neugroschel (New York: Seabury, 1978), 185.

7. In his chapter "Immunitary Democracy," Roberto Esposito lists Canetti among a number of thinkers he identifies as "the great twentieth-century tradition of negative anthropology—from Helmuth Plessner to Arnold Gehlen and Niklas Luhman," for whom "the category of immunization, in its head-on confrontation with that of community, was the most fruitful interpretative key for modern political systems." Roberto Esposito, *Terms of the Political: Community, Immunity, Biopolitics*, trans. Rhiannon Noel Welch (New York: Fordham University Press, 2013), 39. Referring specifically to Canetti's premise in *Crowds and Power*, Esposito writes: "Elias Canetti also reminds us, nothing scares the individual more than being touched by what threatens to cross his or her individual boundaries" (40). A few pages later, he credits Canetti with an insight that helps articulate Esposito's own diagnosis of the contemporary in terms of a spreading of what he calls the "immunitary dispositif" to "all sectors and languages of our lives" as if "that fear of being even accidentally grazed has been made worse, that fear that Elias Canetti located at the origin of our modernity in a perverse short circuit between touch [*tatto*], contact [*contatto*], and contagion [*contagio*]. The risk of contamination immediately liquidates contact, relationality, and being in common" (59).

8. *Die Blendung* (literally, *The Blinding*, published in translation first as *Babel Tower / La Tour de Babel*, then as *Auto-da-fé*), was the first and only novel Canetti wrote, published in Austria in 1935. The long silence he imposed on himself was punctuated by a few plays (*The Wedding, Comedy of Vanity*, etc.) and ended with the lengthy book on crowds and the autobiographical volumes. A few collections of essays, notes, and aphorisms, of which some are posthumous, complete the Canettian oeuvre. I am using here the English edition *Auto-da-fé* in the translation of C. V. Wedgwood (London: Picador, 1978).

9. "Cette œuvre d'une vie ne se laisse pas plus facilement résumer que *La Recherche du Temps Perdu*." Historian Pierre Nora in his review of the book, "Un Tocqueville du vingtième siècle," *La Quinzaine Littéraire*, April 15, 1966, 20.

10. One of the readers who was susceptible to be struck by Canetti's idiosyncratic bibliography was George Steiner, author of *After Babel*, who noted that it "ranges from Tertullian's *De Spectaculis* to A. Dalzel's *History of Dahomey* (1793) and P. E. Williams' *The Vailala Madness* (Port Moresby, 1923)." Steiner, "Canetti's Crowd," *Encounter*, December 1962, 86.

11. Hansjakob Werlen, "Destiny's Herald: Elias Canetti's *Crowds and Power* and Its Continuing Influence," in *Critical Essays on Elias Canetti*, ed. David Darby (New York: G. K. Hall, 2000), 174. Later on, he completes the diagnosis of the

book's difficulty with the no less insightful remarks: "The crossing of boundaries in *CP* is not restricted to the appropriation of various discourses. Canetti's essay crosses all chronological and geographic limits, the demarcation between the real and the imagined, and, most importantly, the schism between Western and non-Western consciousness, between rationalist thought and mythic imagination. It is this appropriation of anything and everything to document the core axioms of *CP* that makes the reception of Canetti's essay so difficult" (ibid., 182).

12. Before Canetti, "mob was the word for the crowd when it threatened civilized living; crowd was the word for the mob while it gathered its strength between riots; civilization was the word for what the crowd threatened; rule was the word for what kept the crowd from becoming a mob; riot or revolution the word for the mob's own life. Even when the crowd was seen to be manipulated by its leaders for their own ends, it was always typically concern for the victims of those ends, and not for the crowd itself, which predominated." See J. S. McClelland, *The Crowd and the Mob: From Plato to Canetti* (London: Unwin Hyman, 1989), 311.

13. There are, for instance, fascinating accounts of the rain dances of the Pueblo Indians, or of the Muharram festival of the Shiites; a provocative analysis of Islam as a religion of war, followed by sections on "Catholicism and the Crowd" and "the Holy Fire in Jerusalem"; the penultimate section "Socialism and Production" precedes a return to the archaic in the disturbing account of "the Self-Destruction of the Xosas."

14. Canetti offers a corrective to Freud's famous analysis of the former president of the senate in Dresden, hardly mentioning Freud's name: in the German original, Freud's name does not even appear; in the English translation, he is granted acknowledgment in a footnote, but not in the bibliography.

15. If this is unsettling to some readers, it might not be to others: in a positive review of *Crowds and Power*, British historian Veronica Wedgwood writes: "We are all of us glad to survive dangers in which others have perished, and this is not mere relief. If we are honest with ourselves we are aware also of a sense of triumph in being still alive when others are dead. Education and good manners may instantly stifle this feeling, but no one who has experienced an air-raid can honestly deny its existence." C. V. Wedgwood, "The Quest for Power," *Daily Telegraph and Morning Post*, September 28, 1962.

16. "When a command is passed on it is as though a man pulled out an arrow which had hit him, fitted that same arrow to his bow and shot it again. The wound in his body heals, but it leaves a scar. Every scar has a story; it is the mark of a particular arrow" (*CP*, 308).

17. Consequently, as critics have remarked, a free person remains a hypothesis at best, since in real life such a person does not exist, if only by virtue of having been a child.

18. I am referring to Elias Canetti's book *Kafka's Other Trial: The Letters to Felice* (1969), trans. Christopher Middleton (New York: Schocken, 1974), and the essay "The Writer's Profession," in *The Conscience of Words* (New York: Seabury, 1979), 236–246.

19. In an apposite formulation, David Darby suggests that metamorphosis is for Canetti "the potentially inexhaustible regenerative capacity that all animate beings possess to reinvent and transform themselves and their world in defiance

of specialization, stagnation, petrification, and death." David Darby, introduction to *Critical Essays on Elias Canetti*, ed. Darby (New York: G. K. Hall, 2000), 3. These themes, it might be worth pointing out, are central to Gilles Deleuze and Félix Guattari's *Capitalism and Schizophrenia*, and metamorphosis translates for them as *deterritorialization* and *becomings*. (Unsurprisingly, Canetti appears in a footnote in *Anti-Oedipus*.) See Deleuze and Guattari, *Capitalism and Schizophrenia*, trans. Robert Hurley, Mark Seem, and Helen R. Lane (Minneapolis: University of Minnesota Press, 2000). For other interpretations of "metamorphosis" in Canetti's work see J. P. Stern, "Canetti's Later Work," in Darby, *Critical Essays on Elias Canetti*, 239–249, and Friederike Eigler, "Fissures in the Monument: Reassessing Elias Canetti's Autobiographical Works," ibid., 261–276.

20. Iris Murdoch, "Mass, Might and Myth" in *The Spectator*, September 1962, republished in Iris Murdoch, *Existentialists and Mystics: Writings on Philosophy and Literature*, ed. Peter J. Conradi (London: Allen Lane, 1997), 187–193, here 188.

21. Steiner, "Canetti's Crowd," 85–87.

22. Murdoch, *Existentialists and Mystics*, 187.

23. "Théories que pour discuter, il faudrait la compétence d'un collège d'historiens, de sociologues, de psychanalystes et de philosophes." Nora, "Un Tocqueville du vingtième siècle," 20.

24. Iris Murdoch, "Mass, Might and Myth," *The Spectator*, September 1962, republished in Murdoch, *Existentialists and Mystics*, 191.

25. Jacques Cabau, "Le chef et le sorcier," *L'Express*, April 17, 1966, 96–97.

26. Wedgwood, "The Quest for Power."

27. Frenzel and Pross were among the earliest reviewers of *Crowds and Power* in German. Although they praise Canetti's originality and the readable style, emphasizing the theory of command as the most important aspect of the book, they deplore the choice of "Masse" / "Vermassung" as objects of investigation, because they can only generate thought bogged down in cliché. Harry Pross, "Das dümmste Schlagwort des Jahrhunderts," *Süddeutsche Zeitung*, June 15, 1960, and Ivo Frenzel, *Hessischer Rundfunk*, August 14, 1960.

28. See Ernst Fischer, "Anmerkungen zu Ernst Fischers Aufsatz über Elias Canettis Masse und Macht," *Literatur und Kritik* 7, no. 1 (1966): 12–20; Wolfgang Hädecke, "Bemerkungen zu Elias Canettis Masse und Macht," *Literatur und Kritik* 2, no. 20 (1967): 599–610.

29. The conclusion of his review is unequivocal about the book's groundbreaking value as a companion into the twenty-first century: "Für den Eintritt ins neue Zeitalter der Aufklärung, an dessen Schwelle wir uns auf den Ausgang des 20. Jahrhunderts hin befinden, um den 21. den Weg zu bereiten, ist Canettis Buch eine gewichtige Basis" (Canetti's book is a significant basis for entering the new age of the Enlightenment, at the threshold of which we find ourselves at the end of the twentieth century, ready to prepare the way into the twenty-first). Karl Rauch, "Von der Problematik des Befehlens: Zu Elias Canettis Buch über Masse und Macht," *Telegraf* 15, no. 201 (August 28, 1960), 20, my translation.

30. Steiner, "Canetti's Crowd," 87.

31. "Schon wieder in Vergessenheit geraten," quoted in Dieter Dissinger, "Erster Versuch einer Rezeptionsgeschichte Canettis am Beispiel seiner Werke

Die Blendung und *Masse und Macht*," in *Canetti lesen: Erfahrungen mit seinen Büchern*, ed. G. Göpfert (Munich: Carl Hanser, 1975), 103.

32. Werlen, "Destiny's Herald," 172. In support of this claim, Werlen cites an obituary in *Der Spiegel* (August 22, 1994) as echoing a commonly heard judgment after Canetti's death: "He never found his niche or pedestal in German literature of this century. He was too individualistic and also always too demanding to achieve this stature." Quoted in "Destiny's Herald," 173, Werlen's translation.

33. Ibid., 172.

34. "Introduction," *Thesis Eleven* 45 (1996): iii.

35. John McClelland, "The Place of Elias Canetti's *Crowds and Power* in the History of Western Social and Political Thought," *Thesis Eleven* 45 (1996): 16. McClelland continues: "Those of us who first read *Crowds and Power* in the early sixties will never forget the sense of bewilderment that the book caused us. We had no doubt that we had something important in our hands. It sounded a bit oracular at times, but we easily forgave this, because Canetti was offering some kind of original explanation of the great horrifying events of the twentieth century. . . . But the problem still remained of deciding what it was, in general, that Canetti was trying to say. The details of *Crowds and Power* are marvelously clear and direct, and its erudition is part of its charm, but the problem remained of deciding what all the detail added up to? Another way of putting the problem is to say that it was very difficult to decide what subject *Crowds and Power* was part of."

36. Some more recent notable work on Canetti, mostly volumes of collected essays, should be mentioned: Herbert G. Göpfert, ed., *Essays in Honor of Elias Canetti*, trans. Michael Hulse (New York: Farrar, Straus and Giroux, 1987); John Pattillo-Hess, ed., *Canettis Masse und Macht, oder, Die Aufgabe des gegenwärtigen Denkens* (Vienna: Österreichischer Bundesverlag, 1988); Michael Krüger (ed.), *Einladung zur Verwandlung: Essays zu Elias Canettis "Masse und Macht"* (Munich: Hanser, 1995); Judith Veichtlbauer and Penka Angelova, eds., *Pulverfass Balkan: Mythos oder Realität: Internationales Symposium Rousse, Oktober 1998* (Sankt Ingbert: Röhrig Universitätsverlag, 2001); and Kurt Bartsch and Gerhard Melzer, eds., *Elias Canetti* (Graz: Droschl, 2005) (sadly, the bibliography of Bartsch and Melzer, *Elias Canetti*, contains many errors). See also W. C. Donahue, "The End of History: 'Eschatology' in Elias Canetti's Masse und Macht," in *Fin de siècle, fin du millénaire: Endzeitstimmungen in der deutschsprachigen Literatur*, ed. Hans-Jörg Knobloch and Helmut Koopmann (Tübingen: Stauffenburg, 2001), 113–135; and Françoise Kenk, *Elias Canetti: Un auteur énigmatique dans l'histoire intellectuelle; Enquête* (Paris: Harmattan, 2003).

37. McClelland, "The Place of Elias Canetti's *Crowds and Power*," 26.

38. Ibid.

39. Ibid., 21–24.

40. Werlen, "Destiny's Herald," 175.

41. Ibid.

42. Axel Honneth, "The Perpetuation of the State of Nature: On the Cognitive Content of Elias Canetti's *Crowds and Power*," *Thesis Eleven* 45 (1996): 69. I will return to Honneth's article in due time.

43. Ibid., 70 (emphasis added).

44. See Stern, "Canetti's Later Work."

45. Ibid., 244. Stern also formulates questions that refer to other thinkers difficult to situate—for the same or similar reasons—thinkers whose work triggered very different reactions (Nietzsche is a good example). Stern readily acknowledges that such questions as the ones enumerated above are not just "a matter of retrospective criticism but of contemporary concern. Can we really rest content with designating Freud or Lévi-Strauss—or Nietzsche, for that matter—as mythopoeticists?" And then he proceeds with a diagnosis of academic practices: "The uncritical use of 'anthropological' fictions, our heritage from the troubled Twenties and Thirties, has acquired a new academic respectability: then and now we are surrounded by enquiries in which metaphors replace theory and analogies explanation. Anyone intent on doing away with distinctions between fiction and philosophy should read *Crowds and Power* to see what discord follows" (ibid., 246).

46. The interview was published in the 1996 issue of *Thesis Eleven* (on Canetti) mentioned above, under the title "Elias Canetti: Discussion with Theodor W. Adorno."

47. Is this a playful allusion to Rousseau and his barely literate domestic partner Thérèse Levasseur?

48. For a detailed reception history *of Die Blendung* in the first fifty years after its publication, see Dieter Dissinger's essay "Erster Versuch einer Rezeptionsgeschichte Canettis am Beispiel seiner Werke *Die Blendung* und *Masse und Macht*," 90–106, and Herbert G. Göpfert, "The Reception History of *Auto-da-fé*: A Documentation," in Göpfert, *Essays in Honor of Elias Canetti*, 289–297.

49. William Collins Donahue, *The End of Modernism: Elias Canetti's "Auto-da-fe"* (Chapel Hill: University of North Carolina Press, 2001).

50. *MEC*, 545. The ending of this multivolume "comedy" was to have a deeply moral meaning. The characters would end up together in the pavilion ward of an asylum (incidentally, Canetti's apartment overlooked the Steinhof asylum on the outskirts of Vienna), and they would talk to one another: "In their individual isolation, they would find sentences for one another, and these peculiar sentences would have a tremendous *meaning*. It struck me as demeaning them to think of their recovering. None of them was to find his way back to the triviality of everyday life. Any adjustment to us would be tantamount to diminishing them; they were too precious for this because of their unique experiences. On the other hand, their reactions to one another stuck me as sublimely, inexhaustibly valuable. If the speakers of these individual languages had anything to say to one another, anything meaningful for them, then there was still hope for us ordinary people, who lacked the dignity of madness" (*MEC*, 546).

51. "In Kolmar, I spent an entire day in front of the Grünewald altar. I didn't know when I had come, and I didn't know when I would leave. When the museum closed, I wished for invisibility, so that I might spend the night there. I saw Christ's corpse without plaintiveness; the dreadful state of his body struck me as true. Faced with this truth, I realized what had bewildered me about crucifixions: their beauty, their transfiguration. Transfiguration belonged to an angelic concert, not on the cross. The thing that people had turned away from, horrified, in real life, could still be grasped in the painting: a memory of the dreadful things that people do to one another" (*MEC*, 472–473).

52. Werlen, "Destiny's Herald," 173.

53. Canetti, *The Secret Heart of the Clock*, 25.

54. Ibid., 67.

55. I am using here Hayden White's well-known term from *Metahistory: The Historical Imagination in Nineteenth-Century Europe* (Baltimore: Johns Hopkins University Press, 1975).

56. "Que le lecteur se rassure: il est facile, trop facile, d'interpréter Canetti à la lumière de l'Oedipe. Cette relation passionnelle à sa mère, . . . et tant d'inépuisable culpabilité—et tous ces aveugles, ces infirmes qui hantent les abords de l'œuvre, et l'œuvre elle-même. Oui, Canetti est Oedipe, il le sait, il en joue, il en fait un leurre, un miroir aux alouettes: il les voit venir, les analystes. . . . Qui ne reconnaîtrait Freud en l'homme à qui il tire la langue?" Roger Gentis, *La folie Canetti* (Paris: Maurice Nadeau, 1992), 93.

57. See the wonderful article by Jakob Norberg, "The Black Book: Karl Kraus's Etiquette," *Modern Austrian Literature* 40, no. 2 (2007): 45–64.

58. Canetti describes the experience of being in Kraus's audience as a crowd experience; ironically, however, this is a Freudian crowd, mesmerized by a charismatic leader. One enjoyed not only recognizing Kraus's rhetorical strategies—"he supplied both accusations and crushed everyone"—but also "feeling the tremendous resonance known as a crowd, in which one no longer bruises oneself on one's own limits" (*MEC*, 464).

59. As we shall see shortly, Canetti was adamant in his refusal of Freud's theory of sublimation.

60. Peter Gay, *Weimar Culture: The Outsider as Insider* (1968; New York: W. W. Norton, 2001).

61. Grosz, too, offered an interesting account of Berlin life during the same period in his autobiography, first from the perspective of the young caricaturist in his thirties during the Weimar era, and as he moved to America in January 1933, a few days only before Hitler's appointment as chancellor of Germany. In America he becomes very critical of the brand of satire he had practiced in Berlin, so he made conscious efforts to give up his "European arrogance" in favor of an "American superiority": "Unfortunately I myself was merely one of those puffed up frogs instead of a normal illustrator, and my drawings were caricatures of a slanted, crooked world, seen and interpreted from the pseudo-scientific viewpoint of Marxism and Freudianism. That stuff, I felt, belonged to the past; and had the Germans not burnt it, I myself might have heaped it up and put a match to it." George Grosz, *Ein kleines Ja und ein grosses Nein* (1946); quoted from the English edition, *George Grosz, an Autobiography*, trans. Nora Hodges (New York: Macmillan, 1983), 253.

62. See Helmut Lethen's *Cool Conduct: The Culture of Distance in Weimar Germany* (2002; California Scholarship Online, 2012), and, from his sources, Helmuth Plessner's *Grenzen der Gemeinschaft: Eine Kritik des sozialen Radikalismus* (1924; English translation, *The Limits of Community: A Critique of Social Radicalism*, trans. and intro. Andrew Wallace [New York: Humanity Books, 1999]).

63. Ironically, Canetti's evocation of English mores in *Party in the Blitz*, to which I will turn shortly, would sound like paraphrases of Plessner's prescriptions. See Canetti, *Party in the Blitz: The English Years* (New York: New Directions, 2005).

64. "Most important for him was that he could tell me, in *his* Berlin, about his innocent ways, his love for his youth, and that I listened" (*MEC*, 511).

65. "Gegen diese vereinte Not und Bedrängnis durch Namen setzte ich jeden Menschen, der keinen hatte, jeden Namens-Armen." Elias Canetti, *Die Fackel im Ohr: Lebensgeschichte 1921–1931* (Munich: Hanser, 1993), 336.

66. Canetti uses the word *Macht* (as in the title *Masse und Macht* [*Crowds and Power*]), which refers not to the capacity or skill to speak, to articulate (*Ausdrucksfähigkeit*), but to the power he sees as inherent to communication.

67. Canetti, *Party in the Blitz*, 14.

68. Ibid.

69. Ibid., 20–21 and 14–15, respectively.

70. Canetti's wife, Veza, wrote a wonderful novel (only published posthumously) about a couple who, like themselves, have to flee the Nazi occupation. A remarkable piece of writing in its own right, *The Tortoises* is a very moving companion to Canetti's writings, not least because she muses on the tribulations of an exiled writer: "It is the poet who is hardest hit of all. The language is his soul, the characters he creates are his body. He can draw breath only where his language is alive, and where he no longer understands and is not understood his life is extinguished" (ibid., 20). Her heroine, the thoughtful Eva, gives us a different perspective on England (than the one Canetti provides in *Party in the Blitz*); for her, the English temperament is precisely the opposite of the stifling atmosphere under Nazi occupation. She anticipates eagerly and somewhat incredulously their departure with thoughts of a regained freedom and a dignified life:

> In England, they will collect themselves. There, people are serious and one can find one's true self.
>
> How she longs here for the English character, which is so scoffed at. Because these are people who never lose control. They are a people isolated from the rest of the world on an island. Her heart becomes light; these people are as if chosen. They whisper rather than talk. They bestow smiles rather than praise. Civility is ingrained in them and is a part of their beauty. The women walk as if on soft carpets, they hold their heads proudly, but there is graciousness in their eyes. It is difficult here to imagine that a country exists where they want to dig flowerbeds, and not graves.

Veza Canetti, *Die Schildkröten* (1999); *The Tortoises*, trans. Ian Mitchell (New York: New Directions, 2001), 58.

71. Canetti, *Party in the Blitz*, 15.

72. Canetti, *Kafka's Other Trial*, 48.

73. Ibid.

74. What Canetti has to say about children in *Crowds and Power* speaks to this quite eloquently: "The depth of the impression which commands make on children and the tenacity and fidelity with which they are preserved owe nothing to the qualities of the individual child; intelligence or exceptional gifts have nothing to do with it. No child, not even the most ordinary, forgets or forgives a single one of the commands inflicted on it" (*CP*, 306). Archetypically a relationship of unconditional mutual love, on Canetti's unforgiving account the mother-child rapport is one in which the mother "domesticates" the command by nurturing the child: "In the three basic relationships I have cited a kind of bribery is practiced:

a master feeds his slave or his dog and a mother her child. . . . Domesticating the command means linking it with a promise of food" (*CP*, 307).

75. Canetti, *Kafka's Other Trial*, 110.

76. This is a quote from Christian Dietrich Grabbe's *Hannibal* ("Ja, aus der Welt werden wir nicht fallen. Wir sind einmal darin") that Freud uses in the opening of *Civilization and Its Discontents* to support his point that the "oceanic feeling" invoked by his friend Romain Roland has to be intellectualized, accounted for in terms of something in this world, without recourse to the metaphysical (i.e., religion). Sigmund Freud, *Civilization and Its Discontents* (New York: W. W. Norton, 1962), 11.

77. Cf. Ludwig Wittgenstein, *Philosophical Investigations: The German Text with a Revised English Translation: German Text, with a Revised English Translation*, trans. G. E. M. Anscombe, 3rd ed. (Malden: Wiley-Blackwell, 2001), no. 18. "Our language may be seen as an ancient city: a maze of little streets and squares, of old and new houses, and of houses with additions from various periods; and this surrounded by a multitude of new boroughs with straight regular streets and uniform houses."

78. "In the most diverse, seemingly farfetched ways, I tried to approach what I had experienced as a crowd. I sought crowds in history, in the histories of all civilizations" (*MEC*, 490). "I wanted to find testimony to the existence and effect of crowds in all realms of life" (*MEC*, 491).

79. With this allusion I am loosely assuming here a tension between the ideas on language in Wittgenstein's *Philosophical Investigations*, and in Derrida's so-called deconstruction, for instance in "Signature Event Context," in *Limited Inc.*, trans. Samuel Weber and Jeffrey Mehlman (Evanston, Ill.: Northwestern University Press, 1988), 1–23. See the essay by Toril Moi, "'They Practice Their Trades in Different Worlds': Concepts in Poststructuralism and Ordinary Language Philosophy," *New Literary History* 40, no. 4 (autumn 2009): 801–824.

80. Wittgenstein, *Philosophical Investigations*, no. 240 onward.

81. "In my isolation at the edge of the city, an isolation that I had good reasons for seeking and to which I own what little my years in Vienna produced, I remained in contact—even unwillingly—with that most urgent, most unsettled, most enigmatic phenomenon. At times that I did not choose myself, it talked away at me, forcing me back to my project, which I might have escaped by seeking refuge in more comfortable problems" (*MEC*, 493).

82. See Robert Gibbs, *Correlations in Rosenzweig and Levinas* (Princeton, N.J.: Princeton University Press, 1992).

83. His lack of interest in singularity also situates his crowd theories in tension with the notion of "multitude" that more recent thinkers like Paolo Virno and Michael Hardt and Toni Negri borrow from Spinoza. See Paolo Virno, *A Grammar of the Multitude: For an Analysis of Contemporary Forms of Life* (New York: Semiotext(e), 2004); Michael Hardt and Antonio Negri, *Multitude: War and Democracy in the Age of Empire* (New York: Penguin Random House, 2005). Strikingly, Canetti has a vested interest in the leaderless crowd, like these thinkers, but his critique of (what might be summarized as) authenticity prevents him from paying attention to the individuality of the group members.

84. I borrow the title of this section from Stanley Cavell's wonderful essay "The Avoidance of Love: A Reading of King Lear," in *Must We Mean What We*

Say? A Book of Essays, updated ed. (Cambridge: Cambridge University Press, 2002), 267–357. I will however content myself to allude to Cavell's focus on blindness in Shakespeare's play, which speaks to Canetti's use of blindness—both a literal and a metaphorical use—in *Die Blendung* and in his own reflections on *King Lear* in his diary *The Secret Heart of the Clock*, 62–64.

85. This is not unlike biblical descriptions of hell, pictured in terms of physical torments which are in fact allegories of psychological suffering.

86. Cf. Deleuze and Guattari's distinction between the aims of philosophy (elaboration of concepts) and those of literature (production of affect) in *What Is Philosophy?* (New York: Columbia University Press, 1996). If Canetti invents a new language for describing crowds and power, it is a language of metaphors that the *Dichter* puts at the disposal of the moralist.

87. Canetti shows in some detail that Freud had "no useful tools for his enterprise," having spent his life pursuing lengthy treatments of his patients in a medical office. His source for the description of the crowd, Canetti points out when summarizing the beginning of *Group Psychology and the Analysis of the Ego*, was Le Bon (who was influenced by Taine's *History of the French Revolution* and who "recalled the early working-class movement and probably the Paris Commune as well") and his own distasteful experience of the crowd when he was almost sixty and he witnessed the war enthusiasm in Vienna. Here too Canetti is quick to point that there are more than one varieties of crowds: "Understandably, he defended himself against this sort of crowd, which I, too, had known as a child" (*MEC*, 407).

88. "As you speak of Freud—I am the first to admit that the innovative way in which Freud approached things, without allowing himself to be distracted or frightened, made a deep impression on me in my formative period. It is certainly the case that I am now no longer convinced of some of his results and must oppose some of his special theories. But for the way he tackled things, I still have the deepest respect." "Elias Canetti: Discussion with Theodor W. Adorno," *Thesis Eleven* 45 (1996): 1–2.

89. Freud, *Civilization and Its Discontents*, 12. This is exactly what Canetti reproached him with, the absence of *recognition* of the crowd phenomenon in *Group Psychology*.

90. Theodor W. Adorno, "Freudian Theory and the Pattern of Fascist Propaganda," in *The Culture Industry: Selected Essays on Mass Culture*, Routledge Classics (New York: Routledge, 2001), 140–141.

91. Ibid., 141.

92. I am referring to Lionel Trilling, *Sincerity and Authenticity* (Cambridge, Mass.: Harvard University Press, 1972), and Robert Pippin, *Modernism as a Philosophical Problem: On the Dissatisfactions of European High Culture*, 2nd ed. (Malden, Mass.: Blackwell, 1999). For authenticity as narcissism see, among others, Charles Taylor, *The Ethics of Authenticity* (Cambridge, Mass.: Harvard University Press, 1992). An interesting partner in this conversation might be the graphic artist George Grosz, who claimed in his autobiography that in America, "I lost my European arrogance, or rather I traded it for what I thought was American superiority" (Grosz, *George Grosz, an Autobiography*, 250).

93. Freud, *Civilization and Its Discontents*, 49.

94. "A company of porcupines crowded themselves very close together one cold winter's day so as to profit one another's warmth and so save themselves

from being frozen to death. But soon they felt one another's quills, which induced them to separate again. And now, when the need for warmth brought them nearer together again, the second evil arose once more. So that they were driven backwards and forwards from one trouble to the other, until they had discovered a mean distance at which they could most tolerably exist." Schopenhauer, *Parerga and Paralipomena*, part 2, 31, "Gleichnisse und Parabeln," quoted in Sigmund Freud, *Group Psychology and the Analysis of the Ego*, trans. James Strachey (New York: Bantam Books, 1965), 41n1.

95. Ibid., 43.

96. Ibid.

97. Ibid., 43.

98. I am here in partial agreement with Axel Honneth, who attributes the strength of Canetti's theory to "the great distance Canetti maintains to every psychoanalytic attempt to explain the crowd phenomenon," but that he also "has to pay a not inconsiderable price for the attempt to achieve a cognitive gain by means of reduction of the object." Honneth shows that "what remains, as it were, of the Freudian structural model in his approach is only the "id" and the "ego"; in addition to the "ego ideals," the "superego" has thus also disappeared from the human person, so that the latter is left in the end without a trace of those sanctioning emotions which Freud comprehended as the outcome of moral learning. That is why the subjects with which Canetti reckons in his crowd analysis possess, in short, neither moral feelings nor even moral beliefs" (Honneth, "The Perpetuation of the State of Nature," 77). If there is no superego, it seems unlikely that there would be an ego, since the latter emerges from the confrontation of the id with reality, internalized as the superego. This suggests that the comparison with Freud is productive only to the extent that we accept that people, as Canetti sees and pictures them, are fundamentally incomplete (the "names" in Berlin "striking at others with themselves" are a case in point). Honneth is right to say that by depriving individuals of a superego, Canetti deprives his crowd-theory of a fundamental aspect that Freud did not neglect, namely the role of moral ideals and feelings in the formation of a crowd (leading to a revolution or to a strike, for example). But this only shows, however disappointing it may sound, that Canetti was ultimately not interested in the real, specifically historical crowd ("I knew I would never need to read anything about the French revolution"), but rather in the imaginary investments of a crowd and its potential to redeem the social. I would also add that the absence of an ego ideal makes the leader irrelevant to the formation of a crowd—an important point to Canetti—but the question how certain crowds come to be manipulated by charismatic figures is not one that he cares to address, except to say that the leader communicates with only one member of the crowd, who then relays the message horizontally; due to the proverbial "quickness of crowds," what is communicated then reverberates throughout the multitude.

99. Derived from Plautus, *Asinaria* II, iv, 88.

100. Freud, *Civilization and Its Discontents*, 69–70.

101. Ibid., 112.

102. "Sehr leicht wandelt einen Europäer ein Gefühl von Erhabenheit ein, wenn er Berichte wie die folgenden auf sich wirken lässt. Es ist aber ratsam, sich in einiger Bescheidenheit zu gedulden, bis man mehr über sie erfahren hat. Es steht dem Europäer des 20. Jahrhunderts schlecht an, sich über Barbarei erhaben

zu dünken. Die Mittel seiner Machthaber mögen wirksamer sein. Ihre Absichten unterscheiden sich oft in nichts von denen afrikanischer Könige." Elias Canetti, *Masse und Macht* (1960; reprint, Munich: C. Hanser, [1994]), 487.

103. Jürgen Kocka, "Ursachen des Nationalsozialismus," *Aus Politik und Zeitgeschichte* 25, no. 80 (June 21, 1980): 11.

104. David Blackbourn and Geoff Eley, *Mythen deutscher Geschichtsschreibung: Die gescheiterte bürgerliche Revolution von 1848* (Berlin: Ullstein, 1980).

105. David Blackbourn and Geoff Eley, *The Peculiarities of German History: Bourgeois Society and Politics in Nineteenth-Century Germany* (Oxford: Oxford University Press, 1984). For a detailed overview of these positions and the controversy aroused by this book see Geoff Eley, *From Unification to Nazism: Reinterpreting the German Past* (Boston: Allen & Unwin, 1986), especially chap. 10, "What Produces Fascism: Pre-Industrial Traditions or a Crisis of the Capitalist State?," 254–283.

106. "This generation remembered the war as the great prelude to the breakdown of classes and their transformation into masses. War . . . became the symbol for death, the great equalizer and therefore the true father of a new world order." Hannah Arendt, *The Origins of Totalitarianism* (1948; reprint, San Diego: Harcourt, 1994), 239. See also David Roberts's article "Crowds and Power or the Natural History of Modernity: Horkheimer, Adorno, Canetti, Arendt," in *Thesis Eleven*, 39–68.

107. Ibid., 465–466.

108. Ibid.

109. As he appears in the writings of Paul Celan, Jacques Derrida, Primo Levi, and others.

110. Emmanuel Levinas makes the same move in *Autrement qu'être ou au-delà de l'essence*, which he dedicates to the millions of Jews killed by National Socialists, but then warns against Zionist violence ("This is the image of the usurpation of the entire earth"), figuring the Jew both as victim and perpetrator. Emmanuel Levinas, *Autrement qu'être ou Au-delà de l'essence* (1974; reprint, Paris: Le Livre de Poche, 2004). Judith Butler discusses Levinas's gesture in "Ethical Ambivalence," in *The Turn to Ethics*, ed. Marjorie B. Garber, Beatrice Hanssen, and Rebecca L. Walkowitz (New York: Routledge, 2000), 15–29.

111. Murdoch, *Existentialists and Mystics*, 191.

112. Ibid.

113. By contrast, Canetti enjoins, "you have to imagine this city with its coffeehouses and their floods of I-talk, protestation, confession and self-assertion. All these people were bursting with self-pity and self-importance. They all lamented, bellowed and trumpeted. But all banded together in small groups, because they needed and tolerated each other for their talk. Everything was discussed, the newspapers provided the main topic of conversation. This was a time when a great deal was happening and when people sensed that much more was *in the offing*" (*MEC*, 686).

Chapter 3

An abbreviated version of this chapter appeared in *Modern Language Notes* 129, no. 5 (2014): 1170–1198.

1. This novel was read by most critics in light of, and in line with, the Angry Young Men's novels of the 1950s.

2. As against, so the argument goes, the identity politics and charisma implicit in Foucault's ethos. See Amanda Anderson, *The Powers of Distance: Cosmopolitanism and the Cultivation of Detachment* (Princeton, N.J.: Princeton University Press, 2001), and *The Way We Argue Now: A Study in the Cultures of Theory* (Princeton, N.J.: Princeton University Press, 2006).

3. And he continues: "It is no wonder that friendship has been relegated to private life and thereby weakened in comparison to what it once was. . . . Indeed from an Aristotelian point of view a modern liberal political society can appear only as a collection of citizens of nowhere who have banded together for their common protection. They possess at best that inferior form of friendship which is founded on mutual advantage," says MacIntyre referring to the different forms of friendship identified by Aristotle in *The Nicomachean Ethics*. Alasdair C. MacIntyre, *After Virtue: A Study in Moral Theory* (Notre Dame, Ind.: University of Notre Dame Press, 2003), 156.

4. Geoffrey Bennington, *Interrupting Derrida* (New York: Routledge, 2000), 112.

5. Jacques Derrida, *Politics of Friendship*, trans. George Collins (New York: Verso, 2005), 252.

6. A conspicuous absence among Barthes's references is Kant. Given Barthes's unsystematic treatment of his topics, this is hardly surprising; but the reader familiar with *The Metaphysics of Morals* will readily recall his treatment of love and friendship in "On the Most Intimate Union of Love with Respect in Friendship." In the penultimate chapter of *Politics of Friendship*, Derrida discusses this text at some length (253 ff.).

7. Roland Barthes, *Sade, Fourier, Loyola* (Paris: Éditions du Seuil, 1970), 174, quoted in *CVE* (170) and in *N* (58). The marquis plays on the double meaning of the French *linge*, "linen" and "underwear." "Un principe de délicatesse" has here the sense of a capacity to make fine distinctions.

8. Yet again this brings to mind Cavell, now with his discussion in *Must We Mean What We Say?* of the meaning of "attunement" (*übereinstimmen*) in Wittgenstein's *Philosophical Investigations*.

9. In *The Highest Poverty*, Giorgio Agamben corroborates and expands on many of the points about coenobitic life that Barthes contents himself to make in passing. "It can appear surprising," he opens §1.4, "that the monastic ideal, born as an individual and solitary flight from the world, should have given origin to a model of total communitarian life." Relying on Cassian's text *Cenobitic Institutions*, he compares Aristotle's polis and the monastery (they both have the "perfect life" as their goal), and then spells out the important difference between a monastery and cenoby: "In the *Conlationes* (or *Conferences*), Cassian therefore distinguishes the monastery from cenoby, because a monastery 'is the name of the residence and does not imply more than the place where the monks live. "House of cenobites" points to the character and the way of life of the profession. The residence of a simple monk can be called a monastery. But a place cannot be termed a house of cenobites unless one means a community of many people living together [*plurimorum cohabitantium . . . unita communio*]' (Cassian 2, pp. 22/191). Cenoby does not name only a place, but first of all a form of life" (§1.

Birth of the Rule, 1.4). Giorgio Agamben, *The Highest Poverty: Monastic Rules and Form-of-Life* (Stanford, Calif.: Stanford University Press, 2013).

10. Claude Coste, "Présentation," in *CVE*, 25.

11. "Never forget, in any use of the word, to connect criticism and crisis: criticism (literary, in particular), aims to put in crisis," he adds (*CVE*, 179).

12. Barthes's note reads: "Hupar (grec): vision qu'on a étant éveillé" (Hupar (Greek): vision that one has while awake). My translation.

13. Fiche 64: "Pathos: c'est en somme l'Imaginaire (affectif)." Barthes's note: "Pathos: it is after all the [affective] Imaginary." My translation.

14. Sophia (grec): savoir, sagesse pratique, puis sagesse. Barthes's note: "Sophia (Greek): knowledge, practical wisdom, then wisdom." My translation.

15. To the extent that there is community in Nietzsche, Eugene Goodheart reminds us, it is the utopia of "an anti-community of artists, each creating his own world of beauty and power, which he governs with absolute authority." Eugene Goodheart, *The Skeptic Disposition: Deconstruction, Ideology, and Other Matters* (Princeton, N.J.: Princeton University Press, 1984), 82. In this sense, his impressions of Venice are quite telling: "Hundreds of profound lonelinesses together form the city of Venice: this is its charm, a picture for the men of the future." Ibid. quoted in Karl Jaspers, *Nietzsche: An Introduction to the Understanding of His Philosophical Activity* (Tucson: University of Arizona Press, 1965), 283.

16. Iris Murdoch, *The Bell* (1958; reprint, Harmondsworth, U.K.: Penguin, 1999), 71. Hereafter cited parenthetically as *B*.

17. Murdoch, "Against Dryness," in Murdoch, *Existentialists and Mystics*, 287. The same essay elaborates on her discontent with the contemporary state of affairs in philosophy: "What have we lost here? And what have we perhaps never had? We have suffered a general loss of concepts, the loss of a moral and political vocabulary. We no longer use a spread-out substantial picture of the manifold virtues of man and society. We no longer see man against a background of values, realities, which transcend him. We picture man as a brave naked will surrounded by an easily comprehended empirical world. For the hard idea of truth we have substituted a facile idea of sincerity. What we have never had, of course, is a satisfactory Liberal theory of personality, a theory of man as free and separate and related to a rich and complicated world from which, as a moral being, he has much to learn. We have bought the Liberal theory as it stands, because we have wished to encourage people to think of themselves as free, at the cost of surrendering the background" (ibid., 290).

18. Murdoch quoted in W. K. Rose, "An Interview with Iris Murdoch," *Shenandoah* 19 (winter 1968): 5.

19. MacIntyre, *After Virtue*, 163.

20. Iris Murdoch's biographer Peter Conradi shows, for instance, how the geography of Imber Court is indebted to Plato and Dante, and he analyzes the novel's Platonism, focusing mostly on Michael. David Beams sees this novel as an allegory, linking Dora to the New Testament as grace supplanting the Old Testament law. Elizabeth Dipple emphasizes the divide between the community's regulations and its self-centered members with their repressed sexuality. G. S. Fraser, one of the early commentators on the novel, sets in contrast the enduring convent and the amateurish community at Imber Court, showing that

the latter "expires of unreality." In the same vein Albert Gérard is critical of the "prideful refusal" of the community members to recognize the existence of others, and James Hall claims that Dora exposes the hypocrisy of the community, while also showing the value of trying for goodness. And so on. Multiplying critical examples would only add variations to what I see as a common trend in the readings of this novel, namely, an emphasis on individual plot elements or characters to the detriment of the community as a project. See Peter Conradi, *Iris Murdoch: The Saint and the Artist* (New York: HarperCollins, 2001); David Beams, "The Fortunate Fall: Three Actions in *The Bell*," *Twentieth Century Literature* 34, no. 4 (1988): 416–433; Elizabeth Dipple, *Iris Murdoch: Work for the Spirit* (London: Methuen, 1982); G. S. Fraser, "Iris Murdoch and the Solidity of the Normal," *International Literary Annual*, no. 2 (1959): 37–54; Albert Gérard, "Iris Murdoch," *La revue nouvelle*, no. 39 (June 1964): 640–663; James Hall, "Blurring the Will: The Growth of Iris Murdoch," *ELH* 32 (June 1965): 256–273.

21. Antonia Susan Byatt, *Degrees of Freedom: The Novels of Iris Murdoch* (London: Chatto and Windus, 1965), 73–105, here 73.

22. See, for instance, Michael Levenson, "Iris Murdoch: The Philosophic Fifties and *The Bell*," *Modern Fiction Studies* 47, no. 3 (fall 2001): 558–579.

23. Iris Murdoch's philosophical essays were edited by Peter Conradi (also her biographer, and author of a wonderful critical study of her fiction, *Iris Murdoch: The Saint and the Artist*) in Murdoch, *Existentialists and Mystics*, which includes many of her early essays as well as the three more famous pieces collected in the shorter volume *The Sovereignty of Good* (London: Routledge, 1970). Murdoch's more mature philosophical work was published in *Metaphysics as a Guide to Morals*, first given as the Gifford Lectures. For a contextualization of her philosophical ideas, see Michael Levenson's article "Iris Murdoch: The Philosophic Fifties and *The Bell*."

24. See for instance her essays "The Sublime and the Beautiful Revisited" and "Vision and Choice in Morality," both in *Existentialists and Mystics*.

25. "Metaphysics and Ethics," in Murdoch, *Existentialists and Mystics*, 72. This mode of evaluation is not only characteristic of ordinary language philosophers, but also Murdoch suggests, corresponds to a typically English mentality: "The logical formula presented by the modern moral philosopher is on the whole a satisfactory representation of the morality most commonly held in England. The simplest moral words ('good' and 'right') are selected for analysis, their meaning is divided into a descriptive and an evaluative part, the descriptive part representing the factual criteria, the evaluative part representing a recommendation. And once the largely empirical disagreements about application of principles and classification of cases have been cleared up, ultimate moral differences will show as differences of choice and recommendation in a common world of facts. What the modern moral philosopher has done is what metaphysicians in the past have always done. He has produced a model. Only it is not a model of any morality whatsoever. It is a model of his own morality" (ibid., 67).

26. "The Idea of Perfection," in Murdoch, *The Sovereignty of Good*, 13.

27. Murdoch, *Existentialists and Mystics*, 269. I might add here that this broad opposition is still relevant in the moral philosophy of the past decades, liberalism vs. communitarianism; in religious ethics as autonomy vs. situatedness. See Maria

Antonaccio, *Picturing the Human: The Moral Thought of Iris Murdoch* (Oxford: Oxford University Press, 2000).

28. Murdoch, *Existentialists and Mystics*, 268 (my italics), 269–270.

29. Ibid., 72–73. Broadening the field and vocabulary of moral philosophy is something contemporary philosophers have given Murdoch credit for. Charles Taylor, for instance, opens the first chapter of *Sources of the Self* with an outline of his project of displacing and broadening the framework of inquiry from a rule-based morality to an ethics that pays heed to broader considerations, and mentions Iris Murdoch as a model: "Much contemporary moral philosophy, particularly but not only in the English-speaking world, has given such a narrow focus to morality that some of the crucial connections I want to draw here are incomprehensible in its terms. This moral philosophy has tended to focus on what it is right to do rather than on what it is good to be, on defining the content of obligation rather than the nature of the good life; and it has no conceptual place left for a notion of the good as the object of our love or allegiance or, as Iris Murdoch portrayed it in her work, as the privileged focus of attention or will." Charles Taylor, *Sources of The Self: The Making of the Modern Identity* (Cambridge, Mass.: Harvard University Press, 1989), 3. Many other contemporary philosophers have engaged Murdoch's thought and given her credit for the depth of her insights and the relevance—today, still—of her critiques and positions. Maria Antonaccio's *Picturing the Human* is an in-depth assessment of her philosophical writings. See also the essays by Charles Taylor, Cora Diamond, Elizabeth Dipple, Stanley Hauerwas, William Schweiker, and Martha Nussbaum in Maria Antonaccio and William Schweiker, eds., *Iris Murdoch and the Search for Human Goodness* (Chicago: University of Chicago Press, 1996). Moral philosopher Susan Wolf prefaced her 1990 book *Freedom within Reason* with the acknowledgment that "P. F. Strawson's 'Freedom and Resentment' and Iris Murdoch's *The Sovereignty of Good* were immeasurably important in focusing my interest in and shaping the views on freedom and responsibility that are developed here." Susan R. Wolf, *Freedom within Reason* (New York: Oxford University Press, 1990), ix.

30. Murdoch, "Vision and Choice in Morality," 87.

31. Inspired by an episode in chapter 34 of *Histoire lausiaque*, Barthes discusses this type of character under the heading "Éponge" (sponge). The term refers to the derogatory phrase "l'éponge du couvent" (the sponge of the monastery), which identifies a nun who is exploited and marginalized in the monastery and who disappears when through a turn of events she is heralded at the local saint. For Barthes the sponge represents a fascinating element in any community—more interesting in the fantasy of community is not whom it includes, he says, but whom it excludes (*CVE*, 119). "C'est le statut contradictoire du paria: rejeté et intégré, intégré comme déchet. Peut-être pas de communauté sans déchet intégré" (It is the contradictory status of the pariah: rejected and integrated, integrated as residue) (ibid.). Three pages later, Barthes makes some precisions that describe the paradox of the integrated reject in terms of an immunization dispositif (familiar to readers of Roberto Esposito): "Point sur lequel la communauté fixe la maladie . . . et de la sorte l'exorcise, s'en débarrasse. J'intègre l'anomique en codant sa place d'anomique. Je le récupère à une place sans danger = ce que fait le pouvoir, s'il est astucieux, avec les marginalités" (A point to which the community

attaches illness . . . and thus exorcises it, gets rid of it. I integrate the lawless encoding its place as anomie. I recuperate it in a safe place = this is what power does, if it is clever, with marginalities) (ibid., 122). For a comprehensive treatment of this figure, see Goh, *The Reject.*

32. The most obvious example here can be lifted from Murdoch's essay "The Idea of Perfection": M, a mother initially disappointed by her son's choice of a wife, gradually comes to change her opinion about her daughter-in-law, and to see her in a different light without the former having actually changed. What has prompted the alteration of vision is M's willingness to be just and loving, her attention to the reality of the other person, rather than to her own prejudice (17ff.). The central concept of morality, Murdoch proposes later, is the "'individual' thought of as knowable by love" (*Sovereignty*, 30).

33. Quoted in Roland Barthes, *Le discours amoureux: Séminaire à l'école pratique des hautes études, 1974–1976*, ed. Claude Coste (Paris: Seuil, 2007), 523 (my translation).

34. "Without showing it, Michael was immensely touched and a little rueful about the boy's evident admiration for him. Toby saw him as a spiritual leader. While knowing how distorted this picture was, yet Michael could not help catching, from the transfigured image of himself in the boy's imagination, an invigorating sense of possibility. He was not done for yet, not by any means" (*B*, 139).

35. Barthes then mentions some of the rules of distance meant to prevent eroticism in coenobitic communities, as he finds them in the writings of Pacôme de Tabennensis, the founder of coenobitism. These "propedeutic rules for channeling desire" are very detailed in their attention to the "isolated body, minutely enveloped in distance" ("Distance," in *CVE*, 110–113).

36. Tact, Stanley Cavell reminded his students in a spring 2010 seminar at Duke University, is not avoidance; enumerating instances of tact in the activity of the surgeon, the pianist, the parent raising a child, the jeweler polishing a diamond, he reluctantly defined it as "the application of a tremendous amount of force with a tremendous amount of precision." This would be a compelling articulation of the power of the Abbess, which Michael can only intuit.

37. Reading the novel in light of Barthes's *dossiers*, it is possible to see in Nick the integrated reject whose suicide exposes the community as an exclusionary one, and thus unworks its project as one unselfconsciously pursuing a certain commonality. In Nick's death, the community confronts its limit; paradoxically, it becomes a more authentic community (this time in Nancy's sense of an inoperative community) when it disbands.

38. To follow up on my previous note: Michael's recognition of the debt he should have recognized toward Nick changes fundamentally the notion of community at work here: from one conceived around something in common to a sense of debt as a founding principle (see Roberto Esposito's emphasis on the etymology of the *munus* as law and debt in *Terms of the Political*).

39. Iris Murdoch, "The Sublime and the Beautiful Revisited," first published in *Yale Review* (December 1959), reprinted in Murdoch, *Existentialists and Mystics*, 261–287.

40. See C. Fred Alford, "Emmanuel Levinas and Iris Murdoch: Ethics as Exit?," *Philosophy and Literature* 26 (2002): 24–42.

41. "After Nick's death, he was for a long time quite unable to pray. He felt indeed as if his belief in God had been broken at a single blow, or as if he had discovered that he had never believed. He absorbed himself so utterly, so desperately, in the thought of Nick that even to think about God seemed an intrusion, an absurdity. . . . He thought of religion as something far away, something into which he had never really penetrated at all. He vaguely remembered that he had had emotions, experiences, hopes; but real faith in God was something utterly remote from all that. He understood that at last, and felt, almost coldly, the remoteness. *The pattern which he had seen in his life had existed only in his own romantic imagination. At the human level there was no pattern.* 'For as the heavens are higher than the earth, so are my ways higher than your ways and my thoughts than your thoughts.' And as he felt, bitterly, the grimness of these words, he put it to himself: there is a God, but I do not believe in Him" (*B*, 288–289, my italics). Whether this estrangement from religious belief is permanent or not remains an open question; what seems to matter is that it helps Michael to gain a new awareness of fellow human beings.

42. Iris Murdoch, "On God and Good," in *The Sovereignty of Good* (London: Routledge, 1970), 67.

43. My italics. As an example, she adds: "Repentance may mean something different to an individual at different times in his life, and what it fully means is a part of this life and cannot be understood except in context." Murdoch, "The Idea of Perfection," in *The Sovereignty of Good*, 26.

44. Ibid., 29.

45. There might be a finer line than already acknowledged between Levinas's claim that metaphysics precedes ontology (especially if one tries to imagine how it could be translated into a living ethical practice) and Murdoch's idea, developed especially in the later work (the Gifford lectures), of metaphysics as *a guide* to morals. In an essay published in 1957 already, entitled "Metaphysics and Ethics," she begins her critique of contemporary moral philosophy for its elimination of metaphysics from ethics, on the ground that "if we cannot establish transcendent metaphysical structures by philosophical argument then such structures cannot be the basis of ethics"; in Murdoch's view, "this is not yet to say that the notion of *belief* in the transcendent can have no place in a philosophical account of morality." Murdoch, "On God and Good," 65. In "On 'God' and 'Good,'" she proposes that one needs to imagine other methods for channeling spiritual energy on the religious model of prayer directed to God as a source of power which has, for the believer, real meaning. Some alternatives in a secular world might include the contemplation of art, the company of good persons or focus on the idea of goodness itself.

46. Murdoch, "The Idea of Perfection," 37.

47. "Do I not know that in the realm of the subject, there is no referent?" Barthes, *Roland Barthes par Roland Barthes*, 60 (my translation). Murdoch's critical essay "Derrida and Poststructuralism" is part of her Gifford Lectures, published as *Metaphysics as a Guide to Morals* (185–217).

48. Murdoch, "Mass, Might and Myth," *The Spectator* (September 1962), republished in Murdoch, *Existentialists and Mystics*, 191.

49. Interview with Bryan Magee in Murdoch, *Existentialists and Mystics*, 15.

50. Murdoch, "Vision and Choice in Morality," 90–91.

Introduction to Part II

1. Fredric Jameson, "Prussian Blues," *London Review of Books* 18, no. 20 (October 17, 1996): 3–7.

2. Martin Heidegger, *Being and Time*, trans. John Macquarrie and Edward Robinson, with a new foreword by Taylor Carman (New York: Harper Perennial, 2008), 141–142.

3. Ibid., 166. The notion of *das Man* is one of the ways Heidegger marks his distance from the Cartesian ego: the "I" in Descartes's sense manifests itself in an ontic sense, whereas the subject of everyday Dasein in the ontological sense central to Heidegger's philosophical project is "the they" [*das Man*]. If *das Man* is explicitly an existential (an ontological category, in which all others—past, present, and future—are congealed without differentiation), *distantiality*, the performance of difference in the realm of everyday life, appears more problematically to point both to an existential (an ontological difference) and to an existential (an ontic actualization).

4. Ibid., 163–164. One of the striking characteristics of everyday Dasein is its inauthenticity (it is alienated from Being to the point where "Dasein itself is not"); it has what Heidegger calls a "pre-ontological" understanding of Being. The paradox is that this pre-ontological understanding should become the point of departure of his ontology.

5. Ibid., 211.

6. Ibid., 219. I believe this passage puts in perspective the stark contrast that some of Heidegger's readers have established between *"the they"* and distantiality, where *das Man* is understood as the set of norms we belong to, and *Abständigkeit* as the differences that set us apart. See, for example, David Egan, "*Das Man* and Distantiality in *Being and Time*," *Inquiry* 55, no. 3 (June 2012): 289–306. On one hand, *das Man* is described as public and anonymous, thus lacking particularity; on the other, as this passage suggests, it is possible to experience "being-with-one-another in the 'they,' " which puts that competitive and suspicious tinge characteristic of distantiality on what would otherwise remain impersonal. In other words, I see *das Man* not simply as another word for inherited doxa (popular beliefs, what *one says*, what *one does*, which refers to the lowercase *man* in German, "one" in English, *on* in French), which it certainly is, but also referring more generally to an unexamined mode of life driven by a strictly pragmatic concern with externalities, untroubled by questions that transcend the mundane.

7. Ibid., 216.

8. Ibid., 217.

9. Jameson, "Prussian Blues."

10. Heidegger, *Being and Time*, 167.

11. Both Ernaux and Grass have expressed affinities with the work of Pierre Bourdieu: Ernaux has often described how the latter's sociological analyses gave legitimacy to her experiences, thus symbolically authorizing her writing, while Grass talked about his appreciation for Bourdieu's work, pointing to similarities between *La misère du monde* and his own *Mein Jahrhundert*. I will return to these points shortly.

12. Nancy, *Being Singular Plural*, 9.

13. Heidegger, *Being and Time*, 154.

14. Nancy, *Being Singular Plural*, 11.

15. Heidegger, *Being and Time*, 216–217.

16. Nancy, *Being Singular Plural*, 19.

17. Ibid., 20. This ties into Nancy's critique of *das Man* in the section "The Measure of the 'With,' " 82.

18. Annie Ernaux's diary of the outside is the mirror image of Benjamin's *Berlin Childhood around 1900*. Whereas Benjamin erects an imaginary mausoleum to his childhood, modeled on the parental home, because his exile offers him no bearings, she does not look back any longer—the "family ethnography" is her own farewell to the familial environment—but engages in a painstaking process of mapping her new surroundings. Walter Benjamin, *Berlin Childhood around 1900*, trans. Howard Eiland (Cambridge, Mass.: Belknap Press of Harvard University Press, 2006).

Chapter 4

1. Adorno, Nachwort (afterword) to *Berliner Kindheit um 1900* (Frankfurt: Suhrkamp Verlag, 1950), 176–80. The translation here is based on the text in Adorno, *Gesammelte Schriften* (Collected Writings), vol. 20 (Frankfurt: Suhrkamp Verlag, 2003), 1:170–72.

2. Hannah Arendt, "Introduction: Walter Benjamin: 1892–1940," in Benjamin, *Illuminations* (New York: Schocken Books, 1968), 19.

3. Cf. "The Storyteller" and "The Work of Art in the Age of Mechanical Reproduction," in *Illuminations*.

4. An apt metaphor for the essay's breaking the spell of beginnings and endings is the moment, evoked in the first section, "Loggias," of the child's encounter with the day: "The morning, whenever I encountered it on our loggia, had already been morning for so long that it seemed more itself there than at any other spot. Never did I have the chance to wait for morning on the loggia; every time, it was already waiting for me. It had long since arrived—was effectively out of fashion—when I finally came upon it." Walter Benjamin, *Berlin Childhood around 1900*, trans. Howard Eiland (Cambridge, Mass.: Belknap Press of Harvard University Press, 2006), 41. Hereafter cited parenthetically as *BC*.

5. Such a gesture is a rarity in Benjamin's writing, as the reader of "The Task of the Translator" is aware: for Benjamin, the concept of the receiver is detrimental to any thinking about art, since all the latter does is to posit man's physical and spiritual existence: "In none of its works," however, "is it concerned with his response. No poem is intended for the reader, no picture for the beholder, no symphony for the listener." "The Task of the Translator," in *Illuminations*, 69. The status of *Berliner Kindheit um 1900* is ambiguous: is it really meant for a readership, Benjamin's farewell text—not only to Berlin, but to life (since it is known that during the time of its writing, he attempted suicide several times), in other words, a testament in which speaks a voice already, rather than a person, hence the distanciation implied in the phrase "der, von dem hier die Rede ist" instead of the use of the first-person pronoun?

6. Walter Benjamin, *Schriften* (Frankfurt: Suhrkamp Verlag, 1995), 7:385, 7:1 (my italics). Hereafter cited parenthetically as *S*. Some of the fragments did not make it into the published English translation, and so I have rendered them into English myself.

7. Blanchot, in "La parole quotidienne," comes close to Benjamin when he defines the everyday as that which we never see for the first time.

8. There is a deeply moving Benjaminian echo in the incantation, penned by Peter Handke, that accompanies the writing hand at the beginning of Wim Wenders's film *Der Himmel über Berlin* (*Wings of Desire*): "Als das Kind Kind war, / Wusste es nicht, / Dass es Kind war, / Alles war ihm beseelt . . ." (When the child was a child, / He didn't know / He was a child, / To him everything carried a soul . . .). The child's unselfconscious enchantment, the surrounding things endowed with souls, the nostalgia of the angel—reminiscent of Benjamin's own angel of history—for the "now," not that of recognizability, but of full physical presence in a moment, make of Wenders's film an apt response to Benjamin's *Berlin Childhood* from across the century.

9. Benjamin, *Briefe*, 1:56, quoted in Arendt, "Introduction," 20. Note a strikingly similar passage in Blanchot's *L'attente, l'oubli*: "La pression de la ville: de toutes parts. Les maisons ne sont pas là pour qu'on y demeure, mais pour qu'il y ait des rues, et dans les rues, le mouvement incessant de la ville" (The pressure of the city, from all sides. Houses are not there for living in, but so that there may be streets, and in the streets, the incessant bustle of the city). *L'attente, l'oubli* (Paris: Gallimard: 1971), 19 (my translation).

10. Benjamin, *Briefe*, 1:56, quoted in Arendt, "Introduction," 21.

11. Benjamin, quoted in Richard Sieburth, "Benjamin the Scrivener," *Assemblage* 6 (1988): 11; suspension points in the original. This essay offers a compelling analysis of the generative presence of thresholds in *The Arcades*, one that is highly relevant to the Berlin childhood fragments.

12. Benjamin, *Schriften*, 1:xix, quoted in Arendt, "Introduction," 12.

13. Benjamin, *The Arcades*, 462–463 (section N3,1).

14. Here I am using a Heideggerian term as a way to suggest that Benjamin's understanding of the thing as something that can gather and contain, virtually, everything else, comes close to Heidegger's understanding of the thing in his essays "The Thing" and "The Origin of the Work of Art." Interestingly, their respective examples of thing-as-gathering are symmetrical in a symbolic way: Heidegger's is the bridge, Benjamin's the arcade.

15. Benjamin, quoted by Howard Eiland in the introduction to the English translation of *Berlin Childhood*, xii.

16. Arendt, "Introduction," 11–12. She also shows, not without humor, that Benjamin was "a critic and an essayist who regarded even the essay form as too vulgarly extensive and would have preferred the aphorism if he had not been paid by the line" (ibid., 23).

17. This section was preserved only in the 1932–1934 version, published in the English version of Benjamin, *Berlin Childhood*, 140–142.

18. In *The Hidden Dimension* (Garden City, N.Y.: Doubleday, 1966), Edward Twitchell Hall uses the term *proxemics* as the ensemble of observations and theories concerning the usage one makes of space as a specific cultural product: in other words, as a dialectics of distance. Barthes, as I point out further on, uses it in a slightly different way.

19. Like the reading box, the Chinese painter only survived in the 1932–1934 version.

20. Waiting is a leitmotif in *Berliner Kindheit*, as the sections *Loggien* and *Wintermorgen*, among others, suggest.

21. In Szondi's reading, Benjamin, unlike Proust (who sets off in quest of the past in order to escape from time altogether), seeks the future in the past; his memory encounters a manifestation of childhood "in the office of the seer who foretells the future." Szondi therefore suggests that Benjamin's *Berlin Childhood* is the exact counterpart of Proust's Parisian childhood: "Proust listens attentively for the echo of the past; Benjamin listens for the first notes of a future which has meanwhile become the past. Unlike Proust, Benjamin does not want to free himself from temporality; he does not wish to see things in their ahistorical essence. He strives instead for historical experience and knowledge. Nevertheless, he is sent back into the past, a past, however, which is open, not completed, and which promises the future. Benjamin's tense is not the perfect, but the future perfect in the fullness of its paradox: being future and past at the same time." Peter Szondi, "Hope in the Past: On Walter Benjamin," trans. Harvey Mendelsohn, *Critical Inquiry* 4, no. 3 (spring 1978): 499.

22. Benjamin, quoted in Richter, *Thought-images: Frankfurt School Writers' Reflections from Damaged Life* (Stanford, Calif.: Stanford University Press, 2007), 214.

23. In section "Blumeshof 12," for instance, he describes his grandmother's bourgeois interior: "Here reigned a type of furniture that, having capriciously incorporated styles of ornament from different centuries, was thoroughly imbued with itself and its own duration. Poverty could have no place in these rooms, where death itself had none. There was no place in them to die; and so their occupants died in sanatoriums" (*BC*, 88).

24. Benjamin, *Schriften*, 632, quoted in Arendt, "Introduction," 29.

25. Ibid., 420.

26. Gerhard Richter and J. M. Gagnebin suggest that the intimation of a politics of the reusable, developed in Benjamin's other texts, is not absent from these late reminiscences. The social geography privileged in *Berlin Childhood* remains ambiguous, Gagnebin suggests: "Lieux qui sont autant de seuils, d'accès à l'autre monde terrifiant et fascinant du travail et de la pauvreté, osons le mot: du prolétariat. Même ambiguïté en relation au 'malheur,' c'est-à-dire, pour un enfant de la classe bourgeoise, à tout ce qui pourrait détruire la propriété privée et, en un secret attrait, menacer la toute-puissance parentale: les voleurs, les incendiaires, les révolutionnaires" (Places that are like many thresholds, providing access to the other, terrifying and fascinating world of work and poverty, of—let us dare use the word—the proletariat. Same ambiguity with regard to "misfortune," that is, for a child from the bourgeois class, to anything that could destroy private property and, secretly attractive, that would threaten parental omnipotence: robbers, arsonists, revolutionaries). J. M. Gagnebin, *Histoire et narration chez Walter Benjamin* (Paris: L'Harmattan, 1994), 122 (my translation). By privileging these social zones of indeterminacy, *Berliner Kindheit* not only gives an idiosyncratic historical representation of Berlin around 1900, but he might allude to a politics of the periphery, of the threshold, of the discarded. A suggestive passage in *One-Way Street* registers with the image of the historian as ragpicker, with its evocation of children's recuperation of useless odds and ends for their own playful purposes,

not unlike the "perruque" strategies of recycling creatively discarded materials described by de Certeau in *L'invention du quotidien*, strategies meant to undermine the capitalist system by introducing creativity at the heart of rigid structures and thus unsettle them. See Benjamin, "One-Way Street," in *Reflections*, ed. Peter Demetz, trans. Edmund Jephcott (New York: Schocken, 2007), 68–69.

27. Benjamin, "Franz Kafka," in *Illuminations*, 133–134.

28. Ibid., 134. And the second, shorter essay on Kafka concludes not with praise for his attentiveness ("the natural prayer of the soul" in which "he included all living creatures, as saints include them in their prayers"), but with amazement in the face of Kafka's embracing of failure: "To do justice to the figure of Kafka in its purity and peculiar beauty one must never lose sight of one thing: it is the purity and beauty of a failure. The circumstances of this failure are manifold. One is tempted to say: once he was certain of eventual failure, everything worked out for him en route as in a dream. There is nothing more memorable than the fervor with which Kafka emphasized his failure." Benjamin, "Some Reflections on Kafka," in *Illuminations*, 144–145.

29. Franz Kafka, "The Cares of a Family Man," in *The Complete Short Stories* (London: Vintage Books, 2005), 429.

Chapter 5

1. Annie Ernaux, *Journal du dehors* (Paris: Gallimard, 1993), and Annie Ernaux, *La vie extérieure* (Paris: Gallimard, 1999). I will hereafter reference the former with the abbreviation *JD*, quoting from the English version, *Exteriors*, trans. Tanya Leslie (New York: Seven Stories, 1996). For the purposes of my argument here, I will occasionally refer to this book with the literal translation of the title, *Diary of the Outside*. Translations of passages from *La vie extérieure* are my own.

2. Modernity is for Baudelaire "the ephemeral, the fugitive, the contingent, the half of art whose other half is the eternal and the immutable." See Charles Baudelaire, "The Painter of Modern Life," in *The Painter of Modern Life, and Other Essays*, ed. Jonathan Mayne, trans. Jonathan Mayne (Oxford: Phaidon, 1964), 13.

3. Georg Simmel's account of the metropolitan personality foregrounds the psychological basis of the metropolitan type of individuality, which "consists in the *intensification of nervous stimulation* which results from the swift and uninterrupted change of outer and inner stimuli." Georg Simmel, "The Metropolis and Mental Life," in *The Sociology of Georg Simmel*, ed. Kurt H. Wolff (Glencoe, Ill.: Free Press, 1950), 409–410, italics in the original. Marshall Berman's account of modernity famously emphasizes "a unity of disunity: it pours us all into a maelstrom of perpetual disintegration and renewal, of struggle and contradiction, of ambiguity and anguish. To be modern is part of a universe in which, as Marx said, 'all that is solid melts into air.'" Marshall Berman, *All That Is Solid Melts into Air: The Experience of Modernity* (London: Verso, 1983), 15.

4. Henri Lefebvre, *Everyday Life in the Modern World*, trans. Sacha Rabinovitch (New Brunswick, N.J.: Transaction, 1984), 114. For a highly informative article about the planning of the *villes nouvelles* and Ernaux's evolving relationship to Cergy throughout her diaries, see Edward Welch, "Coming to Terms with the Future: The Experience of Modernity in Annie Ernaux's *Journal du dehors*," *French Cultural Studies* 18, no. 1 (2007): 125–136. On this topic, see also Fiona

Handyside, "'J'ai aimé vivre là': Re-Thinking the Parisian Suburbs in Annie Ernaux and Eric Rohmer," *Nottingham French Studies* 48, no. 2 (2009): 43–54.

5. "Looking back, I can now see a link between this enterprise [the diary] and the Alzheimer's disease my mother was suffering from: her memory began to fail, she no longer recognized the people around her. This annihilation of her personality threw me into a state of utter confusion. I feel that writing about the outside world helped ease my grief and keep me in touch with the world that was gradually slipping away from my mother's own consciousness." Ernaux, *JD*, 6–7. In her article "Life, Disrupted," Sonia Wilson shows that parallel to the writing of her unusual diary of the outside, Ernaux also kept a "journal des visites" (to her ailing mother), thus compartmentalizing her experiences. Wilson, "Life, Disrupted: Annie Ernaux's *Journal du dehors* and 'Je ne suis pas sortie de ma nuit,'" *Australian Journal of French Studies* 49, no. 3 (September 2012): 250–266.

6. Janet Wolff, "The Invisible Flâneuse: Women and the Literature of Modernity," *Theory, Culture and Society* 2, no. 3 (November 1, 1985): 37–46, here 41–42.

7. See, for instance, George Sand's joy at managing to transform herself into a person—"solid on the pavement"—who could enjoy the paradoxical freedom to pass unnoticed is quite suggestive: "So I had made myself a *redingote-guérite* in heavy gray cloth, pants and vest to match. With a gray hat and large woolen cravat, I was a perfect first-year student. I can't express the pleasure my boots gave me: I would gladly have slept with them, as my brother did in his younger age, when he got his first pair. With those little iron-shod heels, I was solid on the pavement. I flew from one end of Paris to the other. It seemed to me that I could go round the world. And then, my clothes feared nothing. I ran out in every kind of weather, I came home at every sort of hour, I sat in the pit at the theater. No one paid attention to me, and no one guessed at my disguise. . . . No one knew me, no one looked at me, no one found fault with me; I was an atom lost in that immense crowd." Quoted in Ellen Moers, *Literary Women: The Great Writers* (Oxford: Oxford University Press), 12.

8. Walter Benjamin, "On Some Motifs in Baudelaire," in *Illuminations*, 169.

9. Wolff, "The Invisible Flâneuse," 45.

10. Deborah L. Parsons, *Streetwalking the Metropolis: Women, the City and Modernity* (Oxford: Oxford University Press, 2000).

11. Ibid., 6.

12. Ibid., 27. In an early entry of the *Journal*, Ernaux notes in passing that her safety in certain public spaces is by no means guaranteed, thus noting another aspect that is likely to set the flâneuse apart: "As I leave the elevator in the underground garage, third level down, I am greeted by the rumble of the air extractors. Nobody would hear a woman scream if she was being raped." Ernaux, *JD*, 25–26. In other words, the anonymity of the public space that the flâneur seeks and revels in, might have a more ambiguous quality for his female counterpart. Corroborating Ernaux's anxiety, Robin Tierney points to a serendipitous illustration of similar apprehensions in the opening scene of Eric Rohmer's 1987 film *L'Ami de mon amie*—"serendipitous" not only because it corroborates Ernaux's anxiety but also because it is set in Ernaux's own *ville nouvelle*, Cergy-Pontoise—which features Lea introducing herself to Blanche in a café and proposing to have lunch together: "If I sit by myself some jerk will always come along and try to pick me

up," she explains. And Tierney adds, echoing George Sand: "Lea is not allowed the protection of anonymity, and must take precautions that foreclose the freedom of solitude." Robin Tierney, "Lived Experience at the Level of the Body: Annie Ernaux's 'Journaux Extimes,'" *SubStance* 35, no. 3 (2006): 115.

13. Lefebvre, *Everyday Life in the Modern World*, 73.

14. Benjamin, "Baudelaire, or the Streets of Paris," in *Reflections*, 156.

15. In an interview with Alison S. Fell and Edward Welch, she pointed out that she continued, after the success of *La Place* in 1984, to live and teach as before, despite her access to other social circles. See "Interview with Annie Ernaux," *Nottingham French Studies* 48, no. 2 (2009): 6–9.

16. Pierre Bourdieu, *Esquisse pour une auto-analyse* (Paris: Raisons d'agir, 2004), 127.

17. Annie Ernaux, "Raisons d'écrire," *French Nottingham Studies* 48, no. 2 (2009): 11 (my translation).

18. Ibid., 12.

19. It is useful here to unwrap what Bourdieu means by this notion, since it sheds light on the identification at work in Ernaux's diaries. In the preface to *The Logic of Practice*, the French sociologist explains: "The reification of the object of science in the essential otherness of a 'mentality' presupposes triumphant adherence to a non-objectified subject. Distance is not abolished by bringing the outsider fictitiously closer to an imaginary native, as is generally attempted; it is by distancing, through objectification, the native who is in every outside observer that the native is brought closer to the outsider" (20). In this logic resides, according to Bourdieu, the very raison d'être and the ethical significance of sociology as a practical discipline: "In contrast to the personalist denial which refuses scientific objectification and can only construct a fantasized person, sociological analysis, particularly when it places itself in the anthropological tradition of exploration of forms of classification, makes a self-reappropriation possible, by objectifying the objectivity that runs through the supposed site of subjectivity, such as the social categories of thought, perception and appreciation which are the unthought principle of all representation of the 'objective' world. By forcing one to discover externality at the heart of internality, banality in the illusion of rarity, the common in the pursuit of the unique, sociology does more than denounce all the impostures of egoistic narcissism; it offers perhaps the only means of contributing, if only through awareness of determinations, to the construction, otherwise abandoned to the forces of the world, of something like a subject." Pierre Bourdieu, *The Logic of Practice*, trans. Richard Nice (Stanford, Calif.: Stanford University Press, 1990), 20–21.

20. Continuing the thought pursued in the concluding lines of the preface to *The Logic of Practice*, he adds: "Paradoxically, perhaps nothing nowadays appears more hateful than this interchangeable self that is revealed by the sociologist and socio-analysis (and also, though it is less apparent, and so better tolerated, psychoanalysis). Whereas everything prepares us to enter the regulated exchange of narcissisms, of which a certain literary tradition has established the code, the effort to objectify this 'subject' which we are led to think universal because we have it in common with all those who are the product of the same social conditions encounters violent resistance. Anyone who takes the trouble to break with the self-indulgence of nostalgic evocations in order to make explicit

the collective privacy of common experiences, beliefs and schemes of thought, in other words some of the unthought which is almost inevitably absent from the sincerest autobiographies because, being self-evident, it passes unnoticed and, when it surfaces in consciousness, is repressed as unworthy of publication, is liable to offend the narcissism of the reader who feels objectified, despite himself, by proxy and, paradoxically, all the more cruelly the closer he is to the author of the work of objectification—unless the chatharsis induced by the awakening of consciousness is expressed, as sometimes happens, in liberated and liberating laughter." Pierre Bourdieu, *Pascalian Meditations* (1997), trans. Richard Nice (Stanford, Calif.: Stanford University Press, 2000), 33–34.

21. Thus Benjamin quotes from *The Condition of the Working Class in England* both in the *Arcades*, and in "On Some Motifs in Baudelaire": "There is something distasteful about the very bustle of the streets, something that is abhorrent to human nature itself. Hundreds of thousands of people of all classes and ranks of society jostle past one another; are they not all human beings with the same characteristics and potentialities, equally interested in the pursuit of human happiness? . . . And yet they rush past one another as if they had nothing in common or were in no way associated with one another. Their only agreement is a tacit one: that everyone should keep to the right of the pavement, so as not to impede the stream of people moving in the opposite direction. No one even bothers to spare a glance for the others. The greater the number of people that are packed into a tiny space, the more repulsive and offensive becomes the brutal indifference, the unfeeling concentration of each person on his private affairs." Walter Benjamin, *Illuminations* (New York: Schocken, 1968), 166–167. A version of this passage also appears in convolute M of the *Arcades* ("The Flâneur"), where Benjamin quotes an additional sentence, in which Engels generalizes the indifference of the street to the whole of society: "'And however much one may be aware that this isolation of the individual, this narrow self-seeking, is the fundamental principle of our society everywhere, it is nowhere so shamelessly barefaced, so self-conscious, as just here in the crowding of the great city'" (Engels quoted in *The Arcades*, 427–428 (section M5a,1).

22. Benjamin, *Illuminations*, 167.

23. As Michael Sheringham points out in *Everyday Life*, Ernaux's "ethnowriting" can be placed in conversation with the "proximate ethnographies" of her contemporaries Maspéro and Réda and with the ethnographic turn in anthropology in the 1980s. Michael Sheringham, *Everyday Life: Theories and Practices from Surrealism to the Present* (Oxford: Oxford University Press, 2006), chap. 8, 292–360.

24. See Georges Perec, *La vie mode d'emploi* (Paris: Hachette, 1978).

25. For a more recent analysis of muted forms of subversion, see James Scott, *La domination et les arts de la résistance* (Paris: Editions Amsterdam, 2009).

26. Ernaux, "Raisons d'écrire," 13.

27. Sheringham, *Everyday Life*, 66.

28. Lefebvre, *Everyday Life in the Modern World*, 83, suspension points in the original.

29. One of the most acerbic critiques in Lefebvre's book is mounted in a section on "la presse féminine et spécifiquement la 'presse de coeur.'" *Critique de la vie quotidienne* (Paris: L'Arche, 1977), 84–85.

30. Benjamin, *Reflections*, 156.

31. See Erving Goffman, *The Presentation of Self in Everyday Life* (Garden City, N.Y.: Doubleday, 1959), 208–238.

32. For a lucid analysis of this phenomenon, see also Bertrand Ogilvie, *L'homme jetable: Essai sur l'exterminisme et la violence extrême* (Paris: Éditions Amsterdam, 2012).

33. Guillaume le Blanc, *Que faire de notre vulnérabilité?* (Paris: Bayard, 2011), 40 (my translation).

34. Ibid.

35. Ibid., 121.

36. Ibid., 137.

37. Ibid., 42. Occasionally she distances herself from public figures or intellectuals who appear on television or other media, commenting on the public display of false empathy with the poor, or the smug expression of contented belonging to a circle of engaged intellectuals. . . . In counterpoint to such entries are remarks such as the following, that she makes looking at the discolored hands of an African man: "That too is the sign of an intellectual: never to feel the need to dissociate oneself from one's quivering hands that have been damaged by work." Ernaux, *JD*, 38.

38. Le Blanc: "Il n'y a pas d'exclu extérieur. L'exclu est toujours un exclu intérieur, quelqu'un qui se trouve dans les franges d'un territoire, qui ne peut appartenir au moindre groupe alors qu'il s'y trouve inexorablement ramené" (107). "Car le dehors n'existe pas comme une zone tampon autonome mais bien comme un effet du dedans. Le dehors existe au-dedans comme cette zone que le dedans veut situer au-dehors. Il est, pour ainsi dire, ce qui dans le dedans se voit contraint à ne pas lui appartenir et devient, de ce fait, flottant, sans attache." Le Blanc, *Que faire de notre vulnérabilité?*, 148.

39. Ibid., 51.

40. Ibid., 74–75.

41. Jacques Rancière, *Le partage du sensible: Esthétique et politique (*Paris: La Fabrique Éditions, 2000).

42. Le Blanc credits S. Quesemand Zucca, *Je vous salis ma rue: Chroniques de la désocialisation* (Paris: Stock, 2007), for the inspiration of this compelling passage: "Se découvrir flottant, privé de solidité, d'assise, c'est se sentir hors du commun dans un monde de pas perdus, dans un vestibule de courants d'air. Le clochard qui mendie au bout de la rue est une vie dans un carrefour de vents. Une vie, c'est-à-dire un corps qui a perdu toute teneur sociale et qui ne tient plus qu'à la possibilité vitale d'occuper un bout de trottoir, impossible abri en miniature dans lequel il faut chercher à ne pas se laisser absorber, asphaltiser." Quoted in Le Blanc, *Que faire de notre vulnérabilité?*, 44–45.

43. We have come full circle here from Orwell's identification with the tramps in *Down and Out in Paris and London.*

44. Le Blanc, *Que faire de notre vulnérabilité?*, 170.

45. Strikingly, Alfred Döblin's description of an album of death masks echoes le Blanc's words: "In the presence of these dead faces, one feels that they are not only silent and enclosed within themselves, but that they are also diminished, that they have become objects in alien hands. They *were* at one time active, and that was what formed their faces." Alfred Döblin, "Faces, Images, and Their Truth" (1929), in August Sander, *Face of Our Time* (Munich: Schirmer/Mosel, 2003), 9.

46. Le Blanc, *Que faire de notre vulnérabilité?*, 45. See here Éric Chauvier, *Anthropologie de l'ordinaire: Une conversion du regard* (Toulouse: Anacharsis, 2011).

47. See Deleuze and Guattari, *Capitalism and Schizophrenia*, vol. 1, *Anti-Oedipus*.

48. I am borrowing here some of the vocabulary of affect proposed by Sianne Ngai in her wonderful book *Ugly Feelings* (Cambridge, Mass.: Harvard University Press, 2007). See, in particular, her discussion of Philip Fisher's *The Vehement Passions*, 188–189.

49. Ibid.

50. The 1969 playlet *Breath* famously opens with the following stage directions: "Faint light on stage littered with miscellaneous rubbish." See Samuel Beckett, *Breath and Other Shorts* (London: Faber and Faber, 1971).

51. In a conversation with Günter Grass, to which I will return toward the end of this chapter, Pierre Bourdieu has drawn attention to the danger of becoming overwhelmed and aestheticize the suffering of other people. Referring to the collective volume *The Weight of the World*, in which a group of sociologists collected and analyzed testimonies of working-class individuals, he cautioned about the danger of losing distance: "The person who hears these stories directly from the one who experienced them is often wiped out by them or overwhelmed, and it isn't always possible to maintain one's distance from them. . . . One of our rules was that there would be no turning of the stories into 'literature.' This may seem shocking to you, but there is a temptation, when one is dealing with dramas like these, to write well. The rule here was to be as brutally pragmatic as possible, to allow these stories to retain their extraordinary, and almost unbearable, violence." Pierre Bourdieu and Günter Grass, "A Literature from Below," trans. Deborah Triesman, *The Nation*, July 3, 2000, 25–28.

52. Le Blanc, *Que faire de notre vulnérabilité?*, 71.

53. Ibid., 154. Le Blanc's analysis elaborates on Cora Diamond's *L'importance d'être humain* (Paris: PUF, 2011).

54. Le Blanc, *Que faire de notre vulnérabilité?*, 139–141.

55. Pierre Zaoui, *La discrétion, ou l'art de disparaître* (Paris: Autrement, 2013), 10 (my translation).

56. Zaoui thus echoes Barthes's claim that his focus on community in *Comment vivre ensemble* was his "façon d'être présent dans les luttes de [son] temps" and Kristeva's emphasis on her former professor's delicacy in a "world of visibility, saturated with images."

57. Ibid., 107.

58. Ibid.

59. Ibid., 108.

60. Ibid., 110.

61. Ibid., 37.

62. Nancy K. Miller calls "auto-identification" the "identification with which others return one to oneself, often, a younger self." See "Autobiographical Others: Annie Ernaux's *Journal du dehors*," *Sites: The Journal of Twentieth-Century/Contemporary French Studies* 2, no. 1 (1998): 127–139, 131.

63. See Michael Sheringham, *French Autobiography: Devices and Desires; Rousseau to Perec* (Oxford: Clarendon, 1993).

64. Annie Ernaux, "Vers un Je transpersonnel," *RITM: Recherches interdisciplinaires sur les textes modernes*, no. 6 (1993): 219. In "The Law of Community," Roberto Esposito comments on the full passage from Rousseau that Ernaux has placed at the beginning of her diaries: "Community is what we need the most, as it is a part of our very selves: 'Our sweetest existence is relative and collective, and our true self is not entirely within us.' Even the sustained declaration of his own solitude, upon which he almost obsessively insists in his final works, resounds with a silent revolt against the absence of community. Rousseau is alone because community does not exist, or, better, because all existent forms of community are nothing but the opposite of the only authentic one. In response, Rousseau protests against solitude as the negative imprint of an absolute need for sharing, which, however paradoxically, appears in his work as the written communication of his impossibility to communicate. Writing thus assumes the character of 'solitude for others,' of a 'substitute for the human community that is unrealizable in social reality.' " Esposito, "The Law of Community," in *Terms of the Political*, 16.

65. Zaoui, *La discrétion*, 14.

66. Ernaux, "Raisons d'écrire," 14.

Chapter 6

1. Günter Grass, *My Century*, trans. Michael Henry Heim (New York: Harcourt, 1999), 1. I will also be using the German edition of the text, *Mein Jahrhundert* (1999; reprint, Munich: Deutscher Taschenbuch Verlag, 2002).

2. The device of expanding the time frame of his book to a whole century by including characters of various ages is something Grass explored in other texts. Writing about *Too Far Afield*, for instance, Julian Preece refers to the role of this technique: "By adding the biographies of the parents of the two septuagenarian leading characters, Grass effortlessly encompasses the whole century: the idea of Fonty and Hoftaller recalling their past existences as Fontane and Tallhover gives him a way of treating up to 200 years at once. Grass has never found one time sequence enough." Julian Preece, *The Life and Work of Günter Grass: Literature, History, Politics* (London: Palgrave Macmillan, 2004), 194.

3. I see the vast panorama created by the "frescoes" in Grass's fragmentary book matched by the gigantic canvases of Anselm Kiefer; there is a sense in which the texture of everyday stories and voices in *My Century* might be found to have a kind of "objective correlative" in the flesh of the ruins that are ever so present in Kiefer's work. See, for example, their representation of the "rubble women" (Kiefer's *Trümmerfrauen*, and Grass's entry for 1946 in *Mein Jahrhundert*, respectively).

4. It is worthwhile noting that the Polish poet Aleksander Wat set a precedent to Grass's choice of title—his *My Century* was published posthumously in 1977—and that his powerful memoir sheds light on the implicit claims to representing, by way of an account anchored in one's autobiography, one's entire epoch. I will return to it in due time.

5. Günter Grass, quoted in Preece, *The Life and Work of Günter Grass*, 188.

6. For a comprehensive review of the critical literature generated by Günter Grass's work, see Siegfried Mews's very useful book *Günter Grass and His Critics: From "The Tin Drum" to "Crabwalk"* (Rochester, N.Y.: Camden House, 2008).

7. Philosopher and political science professor Iring Fetscher, whose review I discuss below, concurred with the evaluation of a penetrating "Grass sound" in the book, despite the diversity of topics.

8. This concern was raised mostly by American reviewers, including Peter Gay, John Simon, and Ian Buruma. See Peter Gay, "A Cloud of Witness," *New York Times Book Review*, December 19, 1999, 9; Peter Gay, "The Fictions of Günter Grass," *New York Times*, August 20, 2006, Opinion sec., http://www.nytimes.com/2006/08/20/opinion/20gay.html?mcubz=1; John Simon, "Sturm und Drang," *Washington Post*, December 19, 1999; and Ian Buruma, "The Tin Ear," *New Republic*, January 31, 2000, 33–34.

9. See Wolfgang Weber, "My Century? A Review of Günter *Grass'* Latest Novel, *Mein Jahrhundert*," *World Socialist Web Site*, February 8, 2000, http://www.wsws.org/articles/2000/feb2000/gras-f08.shtml, and Richard Bernstein, "100 Years of Certitude: Günter Grass's History," *New York Times*, January 5, 2000, http://www.nytimes.com/2000/01/05/books/books-of-the-times-100-years-of-certitude-gunter-grass-s-history.html.

10. Iring Fetscher, "Kritik—Günter Grass sein Jahrhundert," *Neue Gesellschaft/Frankfurter Hefte*, no. 46 (1999): 850–852.

11. Weber, "My Century? A Review of Günter Grass' Latest Novel."

12. Simon, "Sturm und Drang."

13. Peter Gay, "A Cloud of Witness" and "The Fictions of Günter Grass." In contrast to Bernstein's evaluation, Wolfgang Weber credits Grass's presentation of events "from below," "from changing, unexpected viewpoints" with "unforgettable" scenes presented in "a concise and striking manner"; "the stories about the first half of the century are also linguistically colourful and multifaceted, allowing history to be re-lived and re-considered."

14. Buruma, "The Tin Ear," 33–34.

15. When it comes to German history and literature about it, this statement is perhaps more contentious than it might appear, as the reception of books like Jonathan Littell's *Les bienveillantes* (Paris: Gallimard, 2006), among others, has amply demonstrated.

16. Nikita Khrushchev (1894–1971) was First Secretary of the Communist Party (1953–1964) and premier of the Soviet Union (1958–1964). While in this confidential speech he was careful to protect the spirit of Lenin, he attacked the crimes committed by Stalin and his closest associates. The text is accessible online, at http://www.historyguide.org/europe/khrush_speech.html (accessed October 12, 2017).

17. Michael Heim's rendition of this passage reads: "One praised the other's play *The Measures Taken* ironically as 'the verbal universe of a true Ptolemean,' then immediately exonerated both of them, sinners that they were, with a quotation from his own great poem 'To the Coming Generation.'" This translation confuses the authorship of the two cited texts, implying that they do not belong to the same author, Brecht, and also leaves out the mention of Kleist's grave. I have not modified Heim's translation of the fragment from Brecht's poem.

18. Ironically, he committed suicide not long after saying that.

19. Monika Shafi, "'Gezz will ich ma erzählen': Narrative and History in Günter Grass's *Mein Jahrhundert*," ed. Paul Michael Lützeler and Stephan K. Schindler, *Gegenwartsliteratur* 1 (October 2002): 39–62, 40.

20. Ibid., 53.
21. Ibid., 53–54.
22. Ibid., 54–55.
23. Aleksander Wat, *My Century: The Odyssey of a Polish Intellectual*, trans. Richard Lourie (Berkeley: University of California Press, 1988).
24. Ibid., 291.
25. Ibid., 152.
26. Ibid.
27. Anne Fuchs, *Phantoms of War in Contemporary German Literature, Films and Discourse: The Politics of Memory* (New York: Palgrave Macmillan, 2008), 161.
28. See their coedited issue of *German Life and Letters*, especially the coauthored Anne Fuchs and Mary Cosgrove, "Introduction," *German Life and Letters* 59, no. 2 (2006): 163–168.
29. The term "postmemory" was coined by Marianne Hirsch, *Family Frames: Photography, Narrative, and Postmemory* (Cambridge, Mass.: Harvard University Press, 1997), 22, quoted in Fuchs and Cosgrove, "Introduction," 166.
30. Susan Sontag, quoted in Fuchs and Cosgrove, "Introduction," 164–165.
31. As the brief literature review has suggested, various readers proposed different generic categories to describe *My Century*, such as novel, short story, vignettes, fragments, and anecdotes. In support of their characterization as anecdotal stories, Richard Schade emphasizes the "decidedly anecdotal narrative," akin to a "micro-historical presentation of events." Richard E. Schade, "Günter Grass's *Mein Jahrhundert*: Histories, Paintings, and Performance," *Monatshefte* 96, no. 3 (fall 2004): 410.
32. Catherine Gallagher, *Practicing New Historicism* (Chicago: University of Chicago Press, 2000), 51.
33. See Geoff Eley, "Foreword," in *The History of Everyday Life: Reconstructing Historical Experiences and Ways of Life*, ed. Alf Lüdtke (Princeton, N.J.: Princeton University Press, 1995), vii.
34. Ibid., viii.
35. Günter Grass and Pierre Bourdieu, "A Literature from Below," trans. Deborah Treisman, *The Nation*, July 3, 2000, 25–28.
36. Might this count as what Lefebvre hoped would save us from the oppression of the everyday, namely the resuscitation of the festival?
37. Rebecca Braun, *Constructing Authorship in the Work of Günter Grass* (Oxford: Oxford University Press, 2008), 143.
38. Alfred Döblin, "Faces, Images, and Their Truth" (1929), in August Sander, *Face of Our Time* (Munich: Schirmer/Mosel, 2003), 11.
39. Ibid., 15.

Chapter 7

1. Peter Sloterdijk, *You Must Change Your Life* (2009), trans. Wieland Hoban (Cambridge: Polity, 2013), 62.
2. Ibid.
3. Ibid., 63, my italics.
4. Roberto Esposito, "Immunization and Violence," in *Terms of the Political* (New York: Fordham University Press, 2013), 59.

5. Sloterdijk, *You Must Change Your Life*, 451.

6. Ibid., 451.

7. I am not suggesting that the two notions, "the subject" and "the self," are interchangeable. One way of understanding the difference between them is by relying on Alexander Nehamas's distinction in *The Art of Living* between two conceptions of philosophy: a theoretical and systematic one that distrusts personal style and idiosyncrasy; and a more personal one that requires style, "composed in a self-conscious literary manner." Alexander Nehamas, *The Art of Living: Socratic Reflections from Plato to Foucault* (Berkeley: University of California Press, 1988), 3. Nehamas enumerates in this category Montaigne, Pascal, Schopenhauer, Nietzsche, Kierkegaard, and Foucault, among others; like these, Sloterdijk could also be considered by systematic philosophers as a "poet" or a literary figure. The autonomous "subject" of theoretical philosophy has received much bad press in the last century; famously, Jean-Luc Nancy asked, in a 1986 text, "What comes after the subject?," a question to which most recently Irving Goh has responded: the reject. See Irving Goh, *The Reject: Community, Politics and Religion after the Subject* (New York: Fordham University Press, 2015). For the philosophers of the art of living, the "self" has always been "a constructed unity" (as Nehamas puts it). Although I would situate Sloterdijk in this second category, the figure of the athlete featured in *You Must Change Your Life* has (what one might call) a strong sense of self, and often seems to assume the allure of a subject.

8. "An ethics is possible only when—with ontology (which always reduces the Other to the Same) taking the backseat—an anterior relation can affirm itself, a relation such that the self is not content with recognizing the Other, with recognizing itself in it, but feels that the Other always puts it into question to the point of being able to respond to it only through a responsibility that cannot limit itself and that exceeds itself without exhausting itself." Maurice Blanchot, *The Unavowable Community* (New York: Station Hill, 1988), 43. With this claim, Blanchot positions himself closer to Levinas, who places metaphysics before ontology, than to Heidegger, who allegedly uses the inclusive "we" too easily when he insists on the sociability of Dasein, which denies the existence of a solitary subject prior to collective existence.

9. Sloterdijk, *You Must Change Your Life*, 452.

10. For a critical analysis of Sloterdijk's partial reading of Kafka, see Chris Danta, "Acrobatics and Ascetics: Peter Sloterdijk and the Aesthetics of Verticality," *European Journal of English Studies* 19, no. 1 (April 2015): 66–81.

11. In an otherwise superlative review of *You Must Change Your Life*, Keith Ansell-Pearson also expresses reservations vis-à-vis Sloterdijk's choice of Zarathustra as the model of self-becoming through the command of demanding the impossible of oneself: "I prefer the Nietzsche who calls for modesty in moral matters, who labors against moral fanaticism, and who remains focused on the smallest and closest things." This is a reiteration of an earlier point, about the neglected books of Nietzsche's middle period, where he favors "an approach to self-cultivation and social transformation based on the need for slow cures and small doses, amounting to a veritable philosophy of the morning, which presages so many new dawns, dawns of knowledge and self-overcoming." Instead of those "witty and graceful" books, as Michel Foucault called them, Sloterdijk

relies on the 1887 *Genealogy of Morals*, making of asceticism his theory's cornerstone. After belaboring this point, the review ends on a tactful note that sees in Sloterdijk's omission of the subject and the ethical relationship that is community a gesture of openness and anticipation of the readers' continuation of the work: "Sloterdijk leaves it to us, his readers, to work out the ethical and political details of this ecological conception of a new future humanity." Keith Ansell-Pearson, "Philosophy of the Acrobat: On Peter Sloterdijk," *Los Angeles Review of Books*, July 8, 2013, http://lareviewofbooks.org/review/philosophy-of-the-acrobat-on-peter-sloterdijk.

12. See, in addition to Guillaume le Blanc's books referenced in the previous chapter, David Le Breton, *Disparaître de soi: Une tentation contemporaine* (Paris: Métailié, 2015).

13. Galgut's passage continues: "The words come to him from a long way off. He puts the book down and stares at peculiar long-legged insects on the surface of the river, they dart frantically back and forth, living out their whole lives in a space of one or two meters, they know nothing about him or his troubles, even now they're unaware of him watching, their otherness to him is complete" (*In a Strange Room*, 47). He chooses to leave out the following sentences from Faulkner's novel: "I don't know what I am. I don't know if I am or not" and end, after a short deliberation, affirmatively: "And then I must be, or I could not empty myself for sleep in a strange room." William Faulkner, *As I Lay Dying* (New York: Vintage, 1957), 76. Why does Galgut cut the passage, dwelling on the doubt rather than on the resolution? His point, I believe, is about the possibility of living without awareness of other people's lives, although side by side, as the insects who are completely oblivious of his existence. During his trip through Lesotho, Damon makes a similar point, noticing "people living out their whole lives in one small portion of the earth, oblivious to anything beyond" (*In a Strange Room*, 43).

14. Chris Roper, "The Strangest of Rooms and Places," *Mail & Guardian*, May 7, 2010, http://mg.co.za/article/2010-05-07-the-strangest-of-rooms-and-places.

15. Sloterdijk, *You Must Change Your Life*, 4.

16. Ibid., 110.

17. Ibid., 40–61.

18. In the *Paris Review*, the short stories appeared separately.

19. Kianoosh Hashemzadeh, "An Interview with Damon Galgut," *Conjunctions: A Web Exclusive*, http://archive.is/NVnxc (accessed March 10, 2017, my italics).

20. Jacques Rancière, "The Thread of the Novel," *Novel: A Forum on Fiction* 47, no. 2 (2014): 197.

21. Ibid., 203.

22. Ibid., 205. A page later, Rancière concludes: "Modern fiction has no proper mode of linkage. . . . The fictional sacrifice of Emma, Albertine, or Septimus—among many others, from Jude the Obscure to Joe Christmas—is also a structural condition for settling the relationship between truth and plot" (206).

23. Hashemzadeh, "An Interview with Damon Galgut."

24. This is a view of the subject that Sloterdijk could have borrowed from Nietzsche. See Robert Pippin's work on Nietzsche, and his dialogue with Alexander Nehamas from which emerges the view of the self as an assembly of drives,

in which one takes the upper hand and, like a conductor, coaxes the others to follow heed. I have in mind here two essays: Robert Pippin, "Self-Interpreting Selves: Comments on Alexander Nehamas's *Nietzsche: Life as Literature*," *Journal of Nietzsche Studies* 45, no. 2 (summer 2014): 118–133, and the response, Alexander Nehamas, "Nietzsche, Drives, Selves, and Leonard Bernstein: A Reply to Christopher Janaway and Robert Pippin," *Journal of Nietzsche Studies* 45, no. 2 (summer 2014): 134–146.

25. In an interview, Galgut conceded that the narrative shift between the first and the third person might have been an influence of his training in acting, accompanied by a reflection on the capacity of the director to move in and out of the stage action.

26. Philippe Lejeune, *Le pacte autobiographique* (Paris: Seuil, 1975).

27. Galgut in Hashemzadeh, "An Interview with Damon Galgut."

28. A brief passage in the novel sheds light on the subjective nature and partiality of such gestures: "What he is looking for, he himself doesn't know. At this remove, his thoughts are lost to me now, and yet I can explain him better than my present self, he is buried under my skin" (67). The distance between the narrating and the narrated self increases hindsight, making possible an explanation in light of what happened before and after, endowing the moment with a meaning that is paradoxically alien to the "thoughts" that memory has sifted away.

29. Galgut in Hashemzadeh, "An Interview with Damon Galgut."

30. "I'm after memory not because I believe my lost memories are of any importance to my country. It's more in the nature of a grabbing off to the essence of consciousness itself, if that doesn't sound too overblown. I'm doing something quite unfashionable in South African terms, really" (ibid.).

31. This is different from his earlier novel *The Good Doctor* (New York: Grove, 2003), in which local conflicts impinge on the plot.

32. Reading Deleuze and Guattari, Roberto Esposito quotes from *A Thousand Plateaus*: "A fascination for the outside? Or is the multiplicity that fascinates us already related to a multiplicity dwelling within us?" Esposito, "Immunization and Violence," 122.

Conclusion

1. Peter Sloterdijk, "Warten auf den Islam," *Focus Online*, no. 10, March 6, 2006, http://www.focus.de/kultur/medien/essay-warten-auf-den-islam_aid_216305.html (my translation).

2. Slavoj Žižek, *Against the Double Blackmail: Refugees, Terror and Other Troubles with the Neighbors* (London: Penguin Random House, 2016), 74.

3. See Wallace's introduction to Plessner, *The Limits of Community*, where he offers an overview of Plessner's intellectual trajectory, from the critique of community to his philosophical anthropology, as developed in *The Levels of Organic Being*). Helmuth Plessner, *The Limits of Community: A Critique of Social Radicalism*, trans. and intro. Andrew Wallace (New York: Humanity Books, 1999).

4. Plessner's thoughtful pages on tact acquire particular relevance. Tact, he writes anticipating Zaoui, is "the willing openness to see others and, in so doing, to remove oneself from the field of vision; it is the willingness to measure others according to their standards and not one's own . . . the eternally alert respect before the other soul; . . . it never permits too much closeness nor too much

distance." Plessner, *The Limits of Community*, 163–164. I will return to this work shortly.

5. Žižek, *Against the Double Blackmail*, 83.

6. Ibid., 77.

7. Ibid., 79.

8. Ibid.

9. Paul Bloom, *Against Empathy: The Case for Rational Compassion* (New York: Ecco, 2016).

10. Symptomatic of this shift is the notion of *délicatesse* itself, which, as I have suggested, is first recuperated from the dying "art de vivre bourgeois" as an anachronism (like Adorno's tact), but then defined through a proliferation of illustrations lifted from various literary sources.

11. Plessner, *The Limits of Community*, 163, 166, 164.

12. Ibid., 164.

13. Ibid., 168.

14. In this spirit, Stanley Cavell speaks in *A Pitch of Philosophy* (Cambridge, Mass.: Harvard University Press, 1996) of the "arrogation of voice."

15. George Orwell, "Reflections on Gandhi," in *A Collection of Essays* (San Diego: Harcourt Brace Jovanovich, 1981), 176.

16. And Orwell specifies: "But it is not necessary here to argue whether the other-worldly or the humanistic ideal is 'higher.' The point is that they are incompatible" (ibid.)

17. It would be rather difficult to imagine the contours of such a philosophical argument when conducted by means of the literary. One would most likely need to draw inspiration from more radical literary or narrative experiments than the ones that have been central to this book. See my review of Goh's book *The Reject* in *Modern Language Notes* 130, no. 5 (2015): 1242–1247.

18. On this topic, see also Charles Taylor's *Ethics of Authenticity* (Cambridge, Mass.: Harvard University Press, 1992).

19. Martin Heidegger, *Being and Time*, trans. John Macquarrie and Edward Robinson, with a new foreword by Taylor Carman (New York: Harper Perennial, 2008), 218.

20. Ibid., 151–152.

21. Alberto Giacometti, *City Square* (also known as *Piazza*, or *City Square II*), 1948, bronze, Museum of Modern Art, New York, N.Y.

22. M. C. Escher, *Relativity*, 1953, lithograph (see front book cover).

23. See Marian Simon, *Ființare*, 2015, https://i1.wp.com/artasim.ro/wp-content/uploads/2015/08/8.jpg, accessed August 22, 2017.

INDEX